The Inherence of Human Dignity

The Inherence of Human Dignity

Foundations of Human Dignity, Volume 1

Edited by
Angus J. L. Menuge
Barry W. Bussey

ANTHEM PRESS

Anthem Press
An imprint of Wimbledon Publishing Company
www.anthempress.com

This edition first published in UK and USA 2021
by ANTHEM PRESS
75–76 Blackfriars Road, London SE1 8HA, UK
or PO Box 9779, London SW19 7ZG, UK
and
244 Madison Ave #116, New York, NY 10016, USA

British Library Cataloguing-in-Publication Data
A catalogue record for this book is available from the British Library.

Library of Congress Control Number: 2020952918

ISBN-13: 978-1-78527-648-4 (Hbk)
ISBN-10: 1-78527-648-4 (Hbk)
ISBN-13: 978-1-78527-651-4 (Pbk)
ISBN-10: 1-78527-651-4 (Pbk)

Cover image: Photograph by Barry W. Bussey

This title is also available as an e-book.

To

John Warwick Montgomery
for his pioneering contributing work Human Rights and Human Dignity *(1986) wherein he reminded us:*

The Bible leaves no doubt that the panoply of human rights derive from man's status as creature of God, made in His image. The sun shines and the rain falls on the just and the unjust (Matt. 5:45): believers have no more human rights over against unbelievers than the latter have over against them.

To

Vicki Menuge
for a life of sacrificial service, raising fine children and caring for her mother

To

LaVonna Bussey
for her unselfish commitment and dedication to her children, grandchildren, parents and parents-in-law

CONTENTS

Law and Religious Liberty, Volume 2

INTRODUCTION

Angus J. L. Menuge

Whither Dignity?

In recent years, there has been a veritable explosion of scholarship on the topic of human dignity, reflected in numerous conferences (e.g. the 2019 IVR World Congress in Lucerne), monographs (e.g. Rosen 2012; Kateb 2014; Barak 2015) and edited collections (e.g. McCrudden 2013; Düwell et al. 2014; Debes 2017). Yet there is an amply justified concern that the modern human rights movement is losing steam, and one reason for this is scepticism about the very idea of human dignity that allegedly grounds these rights (Rosen 2013). Such scepticism is not new, of course. Immanuel Kant (1724–1804) argued that rational beings are 'elevated above any price' by 'an inner worth, i.e. *dignity*' (2012 [1786], 4:434–4:435, 46, emphasis original). But Arthur Schopenhauer (1788–1860) countered that the lofty phrase 'dignity of man' has merely served as 'the shibboleth of [...] perplexed and empty-headed moralists who concealed behind their expression their lack of any real basis of morals' (1965 [1840], 100). Yet newer sources of scepticism are more surprising because they succeed the confident assertion, in the 1948 Universal Declaration of Human Rights (UDHR), of 'the inherent dignity and [...] the equal and inalienable rights of all members of the human family' (United Nations 1948).

One problem, emphasized by John Tasioulas in his plenary address in Lucerne, is that dignity claims have been trivialized, and so we have lost track of the original vision adopted by the drafters of the UDHR. As Clint Curle explains in Volume II, the historical context of the UDHR is vital to understanding its approach to human dignity. Vivid in many people's memories were the Nazi programs of mass extermination, 'barbarous acts which have outraged the conscience of mankind' (United Nations 1948). So it is not surprising that the focus of the UDHR was securing the right never to endure such cruel and unusual treatment again. But many people in Western democracies in the twenty-first century have no memory of such atrocities, and dignity claims have now so proliferated that almost any human desire is asserted as a human right. For example, regardless of what one may think about transgender issues, it is hard to take seriously the idea that the framers of the UDHR would agree with the claim, in a recent Canadian case, that a biological man self-identifying as a 'trans woman' had a human right to Brazilian waxing of the genitals (Murphy 2019). Worse, the set of rights claims can no longer be made logically consistent. The dignity of life contends with the dignity of autonomy used to justify abortion and euthanasia. And while some locate dignity in free speech and religious conscience, others contend that dignity demands the curtailment of offensive speech and the acceptance by religious communities of lifestyles which their tradition does not condone. If dignity can be used to defend conflicting and even mutually exclusive claims, of what use is the idea?

A second worry is that dignity is an ambiguous notion, making it difficult to find a widely shared understanding of its relevant meanings. As Michael Rosen documents, dignity has a rich and multivalent history, with at least four different meanings: (1) rank or status, (2) intrinsic value, (3) dignified behaviour and (4) respect (2012, 114). As a result, discussions of 'dignity' are easily derailed by conflation of, or equivocation between, distinct meanings of the term. The result is confusion and misunderstanding which may encourage those of a practical persuasion to conclude that dignity is an unproductive notion. If we are to avoid this defeatist conclusion, it is vitally important to isolate, and sharply define, the specific meanings of 'dignity' that are relevant to human rights discourse and protections.

That takes us to the third and most fundamental problem: assuming we have a clear understanding of the relevant meaning of 'dignity', we must then show that our discourse is *justified*, that is, that it can somehow be validated. A traditional ontological approach is to locate dignity in some characteristic of human nature. Yet, given the controversies over human nature (including even whether there is such a thing), others seek to ground dignity in facts of human experience, still others in our linguistic and behavioural practices, both inside and outside the law. Regardless of the approach, such accounts try to explain the origin of our concept of dignity (*its source*), and in what dignity consists (*its nature or meaning*). In other words, these accounts are looking for the foundations, or grounding, of the concept of human dignity, much as Kant, in *The Critique of Pure Reason*, argued that we need to provide a 'deduction' of our basic categories of thought (e.g. substance, causation, community) to show that they are more than useful fictions, that they actually apply to the world in which we live.

The Conceptual Foundations of Human Dignity

This issue of justifying the concept of human dignity is the focus of the present volume. But even if human dignity is grounded in reality, it is a further and important question how useful this notion is for legislation. So that is the focus of our second volume, which explores the implications of human dignity for legal practice.

The word 'dignity' derives from the Latin *dignitas*, meaning worth, and the history of thinking about human dignity has centred on which, if any, human beings have special worth not possessed by other creatures. In ancient societies, dignity was typically restricted to those with elevated rank or status: only such people qualified as 'dignitaries' or 'worthies'. Yet, both classical ideas of natural rights and Judeo-Christian teaching provided an impetus towards the idea that dignity is equally shared by all human beings. For example, the stoics grounded dignity in our rational nature, making social class irrelevant, at least in principle. And the Bible affirms that all human beings have special worth because they are uniquely made in the image of God. But only more recently, in the UDHR, do we see a clear articulation of the demand to recognize dignity that is inherent, equal and universal.

While it sets an ambitious agenda for moral and legal reform, the UDHR also leaves us with many problems. It does not say, precisely, what the phrase 'inherent dignity' means. Nor does it tell us what sort of thing, or characteristic, human dignity is. And we do not learn the source of human dignity or what makes it reasonable to believe that it exists. In short, the UDHR asserts the existence of an inherent, equal and universal dignity, but it neither explains nor defends that claim. So, in the first part of this book, seven chapters wrestle with these fundamental questions of how we ground the notion of inherent human dignity, by clarifying its meaning, nature, source and justification.

Yet the very idea of inherent dignity is by no means uncontroversial. Even its supporters disagree about the best way to understand that notion, and it faces opposition from competing accounts which deny that dignity is inherent and doubt whether human beings have any special worth. So the second part of the book is devoted to a consideration of competing concepts of human dignity. It considers the best way to understand inherent human dignity and how to respond to the competing ideas that dignity is merely a construct, one that it created by acts of interpretation and which may be conferred or removed by acts of legislation. It also considers the impact on our understanding of human dignity of extending dignity to artificial intelligence.

Grounding Human Dignity

So we begin with the exegetical problem: just what, precisely, did the framers of the UDHR mean by the phrase 'inherent dignity'? Is the underlying concept a secular one, or is it, at least implicitly, a religious one? In the opening chapter, Laura Kittel devotes her attention to these questions and argues that, despite the religious orientation of some of the key drafters of the UDHR, they aimed at a notion of human dignity that could be understood independently of any transcendent source it may ultimately have. Kittel argues that the notion of dignity found in the UDHR should be distinguished both from an 'old' idea of dignity, derived from such religious teachings as the *imago Dei*, and from a 'newer' idea of dignity as something which is merely conventional and socially constructed. Instead, the UDHR contends for a notion of inherent human dignity that is designed to be appealing to both religious and secular people.

Matters are made more difficult by the fact that the UDHR does not comment on the origin or grounding of the notion of human dignity which it employs. We are not informed of the source or authority which bestows dignity or told in what, exactly, that dignity consists. So, even if we can settle the controversial question of what the framers of the UDHR meant by 'human dignity', it is a further question whether, and if so, how, that concept can be justified. In Chapter 2, Keith Thompson argues that the modern notion of human dignity is not grounded in the natural rights of either Greco-Roman or eighteenth-century thought. He maintains that, even if it is not explicitly acknowledged in the documents themselves, a major factor in the acceptance of the modern notion of universal human dignity is the influence, conscious or not, of religious teachings about reciprocity, the *imago Dei* and the *imitatio Dei*. His concern, however, is that acceptance of these religious teachings is waning in the West, and he challenges philosophers and legal theorists to propose alternative, secular accounts of human dignity to sustain continued support of human rights.

To be sure, a religious account of inherent human dignity faces many objections, not only from secular thinkers like Ruth Macklin (2003) and Steven Pinker (2008) who claim that it is a redundant and indefensible notion, but also from some theologians who maintain that dignity is not inherent but relational. And even if these objections can be addressed, there is the residual concern that a theistic account of human dignity will not be appealing to secular thinkers. In Chapter 3, David Guretzki considers the force of these objections. He concedes that there are problems with the idea of *inherent* human dignity as this notion suggests human value can be understood independently of human relationships. As an alternative, he proposes that the *co-inherence* and *co-relativity* of human dignity – ideas derived from Karl Barth's relational anthropology – could provide common ground between secular and theistic approaches that will help support their shared commitment to human rights protections.

Yet, even if such an account is plausible, this does not settle the question of justification, at least for those hoping to ground our dignity discourse in ontology. For the question remains whether that account is likely to be true in a godless world or whether it is better located in a theistic universe. Recently, Erik Wielenberg (2014) has made a strong case that human dignity and worth can plausibly be grounded in a world without God. In Chapter 4, Wielenberg makes a move symmetrical to Guretzki's suggestion of a theological basis for dignity that will be plausible for secularists, by proposing a secular account of human dignity which will also be appealing to religious thinkers. Wielenberg contends that in virtue of their mental capacities, normal adult humans have a special worth (*psychological worth*) not shared by members of other species. However, he argues, this does not imply that those human beings who lack these capacities have no worth at all. They may still have value because of what they represent (*symbolic worth*) or because they are the kind of being which, if it develops normally, will acquire psychological worth (*potential worth*). Wielenberg defends this account against Singer's charge that special human dignity is *speciesist* and argues that competing theistic accounts of human dignity are inadequate.

However, in Chapter 5, Paul Copan argues that in a godless world of valueless processes, we have no good reason to think that human dignity would exist. Wielenberg and Copan are both moral realists, and their intuitions strongly affirm the reality of human dignity. But Copan argues that their shared intuitions are unlikely to be reliable if there is no God and that the assertion of human dignity in a godless world leaves us with a large number of unexplained brute facts. By contrast, granted God's existence, Copan argues that we can provide a plausible explanation of human worth.

As an alternative to an analytic philosophical approach, Claudia Mariéle Wulf contends that we may locate the essence of human dignity via an existential and phenomenological investigation (Chapter 6). In this way we discover dignity both negatively (in discerning what constitutes its violation) and positively (through recognition of its affirmation). Moreover, in this approach, dignity is found not by conceptual analysis, but by attending closely to those experiences in which it is transgressed or upheld.

Hendrik Kaptein provides another alternative to conceptual analysis (Chapter 7). Rather than starting from the top, with an abstract account, we can start at the bottom, with close attention to the types of communication and conduct which intuitively support (or undermine) human dignity. What is it that we may say or do that promotes or undercuts human dignity? Kaptein considers 10 formal commandments which, if followed, tend to uphold what we pre-reflectively recognize as human dignity. By providing more data to work with, this inductive approach may also help us to find a better conceptual account of human dignity.

Competing Concepts of Human Dignity

Amongst those sympathetic to a robust understanding of human dignity, one classic dispute centres on whether dignity is rooted in human flourishing (the 'well-being theory') or in human autonomy (the 'agency theory'). Defending the second position, in Chapter 8, Åsbjørn and Bjarne Melkevik contend that, as it has been developed by Alan Gewirth, the well-being theory of dignity contributes to the disturbing 'decay of agency' in modern legal systems and may even be self-defeating. The alternative they propose rests on an antinomian reading of Kant's theory, according to which rational people are to be their own lawmakers, thereby profoundly limiting the scope of legislative activity.

By contrast, in Chapter 9, Michał Rupniewski defends a personalist conception of human dignity. Personalism takes the person (rather than impersonal facts and processes) as the starting point of inquiry into reality, and this includes inquiry into the purpose and justification of law. Rupniewski rejects the idea that personalism is dependent on a theistic worldview or speculative metaphysics. In his view, both secularists and theists can agree on the irreducible reality of persons, and both can discover the nature of dignity by reflection on the nature of human action and discourse. Rupniewski agrees with Jeremy Waldron (2012) and Stephen Riley (2017) that law, and the rule of law, are understandable only when closely, and not just contingently, linked to human dignity. He sees human dignity as foundational to law, and not just one of many values realized through, or protected by, the law. But there is more: Waldron and Riley do not go far enough, in his view. What is needed, as supplied by the works of Karol Wojtyła (1979) and Tadeusz Styczeń (2012), is for the law to be cognizant of the structure of human action (including the way a person transcends himself by being both subject and object of his actions) and of the respect due to persons. These considerations of meta-ethics and philosophical anthropology can then be operationalized in jurisprudence and yield a new type of personalist jurisprudence based on the reality of human action.

While the Melkeviks and Rupniewski emphasize in different ways our agency, the UDHR notes that human dignity is a characteristic of all members of the 'human family', and one may wonder whether the notion of autonomy that prevails in modern cultures and many legal decisions adequately captures the social embeddedness of human beings. As Nicholas Aroney argues in Chapter 10, the law must seek ways to balance individual rights with the rights of communities, particularly because people often find their identity in a community – as a member of a church, movement, political association and so on. This is especially important when the demand for individual rights is in tension with the rights of an entire community. For example, according to the 1966 International Covenant on Civil and Political Rights (ICCPR), the rights of individuals not to be discriminated against on the basis of protected attributes (ICCPR Articles 2 and 26) must be harmonized with the rights of human beings to manifest their religious beliefs, enjoy their own culture and use their own language in community with others (ICCPR Articles 18 and 27). Aroney argues that we can resolve these issues only by gaining a better understanding of the social ontology presupposed by human rights law. On this understanding, dignity is not a characteristic of human 'atoms' conceived in isolation from one another but is rather grounded in our common nature as social, relational beings.

While the Melkeviks, Rupniewski and Aroney all locate dignity in some aspect of human nature, others doubt that dignity has a sufficiently objective basis to be a useful legal concept. In Chapter 11, Friedrich Toepel rejects the conclusion that human dignity must have a certain definitive content in law according to a particular moral system. He argues those reaching such a conclusion are committing a fallacy by deriving an institutional fact from another institutional fact, namely the existence of a norm in one system of norms from the existence of the norm in another system of norms. Such an inference is a fallacy because an institutional fact exists only relative to a particular system of norms. The practical significance is that there are many different understandings of human dignity in different cultural settings and the term 'human dignity' should not be used in law. Rather, definitions of indispensable elements of personhood should be used in an unambiguous way.

In the background, a major philosophical controversy driving competing conceptions of human dignity is the classic debate between realism and nominalism in ethics. In Chapter 12, Scott Smith explores the divide between realists, who maintain the real existence of moral universals, such as justice, and nominalists, who claim that only moral particulars exist, such as this just action or that just person. He points out that without universals, we cannot say that the dignity of human beings is defined by some shared essence. So there is no such thing as dignity per se, but only many *dignities*, with nothing in common. Smith argues that if we cannot say what it is that grants all human beings dignity, it is hard to avoid the conclusion that dignity is a mere *construct*, something created by human activities, such as legal interpretations or acts of legislation. He concludes that if we are to uphold a robust understanding of inherent human dignity, we must maintain that it is an objectively real, moral universal.

With the explosion of progress in artificial intelligence (AI), we face the question of whether dignity should be extended to some non-human artefacts. In the closing chapter of this volume, Andy Steiger considers the competing visions of Alan Turing and Michael Polanyi. Turing and more recent thinkers like Ray Kurzweil defend strong AI, the thesis that machines can have their own intelligence, and if this is so, it is plausible to conclude that we may need to extend human dignity to artificial systems. However, Steiger argues that these claims are premised on a flawed, reductive physicalist ontology of human persons. What is wrong with strong AI, according to Steiger, is its failure to recognize the importance of a being's purpose and its implicit reduction of interpersonal I-Thou relationships to mere I-It relationships between persons and objects. Treating a person as a thing, or as a mere collection of functions, denies that person's dignity, and the actual result of humanizing AI is the dehumanization of humankind.

Origin of the Present Volumes

At the 2009 IVR World Congress meeting in Beijing, several of us discussed the paradox that while the main topic of the IVR meeting was human rights, there was a lack of sustained attention to the philosophically most important question: Can we identify and defend a sufficient grounding in reality for our claims about human rights? I was then asked to organize a special workshop focused on that very topic for the 2011 IVR World Congress meeting in Frankfurt. Papers delivered there, combined with others that were specially solicited, issued in the study *Legitimizing Human Rights* (Menuge 2013).

As the range of our contacts continued to grow, we decided we should focus more closely on the nature and importance of religious liberty and its connection to human rights and human dignity. This was the topic of another special workshop I led at the IVR World Congress meeting in Washington, DC, in 2015. Resulting papers plus some additional ones yielded the volume *Religious Liberty and the Law* (Menuge 2017).

Yet we still felt that we had not focused closely enough on the nature and implications of human dignity, and although that idea has proven elusive, we thought that this was the most important notion to tackle next. By good fortune, the IVR committee announced that dignity was one of its leading themes for the 2019 meeting in Lucerne. By this stage, we had considerable international connections, and we wanted to have a large and prestigious presence at the conference and cover both fundamental philosophical questions and also a careful examination of the implications of various notions of dignity for a range of ongoing, high-profile legal controversies. Given the scope of our study, our steering group wisely agreed that our special workshop and subsequent publications needed two leaders, and due to his strong background in law, Barry W. Bussey was selected to join me as co-chair and co-editor.

In Lucerne, over the course of two days and many hours, we had a wide-ranging discussion of the nature, value and ramifications of human dignity. We heard from many ideological perspectives, and there were significant agreements and disagreements about the best way to ground and apply human dignity. While our first thought had been to take these presentations and other papers we had solicited to produce a single, comprehensive tome, it soon became clear that the best way to arrange the material was in a two-volume set, with the first volume devoted to theoretical issues and the second to their practical consequences for a variety of legal controversies and especially for cases involving religious liberty issues.

Acknowledgements

First, I would especially like to thank my wonderful wife Vicki, for agreeing to travel with me to Lucerne to attend the 2019 meeting of the IVR World Congress. We had a remarkable trip together, and before the conference we enjoyed many memorable times in Austria and Switzerland. Special thanks also go to Barry Bussey (who also travelled with his wife) for agreeing to co-chair our special workshop and co-edit the subsequent volumes of essays. And many thanks as well to his assistant, Amy Ross, who has been invaluable in the editing process. I would also like to express my sincere gratitude to the steering committee – Andrew Bennett, Barry Bussey, Dallas Miller, Dwight Newman and Ray Pennings – for their advice and support in guiding this project from concept to completion. Many thanks also to the contributors to our special workshop and to the other writers so kindly offering their work to our volumes on special dignity, for their diligence and attention to detail.

Finally, Barry Bussey and I wish to acknowledge with deep gratitude the generous support we received through CARDUS, an independent, faith-based, Canadian think tank devoted to the support of human flourishing and religious freedom. This support made our initial special workshop possible and also assisted in the publication process.

References

Barak, Aharon. 2015. *Human Dignity: The Constitutional Value and the Constitutional Right*. Cambridge: Cambridge University Press.

Debes, Remy, ed. 2017. *Dignity: A History*. Oxford: Oxford University Press.

Düwell, Marcus, Jens Braarvig, Roger Brownsword and Dietmar Mieth, eds. 2014. *The Cambridge Handbook of Human Dignity: Interdisciplinary Perspectives*. Cambridge: Cambridge University Press.

Kant, Immanuel. 1965 [1781]. *Critique of Pure Reason*. Translated by Norman Kemp Smith. New York: St. Martin's.

———. 2012 [1786]. *Groundwork of the Metaphysics of Morals*, rev. ed. Edited by Mary Gregor and Jens Timmermann. Cambridge: Cambridge University Press.

Kateb, George. 2014. *Human Dignity*. Cambridge, MA: Belknap – an Imprint of Harvard University Press.

Macklin, Ruth. 2003. 'Dignity Is a Useless Concept'. *British Medical Journal* 327, no. 7429 (20 December): 1419–20.

McCrudden, Christopher, ed. 2013. *Understanding Human Dignity*. Oxford: Oxford University Press.

Menuge, Angus J. L., ed. 2013. *Legitimizing Human Rights: Secular and Religious Perspectives*. Farnham, Surrey: Ashgate. Reprinted 2016. Milton Park: Routledge.

———, ed. 2017. *Religious Liberty and the Law: Theistic and Non-Theistic Perspectives*. Milton Park: Routledge.

Murphy, Rex. 2019. 'B.C. Groin Waxing Case Is a Mockery of Human Rights'. *National Post*, 19 July. https://nationalpost.com/opinion/rex-murphy-b-c-groin-waxing-case-is-a-mockery-of-human-rights.

Pinker, Steven. 2008. 'The Stupidity of Dignity'. *New Republic*, 28 May. https://newrepublic.com/article/64674/the-stupidity-dignity.

Riley, Stephen. 2017. *Human Dignity and Law*. London: Routledge.

Rosen, Michael. 2012. *Dignity: Its History and Meaning*. Cambridge, MA: Harvard University Press.

———. 2013. 'Dignity: The Case Against'. In *Understanding Human Dignity*, edited by Christopher McCrudden, 143–54. Oxford: Oxford University Press.

Schopenhauer, Arthur. 1965 [1840]. *On the Basis of Morality*. Indianapolis, IN: Hackett.

Styczeń, Tadeusz. 2012. *Dzieła zebrane, T.2. [Collected Works, V. 2]*. Edited by K. Krajewski. Lublin: Towarzystwo Naukowe KUL.

United Nations. 1948. *Universal Declaration of Human Rights.* http://www.un.org/en/universal-declaration-human-rights/index.html.

Waldron, Jeremy. 2012. *Dignity, Rank, and Rights.* Edited by Meir Dan-Cohen. Oxford: Oxford University Press.

Wielenberg, Erik J. 2014. *Robust Ethics: The Metaphysics and Epistemology of Godless Normative Realism.* Oxford: Oxford University Press.

Wojtyła, Karol. 1979. *The Acting Person.* Translated by Andrzej Potocki. Dordrecht: D. Riedel.

Part I

GROUNDING HUMAN DIGNITY

Chapter One

HUMAN DIGNITY IN THE UNIVERSAL DECLARATION OF HUMAN RIGHTS: 'OLD' OR 'NEW'?

Laura Kittel

This chapter examines the doctrine in the Universal Declaration of Human Rights (UDHR 1948) that human beings have a special, inherent dignity. In what, exactly, is this dignity grounded? Is dignity inborn, or is it conferred by an external authority? Is it natural or conventional? What is the significance of this concept of dignity for understanding human rights in the twenty-first century? In seeking answers to these questions, the drafters of the UDHR shall be consulted, as well as relevant perspectives from other contributors, starting with eighteenth-century framers of rights documents in the United States. Their innovations on rights and liberty will provide the necessary background for understanding the twentieth-century notion of human dignity.

As indicated by the term 'inherent', the Universal Declaration's drafters held that dignity belongs to human beings by virtue of their nature as human beings. However, they did not ground this understanding of human nature in a divine source such as the Creator, as appears to be the case with certain eighteenth-century rights documents like the US Declaration of Independence. This was a conscious choice on the part of the drafters so that the Universal Declaration would be secular and therefore its endorsement would not require acceptance of any particular religious worldview. At the same time, the UDHR communicates the idea that dignity and rights are inherent, rather than conventional or bestowed upon individuals by the state. This suggests a third way of viewing the modern notion of human dignity: not as the 'old' notion that was more or less explicitly grounded in religious concepts of human nature, nor as a 'new' notion that is conventional, constructed and conferred by the state. Instead, according to the Universal Declaration, human dignity simply signifies that every person is worthy of respect and that this worth is inherent rather than constructed. Although this does not resolve the tension between declaring dignity to be inherent on the one hand and declining to specify grounds on the other, the Declaration's concept of inherence does point towards certain limits in considerations of dignity to preserve its universal and objective nature.

The main aim of this investigation is to examine the notion of human dignity, particularly in the Universal Declaration, to derive an account of this concept that is historically and conceptually accurate. The 'old' and 'new' concepts of human dignity mentioned earlier and controversies surrounding them have arisen, in the context under consideration in this chapter, from the *Obergefell v. Hodges* (2015) decision of the US Supreme Court that legalized same-sex marriage across the country. The 'old' notion of human dignity, typically grounded in religious concepts of human nature, is said to be under duress as a result of the *Obergefell* decision. For many people, this 'old' dignity is grounded in the Christian understanding that all human beings are created in the image and likeness of God (*imago Dei*) and therefore are of inherent worth, as Justice Clarence Thomas argues in his dissenting opinion in *Obergefell v. Hodges* (2015, 17). According to this view, human beings are entitled only to the natural rights that follow from this grounding in God's image. Rights must conform to God's moral law and in this case to God's design for marriage, which is said to be between one man and one woman. Proponents of this view and perhaps some legal commentators in general are concerned that with the *Obergefell* decision, a 'new' notion of human dignity has been established that is conventional, constructed and conferred by the state (1–18; Yoshino 2015). Presumably one of the main concerns with this is that if dignity is conferred by the state, then the state could take away that dignity, which would also result in the loss of human rights since rights are based on that dignity.

Returning to the aim of this chapter, however, it is not to evaluate every argument presented in the *Obergefell* decision, to engage in theological debates about the appropriate definition of marriage, nor is it to expressly argue the case for or against same-sex marriage. Rather, the main goal of this study is to gain a deeper understanding of the meaning of human dignity, especially in the UDHR, which does not conform to either of the 'old' or 'new' understandings, and to suggest that this meaning presents not only a third way of viewing human dignity in the twenty-first century but that it is the way human dignity should be viewed in politics. Our investigation begins with an exploration of the 'old' human dignity that is found at least implicitly in eighteenth-century American rights documents, along with the concept of liberty. Then we shall evaluate some aspects of 'new' and 'old' dignity in contrast with the notions of human dignity found in the Universal Declaration. In fact, there is more than one notion of human dignity in the UDHR: the first is inherent dignity and the second is achieved dignity. As mentioned earlier, the former is inborn; but the latter concept of dignity is fulfilled when human beings are able to realize or achieve all 30 rights in the Universal Declaration, which are said to constitute a dignified human life. Both types of dignity are integral to understanding human rights in the twenty-first century. However, our investigation begins with the eighteenth century, to which we now turn.

Human Dignity, Rights and Liberty in the Eighteenth Century

Before unpacking human dignity in the UDHR, it is important to address certain points raised in the *Obergefell* decision relating to the eighteenth-century or 'old' notions of human dignity and of liberty, as they have a bearing on how human rights are understood. Justice Thomas argues that when the framers wrote that all human beings were created equal and were 'endowed by their Creator with certain unalienable Rights', they were referring to the Christian belief that human beings have inherent worth because they are made in the image of God (2015, 17). However, the US Declaration of Independence (1776) neither mentions human dignity nor rests that concept upon the *imago Dei*; for that matter, neither does the US Constitution (1787) nor does the Bill of Rights (1789). Historian Remy Debes contends that the moralized concept of human dignity, in which dignity signifies the fundamental moral worth of all human beings, was not in use in political discourse until the UDHR introduced it in 1948 (2017, 1–2; see also McCrudden 2008 and Habermas 2010). Prior to this, until around 1830–50, Debes explains that human dignity was largely understood in terms of social status or rank, for example, in relation to nobility, power, gentlemanly bearing or status within the church – not 'some fundamental, unearned, equally shared *moral* status among humans' (2017, 2, emphasis original). This could explain why there is no direct reference to human dignity or the image of God in the eighteenth-century American rights documents. The historical evidence suggests that human rights have been retrospectively invested with the moralized notion of human dignity via the UDHR, but Jürgen Habermas contends that there has likely been an intimate, though implicit connection between the two concepts of rights and dignity 'from the beginning' (2010, 466). Nevertheless, historians observe that the 'universalization process', whereby dignity came to signify the innate moral worth of the human person in politics, primarily occurred during the nineteenth century, culminating in the twentieth (LaVaque-Manty 2017; see also Debes 2017, McCrudden 2008). The 'old' concept of human dignity, then, is properly dated to the UDHR, which further suggests that the authoritative document on the matter is in fact the Universal Declaration.

There is another concept in *Obergefell* that would benefit from a more accurate understanding, that of liberty. The concept of liberty is relevant to that of dignity in *Obergefell* in that it appears to be the value within which dignity is largely articulated in the majority decision, and it also has a bearing on the types of rights (e.g. positive and/or negative) that are thought to be relevant to the eighteenth-century American documents, and therefore to those of the present day. Jonathan Kahn explains that Justice Anthony Kennedy's majority opinion in *Obergefell* situates dignity as a constitutional value in the doctrine of substantive due process (SDP), which is derived from the Fourteenth Amendment's guarantee that the state will not deprive anyone of liberty without the due process of law. In this view, the concept of liberty contains 'fundamental values and rights so important that any law affecting them must be subject to a close and searching review by the Court to ensure that they are not being improperly infringed' (Kahn 2015). In Kennedy's opinion in *Obergefell*, human dignity is among these values. Justice Clarence Thomas, on the other hand, locates dignity in the notion of human beings as created in the image of God, which suggests a different relationship to liberty, wherein dignity exists prior to, rather than following, liberty. Perhaps part of the problem here is that the 'new' and 'old' concepts of human dignity, highlighted, respectively, in the judges' opinions mentioned earlier, are elaborated alongside one another in a way that does not make clear whether the old concept has been subsumed under the new, or whether the two concepts of human dignity can coexist together and in what way.

In any event, in evaluating the old concept of human dignity, it is important to likewise evaluate the notion of liberty to which it is said to correspond. Justice Thomas argues that 'in the American legal tradition, liberty has long been understood as individual freedom *from* governmental action, not as a right *to* a particular governmental entitlement' (2015, 7, emphasis original). He argues that the liberty of the eighteenth century was negative, meaning that it consisted of freedom from government interference and its arbitrary exercise of power. More narrowly, he maintains, this concept of liberty harkens back to the definition found in the Magna Carta (1225), where it consisted of freedom from physical restraint (Thomas 2015, 4–9). According to Justice Thomas, the framers' concept of liberty did not include government recognition of rights much beyond the scope of already extant natural rights, nor could the government be called upon to provide benefits (10–13). In other words, liberty was not recognized in a positive sense where the government provided citizens with certain benefits based on their rights. On the contrary, the framers understood liberty not only in the negative sense, but also in the positive sense as the provision of rights or entitlements. In fact, Edmund Randolph explains that he and his fellow delegates at the Constitutional Convention (25 May–17 September 1787) were tasked to work on 'rights modified by society' because states had already secured natural rights (Levy 2005, 15). Among those rights were the right to form a militia and keep and bear arms (Second Amendment) and the right not to house soldiers in one's home (Third Amendment). Thus, in their own words, the framers saw the creation of the US Constitution (1787) and Bill of Rights (1789) as establishing 'rights modified by society', as securing rights beyond those that are said to be natural.

The framers understood not only that the creation of a new nation involved freedom from government interference and the protection of certain fundamental natural rights, but also that a functioning society required the provision of government entitlements or benefits. In fact, as Billy D. Walker explains, since seventeenth-century colonial America, local governments have drawn upon property tax as a resource for those provisions (1984, 265). The practice of taxation has its roots in the ancient world. There was a land tax in Athens as far back as 596 BC (ibid.). The Romans likewise taxed their subjects, especially lands that they had conquered. England was taxed under the Romans and continued the practice after the Norman conquest of 1066, instituting a more structured taxation system in the twelfth century (266). Walker argues that the history of the property tax is in fact intertwined with the establishment of free, universal, compulsory education that originated with the sixteenth-century Protestant Reformation. Protestants in both Germany and England believed that this education was necessary to protect the well-being of the state against rising secular nationalism, to enable people to read Scriptures on their own and to counterbalance the dominance of the Catholic Church in education (ibid.). In fact, the first modern public schools were founded in Germany and funded by property and other taxes. In 1524, Martin Luther's plans for a public school system were enacted in Magdeburg, and in 1528, Saxony put in place a similar system under the advice of Philip Melanchthon (ibid.). In England by 1600, Henry VIII and Edward VI instituted Anglican authority over education, creating 360 grammar schools across the country (267). After the English Civil War of 1649, the Puritans were in a position to promote public schools, but were shortly thereafter compelled to leave for America; by 1660, three Puritan colonies – Massachusetts Bay, Connecticut and New Haven – established laws to enact public school systems funded by local property taxes (267–68). However, in the rest of the colonies, people viewed levying taxes to support public schools as an infringement of their property rights, and thus the practice was widely opposed until the latter part of the eighteenth century (271–72).

Despite the opposition, Thomas Jefferson was one of the proponents of raising taxes for public schools during the Revolutionary period. Historical sources show that by 1779, if not earlier, Jefferson wanted resources to be allocated to public schools in Virginia so that they could serve as the primary means of education, rather than church or private schools (Walker 1984, 272–73). In a letter, Jefferson (1786b) wrote, 'I think by far the most important bill in our whole code is that for the diffusion of knowledge among the people. No other sure foundation can be devised for the preservation of freedom, and happiness'. He argued that public education is not only essential for preserving liberty (and happiness) but that it is the *most* important bill in the entire code of Virginia, even above those that would, for example, secure people's property rights and their freedom from government intrusion. He encourages the letter's recipient, George Wythe, to 'establish and improve the law for educating the common people' (Jefferson 1786b). Further, Jefferson contends that 'the tax which will be paid for this purpose [public education] is not more than the thousandth part of what will be paid to kings, priests and nobles who will rise up among us if we leave the people in ignorance' (Jefferson 1786b). Contrary to Justice Thomas's argument in *Obergefell*, then, the framer of the US Declaration of Independence, Thomas Jefferson, also conceived of liberty in positive terms as requiring the state to provide citizens with certain rights or benefits.

In fact, rather than declaring the rights to life, liberty and property, as Justice Thomas (2015, 4–6) argues in attempting to clarify the meaning of liberty in the Bill of Rights, Jefferson enshrined the rights to 'Life, Liberty, and the pursuit of Happiness' in the US Declaration of Independence. The notion of pursuing happiness provides a more expansive definition of freedom than that of being free from physical restraint. As I have argued elsewhere (Kittel 2019, 28–52), in the Declaration, the pursuit of happiness has a double meaning: first, it encompasses the moral right of the individual to pursue happiness for himself or herself, and the second is Jefferson's desire for people to recognize that the pursuit of happiness is also a communal enterprise, meaning that people are to undertake actions to benefit others as well as the state (White 1978, 233). Michael Zuckert contends that the rights to life and liberty, along with that to property (although not included in the Declaration), comprise a notion of personal sovereignty, in which a person has rightful say over his or her life, actions and possessions. Zuckert concludes that these particular rights amount to 'a comprehensive right to pursuit of happiness, i.e., the right to pursue a shape and way of life self-chosen' (2000, 66). However, these rights are not absolute or unlimited, but are constrained by considerations of the public good. In his *Essay Concerning Human Understanding* (1689), John Locke argues that the 'careful and constant pursuit of true and solid happiness', wherein people suspend their desires and will to act until they have examined whether those desires are good or evil, and have chosen the good, is the 'necessary foundation of our *liberty*' (1961, 219–20, emphasis added). For Locke, the morally good or virtuous pursuit of happiness is the foundation of liberty. He also argues that natural rights must be exercised within the bounds of natural law, as liberty is not license, or freedom from any and all constraints or substantive moral values

(Locke 1988, 306). At the same time, it is indisputable that the right to pursue happiness includes the right to pursue a way of life that is self-chosen. Does this mean that the state protects only a way of life that is founded on or follows the natural law instituted by God?

On the appropriate relationship between religious beliefs and natural or human rights for many of the most influential framers – Thomas Jefferson and James Madison, the latter of whom drafted the US Constitution (1787), for example – and John Locke, the answer is clear: salvation and politics are separate issues. This brings us to another aspect of liberty as fundamental to the founding notion of it as any other: religious liberty. In authoring the Virginia Statute for Religious Freedom (1786), a forerunner to the First Amendment of the US Constitution, Jefferson presented the principle of separation between church and state and argued that freedom of religion or conscience was a natural right:

> Whereas Almighty God hath created the mind free; that all attempts to influence it by temporal punishment or burthens, or by civil incapacitations, tend only to beget habits of hypocrisy and meanness, and are a departure from the plan of the Holy author of our religion, who being Lord both of body and mind, yet chose not to propagate it by coercions on either, as was his Almighty power to do.

In *Memorial and Remonstrance* (1785), Madison argues similarly that freedom of religion is an inalienable right 'because the opinions of men, depending only on the evidence contemplated by their own minds cannot follow the dictates of other men' (para 1). Religious belief is genuine, Madison contends, only when guided by a person's own reason, conscience and conviction, not force or violence as when it is instituted by the state. Madison explains, 'We maintain therefore that in matters of Religion, no mans [*sic*] right is abridged by the institution of Civil Society and that Religion is wholly exempt from its cognizance' (ibid.). In the same document, he denies that a civil magistrate is 'a competent Judge of Religious Truth; or that he may employ Religion as an engine of Civil policy' (para 5), since salvation, with which religion is concerned, is beyond the concerns of the state. Rather, the basis of all laws, Madison argues, is equality.

Many of these ideas are found in John Locke's *Letter Concerning Toleration* (1689). Locke writes that the toleration of others with different religious beliefs is 'agreeable to the Gospel of Jesus Christ, and to the genuine reason of mankind' and that it is also a necessity (6). In this letter, Locke aims to distinguish between the concerns of civil government and those of religion to determine the boundaries that should rightfully separate the two. The business of civil government is for people to procure, preserve and advance their civil interests, Locke argues, such as 'life, liberty, health, and indolency of body; and the possession of outward things, such as money, lands, houses, furniture, and the like' (6–7). Civil magistrates are restricted to the promotion of these things, and their reach 'neither can nor ought in any manner to be extended to the salvation of souls' or the care that each human being undertakes towards his or her own soul (7). Locke argues, 'All the life and power of true religion consist in the inward and full persuasion of the mind; and faith is not faith without believing' (ibid.). If people are forced to accept religious views by laws, they do not really have faith; the power of religion is found precisely in its voluntary nature.

Madison (1785) contends that religious believers should bear with those who do not share their faith. He writes, 'Whilst we assert for ourselves a freedom to embrace, to profess and to observe the Religion which we believe to be of divine origin, we cannot deny an equal freedom to those whose minds have not yet yielded to the evidence which has convinced us' (para 4). In other words, people who do not share a particular religious worldview have the same rights and freedoms as those who do. Complementing this view, Thomas Jefferson argues in his *Notes on Virginia* (1781) that people's rights do not depend upon their religious beliefs (1999, 392–96). Natural rights and those modified by the state are not predicated upon whether people believe in God or follow His precepts as set forward by any Christian denomination. Given their views on religious liberty and on pursuing happiness, these framers appear to have endorsed a way of life in which a person cultivates moral and intellectual virtues and follows an educated conscience – they did not promote in politics any particular religious doctrine regarding the way a person should properly live.

Although the larger goal of this chapter is to arrive at a deeper understanding of human dignity in the UDHR, it has been necessary to elaborate the 'old' notion of dignity, especially in regards to eighteenth-century liberty, to demonstrate that this notion is substantially different from the way liberty is portrayed by some as only negative in character and wedded to certain Christian doctrines. On the contrary, the 'old' notion of dignity in which human beings have equal, inherent moral worth is more recent, appearing in politics through a gradual shift in thought during the nineteenth century, culminating with its first overt reference in a rights document with the UDHR. As has been demonstrated, evidence for the positive aspects of liberty, wherein the state provides benefits, entitlements or rights to its citizens, can be found in the practice of taxation, which spans history from ancient Greece to the present. The provision of public education is also a well-established tradition that eighteenth-century framers such as Thomas Jefferson supported. The liberty that the framers envisioned thus was both negative *and* positive: it involved not only freedom from government interference, but actions that the government undertook to preserve the rights and well-being of citizens, also found in relation to the right to pursue happiness and bills to establish religious freedom. The concerns that eighteenth-century framers dealt with, such as the nature of rights, liberty and dignity (the latter dealt with more or less implicitly), as well as the appropriate grounding of these concepts, are recurrent questions in politics, as we shall see with the explication of human dignity in the UDHR.

Human Dignity in the Universal Declaration: Inherent and Achieved

Whereas liberty is the overarching concept within which the notion of 'new' dignity has arisen in the *Obergefell* decision, the concept of human dignity in the UDHR is articulated on its own in two distinct forms: (1) inherent dignity, meaning the unearned equal moral worth of all individuals; and (2) achieved dignity, meaning that the rights in the Declaration set forward the standards necessary to be achieved for human beings to live a dignified life (Hughes 2011, 9–11; Donnelly 2013, 15). The first concept, inherent dignity, is the overarching foundation for all the rights in the Universal Declaration and the origin of the 'old' notion of dignity in politics. Inherent human dignity affirms the notion that human beings have objective moral value. Importantly, it is not a right itself or one right among many. As such, inherent dignity is not elaborated in the Universal Declaration as a person's feelings or sense of their own dignity, even though this sense might otherwise be a component of the notion. Inherent dignity signifies rather that no matter how a person feels or has been degraded, they possess an innate worth (Hughes 2011, 13). Human beings do not have to do or achieve anything to prove that they possess equal moral worth. At the same time, the second type of dignity in the UDHR, achieved dignity, *does* mean that certain standards need to be achieved so that people can lead dignified lives; these standards are the rights listed in the 30 articles of the UDHR. The rights that the Universal Declaration's drafters thought necessary for human beings to live a dignified life include rights to liberty, security, legal personhood, privacy, freedom of movement and religion, education, participation in governance, work, leisure, an adequate standard of living and healthcare, and marriage. Human rights in the Universal Declaration were safeguarded with a view towards preventing future Holocausts and other atrocities, and their specific origins during the drafting were frequently attributed to the events of World War II (Morsink 1993, 358). The project of articulating human dignity as inherent and achieved, then, took shape in an atmosphere where that dignity had been gravely violated. The UDHR's ideas that all human beings have inherent moral worth and deserve certain rights to live a dignified life set the international standard for the meaning of human dignity in politics; they must not again slip from humanity's memory or be lost among various other notions of dignity whether 'new' or 'old'.

Before elaborating on these notions of dignity, it is important to observe some of the document's central characteristics for the sake of understanding not only its content and history, but also how the drafters thought it should be viewed. The Commission on Human Rights that undertook the preliminary draft was comprised of 18 members from diverse backgrounds. The first draft of the UDHR proposed in September 1948 included advice from 50 member states (United Nations n.d.). There were significant contributions from a range of nations and representatives though the central contributors were Chinese philosopher Peng Chun Chang, French jurist René Cassin, Lebanese philosopher Charles Malik and American First Lady Eleanor Roosevelt.[1] The UDHR was adopted by the United Nations (UN) General Assembly on 10 December 1948, after less than two years of drafting and debate. It complemented the UN Charter of 1945, set forward the human rights that belong to all individuals across the globe and became part of a new international system in which nations and individuals within them would be

---

[1] For more on contributors, see Glendon (2001, xx, 239). Glendon highlights the contributions of Canadian jurist John P. Humphrey, who drew up the first draft of the declaration; Carlos Romulo of the Philippines; India's Hansa Mehta, who ensured the rights of women were included; Alexei Pavlov of Russia; and Hernán Santa Cruz from Chile, who advocated strongly for social and economic rights.

held accountable for the treatment of their citizens (Glendon 2001, xvi). Consequently, national sovereignty no longer shielded a state and its actors from punishment for domestic behaviour. The drafters did not view the UDHR as legally binding, so they addressed it not to governments in the first instance but, quoting the Preamble, to 'every individual and every organ of [every] society' to serve as an educational tool (Morsink 1999, xxii, 330–31). The UDHR has since been midwife to over 50 legal documents, but the document itself consists of moral rights and principles (xi). That said, the drafters intentionally refrained from endorsing any one system of morality or ultimate reality over another, religious or otherwise; they did not refer in the document to divinely established moral laws or to our responsibilities to keep those moral laws. Instead the drafters sought to protect human life and inherent dignity (as a secularized notion), as well as to put into practice the rights of all human beings, or as Jack Donnelly argues, the rights that all human beings need 'for a life of dignity, a life worthy of a human being' (2013, 15), which of course is the notion of achieved dignity.

Inherent Dignity

Unlike the 'new' dignity produced by *Obergefell* that is conventional, constructed and conferred by the state, the first notion of human dignity in the Universal Declaration is decidedly extant prior to the state. The Universal Declaration was created in response to the 'barbarous acts which have outraged the conscience of mankind', as the Preamble states, implicitly referring to the systematic slaughter of six million Jews during the Holocaust. However, explicit references to both World Wars I and II were removed from the Preamble to stave off the impression that the Declaration was limited only to those historical events (Glendon 2001, 176). Mary Ann Glendon argues that the UDHR rejects legal positivism with the statement in the Preamble that the document recognizes people have inherent dignity and equal rights, which implies that dignity and rights exist prior to the state (ibid.). Legal positivism is the view that there are no rights outside those granted by the state through legislation. Before World War II (1939–45), the positivist view prevailed in the United States, Europe and the Soviet Union (ibid.). However, the widespread outrage over Nazi atrocities indicated that it was human beings themselves and their intrinsic value that had been violated, rather than state-created positive law. The UDHR drafters also knew that to counter these atrocities, which had been legalized by the Third Reich, they would have to appeal to a notion of law that was higher than and prior to the laws of nation states.

As mentioned earlier, those a priori laws were traditionally thought to have a religious basis. In his *Two Treatises of Government* (1689), John Locke argued that divinely established natural law and natural rights existed prior to the creation of the state; further, when people came together to form a government, they limited some of their rights such as natural liberty to maintain government, but only minimally. According to Jerome Shestack (1998), World War II resulted in a revival of eighteenth-century natural rights theory, but this theory was a qualified or modified version. Twentieth-century rights theorists did not wear the 'same metaphysical dress' as their predecessors but they did attempt to find values that have universal aspects (215). For their part, the drafters of the

Universal Declaration, some of whom did have the same 'metaphysical dress' as their predecessors, nevertheless worked through their religious beliefs and commitments to Western notions of natural law to search for values that have universal aspects and ways of articulating these values that would resonate among the global community (Morsink 1999, 284–90). Although the drafters did not endorse one specific view of morality or ultimate reality, for example, Christian, Muslim or Buddhist, they did not enshrine a contingent, historically bound or materialist view either. Glenn Hughes argues that the idea of inherency in the Universal Declaration indicates that there is more to the document than historicism or materialism; in fact, this inherent human dignity suggests first that human beings share a universal human nature and second that they live together in a transcendent reality, albeit one that is not bound to any particular religious doctrine or ecclesiastical commitment (2011, 1, 15–17). As the sources in this and the previous paragraph indicate, human dignity in the UDHR was not granted by the state as it is said to have been with the 'new' notion of dignity, but its stated source was not God-given either.

For many delegates, the journey to articulating a secular vision of human nature and dignity in the Universal Declaration required traversing well-worn paths of religious belief, including reference to Christian natural law theory and the *imago Dei*. Johannes Morsink explains that Article 1 of the Declaration, which encapsulates the notion of inherent dignity in its statement that 'all human beings are born free and equal in dignity and rights', started out in a secular format and returned to one, but along the way referred to nature as an apparent substitute for God (1999, 284). During a working group meeting of the Second Session, delegates from France and the Philippines jointly proposed that Article 1 be amended to read that all human beings are 'endowed by nature with reason and conscience', whereas the original wording simply said that human beings were 'endowed with reason and conscience' (UN ESCOR 1947a, 21). The addition of the phrase 'by nature' appeared in some ways to link the article to Christian natural law theory and thus was later removed. Overt reference to God was introduced by the Brazilian delegation during the Third Committee with the suggestion that the second sentence of Article 1 read: '*Created in the image and likeness of God*, they are endowed with reason and conscience' (UN General Assembly 1948b; Morsink 1999, 285, emphasis original). The Dutch delegates similarly proposed amending the first recital of the Preamble to include divine origins: 'Whereas recognition of the inherent dignity and of the equal and inalienable rights of all members of the human family, based on man's divine origin and immortal destiny, is the foundation of freedom' (UN General Assembly 1948a). The Brazilian and Dutch amendments were withdrawn when widespread opposition to them became apparent, as even religious nations did not want to impose their beliefs on others and did not consider it appropriate to decide such matters of faith by popular vote (Morsink 1999, 285). The drafters were aware of the metaphysical implications of inherent human dignity, but chose to set aside specific reference to the *imago Dei* among other things so that the Universal Declaration could meet its goal of universal appeal.

The 'old' notion of human dignity in politics, which originates with the UDHR, then, is one that has been secularized. This also holds true for Article 16 on the right to marry. Charles Malik, the Lebanese delegate and a Greek Orthodox Christian, suggested during the Second Session of the drafting committee that the article on marriage be amended to read: 'The family deriving from marriage is the natural and fundamental group unit of society. It is endowed by the Creator with inalienable rights antecedent to all positive law' (UN ESCOR 1947b, 11–12; Morsink 1999, 284). The drafters accepted Malik's first sentence but denied the second, divorcing the connection between God and nature that often existed in rights documents since the eighteenth century. Alexandre Bogomolov, a Russian delegate, had reminded the committee that 'many people did not believe in God and that the Declaration was meant for mankind as a whole, whether believers or unbelievers' (UN ESCOR 1947b, 12). The document might not satisfy religious believers in every respect, but it does not attempt to do so; neither does it aim to satisfy every unbeliever. People who subscribe to the notion that human origins are entirely material are also likely to find fault with the document (Hughes 2011, 17). Glenn Hughes argues that the view of transcendence that the UDHR delineates does not entail a specific realm or divine entity, which are often taken to be the most problematic aspects of transcendence; rather, the concept can be understood as a descriptive term in contrast to immanence (16). Hughes contends that this transcendence signifies a 'dimension of *meaning*', not confined to time or space, wherein we experience things like 'our moral longing for perfect justice, or our consciousness of the infinite value of each human person' (ibid., emphasis original). In other words, people can participate in a shared, transcendent realm of meaning while remaining firmly grounded in the spatial and temporal world of everyday life. This transcendence includes the idea that certain features of human existence, such as our purpose, origins, free will and capacity to act morally, are ultimately 'not directly accessible to human understanding' and thus remain mysterious (ibid.). Even though the Universal Declaration does not ground human dignity and rights in a religious worldview, in this manner it still does provide a transcendent grounding of sorts for these concepts.

The notion of inherent human dignity in the Universal Declaration is thus a simple one: human beings possess human rights by virtue of their nature as human beings, where 'by nature' means simply the fact that they are human beings. There is no religious doctrine such as the *imago Dei* invested in the document as a necessary support, although such considerations informed debate about the concept. In the end the document was created to be secular. The drafters thought that people could apprehend basic moral truths independently from religion in ways that were suitable for politics, which was acceptable to those from a variety of religious faiths, including Catholic and Protestant Christians, Jews, Buddhists and Muslims (though fundamentalists found this objectionable) (Morsink 1999, 285). Further, the drafters recognized that the Universal Declaration needed what the concept of inherent human dignity, without an historical or religious grounding, provided: 'a founding explanatory principle that was both universal and pluralistic' (Hughes 2011, 7). The doctrine of simple inherence, as Morsink describes it, enables the notion of human dignity to be flexible enough to accommodate various conceptions of human nature, but at the same time it retains substantive value, so it excludes notions that devalue human beings or misconstrue the Universal Declaration as a value-neutral blank slate (1999, 286–88, 295). The document can accommodate or resonate with many diverse views on human nature and rights, but not all of them. Further, since the document is secular – as is appropriate for establishing a global intergovernmental organization or a modern nation state for that matter – it must be utilized in ways that are compatible with it being non-religious, universal and pluralistic. Although certain faiths or other perspectives might understand their beliefs and values to be reflected in the Universal Declaration, they cannot then tailor the document to fit purposes that contravene its content and spirit. This is one of the limits in considerations of dignity.

Achieved Dignity

The second type of human dignity in the Universal Declaration, achieved dignity, relates to the content of the 30 articles, which together set forward minimal standards necessary for human beings to achieve a dignified life. All the rights in the document must be enacted, accessible or made achievable by every human being. Although some of the rights, as mentioned earlier, were informed by religious or philosophical views concerning how human beings should conceive of their origins, purpose or conduct, the drafters more often than not found philosophical arguments unnecessary for establishing which rights to include in the document (Morsink 1993, 358). Rather, the experiences of World War II under Hitler's National Socialism, particularly the Holocaust, were enough in their minds to justify the rights they enshrined. Indeed, they consulted not only their memories of the war, but a 384-page report on human rights violations compiled by the War Crimes Commission (UN ESCOR 1948; Morsink 1993, 367). During World War II (1939–45), R. J. Rummel contends that the Nazis murdered over 20 million men, women and children of many races and nationalities, not including civilian and military casualties (1992, 11). This figure includes 'handicapped, aged, sick, prisoners of war, forced laborers, camp inmates, critics, homosexuals, Jews, Slavs, Serbs, Germans, Czechs, Italians, Poles, French, Ukrainians, and many others' (ibid.). Hitler did not view human beings as members of the same human family or as possessing inherent dignity, so they did not have equal rights; in fact, Hitler argued that a person's value was determined by his or her 'inner racial virtues', with Aryans being the most valuable (Morsink 1993, 363). The UDHR repudiates this view in every article, starting with the Preamble and Articles 1 and 2, which include affirmations that 'all human beings are born free and equal in dignity and rights' (Article 1) and that 'everyone is entitled to all the rights and freedoms set forth in this Declaration, without distinction of any kind, such as race, colour, sex, language, religion, political or other opinion, national or social origin, property, birth or other status' (Article 2). The principles of inherent human dignity and non-discrimination in these articles characterize the document as a whole, and along with the rest of the rights enumerated, make up a program of rights that is essential to enact, make accessible or achieve for a dignified life; further, these rights are indivisible.

Like rights in the eighteenth century, the human rights that were enshrined in the Universal Declaration were not just so-called negative rights, or freedoms from government interference, they were positive rights requiring government action as well. Human rights theorists in the twentieth and twenty-first centuries such as Henry Shue (1980) and Jack Donnelly (2013) have demonstrated that the distinction between 'positive' and 'negative' rights – wherein the state acts to provide people with certain entitlements as with positive rights, or the state simply refrains from acting, as with negative rights – is a misnomer in the first place. Donnelly argues, 'All human rights require positive action and restraint on the part of the state' (2013, 43, emphasis added). Civil and political rights are often characterized as negative rights, but for people to exercise their right to vote, for example, the state must provide the means to vote in a free and fair election. Prior to this, as Thomas Jefferson observed, if a state wants its citizenry to be informed and capable of making these decisions, it must provide them with a basic education. The drafters of the UDHR were sensitive to issues of state action or inaction in 1948 and instilled rights in the document that did not rely upon maintaining such distinctions.

René Cassin likened the Universal Declaration to the portico of a temple, which is helpful for understanding the types of rights and principles in the document and they shaped a dignified life that was propounded in secular terms. Glendon contends that the four principles of dignity, liberty, equality (non-discrimination) and brotherhood served as the foundation stones of the temple, from which arose the seven steps (statements or recitals) of the Preamble (2001, 174). She explains that for Cassin:

> The main body of the Declaration consists of rights arranged in *four columns*: rights pertaining to individuals as such (Articles 3 through 11); the rights of the individual in relation to others and to various groups (Articles 12 through 17); the spiritual, public, and political liberties (Articles 18 through 21); and the economic, social, and cultural rights (Articles 22 through 27). (Ibid., emphasis original)

Finally, Articles 28 through 30 form the pediment of the temple, serving as a capstone that connects individuals to society and places all the rights within a framework of limits, duties and a peaceful social and political order to facilitate their realization (ibid.). Article 1 itself reflects this unfolding of rights in that it sets forward not only dignity and liberty, but equality and brotherhood. According to Peng Chun Chang, these qualities of Article 1 enable the document from the beginning to communicate the idea that individuals not only have rights, but that they also have duties, which are implied with the article's statement that people should act towards one another in a spirit of brotherhood (UN GAOR 1948, 98).[2] The concepts of fraternity and belonging to a shared human family (the latter is stated in the Preamble) are interwoven with those of dignity, equality (non-discrimination) and liberty.

As the relationship between these rights and principles indicates, the Universal Declaration is meant to be read as a whole, rather than as a collection of rights that can be interpreted individually according to preference. Morsink explains that the drafters maintained that despite these different types of rights there was a fundamental unity to them, expressed in what is called the 'organic unity' of the document (1999, xiv). Glendon contends that the contemporary failure to gain an appreciation of the document as an organic unity, or an integrated body of principles, has led to the prevailing approach today wherein the 30 articles of the Declaration are interpreted 'pick-and-choose cafeteria-style' (1998, 1153). Akhil Reed Amar argues that this approach is also

---

[2] UN GAOR, 3rd Session, 96th plenary meeting, UN Doc. A/C.3/SR.96 (7 October 1948), 98. https://undocs.org/A/C.3/SR.96.

common towards the US Constitution (1787) and Bill of Rights (1789); many American law schools separate the amendments for instruction in different types of courses, and legal scholarship tends not to view the two documents holistically or in the fullness of their relationship to one another (1991, 1132–33). The result is that the significance of these documents tends not to be fully understood. Last, according to the United Nations itself, human rights are interrelated, interdependent and indivisible (OHCHR n.d.). Rights exist in close relationship to one another: advancing or improving conditions for one right positively affects the rest, while abridging one right negatively impacts the others. Not only must the UDHR be interpreted holistically to gain an accurate appreciation of the document, but to achieve human dignity in practice, its 30 articles must also be enacted holistically.

While it is not possible to evaluate the 'new' notion of human dignity arising out of *Obergefell*, it is important to observe one aspect that appears to be problematic for the two primarily objective notions of dignity in the Universal Declaration: dignitary wounds. In *Obergefell*, the plaintiffs seeking to legalize same-sex marriage argued that children of same-sex couples 'suffer the stigma of knowing their families are somehow lesser' (Kennedy 2015, 15). The Supreme Court's decision attempts to remedy those wounds, but as Kennedy argues, 'Dignitary wounds cannot always be healed with a stroke of a pen' (25). In contemplating whether dignitary wounds are legitimate issues for legal redress and where they might fit within the UDHR's constellation of concerns, it is notable that these wounds are observable across multiple cases in history. Perhaps nowhere are dignitary wounds more evident than those created during the Holocaust where Jews were stripped of their possessions, herded into concentration camps and tattooed with identification numbers as indelible signs of their perceived inferiority. The Nazis inflicted dignitary wounds upon Jews to dehumanize and humiliate them and to convince the populace that Jews were in fact worthless so that plans to exterminate them could be carried out. Elie Wiesel, although he does not identify it as such, illustrates this wounding:

> A young Jewish boy discovered the Kingdom of Night. I remember his bewilderment, I remember his anguish. It all happened so fast. The ghetto. The deportation. The sealed cattle car [...]
>
> I remember he asked his father [...] 'Who would allow such crimes to be committed? How could the world remain silent?'
>
> [...] And then I explained to [the boy] how naïve we were, that the world did know and remained silent. (2006, 118)

Dignitary wounds pre-date *Obergefell* and are not immaterial considerations. In fact, these wounds were also cited by Chief Justice Earl Warren in the Supreme Court's *Brown v. Board of Education* (1954) ruling that the practice of racial segregation in public schools following the 'separate but equal' doctrine was in fact unconstitutional (Kahn 2015). Warren argued that 'to separate [children] from others of similar age and qualifications solely because of their race generates a feeling of inferiority as to their status in the community that may affect their hearts and minds in a way unlikely ever to be undone' (1954, 494). A person's sense of his or her own dignity having been violated is worthy of legal and moral redress and could be considered part of the Universal Declaration's overarching concept of inherent human dignity, arising out of the fact that a person has been prevented from achieving a dignified life, that is, accessing the rights essential to it.

The two concepts of human dignity in the Universal Declaration, inherent and achieved, can accommodate the subjective experience of dignity, but it is important that this subjective notion does not eclipse the objective nature of these two concepts. Inherent human dignity – the idea that all human beings have unearned equal moral worth – underwrites all the rights in the document; from this idea it then follows that all human beings are equally entitled to the fulfilment of those 30 articles of rights. The Universal Declaration protects these notions of dignity as though they were facts rather than values that are contestable. However, as Michael Ignatieff points out, the idea that human beings have inherent dignity (by virtue of their nature as human beings) is controversial because it makes a metaphysical claim about human nature and not everyone will agree that human beings possess intrinsic value worth respecting (2001, 54). The Universal Declaration takes a stand against the position that human beings do not have intrinsic value, which for many people might simply be a philosophical problem, but for the Universal Declaration this stance in its most virulent forms is demonstrated by Hitler and other genocidal dictators. The UDHR remedies dignitary wounds first and foremost by securing the objective nature of human dignity, inherent and achieved, as well as by safeguarding human life. This purpose places another important limit on considerations of dignity.

This chapter has presented some of the main issues relating to the 'old' and 'new' concepts of human dignity, arguing that the UDHR is the origin of inherent human dignity in politics, although the religious notion is much older; and that as a result, the old concept of human dignity said to be in conflict with the *Obergefell* decision is perhaps more amenable to it in ways that were not initially apparent. For instance, the old notion of inherent dignity, belonging to the UDHR, is secular rather than religious. It is ultimately founded not upon the *imago Dei*, but upon a broad notion of transcendence that can accommodate a diverse range of religious, philosophical and cultural beliefs. The old notion of inherent human dignity in the UDHR – universal and pluralistic – is accompanied by another concept – that of achieved dignity. Both notions are critical for understanding human rights in the twenty-first century as entailing the realization of positive and negative rights, that is, the full spectrum of human rights, for all human beings equally based on their inherent moral worth. The Universal Declaration also carries forward the eighteenth century's expansive notion of liberty, protecting the individual's right to a self-chosen way of life within the moral parameters set by the document in addition to any moral views or religious beliefs they might hold personally. At the same time, inherent human dignity in the Universal Declaration is unlike the 'new' concept of dignity arising out of *Obergefell* in that it is not conventional, constructed and conferred by the state. Also, unlike this new notion of dignity, the two concepts of human dignity in the UDHR cannot be reduced to the subjective experience of dignity. The drafters addressed dignitary wounds not by protecting dignity simply as a person's own sense of it, but with the knowledge that people have intrinsic moral worth in the first place. Given that they attempt to safeguard humanity from rights violations, provide grounding for human rights, as well as the imperative to achieve or realize those rights, the Universal Declaration's notions of dignity, inherent and achieved, must be preserved against other interpretations.

References

Amar, Akhil Reed. 1991. 'The Bill of Rights as a Constitution'. *Yale Law Journal* 100, no. 5: 81.

Debes, Remy. 2017. 'Introduction'. In *Dignity: A History*, edited by Remy Debes, 1–16. New York: Oxford University Press.

Donnelly, Jack. 2013. *Universal Human Rights in Theory and Practice*, 3rd ed. Ithaca, NY: Cornell University Press.

Glendon, Mary Ann. 1998. 'Knowing the Universal Declaration of Human Rights'. *Notre Dame Law Review* 73, no. 5: 1153–90.

———. 2001. *A World Made New: Eleanor Roosevelt and the Universal Declaration of Human Rights*. New York: Random House.

Habermas, Jürgen. 2010. 'The Concept of Human Dignity and the Realistic Utopia of Human Rights'. *Metaphilosophy* 41, no. 4 (July): 464–80. doi:10.1111/j.1467- 9973.2010.01648.x.

Hughes, Glenn. 2011. 'The Concept of Human Dignity in the Universal Declaration of Human Rights'. *Journal of Religious Ethics* 39, no. 1: 1–24. doi:10.1111/j.1467-9795.2010.00463.x.

Ignatieff, Michael. 2001. *Human Rights as Politics and Idolatry*. Edited by Amy Gutmann. Princeton, NJ: Princeton University Press.

Jefferson, Thomas. 1786a. *An Act for Establishing Religious Freedom*. 16 January. Records of the General Assembly, Enrolled Bills, Record Group 78, Library of Virginia. Richmond, Virginia.

———. 1786b. 'From Thomas Jefferson to George Wythe, 13 August 1786'. Founders Online, National Archives. Accessed 29 September 2019. https://founders.archives.gov/documents/Jefferson/01-10-02-0162.

———. 1999. 'Notes on Virginia: Query XVII'. In *Political Writings*, edited by Joyce Appleby and Terrence Ball, 389–407. Port Chester, NY: Cambridge University Press.

Kahn, Jonathan. 2015. 'The Constitutional Right to Dignity: From Gay Marriage to #Black Lives Matter'. *Conversation*. Accessed 2 February 2020. http://theconversation.com/the-constitutional-right-to-dignity-from-gay-marriage-to-black-lives-matter-44458.

Kennedy, Anthony (Justice). 2015. Opinion of the Court. *Obergefell v. Hodges*, 135 S. Ct. 1732, 576 U.S.

Kittel, Laura. 2019. 'The Pursuit of Happiness and Human Rights: Uncovering Virtues in Human Rights Documents'. PhD diss., University of Notre Dame Australia.

LaVaque-Manty, Mika. 2017. 'Universalizing Dignity in the Nineteenth Century'. In *Dignity: A History*, edited by Remy Debes, 301–22. New York: Oxford University Press.

Levy, Leonard. 2005. *Origins of the Bill of Rights*. New Haven, CT: Yale University Press.

Locke, John. 1689. *First Letter Concerning Toleration*. Translated by William Popple. Accessed 20 January 2020. https://socialsciences.mcmaster.ca/econ/ugcm/3ll3/locke/toleration.pdf.

———. 1961 [1689]. *An Essay Concerning Human Understanding*. Edited by John W. Yolton, vol. 2, Everyman's Library. London: Dent.

———. 1988. *Two Treatises of Government*, student ed. Edited by Peter Laslett. Cambridge: Cambridge University Press.

Madison, James. 1785. 'Memorial and Remonstrance against Religious Assessments, [ca. 20 June] 1785'. Founders Online, National Archives. Accessed 29 September 2019. https://founders.archives.gov/documents/Madison/01-08-02-0163.

McCrudden, Christopher. 2008. 'Human Dignity and Judicial Interpretation of Human Rights'. *European Journal of International Law* 19, no. 4: 655–724.

Morsink, Johannes. 1993. 'World War Two and the Universal Declaration'. *Human Rights Quarterly* 15, no. 2. http://www.jstor.org/stable/762543.

———. 1999. *The Universal Declaration of Human Rights Origins, Drafting, and Intent.* Philadelphia: University of Pennsylvania Press.

Office of the High Commissioner of Human Rights (OHCHR). N.d. 'What Are Human Rights?' *United Nations.* Accessed 15 March 2020. https://www.ohchr.org/en/issues/pages/whatarehumanrights.aspx.

Rummel, R. J. 1992. *Democide: Nazi Genocide and Mass Murder.* New Brunswick, NJ: Transaction.

Shestack, Jerome J. 1998. 'The Philosophic Foundations of Human Rights'. *Human Rights Quarterly* 20, no. 2: 201–34. http://www.jstor.org/stable/762764.

Shue, Henry. 1980. *Basic Rights: Subsistence, Affluence, and U.S. Foreign Policy.* Princeton, NJ: Princeton University Press.

Thomas, Clarence (Justice). 2015. 'Dissenting Opinion'. *Obergefell v. Hodges*, 135 S. Ct. 1732, 576 U.S.

UN ESCOR. 1947a. Comm'n on Hum. Rts, Drafting Comm., 2nd Sess., 9th mtg, UN Doc. E/CN.4/AC.2/SR.9, 21–22 (10 December). https://undocs.org/E/CN.4/AC.2/SR.9.

———. 1947b. Comm'n on Hum. Rts, Drafting Comm., 2nd Sess., 37th mtg, UN Doc. E/CN.4/SR.37, 11–12 (13 December). http://undocs.org/E/CN.4/SR.37.

———. 1948. Comm'n on Hum. Rts, 3rd Sess., UN Doc. E/CN.4/W.20. Used to be UN Doc. E/CN.4/W.19, see UN Doc. E/CN.4/W.20/Corr.1. https://undocs.org/ E/CN.4/W.20/Corr.1.

UN GAOR. 1948. 3rd Sess., 96th plenary mtg. UN Doc. A/C.3/SR.96 (7 October). https://undocs.org/A/C.3/SR.96.

UN General Assembly. 1948a. Draft International Declaration of Human Rights: Netherlands – Amendment to the first paragraph of the preamble. 3rd Sess., 3rd Comm., UN Doc. A/C.3/219 (4 October). https://undocs.org/A/C.3/219.

———. 1948b. Draft International Declaration of Human Rights: Recapitulation of amendments to article 1 of the draft Declaration (E/800). 3rd Sess., 3rd Comm., UN Doc. A/C.3/243, 1 (7 October). https://undocs.org/A/C.3/243.

United Nations. N.d. 'History of the Document'. Universal Declaration of Human Rights. Accessed 9 April 2018. http://www.un.org/en/sections/universal-declaration/history-document/index.html.

Walker, Billy D. 1984. 'The Local Property Tax for Public Schools: Some Historical Perspectives'. *Journal of Education Finance* 9, no. 3 (Winter): 265–88. Accessed 15 January 2020. www.jstor.org/stable/40703424.

Warren, Earl (Chief Justice). 1954. Opinion of the Court. *Brown v. Board of Education of Topeka*, 347 US 483, 74 S. Ct. 686, 98 L. Ed. 873.

White, Morton Gabriel. 1978. *The Philosophy of the American Revolution.* Oxford: Oxford University Press.

Wiesel, Elie. 2006. *Night*, 2nd ed. New York: Hill and Wang.

Yoshino, Kenji. 2015. 'A New Birth of Freedom?: Obergefell V. Hodges'. *Harvard Law Review* 129, no. 1 (November): 147–79. Accessed 17 January 2020. www.jstor.org/stable/24643920.

Zuckert, Michael. 2000. 'Natural Rights in the American Revolution: The American Amalgam'. In *Human Rights and Revolutions*, edited by Jeffrey N. Wasserstrom, Lynn Hunt and Marilyn B. Young, 59–76. Lanham, MD: Rowman & Littlefield.

Chapter Two

HOW DO WE JUSTIFY HUMAN RIGHTS AND DIGNITY?

Keith Thompson

Introduction

In this chapter I discuss the philosophical justifications which underlie human rights and dignity in the Universal Declaration of Human Rights (UDHR) and other international human rights instruments. I write because of concern that the erosion of religious authority in the West may threaten the utilitarian value of the human rights project. While I identify some of the religious premises that can justify human rights and dignity, my purpose is not to highlight those foundations, but to challenge modern legal theorists and political philosophers to explain or justify human rights and dignity in other ways so the power of human rights and dignity is not diminished if the West's retreat from religion continues.

I begin by identifying the existence of natural rights ideas in Greek and Roman philosophy and then discuss the renaissance of those ideas as part of the Enlightenment and their retreat during the age of positivism when Bentham and others assaulted them as 'nonsense upon stilts'. Following the excesses of the Nazis, I note the birth of modern human rights in the middle of the twentieth century and then a reformation of sorts as they morphed into a multiplicity of anti-discrimination and diversity-affirming norms. I suggest this reformation may threaten the original human rights and dignity ideas by splintering them into irreconcilable fragments with no unifying moral power.

I then discuss theory to make sense of human rights and dignity in their twenty-first century context. I ask whether the idea of human dignity underlying the 1948 UDHR project was a postcolonial Western or Christian Trojan horse, or whether it resonated with something deeper and universal in the nature of man as Eleanor Roosevelt and Mary Ann Glendon have argued. And I ask if the idea was always universal, whether the traditional theological and utilitarian supporting arguments can continue to bear its weight in the face of modern challenges.

I conclude that we must find convincing ways to defend human rights in the twenty-first century because they remain a necessary foundation to any peace that protects human dignity. I do not want to accept that the theological justifications of the past have lost their convincing power, but I suggest that an unemotional utilitarian calculus may not be enough to sustain them in the future. I therefore challenge contemporary legal and political theorists to identify passionate arguments with convincing power that can continue to protect human rights.

The History of Human Rights

Some advocates of human rights trace their history to the Greek philosophers, particularly Socrates (d. 399 BC), Plato (428–347 BC) and Aristotle (384–322 BC), and to Cicero (106–43 BC) and Seneca the Younger (4 BC–65 AD) among the Stoics. But the Greek idea of natural rights is different from the ideas expressed in the UDHR since, as in the case of the self-evident equality preached by the American framers, they do not appear to have had any philosophical problem with slavery or the different treatment of the sexes, even though Plato advocated their political equality. Seneca seems to have coined the first generalised egalitarianism since both men and women were rational beings and had an equal capacity for virtue (Sharma 2006, 16; Swidler 1990, 14). But the Christian idea of universal salvation challenged the partition of men into citizen and slave categories. While those ancient ideas may not be far removed from Jefferson's assertion that human equality is self-evident (because of the capacity to reason or because of Christian teaching?), they are distinct from the modern idea that human rights exist as justified claims upon society so that the state must therefore include a claim on the resources of others.

Greek and Roman Versions of Natural Rights and Christianity

The views of Plato and Aristotle about natural rights did not coincide though both discussed them. Miller says Plato saw individuals as under duties as 'an organ of the State', but Aristotle thought of the individual as 'deserving the right which he ought to enjoy in a society based on (proportionate) equality' (Miller 1996, 874; 1995; Baker 1906, 235). Others have pointed out that Aristotle's belief that it was just to allocate resources proportionately (distributive justice) could entrench great inequality because it justified resource allocation according 'to presumed fundamental (natural) rights, due and worth' (Stanford Encyclopedia of Philosophy 2007). Despite Christian challenges, Aristotle's view 'that human beings are unequal by nature' and that they exist in a natural hierarchy endured until the eighteenth century (ibid.). But eventually, the Stoic idea that rational human beings were due the same dignity and respect was developed into a general equality principle in Christianity, even though the Christians did not always live up to their ideals.

Aristotle's natural rights theory also differed from those which were developed by Locke and others in the seventeenth century because Aristotle believed that the polis or state was prior to the individual since individuals could not be self-sufficient if they were separated from the state (Miller 1996, 879). Locke held to the contrary that individuals existed with rights before the state came into existence, though they could not claim rights in twentieth-century terms until there was a state. The difference was that Aristotle believed the individual depended on the state and had rights within it but could not make demands upon it (880).

Though as a leading Stoic Seneca believed that men and women were equal in their capacity for virtue and rationality, his idea was not the same as modern versions of equality either. For though he was consistent in holding that slaves were as capable of virtue as free men, yet there was no offence to justice in confining slaves and women to the role imposed upon them by their social position. Indeed, it was just for 'two equally virtuous human beings' to be assigned different 'officia' based upon their individual dispositions, their 'place in the social structure of the community' and their 'individual fortune at any particular time' (Manning 1973). There was no foundational injustice in the fact that women and slaves were all consigned to places different from that of free men.

Speaking for the US Public Broadcasting Service (PBS), Helmut Koester has framed the origin of modern human rights by discussing the appeal of Christianity. He says Christianity appealed to Roman society because it gave 'even the lowliest slave human dignity and status' (Koester 1998). That dignity and status are evident in Paul's letters where the baptismal formula is that in Christ 'there is neither Jew nor Greek, [...] bond nor free, [...] male nor female' (Gal. 3:28, KJV). For Koester (1998), this was 'a socio-logical formula that define[d an entirely] new community'. New members were invited equally with all others, without disadvantage and with a commandment to love each other. L. Michael White added that in the second and third centuries of the Common Era, Christianity built upon the Roman ethical virtues and improved them, and it answered the questions that people were asking about their deepest human needs (White 1998). Paula Fredriksen said that the church did take care of its needy while the state did not. In the church's infancy, the equality was undeniable and Christianity's broad ethos of community charity combined with its behavioural ethics resonated with lost Roman family values and created a new internal prestige available to all (Fredriksen 1998). In that same PBS documentary, Elaine H. Pagels tied Christianity's care for the needy to its teaching about human potential. Human goodness was limitless because all humans were made in the image of God. That theology conferred 'royal status upon every person' (Pagels 1998).

Human Rights and Dignity – a Product of the Enlightenment?

Many accounts of the history of human rights start with the UDHR after World War II and ignore the efforts of the Greek and Roman philosophers to deduce universal rules of moral behaviour from human nature. Although armchair philosophers during the Enlightenment challenged the divine right of European kings with Greek and Roman natural law and modern social contract ideas, opinion leaders in those countries still took their countries to war, so it is fair to conclude that all the theorising did not generate or inspire a brave new and peaceful world. When new theories of equality were distilled from philosophical ideas thereafter, they could only be implemented following bloody revolutions since the old orders would not give away their dominance willingly, as modern Marxists might have predicted.

It was not until collective mankind surveyed the unparalleled carnage and atrocities of World War II that there was sufficient consensus to seek a better way, although war has still not ended. However, the philosophical consensus achieved after the defeat of the Nazis and the discovery of their Final Solution would ground the modern human rights experiment. But is this post–World War II consensus any more likely to endure than the rediscovery of natural rights during the Enlightenment, and does it have the moral power to inspire men to 'beat their swords into plowshares, and their spears into pruninghooks' (Isa. 2:4, KJV)? Are modern human rights more durable because of the commitments that sustain them? Or are they also going to wither away because they have no clear foundation in absolute truth? There are also questions about whether the first-generation 'blue' human rights set out in the UDHR in 1948 have been diluted and even undermined by second generation 'red' and 'green' human rights (Vasak 1977; cf. Macklem 2015a and 2015b). However, save for some later discussion about the passion achieved by some advocates of those later rights, that question lies beyond the purpose of this chapter. In the next part, I discuss the theological arguments that can be made to justify first-generation human rights and dignity and question whether those arguments will justify and sustain human rights and dignity if religion loses its moral authority.

Do Human Rights and Conceptions of Human Dignity Rely on Religious Belief and Truth?

Randall Peerenboom's (2004a) *Asian Discourses of the Rule of Law* volume featured several authors who suggested that human rights were a twentieth-century Western imperialist project and that modern states using law as a tool enhancing effective administration and economic growth do not need human rights to be safe and politically healthy in economic ways (Peerenboom 2004b, 113–19; Gillespie 2004, 154; Thio 2004, 183; see also Parekh 1997, chapter 5). Mary Ann Glendon, however, has shown that the human rights that came out of Eleanor Roosevelt's (United States) work with P. C. Chang (China), Charles Malik (Lebanon), Carlos Romulo (the Philippines), Hernán Santa Cruz (Chile), Alexei Pavlov (from the USSR as it then was), John P. Humphrey (Canada), Hansa Mehta (India) and René Cassin (France) were not Western in any significant way, particularly since P. C. Chang's foundational 'ren' idea (two-man mindedness) was Confucian at core (2002, 67 and 228). Glendon has also explained that even though Saudi Arabia did not accept there was a right to change religion from Islam in the Qur'an and abstained from the final vote at the UN in 1948, other Muslim nations supported the Declaration and none voted against it.

One may conclude from Cole Durham's work that the existence of the secular 'reciprocity principle' in the world's major world religions (2001, fn 18; see also Lewis 1981, 14–16, 29, 49–59) blunts the suggestion that human rights is a purely Christian project. But that does not mean that human rights and dignity do not rely upon religious ideas for their wide cultural acceptance. Durham has argued both that freedom of conscience and religion rest on respect for the *other* and that such respect is a universal religious tenet (2012). But the reciprocity principle expressed in religious terms is not the only religious idea said to found and justify human rights and dignity.

The most obvious additional religious idea that supports human rights is expressed in the Latin phrase *imago Dei* which refers to the opening chapter of the Hebrew Bible accepted as scripture in Judaism, Christianity and Islam. There, because all humans were created in the image of God, the one true God is the father of all human beings; and because all human beings are thus members of His family, they are literal brothers and sisters. That shared idea of universal human family connection may explain why others should be treated equally even if they do not have the same skills, but it does not explain why they should not kill each other as Cain did Abel in the same shared book of the Hebrew Bible (Genesis 4). Thus the additional religious idea that because humans were created in God's image they must follow and become like Him by imitation (*imitatio Dei*) is also identified in some strains of Christian theology and has analogues in Judaism and Islam, though it is not universally accepted in those faiths.

However, the altruism these religious ideas can generate to support first-generation human rights and dignity is arguably more passionate and enduring than the intellectual assent that flows from the secular utilitarian thought that human rights and dignity can lead to toleration, respect for the other and then world peace. For while Dawkins's (1989) selfish gene can inspire passionate greed and lust for power, no matter how he spins it, the enlightened self-interest he tries to use to explain human altruism does not motivate humans out of bed in the morning to help others with whom they have no connection. Selfishness may inspire advocates of third-generation rights to protect themselves, but it does not explain human care for others when there is no direct and immediate payoff. Nor does it account for cases where there is no payoff at all, for example, when heroes and martyrs lay down their lives for others with no close genetic relation. Without a cause and something approaching religious fervour, it is notoriously difficult to motivate humans to do anything for anyone beyond their immediate kinship group.

In so discussing human altruism, I do not intend to suggest that the passion that justifies religious believers in asserting human rights and dignity is mindless. Quite the contrary. When religious altruism is traced to its source, the fervour I am describing is seated in the sense of obligation and duty that religious commitment invokes. My concern is thus that secular justifications for human rights and dignity do not seem able to generate the passion I believe will be necessary to sustain human rights and dignity.

What I will therefore do in the balance of this chapter is analyse the religious ideas which do motivate passion for human rights and dignity and try to identify elements for passionate development to support human rights. In doing so, I realise that I stand on the shoulders of Cole Durham and Brett Scharffs who have observed the need for 'overlapping justifications' for human rights (2010, 72–77). In my context, their lip service to John Rawls's idea that human society needs 'overlapping consensus' to achieve social justice is ironic since I intend to use religion in my quest, whereas Rawls admonished his readers to set religion aside as an impediment to consensus (1999, 131–32).

The Golden Rule

Earlier in this chapter, I noted from Cole Durham that all religions have, at their core, a belief and commitment to the idea that we should treat others as we would have them treat us. The underlying idea even has a secular analogue – the reciprocity principle. But when expressed in secular terms, this idea generates no passionate reason to care for others. It presents at most an exhortatory admonition. It is to practical altruism what the UDHR is to its successor covenants, the International Covenant on Civil and Political Rights (ICCPR) and the International Covenant on Economic, Social and Cultural Rights (ICESCR). The first expresses principle and an aspiration. The other two are intended for implementation and action. But their call to action is simply a logical progression and a further step in advancing the human rights project. Save for the academic idea and hope that the human rights project may reduce or eliminate war, there is no motivating sense of duty when expressed in reciprocity terms. The theological foundation and sense of duty which flow because of the sustained admonitions of prophetic leaders add gravitas to the reciprocity idea when expressed in a religious context. Without that oomph, the idea falls flat because it is just an idea.

Imago Dei, the Image of God

Though the idea that man was formed in the image of God similarly presents itself as a simple idea, with theological context and development, it becomes a source of motivating power. While a philosopher may analyse it as a bare assertion, the hypothesis that something as sophisticated as a human being must have a model can be inspiring in a religious context. The inspiration comes from the idea that human beings may be genealogically connected with the omnipotent being that created them. The *imago Dei* idea also has more dimensions than the simpler idea that all human beings should be kind to others of their species. Because the *imago Dei* idea suggests that all humans are related and the idea that related humans should care for each other is familiar, it adds to human rights the idea that all humans owe each other a duty of family care regardless of individual capacity. Another way of expressing this duty of family care is evident in the view that parents should care for their children and that siblings should care for each other. That idea resonates because it is familiar and even axiomatic in most human cultures. But the additional idea that children are either genetically disposed to imitate their parents or under a spiritual obligation to do so (*imitatio Dei*) arguably engages human passion more fully.

Imitatio Dei, the Imitation of God

For some Christian theologians, the idea that human beings have a spiritual obligation to copy their God and maker is no more than an aspect or consequence of *imago Dei*. In 'mainstream Judaism and Christianity', since humans are free creatures, they 'have the power to live or not live in a way compatible with the material image of God in [them]' (Power 1997, 131). In this sense, the *imitatio Dei* idea carries little sense of duty. It is no more than the direction imposed on human flesh and bones by genetic destiny, in the same way as it is the destiny of an acorn to become an oak tree. But that *reductio ad absurdum* is unsatisfying because it ignores the human power to reason and choose, which differentiates the human being from the acorn. That the acorn may fulfil its destiny and become an oak tree does not mean that it chose its destiny. It was simply acted upon. Humans can also grow old and die like the acorn/oak tree. But they cannot become like God without exercising their independent human agency and choice to imitate and become like him. To achieve their potential, humans must set personal goals and then reason, choose and act independently in pursuit of those goals. While most of Western Christianity has been happy to engage with the idea of human deification only as a meta-phor, Orthodox theologians have anticipated the deification of man as 'the abrogation of the natural state by a miraculous transformation of our nature' (Russell 2006, 2). C. S. Lewis picked up on this lacuna in Western Christian thought and advanced his vision of human potential in several ways. First, in *The Weight of Glory* in 1949, he said:

> It is a serious thing to live in a society of possible gods and goddesses, to remember that the dullest and most uninteresting person you can talk to may one day be a creature which, if you saw it now, you would be strongly tempted to worship, or else a horror and corruption such as you now meet, if at all, only in a nightmare. All day long we are, in some degree, helping each other to one or the other of these destinations. It is in the light of these overwhelming possi-bilities, it is with the awe and circumspection proper to them, that we should conduct all our dealings with one another, all friendships, all loves, all play, all politics. There are no *ordinary* people. You have never talked to a mere mortal. (2013, 45–46, emphasis original)

And then in *Mere Christianity* in 1952, he wrote that the intention of practical theology was to enable human beings 'to be [...] taken into the life of God'. Lewis then encouraged believer participation in that deification project with an allegory he developed from material provided by his mentor, George MacDonald:

> Imagine yourself as a living house. God comes in to rebuild that house. At first, perhaps, you can understand what He is doing. He is getting the drains right and stopping the leaks in the roof and so on: you knew that those jobs needed doing and so you are not surprised. But presently he starts knocking the house about in a way that hurts abominably and does not seem to make sense. What on earth is He up to? The explanation is that He is building quite a different house from the one you thought of – throwing out a new wing here, putting on an extra floor there, running up towers, making courtyards. You thought you were going to be made into a decent little cottage: but He is building a palace. He intends to come and live in it himself. (2016, 161)

Norman Russell traces what he calls the maturation of the metaphor of deification into a spiritual doctrine of Christianity. The transformation is not just a matter of appearance or the attainment of something that was always within oneself (Russell 2006, 2, 10). When a Christian believer overcomes the evils of his life by imitating the mortal life of Christ, he attains the likeness of God and becomes a partaker of the divine nature through the operation of the Holy Spirit (12–13).

Judaism, Islam, Hinduism and Buddhism, as four of the world's largest religions after Christianity, all have doctrines advocating the improvement or perfection of self, and in Judaism and Islam, the standards for personal integrity have divine coordinates. For example, Norman Russell has noted that 'Rabbinic Judaism had its own version of deification' where 'the "gods" of the [82nd] psalm [...] won immortality through the faithful observance of the Torah' (2006, 11). And though Western critics of Islam like to focus on what they consider the Qur'an's emphasis on the military nature of jihad/struggle, and suggest that prophetic references to the 'greater struggle' against one's base impulses and sin come from unreliable sources (BBC 2009; Hashmi 2016; Perennial n.d.), most contemporary Islamic opinion accepts and follows this personal teaching as the true Islamic gospel (Bonner 2008, 13). 'The goal of the Greater Jihad, the jihad of self, is to "cultivate the attributes of Allah" so that one can reach an inner equilibrium reflecting the Divine Names and Qualities' (Perennial n.d.). Similarly, while integration in Hinduism (Zaehner 1969, 10–12, 24–26, 28–36) and self-mastery in Buddhism (Evola 1996) have different antecedents than the surrender or submission encouraged in Islam (Perennial n.d.), or the self-mastery enjoined in Christianity, Judaism, Hinduism, Buddhism, Christianity and Islam all teach their adherents to overcome adversity and put away their selfish desires and actions in a quest for perfection in and beyond mortal life.

The challenge arising from this summary of the religious ideas that have supported the human rights and dignity project in the minds of the world's religious believers is to identify reasons, including overlapping reasons, to support that project independent of religious beliefs. Several approaches might be taken to that project, including a general survey of philosophy and motivational ideology, and a review of religious ideas that might be suitably secularised for the purpose. However, I will first suggest the twenty-first century reasons why the human rights and dignity project is under threat, recognising that the remedies chosen must respond to that context.

Twenty-First Century Threats to the Human Rights Project

In his 2012 article in the Pontifical Academy's Social Science's Journal, Cole Durham drew attention to 'a looming crisis in defending religious freedom' (2012, 359). While he confirmed that 'religion is here to stay' and is not 'withering away' (362), there is a crisis because our secular Western societies are forgetting how important religious freedom is, even though it has 'a time-tested key for addressing' the most enduring of conflicts (359). Durham's warning that the foundational importance of first-generation human rights is being accorded less weight than more modern social ideas resonates with Martha Nussbaum's (2008) observation that 'in each era of human history [...] the value of equal respect for all human beings needs to be reforged and re-established'. Nussbaum has added that 'history shows us that constant vigilance is required lest th[ese] value[s] be narrowly and partially construed in ways that favour hierarchy [...] the battle for equal respect needs to be refought in each new era' (359–60).

Mary Ann Glendon and Seth Kaplan have echoed Nussbaum's concern in 2019 and have suggested that the need for renewal of common understanding of the importance of all the 1948 UDHR rights is becoming more pressing:

> The international human rights idea is in crisis [and] losing support. Good intentions, honest mistakes, power politics, and plain old opportunism have all played a role in a growing skepticism, and even a backlash. (33)

Their solution, like Nussbaum's, is renewed education so the significance of these foundations is not lost:

> Ultimately, successful human rights promotion depends on attention to the attitudes, ideas, values, relationships, and institutions within which individuals, families, and communities are embedded. As Eleanor Roosevelt put it, documents expressing ideals 'carry no weight unless the people understand them, unless the people demand that they be lived'. And these, as she said in one of her last speeches at the U.N., depend on implementation in lots and lots of 'small places'. (Glendon and Kaplan 2019, 38)

Eleanor Roosevelt's 'small places' undoubtedly included primary and secondary school classrooms, but her vision also required that these elements of Western civilisation get air time in universities where primary and secondary school teachers (and other opinion leaders like journalists and lawyers) receive their education, despite the fact that human rights are not as modern or fashionable as they were when first announced to the world 70 years ago. The challenge for modern university teachers is to find new and imaginative ways of making human rights relevant in the twenty-first century and to invent new and convincing ways of answering claims that human rights are paternalistic, a relic of colonial imperialism (Peerenboom 2004a) or, more simply, just redundant (Tushnet 2001).

How Can We Promote Human Rights and Dignity in the Twenty-First Century?

The first answer is that we must make the original human rights assertions from 1948 relevant in the present. Part of the reason Durham thinks they have become passé is because we have not had a world war for over 70 years. He says the reason 'other rights [...] other state interests [...] [and] transformed equality norms' seem more important than freedom of conscience, speech and association is because the older foundational standards are now taken for granted in the developed world (2012, 360). But if they continue to be eroded by incremental exceptions, the foundations will have gone as surely as if there were another world war. Durham suggests that the blessings of prosperity and peace have anaesthetised the world to the lessons of history.

A first way to make 1948 human rights relevant in the present is to insist that the fragility of our contemporary liberal democratic achievement be measured against the lessons of history in compulsory university education. Contemporary resistance to even well-funded elective courses in Western civilisation in Australia show this is not an easy solution (Sydney Morning Herald 2018; SBS 2018). The instruction will thus have to be enhanced with state-of-the-art technology and analysis designed to hold the attention of all students. While there are balances to be observed when presenting graphic materials to impressionable minds, there is no lack of haunting images, including those General Omar Bradley instructed be taken during the liberation of various Nazi camps at the end of World War II. But there are also non-visual pedagogical ways today's students can be engaged in the history and the reflection required to understand why Durham, Glendon and Nussbaum have all voiced the need to keep this understanding at the centre of contemporary political awareness.

However, the concern I have expressed in this chapter cannot be answered simply by excellent pedagogy. If 1948 human rights are to survive, today's students must be convinced in their hearts and minds there is no other way to preserve human dignity than to uphold these rights ahead of all other human rights virtues. This requires philosophical justifications that can resist the calls for exceptions in favour of other values that Durham has noted. My question is: what will inspire tomorrow's students to uphold human rights and dignity when they no longer believe they were created in the image of God and must imitate his character, including his unbounded love for them all? Can the sense of duty that the *imago Dei* and *imitatio Dei* cause to surge in the breasts of believers in all the world's religions be replicated by secular justifications in a manner just as compelling in the hearts of tomorrow's students?

I therefore conclude with a summary of some religious ideas which have retained some of their motivating power after they have been translated into secular terms. I also review contemporary secular philosophy for any human rights justifications which may contribute any sense of religious duty to the ongoing human rights and dignity project.

Religious Ideas Which Have Survived Translation into Secular Terms

Many self-help books in English significantly connect with the Christian Gospel. The most obvious include Dale Carnegie's *How to Win Friends and Influence People* (1936) and Norman Vincent Peale's *The Power of Positive Thinking* (1952). But there are many other examples, including more recently Stephen R. Covey's *The 7 Habits of Highly Effective People* (1989). M. Scott Peck (*The Road Less Travelled* (1978)) attributes many of his insights to Zen Buddhism despite his Quaker schooling in Greenwich Village near New York City (Epstein 2002), and the earliest books of Daniel Goleman (such as *Emotional Intelligence* (1995)) have drawn both from his Jewish heritage and his study of a variety of meditation systems, including those he encountered while studying in India in the early 1970s. Deepak Chopra (*The Seven Spiritual Laws of Success* (1994)) has similarly drawn from both Hinduism (Maps of India n.d.) and Christianity (*Houston Chronicle* 2008) in his work.

Australian moral philosopher Raimond Gaita, while denying that he is religious (2004, xxvi), has attributed many of his insights about human nature and the worth of an individual human being to the love of an unnamed Catholic nun (xiii). Her example convinced him that

> even people like those patients, who appear to have lost everything that gives sense to our lives, are fully our equals [...] she responded without a trace of condescension and [...] the wondrousness of it compelled me to affirm its rightness. (Ibid.)

'Hitchens is wrong' when he denies that Mother Teresa was a saint (xii–xiii). Gaita affirms that such people move among us and our human capacity for remorse demonstrates that all humans are sacred and owed inalienable human dignity as Kant might explain (xiii–xiv). But even though Gaita devoted his professional life to explaining the human capacity for virtue he experienced in that nun, still he struggled to explain it without God (xxviii). And so I ask again: how are we to affirm the virtue of 1948 human rights and dignity if the motivation inspired by religious understanding and duty has withered away? Is all that we have left logic, and can that sustain the weight of the human rights project in a deconstructionist age when people are not prepared to proceed on the assumed virtue of the premises?

A Challenge and a Conclusion

The consequence of this analysis is that I could not identify a secular justification for human rights that is as motivating as the duty and obligation that flow from religious faith. I want to identify convincing secular justifications for 1948 UDHR human rights that overlap with the religious arguments I have identified because I believe that will ensure the human rights project survives. I therefore challenge human rights lawyers around the world to identify and publish such arguments.

In this chapter, I have explained that natural rights advocacy originated in ancient Greece but that the arguments that justified those rights in the fourth and fifth centuries BC do not assist in justifying the human rights that were declared in the UDHR in 1948 because the rights concerned are not the same. For the ancient Greek philosophers, humans existed in a natural hierarchy, and the more valuable were entitled to a greater allocation of resources as their birthright. The UDHR affirmed that all humans are equal in dignity and entitlement to resources regardless of their birth, family circumstances or even their mental capacity and physical competence. Christianity changed the ancient paradigms beginning in the first century AD.

I then explained how three religious arguments, premised in a theological understanding of human nature, provide convincing justifications for the human rights set out in the UDHR in 1948, though the latter two are stronger than the first. That is because the Golden Rule idea that human beings are obliged to treat others as they would themselves like to be treated is convincing only if the authority of the preacher is accepted. The reciprocity idea by itself does not oblige subscriber compliance. However, the *imago Dei* and *imitatio Dei* ideas oblige believers to treat all other human beings as the children of God because if they do not, there will be a negative consequence in the life to come. Utilitarian calculus cannot provide the sense of duty that threats of punishment or promises of advantage in the life to come stitch into the human heart. The hope that observance and even advocacy of the 1948 human rights of others will result in peace during life is inherently less certain since opportunistic war could outweigh a strategy of respectful restraint at any time.

Since religious ideas have yielded convincing secular arguments when adapted to other purposes, I queried whether the Golden Rule, *imago Dei* and *imitatio Dei* ideas might be adapted to provide compelling secular arguments in favour of 1948 human rights. However, even Richard Dawkins's suggestion that human altruism can be explained as enlightened self-interest does not explain why any human being would want to treat others equally. I thus conclude we have yet to find convincing arguments for human rights that are not premised in religiosity, and I challenge those who agree with me and even those who believe otherwise to prove me wrong.

References

Baker, Ernest. 1906. *The Political Thought of Plato and Aristotle*. London: Methuen.

BBC. 2009. 'Jihad'. 3 August. http://www.bbc.co.uk/religion/religions/islam/beliefs/jihad_1.shtml.

Bonner, Michael. 2008. *Jihad in Islamic History*, Kindle ed. Princeton, NJ: Princeton University Press.

Dawkins, Richard. 1989. *The Selfish Gene*. Oxford: Oxford University Press.

Durham, Cole. 2001. 'The Doctrine of Religious Freedom'. *BYU Speeches*, 3 April. https://speeches.byu.edu/talks/w-cole-durham_doctrine-religious-freedom/.

———. 2012. 'Religious Freedom in a Worldwide Setting: Comparative Reflections'. In *Universal Rights in a World of Diversity: The Case of Religious Freedom*, edited by Mary Ann Glendon and Hans F. Zacher. Pontifical Academy of Social Sciences, Acta 17. http://www.pass.va/content/dam/scienzesociali/pdf/acta17/acta17-durham.pdf.

Durham, Cole, and Brett Scharffs. 2010. *Law and Religion, National, International, and Comparative Perspectives*. New York: Aspen.

Epstein, Robert. 2002. 'M. Scott Peck: Wrestling with God'. *Psychology Today*, 1 November. https://www.psychologytoday.com/au/articles/200211/m-scott-peck-wrestling-god.

Evola, Julius. 1996. *The Doctrine of Awakening, Self-Mastery according to the Earliest Buddhist Texts*, English language ed. Rochester, Vermont: Inner Traditions International.

Fredriksen, Paula. 1998. 'The Great Appeal'. *From Jesus to Christ*. PBS Frontline, April. https://www.pbs.org/wgbh/pages/frontline/shows/religion/why/appeal.html.

Gaita, Raimond. 2004. *Good and Evil: An Absolute Conception*, 2nd ed. London: Routledge.

Gillespie, John. 2004. 'Concept of Law in Vietnam: Transforming Statist Socialism'. In *Asian Discourses of Rule of Law*, edited by Randall Peerenboom, 146–82. London: Routledge.

Glendon, Mary Ann. 2002. *A World Made New*. New York: Random House.

Glendon, Mary Ann, and Seth D. Kaplan. 2019. 'Renewing Human Rights'. *First Things*, February.

Hashmi, S. H. 2016. 'Jihad'. In *Encyclopedia of Islam and the Muslim World*, edited by R. C. Martin. Macmillan Reference USA. https://search-credoreference-com.ipacez.nd.edu.au/content/entry/galeislam/jihad/0.

Houston Chronicle. 2008. 'Deepak Chopra Says Christ's Teaching Reach beyond the Christian Church'. 8 March. https://www.chron.com/life/houston-belief/article/Deepak-Chopra-says-Christ-s-teachings-reach-1675413.php.

Koester, Helmut. 1998. 'The Great Appeal'. *From Jesus to Christ*. PBS Frontline, April. https://www.pbs.org/wgbh/pages/frontline/shows/religion/why/appeal.html.

Lewis, C. S. 1981. *The Abolition of Man*. Glasgow: Collins, Fount Paperbacks.

———. 2013. *The Weight of Glory*. London: William Collins.

———. 2016. *Mere Christianity*. London: William Collins.

Macklem, Patrick. 2015a. 'Human Rights in International Law: Three Generations or One?' *London Review of International Law* 3, no. 1: 61–92.

———. 2015b. *The Sovereignty of Human Rights*. Oxford: Oxford University Press.

Manning, C. E. 1973. 'Seneca and the Stoics on the Equality of the Sexes'. *Mnemosyne*, Fourth Series, 26, Fasc. 2: 170–77.

Maps of India. n.d. 'Dr. Deepak Chopra Biography'. https://www.mapsofindia.com/who-is-who/miscellaneous/dr-deepak-chopra.html.

Miller, Fred D. Jr. 1995. *Nature, Justice, Rights in Aristotle's Politics*. Oxford: Oxford University Press.

———. 1996. 'Aristotle and the Origins of Natural Rights'. *Review of Metaphysics* 49, no. 4: 873–907.

Nussbaum, Martha. 2008. *Liberty of Conscience*. New York: Basic Books.

Pagels, Elaine H. 1998. 'The Great Appeal'. *From Jesus to Christ*. PBS Frontline, April. https://www.pbs.org/wgbh/pages/frontline/shows/religion/why/appeal.html.

Parekh, Bhikhu. 1997. 'Liberalism and Colonialism: A Critique of Locke and Mill'. In *The Decolonisation of Imagination: Culture, Knowledge and Power*, edited by Jan Nederveen Pieterse and Bhikhu Parekh, 81–98. Calcutta: Oxford University Press.

Peerenboom, Randall, ed. 2004a. *Asian Discourses of Rule of Law: Theories and Implementation of Rule of Law in Twelve Asian Countries, France and the U.S.* London: Routledge.

———. 2004b. 'Competing Conceptions of Rule of Law in China'. In *Asian Discourses of Rule of Law*, edited by Randall Peerenboom, 113–45. London: Routledge.

Perennial. N.d. 'The Greater Jihad'. http://perennialvision.org/greater-jihad/.

Power, William L. 1997. 'Imago Dei: Imitatio Dei'. *International Journal for Philosophy of Religion* 42, no. 3: 131–41.

Rawls, John. 1999. 'The Idea of Public Reason Revisited'. In *The Law of Peoples, with 'The Idea of Public Reason Revisited'*. Boston, MA: Harvard University Press.

Russell, Norman. 2006. *The Doctrine of Deification in the Greek Patristic Tradition*. Oxford: Oxford University Press.

SBS. 2018. 'Western Civilisation Degree Arrives at UOW amidst Lean Investment in Indigenous Studies'. 23 December. https://www.sbs.com.au/nitv/article/2018/12/23/western-civilisation-degree-arrives-uow-amidst-lean-investment-indigenous-studies.

Sharma, Arvin. 2006. *Are Human Rights Western?: A Contribution to the Dialogue of Civilizations*. Oxford: Oxford University Press.

Stanford Encyclopedia of Philosophy. 2007. 'Equality'. 27 June. https://plato.stanford.edu/entries/equality/.

Swidler, Leonard. 1990. 'Human Rights: A Historical Overview'. In *The Ethics of World Religions and Human Rights*, edited by Hans Küng and Jürgen Moltmann. Philadelphia, PA: Trinity.

Sydney Morning Herald (SMH). 2018. '"Puerile" Culture War Battering Ramsey Centre Negotiation'. 29 September. https://www.smh.com.au/national/puerile-culture-war-battering-ramsay-centre-negotiations-says-sydney-uni-boss-20180925-p505yc.html.

Thio, Li-Ann. 2004. 'Rule of Law within a Non-liberal "Communitarian" Democracy: The Singapore Experience'. In *Asian Discourses of Rule of Law*, edited by Randall Peerenboom, 183–224. London: Routledge.

Tushnet, Mark. 2001. 'The Redundant Free Exercise Clause?' *Loyola University Chicago Law Journal* 33, no. 1: 71–94.

Vasak, Karel. 1977. 'Human Rights: A Thirty Year Struggle: The Sustained Efforts to Give Force of Law to the Universal Declaration of Human Rights'. *UNESCO Courier* 30, no. 11 (November). Paris: United Nations Educational, Scientific and Cultural Organization.

White, L. Michael. 1998. 'The Great Appeal'. *From Jesus to Christ*. PBS Frontline, April. https://www.pbs.org/wgbh/pages/frontline/shows/religion/why/appeal.html.

Zaehner, R. C., ed. 1969. 'Introduction'. In *The Bhagavad-Gita, with a Commentary Based on the Original Sources*, 5–41 Oxford: Oxford University Press.

Chapter Three

MAY CRITICS OF 'INHERENT DIGNITY' BE ANSWERED? REJOINDERS FROM CHRISTIAN ANTHROPOLOGY

David Guretzki

The Universal Declaration of Human Rights (henceforth, 'Declaration') brought together, in close conceptual proximity, the ideas of inherent human dignity and human rights. The document recognizes 'the inherent dignity and [...] the equal and inalienable rights of all members of the human family', while going on to assert, 'All human beings are born free and equal in dignity and rights' (Declaration 1948). The release of the Declaration focused international scholarly attention on human rights, attention which has not abated in the past decades. However, there is a lesser, but still extensive, examination of the concept invoked in the Declaration – that of inherent human dignity. Though widely appealed to within law, philosophy and theology, the concept of human dignity is increasingly subject to sharp criticism. The question is: Can the concept of inherent human dignity be rescued from its critics?

Preliminary Clarifications

Before hearing from critics of inherent human dignity, two points of clarification are necessary.

First, though it is widely assumed that human dignity grounds human rights in the Declaration, it should be noted that the document never makes explicit that 'inherent human dignity' is in fact the basis of human rights. Dignity *is* declared to be the 'foundation of freedom, justice, and peace', but otherwise, inherent human dignity and inalienable human rights are simply asserted and juxtaposed without clearly attributing one as the cause, root or foundation of the other (Declaration 1948). Indeed, though they could have easily affirmed that human dignity is the basis of human rights, the framers chose not to make this connection explicit. Hughes notes the framers of the Declaration intentionally avoided making assertions about the metaphysical, philosophical or theological basis of human rights, but Gewirth rightly highlights evidence that the principal framers clearly understood 'it is because humans have dignity that they have human rights' (Gewirth 1992, 10).

Despite a friendly disposition towards human dignity as a basis for human rights, the principal authors of the document followed Catholic philosopher Jacques Maritain's advice to produce a practical document that would steer clear, as much as possible, from taking stands on foundational debates (Hughes 2011, 2–3). The Declaration, after all, did not purport to be a religious, theological or philosophical document as much as a practical, legal standard for protecting future generations from re-experiencing the barbarous acts committed during World War II. Foremost in the minds of the committee tasked with writing the Declaration was something like this: Whatever philosophical, metaphysical or theological assumptions we might have, may we not all agree that we must do everything and anything to protect humans from the horrors of this past decade?

Second, and more importantly for our purposes here, once the juxtaposed phrases of 'inherent human dignity' and 'human rights' were released for public consumption, the intentions of the original authors of the Declaration became increasingly irrelevant to how the phrases eventually were interpreted, whether legally, philosophically or even theologically. 'This situation began to change,' Łuków argues, 'when the human rights discourse – i.e. human rights legislation, literature, practices, and institutional arrangements – incorporated the thesis that the rights derive from human dignity' (2018, 313). That is to say, no matter how one may protest that the original Declaration does not make inherent human dignity the basis of universal human rights, much ink has been spilled in past decades making just that correlation.

We should not deny the fact that the introduction of the Declaration did much good for the legal and, indeed, physical protection of human beings around the world. But some 70 years on, it is unsurprising that both the phrases 'inherent human dignity' and 'inalienable human rights' are subject to rigorous philosophical and practical scrutiny. Suspicions of the meaningfulness and usefulness of these ideas were bound to grow when, particularly in past years, those on both sides of major legal and ethical debates have appealed to inherent human dignity as an axiomatic basis for what are otherwise contradictory positions. For example, one only has to point to the worldwide debate on euthanasia, or medical assistance in death (MAID), where the inherence of human dignity is appealed to on both sides. On the one hand, it is because humans have inherent dignity that legalization of assistance in death should be resisted. On the other hand, it is because of inherent human dignity that those seeking assistance in death should be granted their request. Such paradoxical appeals have led one commentator to assert that the current discourse on the legal, ethical and philosophical aspects of human dignity is now in 'utter disarray' (Guyette 2013, 112), leaving one wondering whether the concept can actually be rescued in any practicable sense. In other words, may critics of inherent human dignity be answered?

Of course, before seeking to answer this question, it is necessary to summarize various critiques offered so far. A comprehensive discussion is impossible here, but this chapter will consider five distinct types of critique. As will be argued, despite their differences, the critiques each uniquely point to a fatal flaw in the concept itself, mainly the insistence on human dignity being 'inherent'. In response, it will be argued that while there is scant hope that theists and non-theists will come to an agreement on the nature of human dignity, there may be a possible avenue of exploration that could be serviceable to both, an alternative concept suggested by the Christian theological anthropology of theologian Karl Barth, mainly the two-sided concept of the honour of humans.

Critiquing Inherent Human Dignity: A Typology

Challenges to the concept of inherent human dignity have taken five basic forms. They are designated here as the (1) functional; (2) non-consensus; (3) reductionist; (4) post-modern; and (5) theological (or religious) critiques.

The Functional Critique

The first line of critique is that the concept of human dignity, as commonly appealed to, is functionally redundant (Genuis 2016, 7–8). This critique has especially shown up amongst those seeking to uphold the practical application of human dignity, especially in fields such as law, medicine and social work.

At their harshest, commentators such as Steven Pinker (2008) have derided the concept of human dignity, claiming that it is 'a squishy, subjective notion, hardly up to the heavyweight moral demands assigned to it'.[1] Pinker here takes his cue from bioethicist Ruth Macklin (2003), who argues that 'appeals to dignity are either vague restatements of other, more precise, notions or mere slogans that add nothing to an understanding of the topic' (1419).[2] According to Macklin, most appeals to human dignity simply reiterate that humans should not have personal autonomy reduced or removed. Consequently, if dignity is identified with 'a capacity for rational thought and action', then why not stick to the already widely regarded 'principle of respect for autonomy' (1420)? In other words, these critics ask, why appeal to multiple conceptual entities if an established concept or set of concepts will already do?

Although it is well beyond the scope of this chapter to trace theological reflection on human dignity after the release of the Declaration, similar layering of concepts went on in theological discourse as well. Broadly speaking, in Christian theology leading up to and after Vatican II in both Catholic and Protestant circles,[3] appeals to human dignity rose sharply. And where undertaken, dignity was primarily correlated with the ancient notion of *imago Dei*, namely that humans are created in the image of God.[4] The theo-logic, then, goes something like this: because humans are created in the image of God,

---

[1] It should be noted that the title of Pinker's article, 'The Stupidity of Dignity', is misleading because he nowhere calls the concept of human dignity 'stupid' per se. That said, he unflinch-ingly asserts 'the concept of dignity remains a mess'.

[2] See also Alasdair Cochrane (2010), who argues that bioethics needs to move forward without recourse to the notion of human dignity. He calls for an 'Undignified Bioethics'.

[3] In large part, Orthodox theology has not engaged with notions of human rights and dignity to the same degree, nor with the same presuppositions, as Western theologians. See Clapsis (2011).

[4] It should be noted here that historically the church actually spoke of human dignity as an alter-native to modern discussion of human rights, not as its basis. See Rosen (2018, 91–92).

they have been given a proper dignity within themselves. Dignity, thus, must be protected at all measures.

Compare this theological correlation of human dignity and *imago Dei* with the secular correlation of human dignity and human autonomy. In both cases, critics ask: what is gained by appealing to human dignity which is not already contained in the notion of respect for human autonomy (for secular ethicists) or the *imago Dei* (for theological ethicists)? Amongst theologians, for example, Bernd Oberdorfer hesitates to abandon the notion of human dignity, but instinctively claims that if there is challenge giving content to the modern concept of human dignity, 'the "image of God" concept appears to be perfectly suited to supporting this challenge' (2010, 232). It is not surprising, then, that some regard the notion of human dignity to be a superfluous concept that has only served to increase philosophical, legal or theological complexity rather than bringing functional clarity.

The Non-Consensus Critique

Closely related to the functional account is the 'non-consensus' critique. Critics here have pointed out that 'inherent human dignity' is either asserted as if it is self-evident in meaning or ends up being defined in conceptually and practically incompatible ways. In short, critics argue that as long as there is a significant lack of consensus on what is meant by 'human dignity', the concept fails to provide a sufficient philosophical or theological basis either for human rights or for practical application in legal and professional ethical contexts.

Here, two examples will suffice. On the one hand, Pope John Paul II consistently appealed to human dignity to communicate something specifically theological about humans, mainly that they were created in the image of God.[5] On the other hand, around the same time Beauchamp and Childress championed the notion of dignity as something specifically anthropological, mainly 'self-rule that is free from both controlling interference and from limitations' (2001, 58). One would be hard-pressed indeed to see how these two definitions of human dignity could be easily reconciled, especially when one considers the gap between theistic and non-theistic ways of thinking.

A legal example is also raised by O'Mahony (2012), who argues that the meaning of dignity diverges even within law, depending on whether one is talking about domestic

---

[5] See especially Pope John Paul II (1995). Though beyond the scope of this chapter, it is fascinating that the Roman Catholic Church initially was resistant to human rights discourse, seeing it as a counter-narrative to the Catholic Church's focus on human identity as creatures and servants of God. However, it was during Vatican II that the Catholic Church formally made peace with human rights discourse, adopting both the language of human dignity and human rights into its own documents. Most evident here is Pope John XXIII's 1963 encyclical *Pacem in Terris*; Pope Paul VI's 1965 declaration, *Dignitatis Humanae*; and perhaps most importantly Pope Paul VI's widely regarded 1965 pastoral constitution *Gaudium et Spes*. For an analysis of the context leading to *Dignitatis Humanae*, see Orsy (2014).

or international law. This consequently 'creates disharmony between international and domestic rights protection' (574). As he puts it,

> While the concept of human dignity as a fundamental and foundational value which acts as a source of and justification for human rights receives broad support internationally, the concept of dignity as a human right in itself is less enthusiastically embraced in domestic constitutional laws and the surrounding literature. (561)

This illustrates at least one of the basic problems when making an appeal to human dignity: if there is failure to agree even on its basic meaning, then consensus is surely even more difficult to achieve when approaching the concept from theistic/religious versus secular, or domestic versus international points of view. If it is at all hoped that the concept of 'human dignity' might serve as a kind of bridge concept between various spheres of discourse, the question arises as to the wisdom of appealing to the concept while ignoring fundamental presuppositions of the one making use of it (an important problem explored in more detail by Friedrich Toepel in Chapter 11 of this volume). In other words, the critics ask: Of what use is it to agree on a concept's axiomatic value when clearly it is defined in such fundamentally different ways?

While the lack of basic consensus may seem insolubly problematic, not everyone sees it this way. Hughes, for example, argues that the concept of human dignity, while lacking broad consensus, functions as an 'intrinsically heuristic concept', that is, a concept which points to 'an intelligible reality of which we have some understanding, but whose full or complete content remains, and will always remain to some degree, unknown to us' (2011, 8). It is not necessary, he maintains, that everyone start with an agreed-upon definition of the concept, as long as we agree that it is sufficiently evocative to open the way to future discovery and enable 'filling in' of the concept as we go.[6] The concept of human dignity is, in other words, intended to be an open-ended concept which, despite definitional ambiguity, nevertheless unites people in a common quest, similar to how the human drive for happiness, justice or peace may do the same, differing definitions notwithstanding.

Although this may help soften the non-consensual critique, in the end even heuristic optimists must admit that the problem of definition looms large: for whether at the beginning, middle or end of the process, it is likely the concept will be subject to endless definition and qualification and that it will always be difficult, if not impossible, to find ways to adjudicate existing differences of understanding without yielding wildly different legal and ethical applications. As jurist McCrudden laments,

> The use of 'dignity' beyond a basic minimum core does not provide a universalistic principled basis for judicial decision-making in the human rights context in the sense that there is little common understanding of what dignity requires substantively within or across jurisdictions. The meaning of dignity is therefore context-specific, varying significantly from jurisdiction to

---

[6] Alternatively, Reinbold (2011) speaks of 'inherent human dignity' as a type of 'political myth' that does not need precise definition, but which serves to move dialogue forward towards increased clarity and practice, despite never being full 'closed' in meaning.

jurisdiction and (often) over time within particular jurisdictions. Indeed, instead of providing a basis for principled decision-making, dignity seems open to significant judicial manipulation, increasing rather than decreasing judicial discretion. (2008, 655)

The Reductionist Critique

A third line of criticism pertains more specifically to how the Declaration has spoken of human dignity relative to its intellectual history. In this regard, the Declaration's concept of human dignity being inherent took on a significantly narrower sense than the previous historical trajectory of thought. Critics thus see the Declaration's concept of *inherent* human dignity as a kind of intellectual reductionism.

Though the Declaration declines to define the term, an analysis of the meaning of 'human dignity' so connoted focuses on its *intrinsic, absolute, universal* nature. Dignity is something that exists equally *within* (intrinsic) every human individual (absolute) at all times and in all places (universal). Although there is historical precedent for interiorizing and universalizing dignity in this manner, the concept has historically often been filled out with an understanding of human dignity that is *extrinsic, restricted* and *contingent.*

In his important short history of dignity, Rosen argues that the idea of dignity 'originated as a concept that denoted high social status and the honors and respectful treatment that are due to someone who occupied that position' (2018, 11). Human dignity, therefore, was (and still is) commonly understood as something neither universal in extent nor equal in degree. Thinking here, for example, with an ancient or pre-modern mindset, royalty was understood to have dignity; nobles and aristocrats, less; and peasants, animals and objects, even less, if any at all.

This is not to say earlier notions of dignity were solely defined in terms of status and hierarchy. In Cicero's highly influential *De Officiis* ('On Duties', 1994), he speaks often of dignity in the conventional sense of status, but also of a more general, universal sense of dignity of humans over against the animal kingdom. As he puts it, 'It is vitally necessary for us to remember always how vastly superior is man's nature to that of cattle and other animals. [...] From this we may learn that sensual pleasure is wholly unworthy of the dignity of the human race' (I:30). Thus for Cicero, humans as a whole have a higher status of worth than animals, but for humans to engage in a life devoted to sensual pleasure is to fail to live up to the worth so noted.

This two-sidedness of human dignity – as something both universal *and* contingent – was also present in the works of the medieval Christian philosopher and theologian Thomas Aquinas. On the one hand, Aquinas had a working notion of dignity as universally applicable to all humans, due to being created in the image of God (*imago Dei*). Indeed, in Aquinas's classic definition of 'dignity', it signifies 'something's goodness on account of itself' (as cited in Rosen 2018, 6–7). On the other hand, he also saw dignity more in terms of the 'capacity' of humans rather than as an inviolable, static quality of the human. Thus, according to Aquinas, humans in toto have dignity as image bearers, but only insofar as they have *potential* for dignity do individuals actually reach union with God – the highest possible actualization of human dignity. As Guyette explains, for

Aquinas, 'dignity is dynamic […] It can develop and become stronger when we exercise the gifts of faith, hope, and love, or it can become weaker when we sin and turn away from God' (2013, 118). Dignity, in other words, is simultaneously something that is universally *available*, but can only be said to be contingently *present*. And, of course, for Aquinas, both of these notions of dignity are undergirded by an axiomatic assumption of the existence of God.

Interestingly, the Declaration was one of the first and most widely noted places where the qualifier 'inherent' was added to the phrase 'human dignity'; prior to 1948, it was rare to find human dignity qualified as such.[7] Moreover, human dignity prior to the Declaration was still widely understood as something differing in degree amongst humans. When the concept was used in theological or philosophical contexts, it usually pointed to a socio-political ordering or hierarchy amongst humans, whereas in the Declaration, the concept connoted something akin to a permanent human attribute or characteristic. That dignity was asserted to be 'inherent' to every human being undoubtedly introduced a significant narrowing, if not a substantial change, of concept. Moreover, it ended up being notably disconnected from the breadth of meaning found in its deep intellectual history. This resulted in a kind of unintended selectivity of aspects of the concept that it was hoped would be most universally accepted to the exclusion of other aspects of the concept of human dignity that might not be able to be universally recognized and which are more common in day-to-day perception.

It is evident, therefore, that in its press towards being recognized as a practical universal and ethical standard, the Declaration's use of the term 'inherent human dignity' may have had the paradoxical effect that it actually made it more difficult in the long run to be a serviceable concept precisely because it was abstracted and generalized from the everyday perceptions of dignity (or its lack) that humans identified. Consequently, such reductionism fails to retain the concept's intellectual gravitas needed to undergird the legal and moral protection of human rights so demanded, and/or fails to account for the breadth of deep meanings of dignity both in historical thought and practice.

The weight of this criticism must be felt. Granted, there is no immutable linguistic rule that concepts and language cannot change over history. But without signalling that a change is being demanded, or without referencing the deep history invoked through the use of a philosophically or theologically laden term such as dignity, it is little surprise that invoking a term without redefinition has been deeply problematic.

The Postmodern Critique

Although there are innumerable versions, certainly not all compatible, a fourth line of critique asserts that the notion of inherent human dignity presupposed in the Declaration

---

[7] See the Google n-gram, 'inherent human dignity'. Accessed 18 April 2019. https://books.google.com/ngrams/graph?content=inherent+human+dignity&case_insensitive=on&year_start=1800&year_end=2000&corpus=15&smoothing=3&share=&direct_url=t1%3B%2Cinherent%20human%20dignity%3B%2Cc0.

depends upon a metaphysics held over from a concept of the world as discerned in modernity. This critique is designated simply as the postmodern critique.

Under conditions of modernity, postmodern critics argue, the world was able to be reasonably understood, or more pointedly, subdued through the exercise of human rationality. Modernity presumed that the world, and indeed humanity itself, is orderly, rational and essentially subject to the exercise of reason. The essence of humanity is not to be understood by divine revelation but by inductive, scientific and/or rational investigation of humans, yielding universalized statements or laws that are applicable to all, regardless of age, sex, status, religion, location, culture or history. In this regard, the postmodern critic says, to declare that all individual *homo sapiens* have inherent human dignity is but evidence of the hubris and paradox of the modern spirit: hubristic because it could omnisciently make universal claims of the *character indelebilis* of each human being past, present and future; and paradoxical because it could make a claim contrary to the presupposition of a modern scientific mindset, namely that general conclusions on the nature of anything, humans included, are always provisional and open to further data and analysis.

In contrast to this portrait of a world universally accessible to human rationality and ordering, postmodern thinkers discern particularity and difference within the world. Indeed, Winter argues that 'postmodernism's most profound contribution is its radical insistence on contingency' (1994, 235). In this regard, the idea that human dignity is something that is (1) accessible, (2) uniform and (3) universally distributed is one that could make sense only in a context where the assumptions of Enlightenment rationality hold sway. On the contrary, a deconstruction of this 'view from nowhere' is necessary, as Lyotard famously put it, because of our embodied contingency and the 'loss of credulity of the metanarrative' (1984, xxiv). Every human is bodily situated in a particular time, place, history and culture, making it increasingly implausible to assume that a transcendent universal, such as 'inherent human dignity', could stand in without reserve for every single individual past, present, and future apart from consideration of their actual, concrete situations, that is, apart from the contingencies of their lived existence.

Moreover, the universalism evident in the Declaration also reveals its essentially modernistic political philosophy. As Kateb notes, documents such as the Declaration are 'rather statist (étatiste) [in that they] enshrine the state's authority to abridge rights in the name of morality, order, welfare, and unspecified national purposes' (2014, 29). The socio-political metanarrative of the superiority of the modern nation state, in other words, undergirds the Declaration and makes 'inherent human rights' if not the cause, then at least the metaphysical correlate of modern rights theory. However, postmodern critics are, not surprisingly, incredulous. Though the Declaration was meant to be a modern instrument of liberation of humans from tyranny and oppression, there is increased suspicion, as Gaete trenchantly puts it, that 'the instruments of liberation tend to become means of manipulation' (1991, 150).

Postmodern critics are therefore reasonably sceptical of an appeal to an a priori idea of human dignity while apparently ignoring actual humans in the concrete contingency of their localized experience. In short, the postmodern critic is convinced that what theoretically and practically might count as dignity *here* cannot be assumed to be the same as dignity *there*.

The Theological or Religious Critique

The last line of critique is the theological or religious critique. In a manner of speaking, the postmodern and theological critiques are two sides of a critical coin. If postmodern critics perceive the concept of inherent human dignity as adopting the metaphysical holdover of a modernist worldview, theologians and scholars of religion point out that the Declaration conversely brackets the very theological or religious framework that lent the idea of human dignity its initial weight.

Hughes (2011) notes that the original framers of the document, though seeking to appeal to a variety of world cultures, nevertheless understood that the notion of a universal, inherent human dignity owed itself fundamentally to the deep Western Christian theological and philosophical traditions. He says:

> All [the authors] would have been aware that the twentieth-century ideals and principles of a liberal democratic order and human rights were deeply indebted to the Christian idea of the human being as a person gifted with an inalienable dignity through her created participation in the freedom and self-determination of a transcendent God. Even the Confucianist P. C. Chang, perhaps the most cosmopolitan of the principal drafters and thus well acquainted with Western as well as Eastern cultural traditions, was cognizant of this indebtedness. (6–7; see also Kraynak 2003)

Theological and religious critics here point to arguably two of the most challenging of problems in the notion of dignity as stated in the Declaration. First, if human dignity is universally inherent to the human, from whence is it derived or grounded? And second, how exactly should inherent dignity be characterized? What, in other words, *is* it?

Here secular proponents of inherent human dignity have often argued that the nature of human dignity is either defined by that to which humans ought *not* to be subjected (e.g. torture, starvation, etc.) or else as something that is self-evident: that though we may not be able to fully characterize what dignity is, humans have an intuitive sense of when it is and is not being upheld (Brüning 2013, 155–56). However, Brüning has rightly noted that, in both cases, the notion of inherent human dignity unavoidably brings with it an assumed anthropology which informs either why certain things ought not to be experienced by a human (e.g. why is torture a violation of human dignity?) or even an underlying rationality or logic that makes something appear to be self-evidently true (e.g. what underlying worldview makes the idea of torture a violation of human dignity 'self-evident'?) (Brüning 2013, 156). Here, again, scholars have pushed back that the 'contemporary democratic and liberal ideas of individuals, society, and human rights are historically dependent on the Christian vision of the human person as a being capable of responsible freedom and as having incalculable worth' (Hughes 2011, 6).

One could argue, then, the Declaration's characterization of human dignity as 'inherent' is a paradoxical attempt to be both dependent on and yet free from its theological rootedness. It strives to uphold the concept of humans being of inestimable worth, but it does so by seeking to ground humanity in itself rather than upon a creator or even an ultimate religious or philosophical principle. The notion of inherent human dignity apart from a theological or religious framework, in other words, is finally an exercise in theological, religious and/or philosophical question begging.

It is important to note that Immanuel Kant, widely recognized as the forefather of the modern concept of human dignity as inherent to the human, sought to define human dignity as being erected upon the moral nature of humans. He insisted that even those who did not believe in God could sense the reality of a moral 'ought'. Yet, as Rosen rightly notes, Kant also believed that 'our moral nature comes from the fact that we have been created by God as free beings' (2018, 24). So, though Kant opened the way for secular concepts of the dignity of human beings, even he was unable to avoid the theological conclusion that the human sense of morality came from God, whether individuals believed such a thing or not.

Thus, when the Catholic philosopher Jacques Maritain, one of the Declaration's most influential advisers, was asked whether the framers of the Declaration intended for human dignity to stand as the philosophical basis for human rights, he quipped: 'Yes, we agree about the [inherence of human] rights, but only on condition no one asks us why' (cited in Cullinan 2005). Or to paraphrase Maritain, we can agree that humans have inherent dignity, but only on condition that we bracket theological or religious questions of its ultimate grounding.

Convergences

Although the foregoing critiques of human dignity are wide ranging, at least three points of convergence are notable. First, critics (mostly) perceive that apart from shared senses of the *meaning* or *definition* of dignity, it is difficult, if not impossible, for the concept to be useful in establishing agreement on how it should inform application of human rights, whether in law, ethics or professional practice. This is not an issue unique to the concept of dignity per se; many legal, philosophical or indeed, theological concepts lack common definition. The problem here is that the notion of human dignity as tied to human rights arose precisely *without* an attempt to (re)define it. In this regard, the Declaration sought practical agreement and use of a word without definitional agreement on its meaning. While that may have worked temporarily, it is now clearly evident that practical consensus has given way to substantial philosophical disagreement.

Second, the critiques reveal there is evidence of a significant divide between what might be called 'foundational' versus 'non-foundational' approaches to human dignity. On the one hand, the 'foundationalists' point out that speaking of human dignity in a universalist sense cannot avoid answering what ultimately grounds human dignity. Even the appeal to the 'inherence' of human dignity begs the question of how it is that all humans everywhere can be said to have this common characteristic. On what is that characteristic based, if not some kind of common anthropological definition of the human? Here theistic, religious and, indeed, modern transcendentalists have more in common than not, insofar as they all see some kind of universal grounding of human dignity as something either outside or extrinsic to the human, or as an 'immanent transcendent', as something common to all humans and yet which transcends the contingency of each human situation.

On the other hand, non-foundationalist and various practical approaches to human dignity have questioned the usefulness or functionality of the concept, to see the concept as heuristic or purely practical, or in more radical forms, to see the concept itself as hubristic at worst or as simply having failed to jettison its metaphysical and/or theological roots or metanarratives at best. Taken together, however, foundationalists and non-foundationalists at times have appealed to the deeper intellectual history which often saw both the universal *and* contingent at play in a concept of human dignity. Thus, taken together, the various critiques point to the need to reclaim and reconsider the deeper intellectual roots of human dignity which simultaneously might address the universality of human dignity while recognizing that human dignity works itself out contingently in history, culture and context.

Third, all the critiques, directly or indirectly and to greater or lesser degrees, point to the problematic qualifier 'inherent' when speaking of human dignity. Given that human dignity, whether or not it was so intended by the original framers of the Declaration, has de facto become the touchstone concept for human rights discussion, it is paradoxical that the concept was laden with an adjective that seeks to identify something that is 'internal' or 'intrinsic' to the human rather than something that is extrinsically or relationally defined. Given that modern human rights discourse is all about setting standards for how humans ought or ought not to treat one another, it is puzzling that the contingent, relational, situational, contextual, cultural elements of human history and interaction were downplayed by an appeal to an inner, abstract, universal characteristic apart from human contingency and relationship. Thus, there is a pressing need to rediscover the fuller breadth of the intellectual tradition on human dignity. Perhaps, for example, it is still possible to wed a sense of the intrinsic, universal nature of human dignity to that which is extrinsic and contingent to the human situation as well.

Karl Barth on Honour

At this point in history, the concept of human dignity could be in danger of suffering the death of a thousand qualifications. With the clarity of retrospective vision, seeking to situate human rights on the soil of human dignity may not have been the best decision; at the same time, we need to be careful not to underplay the powerful effect that appeals to protection of human dignity still play in diverse legal and ethical contexts. In this regard, it is likely unwise and impractical to start again with a new concept; more soberingly, it is doubtful that consensus will be achieved on foundational versus non-foundational, or theological versus secular views of human dignity. However, some gains could be possible if all parties acknowledged that the concept of human dignity could be 'thickened' to include consideration that human dignity needs to be understood as having both universal and contingent aspects. But to do so will, in my opinion, need to move away from understanding human dignity solely in terms of inherence.

Here a concept drawn specifically from the Christian theological anthropology of the Basel-based Protestant Reformed theologian Karl Barth (1886–1968), one of the most prolific and most widely studied theologians of the twentieth century, could be fruitful. Barth's concept of *honour* is a rich one that is clearly theological in orientation, but which could be a suggestive conceptual model for theists and non-theists alike to break free from the restrictions which inherence inevitably created.

Barth was publicly outspoken in his critique of the tyrannical human rights abuses of German National Socialism (Gorringe 1999, 158–59), even to the point of being removed from his university teaching post and unceremoniously deported from Germany. Moreover, he lived long enough to see the international conversations on human rights flourish. Yet Barth was cautious, as was the Catholic Church in early years subsequent to the Declaration, about theologically co-opting the language of human rights because it tended to focus too much on the human as an individual rather than as a social being. As Barth once formulated it, 'In the Christian Church we have no option but to interpret [humanity] as fellow-[humanity]' (1960, 319).[8]

For this reason, Barth was moderately critical of the Catholic Church when it began to seek to provide a theological interpretation of human dignity and human rights language in Vatican II documents.[9] More generally, Barth saw modern human rights discourse and its attendant focus on human dignity as in danger of understanding dignity in too absolutized and abstract a fashion (1961, 651). Barth once criticized the idea that human dignity pertains to the majesty of the individual as nothing more than 'enlightened absolutism' (1959, 23).

Rather than speaking of human dignity, Barth preferred instead to speak of the 'honour' of humans, though on occasion he allows that the notion of human dignity in the universal sense as a 'general honour of humanity' is at least partially similar to what the concept of honour demands (1961, 653). In this regard, his use of the term 'honour' was, first, driven by his desire to conform to the patterns of how Christian Scripture spoke of the human and, second, an overarching critique of the individualism of both modern theology and the modern spirit more generally.

Barth's concept of honour has two important aspects. First, honour is something that is *given* or *bestowed*, not something that is an indelible, inviolable part of the human constitution. As Barth put it, 'This is the value which God accords to humans, the honour which He does them. It can only be given them by God. How could humans have it in themselves? How could they take it to themselves? Who else could give it to them?' (1961, 649). In other words, if there is an unwavering, universal aspect of what is today called human dignity, it is not as something universally inherent nor as that which humans own as a possession apart from any other. Dignity, or honour as Barth calls it, is that which one *receives* and *bears* as a gift. In this sense, yes, dignity is universal as a gift to all humans that cannot be lost. As he put it,

---

8   In this and other quotations of Barth to follow, I have taken the liberty of modifying the English translation of 'man' (German, *mensch*) to the more inclusive 'human' or 'humanity'.

9   Some of Barth's criticism of the Catholic Church's co-opting of human rights language can be detected in his *Ad Limina Apostolorum*. See Barth (1968).

The honour itself, precisely because it is not his but the reflection of the glory of God falling upon humans, cannot be lost. It belongs to the *character indelebilis* of their human existence. It is not overlooked, forgotten, nor misunderstood by God, not even where a human tramples it underfoot, or where it is trampled under the feet of others, or where it is misused when human are exalted or think that they can exalt themselves as a demigod. (652)

In short, *all* humans are honoured by God, whether or not they recognize it of themselves or others.

Barth's notion of honour aligns well with attempts to speak of the 'universal', and therefore, inalienable, character of human dignity but is noticeably out of step with the idea that honour, or dignity, is inherent to the human. In the latter case, Barth sees human honour not as something intrinsic to humans but relative to that which is extrinsic to them, namely God the Creator. Human dignity is perpetually bestowed on all but is not an intrinsic, abstract human characteristic any more than human honour of another person changes that person's essential human nature. In other words, for human honour to be meaningful, it must be understood not only as applying to all but as coming to all from outside of oneself in the context of relationship. For Barth, honour comes first from God's relationship with the human but also in the relationships all persons have with their fellow human beings. To honour, in other words, is to consider oneself as, to quote Barth, 'the creature of God before God and from God' and also one who 'lives with his fellows and not as a hermit' (1961, 656). Here Barth's notion of human honour is *asymmetrical* in that humans may honour one another but can do so only derivatively of the ultimate honour given to them by the Creator. We take it for granted that human do not always honour one another, but we should not at all take for granted that God freely chooses to honour humans, whether or not humans do so one to another.

At this point, Barth's notion of honour could be loosely characterized along the lines of what earlier was called a 'foundationalist' or, in this instance, a theological perspective that grounds human dignity not as something inherent to the human but in virtue of the human's ultimate relationship to the Creator. It will be necessary to consider whether Barth's concept might inform non-theistic or non-foundationalist views of human dignity, but at this point it is vital to note that Barth highlights the dynamic relational aspect of honour over against an abstract attribute inherent to the human.

The second important aspect of Barth's notion of honour pertains to the specificity of what God bestows upon humans. As mentioned earlier, Christian theology has traditionally understood that human honour or dignity is discerned by virtue of being created after God's own image and likeness (Gen. 1:27). Extensive treatments of what is similar between God and humans has ensued amongst the theologians. Being created *imago Dei* has often been, in other words, the touchstone theological concept grounding human dignity or honour in God. But Barth, without denying the importance of the biblical testimony to the *imago Dei*, resists an *analogia entis* (analogy of being)[10] and focuses rather upon the *command* of God towards those so created after God's own image and

---

[10] For an extensive analysis of Barth's rejection of the *analogia entis*, see Johnson (2011).

likeness as the locus of honour. Rather than isolating a shared divine and human characteristic, Barth notes that God, after creating humans, immediately *commands* them by giving them a calling and task – a vocation, as he calls it elsewhere in his *Church Dogmatics*. In the Genesis account (Gen. 1:28), that call of vocation and service is God's call to humans first to be fruitful and second to have dominion or co-regency over the world as God's covenant partners. Such a calling reveals a God, as Barth puts it, who 'does not will to be God without humanity' (1961, 654). That God should be a God who commands humans, then, 'is as such an incomprehensible recognition of humanity on the part of God, an expression of His esteem, a distinction' – a distinction such that God 'considers humans worthy that He should confront him as his Commander and stand on his level as Partner with partner' (649).

If the universality of human honour for Barth consists in it being that which is bestowed upon humans from their Creator primarily, the general call to all to be God's covenant partners, and the honour bestowed upon one another as co-humans secondarily, it is the particularity of human vocation and calling that addresses the contingency of human honour. As noted earlier, some critics of human dignity lament that the concept is too abstract or general and lacks an ability to be concretely applied. The reverse of this, of course, is that if human dignity or honour is only to be considered from its particularity, then it fails to function as a basis for setting out general applications, policies or laws for all.

Here Barth provides a concept of human honour that takes into account both the universal and the contingent. Typically for Barth, he moves quickly to the New Testament testimony that in Jesus Christ, God has exalted the honour of humans by taking human form himself – the Christian doctrine of incarnation. As Barth puts it,

> How high is the honour of humanity even as the creature of God and object of His world sovereignty is revealed in the inconceivable fact that God Himself becomes human in Jesus Christ – human in all the limitation in which every other human is also human. [...] What are all human declamations about the intrinsic dignity of humanity compared with the foundation which it is given here according the witness of the Bible? (1961, 654)

Of critical importance for Barth is that Jesus Christ is the only true *analogia entis* and as such, is both the Universal and the Particular: Jesus Christ is the Universal insofar as he is the image of the invisible, unseen, immortal God, but he is also the Particular insofar as Jesus of Nazareth came at a particular time and place in history, into a particular culture and with a specialized and particular calling of God to be the Saviour of all humanity. God is, in other words, the one who is Saviour to all by deigning to be the particular human Jesus.

In this regard, Barth understands Jesus not merely as the archetype or pattern for all humans, but as the very one through whom God honours humans and by which humans lend honour to God. Not only is Jesus the *imago Dei*, but he has been given an eternal calling to be the Saviour and Mediator between all other humans and God the Father himself. Likewise, all humans are, like Jesus, created in the image of God and also called to God's service and are therefore co-participants in God's rule and dominion over creation.

Barth insists that for the concept of honour to be serviceable, it must always be an 'honour in limitation'. While it is true that all humans are equally bestowed with honour by the Creator, the honour of humans is limited to contingent times and places, and humans can fail to live up to the honour bestowed upon all humans universally by the Creator. Here Barth is worth citing at length:

> Honour is distinction. It is the just claim to special, particular and specific recognition. It cannot, then, be a characteristic which might be borne by the human race collectively. It is not a general and equal determination of all human creatures as such. If the term is not to be empty, it must mean the honour of the concrete and therefore always the individual man, the dignity and estimation due to every man, but due to each as this particular man, not merely as a specimen of the race, but directly, personally and exclusively. (1961, 655)

Thus, Barth insists that honour, while given universally to all by God in Jesus Christ, is also something that awaits being manifest in human history. Every human individual, in her or his own way, has opportunity to extend honour not only to God but to one another as an outworking of God's command and call. But the honour so extended, whether to God or to fellow humans, must be continually discerned in the moment, recognizing that what is honourable and dictated by human standards and traditions may or may not ultimately be determined to be honouring to God. Though God is the one who commands universally to all, the response to that command works itself out contingently and in consideration of the time, space, culture and so on in which humans find themselves.

The Promise of Barth's Notion of Honour to Human Dignity/Rights Discourse

It was earlier suggested that Barth's concept of *honour* might be useful for theists and non-theists alike to break free from the restrictions which inherence inevitably created. In this regard, we cannot be under any illusion (1) that there will be a mass conversion to the Christian anthropology suggested by Karl Barth; (2) that a massive cross-disciplinary campaign needs to be launched to replace the language of human dignity with human honour; or (3) that any overtly theologically defined concept will have broad acceptance in an otherwise secularly dominated field of discussion. What might be possible, however, is that Barth's concept of honour could serve as a model for what needs to happen going forward on the theory and practice of human dignity per se. Here three brief lessons learned from Barth's approach could be instructive.

First, and perhaps most importantly, Barth's concept of honour stands as a reminder that the attempt of humans to seek to set standards and practices of behaviour one to another is fundamentally a socio-relational issue. To introduce or rely upon notions of human autonomy and individual rationality (which themselves are inherently individualistic) without at the same time recognizing the inescapable reality that humans are fundamentally social beings is already to begin on the wrong conceptual footing. Whenever appeals to dignity are but reiterations of the affirmation of the 'absolute individual', we are already cast upon a sea of the most radical notions of difference and contingency – hardly a situation from whence common practices and judgements can arise. Attempts to arrive at standards of law and ethics that are applicable to the common good must, then, return to a recognition of the fundamental *sociality* of humans as part and parcel of the exercise of human dignity. To be human is to be co-human. And, theists might add, to be human is to be Creatures honoured by God. In this regard, theists can comfortably work within a notion of human dignity or honour in light of human relationships to God and to one another, while non-theists can, at the very least, recognize that all humans are unavoidably socially and relationally connected to others and that without this fundamental recognition, all appeals to inherent human dignity will finally end up meaning nothing more than 'what I desire or want or need for myself'.

Second, Barth's notion of honour resonates with those critics who see in modern human dignity discourse a reduction, ironically, to the universal. In this regard, Barth's notion of honour seeks to recognize that a serviceable concept of honour (or dignity) must recognize both the universal and contingent aspects of human existence. Undoubtedly, those working outside a theistic framework would reject Christian doctrine of the Incarnation as a conceptual touchstone for human dignity, but Barth's construction nevertheless is instructive in showing how both the Universal and Particular can be upheld. In other words, one should not be forced to appeal solely either to the universal or to the radically contingent aspects of human dignity. Rather, human dignity, or honour, is a dialectical concept (to use a favourite concept of Barth's) that needs always to consider both sides of a tension without reduction or eradication of the tension itself. It is a both/and, not an either/or, concept.

Practically speaking, this means that simply finding a universal definition of human dignity will be no more sufficient to safeguard human rights than to make ad hoc legal or ethical decisions at the level of each and every individual case. Both must come into play for dignity (or honour) to be meaningful. In law that means on the one hand seeking to recognize that human dignity is something constantly to be protected and bestowed, not simply something that *resides* undisturbed in each individual. On the other hand, it also means that the contingencies of culture, traditions, religion and so on must always be considered when seeking to uphold the dignity or honour of people. What is honourable *here* may be different from what is honourable *there*.

Finally, specifically in regard to the conceptual gap between religious/foundationalist and secular/non-foundationalist perspectives on human dignity, Barth, speaking obviously to theists, contends: 'It is not necessary [...] that the honour which comes to humans from God should contradict what humanity itself understands as honour, that it should never in any circumstances be also worldly honour' (1961, 671). In other words, Barth here sets out the principle that there is no reason to assume that non-theistic and theistic perspectives on what does or does not count as human dignity will never coincide. Indeed, Barth epigrammatically puts it thus: 'All honour of humanity is always God's honour' (654). In this regard, the challenge given especially to theists is not to reject practices or rulings of law, ethics and behaviour that are overtly based on non-theistic presuppositions but to recognize that theists and non-theists, foundationalists and non-foundationalists, sometimes in imperfect and faltering ways, actually succeed in protecting the dignity and honour due humans, deep axiomatic divides notwithstanding. Conversely, non-theists must also recognize that though they may be uncomfortable with what appears to them to be outdated modes of religious or metaphysical ways of thinking, common cause for the protection of humans may nevertheless be attempted, if they are but willing to engage in those attempts for the honour of their fellow humans. What must not happen, however, is for one side or the other simply to abandon the other because of a failure to come to fundamental, axiomatic agreement. On the contrary, part of the call for acknowledging the contingency side of the human dignity equation is to recognize the 'one-another-ness' that the notion of human dignity, or honour, implies.

References

Barth, Karl. 1959. *Protestant Thought: From Rousseau to Ritschl*. New York: Harper.
———. 1960. *Church Dogmatics*, Vol. III.2. Edinburgh: T&T Clark.
———. 1961. *Church Dogmatics*, Vol. III.4. Edinburgh: T&T Clark.
———. 1968. *Ad Limina Apostolorum*. Richmond, VA: John Knox.
Beauchamp, Tom L., and James F. Childress. 2001. 'Respect for Autonomy'. In *Principles of Biomedical Ethics*, 5th ed. New York: Oxford University Press.
Brüning, Alfons. 2013. 'Different Humans and Different Rights? On Human Dignity from Western and Eastern Orthodox Perspectives'. *Studies in Interreligious Dialogue* 23, no. 2: 150–75.
Cicero. 1994. *De Officiis*, Vol. I. New York: Oxford University Press.
Clapsis, Emmanuel. 2011. 'Human Dignity in Orthodox Theology – Theology – Greek Orthodox Archdiocese of America'. Accessed 27 April 2019. https://www.goarch.org/-/human-dignity-in-orthodox-theology.
Cochrane, Alasdair. 2010. 'Undignified Bioethics'. *Bioethics* 24, no. 5: 234–41.
Cullinan, John F. 2005. 'Theology of Human Rights'. *National Review* (blog), 8 April. https://www.nationalreview.com/2005/04/theology-human-rights-john-f-cullinan/.
Gaete, Rolando. 1991. 'Postmodernism and Human Rights: Some Insidious Questions'. *Law and Critique* 2, no. 2 (1 September): 149–70.
Genuis, Quentin I. T. 2016. 'Dignity Reevaluated: A Theological Examination of Human Dignity and the Role of the Church in Bioethics and End-of-Life Care'. *Linacre Quarterly* 83, no. 1: 6–14.
Gewirth, Alan. 1992. 'Human Dignity as the Basis of Rights'. In *The Constitution of Rights: Human Dignity and American Values*, edited by Michael J. Meyer and W. A. Parent, 10–28. Ithaca, NY: Cornell University Press.
Gorringe, Timothy J. 1999. *Karl Barth: Against Hegemony*. New York: Oxford University Press.
Guyette, Fred. 2013. 'Thomas Aquinas and Recent Questions about Human Dignity'. *Diametros* 38 (December): 112–26.
Hughes, Glenn. 2011. 'The Concept of Dignity in the Universal Declaration of Human Rights'. *Journal of Religious Ethics* 39, no. 1: 1–24.
Johnson, Keith L. 2011. *Karl Barth and the Analogia Entis*, rpt ed. London: Bloomsbury.
Kateb, George. 2014. *Human Dignity*. Cambridge, MA: Belknap.
Kraynak, Robert P. 2003. '"Made in the Image of God": The Christian View of Human Dignity and Political Order'. In *Defense of Human Dignity: Essays for Our Times*, edited by Robert P. Kraynak and Glenn Tinder, 81–118. Notre Dame, IN: University of Notre Dame Press.
Łuków, Paweł. 2018. 'A Difficult Legacy: Human Dignity as the Founding Value of Human Rights'. *Human Rights Review* 19, no. 3 (1 September): 313–29.

Lyotard, Jean-François. 1984. *The Postmodern Condition: A Report on Knowledge*. Minneapolis: University of Minnesota Press.

Macklin, Ruth. 2003. 'Dignity Is a Useless Concept'. *British Medical Journal* 327, no. 7429 (20 December): 1419–20.

McCrudden, Christopher. 2008. 'Human Dignity and Juridical Interpretation of Human Rights'. *European Journal of International Law* 19: 664–75.

Oberdorfer, Bernd. 2010. 'Human Dignity and "Image of God"'. *Scriptura* 104: 231–39.

O'Mahony, Conor. 2012. 'There Is No Such Thing as a Right to Dignity'. *International Journal of Constitutional Law* 10, no. 2 (30 March): 551–74.

Orsy, Ladislas. 2014. 'The Divine Dignity of Human Persons in *Dignitatis Humanae*'. *Theological Studies* 75, no. 1 (March): 8–22.

Paul II, Pope John. 1995. 'Evangelium Vitae'. 25 March. http://w2.vatican.va/content/john-paul-ii/en/encyclicals/documents/hf_jp-ii_enc_25031995_evangelium-vitae.html.

Pinker, Steven. 2008. 'The Stupidity of Dignity'. *New Republic*, 28 May. https://newrepublic.com/article/64674/the-stupidity-dignity.

Reinbold, Jenna. 2011. 'Political Myth and the Sacred Center of Human Rights: The Universal Declaration and the Narrative of "Inherent Human Dignity"'. *Human Rights Review* 12, no. 2 (June): 147–71.

Rosen, Michael. 2018. *Dignity: Its History and Meaning*, rpt ed. Cambridge, MA: Harvard University Press.

'Universal Declaration of Human Rights'. 1948. Accessed 11 June 2019. https://www.un.org/en/universal-declaration-human-rights/.

Vatican. 2011. 'Pastoral Constitution on the Church in the Modern Word – *Gaudium et Spes*'. 11 April. https://web.archive.org/web/20110411023509/http://www.vatican.va/archive/hist_councils/ii_vatican_council/documents/vat-ii_cons_19651207_gaudium-et-spes_en.html.

Winter, Steven L. 1994. 'Human Values in a Postmodern World'. *Yale Journal of Law & the Humanities* 6, no. 2: 233–48.

Chapter Four

THREE SOURCES OF HUMAN DIGNITY

Erik J. Wielenberg

1. Introduction

One prominent meaning of the word 'dignity' is the value or worth possessed by all human beings in virtue of which they possess certain rights – human rights – such as the right not to be tortured for entertainment and the right not to be enslaved. Various political documents assert the reality of dignity so understood, the most famous of these being the United Nations Universal Declaration of Human Rights (1948), which opens with the assertion that 'recognition of the inherent dignity and of the equal and inalienable rights of all members of the human family is the foundation of freedom, justice and peace in the world'.

My aim here is to sketch a secular account of dignity in this sense. The account is secular in that it does not entail or require the existence of God, though it is, as far as I can see, entirely consistent with the existence of God. Some claim that no such account is plausible. Nicholas Wolterstorff, for instance, declares that 'it is impossible to develop a secular account of human dignity adequate for grounding human rights' (2008, 325; see also Perry 1996 and Stackhouse 1998). A central task of any account of dignity is to identify dignity's ground or basis. As Wolterstorff notes, 'Dignity is not something that just settles down here and there willy-nilly' (2008, 319). Many attempts to identify dignity's basis fail on the grounds that the putative basis is not possessed by all human beings; three particularly challenging cases are infants, those with dementia and the severely cognitively impaired. Immanuel Kant is a popular punching bag here. Wolterstorff, for example, points out that the Kantian proposal that rational agency is the ground of human dignity founders on the fact that 'some human beings [...] do not *have* it – infants and those suffering from dementia, for example' (329, emphasis original; see also Gilabert 2018, 127; Killmister 2017, 2066–69; Li 2019, 187–88; Schroeder 2012, 329–31; and Singer 2009, 573–74).

The secular account of dignity that I sketch here is pluralistic in that I identify three sources of human worth or value that can ground human rights. Some claim that dignity must be possessed to the same degree by all human beings (e.g. see Debes 2017, 1 and Kateb 2011, 5), but I see no good reason to accept such a claim. It is enough for an account of dignity to provide a plausible explanation of the fact that all human beings have value or worth that sufficiently surpasses the value or worth of any known non-human creature to ground the existence of human rights possessed by all human beings. The following analogy may help to illustrate this point.

Suppose you have a collection of wines of various prices. Suppose further that many of the wines range in price from $5 to $20 and the rest range in price from $100 to $200. And suppose you have a fancy wine cellar with a limited capacity. It would be perfectly reasonable to divide your wines into two broad categories – cheap ($5–$20) and expensive ($100 and up) – and treat all the wines in the expensive category with a common minimum level of care. For example, all wines in the expensive category might be placed in the wine cellar whereas all of the cheap wines could be excluded from the cellar. It is entirely reasonable to treat all the expensive wines with the same minimum level of care despite the fact that (let us suppose) no two of them have exactly the same price. My view is that the situation with creatures is analogous to the wine scenario. Human beings are like wines in the expensive category; all other earthly creatures are like wines in the cheap category. Human rights capture the minimum level of respect that all creatures with a certain worth or greater should be treated with; the existence of a shared minimum level of respect – of basic human rights common to all human beings – is in no way threatened by the fact that there is variation in worth within the category of human being.

In what follows I first sketch my account of human dignity. The main task here is to identify distinctive sources of value or worth of human beings. My account is pluralistic in that rather than identifying one ground for the worth of all human beings, I propose three sources of human worth and suggest that for any human being, one or more of the three sources of worth gives that human being enough worth to possess human rights. With a sketch of my account in place, I then consider whether my account is guilty of Peter Singer's charge of speciesism, arguing that it is not. Following that I criticize some theistic alternatives to my account.

2. Three Sources of Human Worth

Consider these excerpts from Adrian Mitchell's (2004) poem 'Human Beings':

> look at your hands
>   your beautiful useful hands
>   you're not an ape
>   you're not a parrot
> you're not a slow loris
>   or a smart missile
>   you're human […]
>   look at your body
> with its amazing systems
> of nerve-wires and blood canals
>   think about your mind
> which can think about itself
>   and the whole universe
>   look at your face

which can freeze into horror
　　or melt into love
　　look at all that life
　　all that beauty
　　you're human.

This poem reminds us that a normal adult human has intellectual and emotional capacities that, as far as we know, far surpass those attainable by any earthly non-human species. Other earthly creatures can suffer and love, but their suffering and love lack the depth and complexity of human suffering and love. Perhaps some other creatures can reason or use language, but the human capacity for reason and language is far more developed than theirs. Perhaps some other creatures can possess primitive forms of artistic creativity, but their creativity lacks the depth and development of ours. Although human beings are in many ways continuous with the rest of nature and, like all living things, products of unguided evolutionary forces, the ancient view that human beings have psychological capacities that set them well apart from all other living creatures is correct. In virtue of such capacities, any normal adult human has a special worth or value that cannot be possessed by any non-human creature that we know of. Let us call this particular sort of value 'psychological worth'.

Not all normal adult human beings possess these psychological capacities to the same degree, so there is some variation in the psychological worth of normal adult humans. Yet, despite this variation, normal adult humans as a class have far more developed psychological capacities than any other known creature and so stand apart from all other creatures in their degree of psychological worth. This worth, in turn, grounds their possession of human rights.

Of course, not all humans are normal adult human beings. Many humans have significantly diminished psychological capacities for one reason or another. Some – infants and children – have not yet fully developed their psychological capacities. Some – the very elderly or those with dementia – have lost their psychological capacities to a significant degree as a result of age or illness. And some – the severely cognitively impaired – have never had and never will have the psychological capacities of normal adult human beings. An important question, then, is: What sort of value or worth do these human beings possess, and what is the source of that value or worth?

To begin to answer this question, let us consider Robert Adams's discussion of a particular category of immoral action – what he calls the morally horrible or abominable. Examples of actions in this category are cannibalism and the making of lampshades from human skin. To account for the morally horrible nature of such acts, Adams proposes that 'a human corpse is a "natural symbol" of the person whose body it was' (1999, 128) and says the following:

> The horror of cannibalism, or of making lampshades of human skin […] lies […] in what is done to the deceased person […] The horrible thing about cannibalism, and about the Nazi lampshades, is that what was the physical basis of a person's life is treated as something much more ordinary […] it is a symbolic violation of the deceased person. (127–28)

A similar line of thought is independently explored by Roland Breeur and Arnold Burms:

> Some objects derive their significance from their material link with a person to whom they belonged or by whom they were handled, used, worn: we usually call these objects 'relics'. Of all relics, the dead human body is without doubt the most fundamental one […] most people think that they should respect or honour it and believe that desecrating it would be cruel, immoral and criminal. (2008, 138)

Like Adams, Breeur and Burms propose that the corpse is a symbol of the living person. But they go beyond Adams in proposing that a living person can be a symbol of another person in virtue of a material or physical connection and in this way the first person can acquire value (139).

Taking a cue from Adams, Breeur and Burms, I propose that a person's corpse has 'symbolic value' in virtue of representing or standing for the person. A human corpse lacks psychological capacities and so has no psychological worth, but it nevertheless has symbolic worth because it stands for the person who did have psychological worth. As the remarks of Adams, Breeur and Burms suggest, this symbolic worth can be quite substantial – substantial enough to make mistreatment of human corpses not just immoral but morally abominable. Such an account allows us to make sense of, for example, the debate over the proper treatment of human remains from the 9/11 attacks on the World Trade Center (Susman 2014). If a person's corpse has this sort of symbolic value, then surely an elderly person with dementia also has a significant amount of symbolic value: the person with diminished psychological capacities symbolizes her former self and hence has symbolic worth.[1] This symbolic worth is substantial enough to set the person with dementia apart, with respect to value, from all non-human creatures, despite her greatly diminished psychological worth. In virtue of this symbolic value (plus their remaining psychological value), human beings with dementia retain their human rights.

The case of the severely cognitively impaired is somewhat different, since such persons never attain the psychological capacities of a normal human adult. Still, it is plausible that such persons to a significant degree stand for or represent typical human adults. One possibility is that they represent the adults that they would have become without their impairment. A less speculative possibility is suggested by Breeur and Burms's proposal that a close material or physical connection can be the basis of a symbolic connection that transfers value from one person to another. Any cognitively impaired human is closely materially connected with non-impaired humans (e.g. his or her parents) and so to some extent symbolizes them. Furthermore, it is crucial to realize that many who fall into the category of the severely cognitively impaired still have psychological capacities which set them well apart from non-human animals. This case is powerfully made by Eva Kittay, a philosopher whose daughter, Sesha, is severely cognitively impaired (2009, 610). One of Kittay's claims is that being loved and parented by a human mother can enhance the cognitive abilities of *all* children, including those who are severely cognitively impaired.

---

[1]   Breeur and Burms discuss an example of just this sort (2008, 136).

She writes: 'Every parent needs schools and other social institutions to ensure that her child can develop her capacities, whatever those capacities may be' (623; for some relevant empirical evidence, see Feniger-Schaal and Joels 2018; Sallisbury and Copeland 2013; and Weiss et al. 2016). And, as Kittay points out, 'we are *all* some mother's child' (2009, 625, emphasis original). So it is important to recognize that there are many human beings that fall well short of the normal adult human with respect to their cognitive abilities and yet have capacities that far outstrip those of any non-human animal (see also Kittay 2008, 153–55).[2]

Finally, consider the case of babies and children. As their psychological capacities grow, so does their psychological value. A newborn baby has a close material connection with its parents and so has a significant degree of symbolic value. Newborns also have a third sort of value which we may call 'potential value'. They possess value or worth *now* in virtue of being the sort of thing that, if it develops normally, will come to have a high degree of psychological worth. Foetuses have this sort of value as well but a lesser degree of symbolic value; as a foetus develops and its psychological capacities emerge and expand, so does its psychological value. This implies what I take to be the correct view that while a week-old human foetus has some value – primarily potential and symbolic value – it has less value than a newborn baby and still less than a typical adult human. While I think that a newborn baby has enough worth to ground human rights, I leave aside here the contentious issue of just when a developing human foetus acquires human rights.

A natural objection to the approach I have sketched is that it is overly permissive, giving too much value to certain things that in truth lack such value. A critic might argue that there are a great many things that represent or symbolize adult humans and so on my view would have a lot of symbolic value and therefore should be treated with the sort of respect that in truth is merited only by actual human beings. Putative examples of such things include dolls and photographs of human beings. My response to this objection is that representation or symbolization comes in degrees. Dolls and photographs represent normal adult humans to some degree, and therefore have some amount of symbolic value, but to a far lesser degree than the higher symbolic value of corpses, humans with dementia or the severely cognitively impaired. I think there are ways of treating dolls and photographs that we tend to find immoral or disturbing, and it is a virtue of my view that it can account for such judgements. Consider, for example, whether it would bother you if urinal mats or toilet paper were manufactured with an image of your face (or your mother's face) on it. Or consider an anecdote I once heard about an angry child who spotted a discarded soda can on the ground, said to his mother 'this is your FACE!' and kicked the can with all of his might. Such an act is obviously a far cry from cannibalism

---

[2] It is also significant, I think, that in making her case for the moral personhood of severely cognitively impaired humans, Kittay emphasizes their *emotional* capacities whereas when Peter Singer makes the case that some non-human animals have cognitive abilities similar to those of some severely cognitively impaired humans he focuses on *intellectual* abilities, such as the ability to understand and use language (see Singer 2009, 568–70).

or making lampshades of human skin, but there is nevertheless something morally troubling about it. I suggest that part of what is morally troubling about the case is that by making the can stand for his mother's face to a small degree, the child is able to then assault his mother to a small degree.[3]

In sum, then, my proposal is that every human being has enough psychological, symbolic and/or potential worth to possess human rights. As I noted earlier, this account is pluralist in that rather than proposing that there is some single ground for the worth of every human being I propose three sources that generate enough worth for every human being to possess human rights.

In the next section I argue that one can hold my view without being guilty of 'speciesism' as that sin is understood by Peter Singer. I also suggest that my account reveals a fundamental flaw in Singer's approach to morality. Following that, I critically examine some theistic alternatives to my approach. Part of my defence of the secular account I have sketched is that some prominent theistic alternatives are inadequate.

3. Speciesism?

In advancing the account described in the preceding section, am I guilty of what Peter Singer calls 'speciesism'? To answer that question, we need some understanding of how exactly Singer understands speciesism. Commenting on the claim that human beings alone have dignity, Singer writes: 'This is really just a piece of rhetoric unless it is given some support. What is it about human beings that gives them moral worth and dignity? If there is no good answer forthcoming, this talk of intrinsic worth and dignity is just speciesism in nicer terms' (2009, 573). This passage suggests that one form of speciesism is asserting that human beings alone have dignity without explaining what it is about humans that gives them alone dignity. The account sketched in the previous section is intended to give precisely such an explanation. So, by endorsing the claim that humans alone have dignity I am not guilty of speciesism as Singer characterized it in this passage.

Elsewhere Singer defines speciesism as 'a prejudice or attitude of bias in favor of the interests of members of one's own species and against those of members of other species' (2000, 33). Notice that this definition of speciesism has to do with how much weight we ought to give to the *interests* of beings of different species whereas the view I have advanced has to do with the *value or worth* of human beings. Furthermore, Singer writes:

> [A] rejection of speciesism does not imply that all lives are of equal worth [...] It is not arbitrary to hold that the life of a self-aware being, capable of abstract thought, of planning for the future, of complex acts of communication, and so on, is more valuable than the life of a being without these capacities. (45)

---

[3]   See also Wolterstorff's discussion of 'going proxy' (2015, 23–24).

The claims advanced in the passage just quoted are entirely compatible with my view. However, not long after the passage just quoted, Singer makes a claim that does conflict with my view: 'As long as we remember that we should give the same respect to the lives of animals as we give to the lives of those human beings at a similar mental level, we shall not go far wrong' (46). This, I think, is mistaken. Consider a case where for some reason we must choose between the life of a woman with severe dementia and the life of a gorilla with roughly the same psychological capacities. In my view, the symbolic value of the woman gives her much greater overall worth than the gorilla, despite their equal psychological worth. But this position is not guilty of speciesism because the basis of the claim that the woman is more valuable than the gorilla is not that the human belongs to the species *homo sapiens* and the gorilla does not, but rather that the woman possesses a significant degree of symbolic worth that the gorilla lacks. Furthermore, the distinction described in the previous section between psychological, symbolic and potential value allows us to identify a weakness that runs throughout Singer's entire approach to morality, which is that he takes it that the value of a being or its life is entirely a function of that being's actual psychological capacities. In other words, Singer assumes that the only value a being can have is what I have called psychological value. It is this narrowness of his approach to morality that leads him to various mistaken conclusions, for example, that we should 'accord the life of a [human] fetus no greater value than the life of a nonhuman animal at a similar level of rationality, self-consciousness, awareness, capacity to feel, etc.' (156).

Singer's approach to morality is just one secular option; the account I sketched in the previous section is part of an alternative secular approach. To the extent that my account is plausible, it reveals important weaknesses in Singer's approach and also shows that a plausible foundation for the reality of special human dignity can be found outside of a theistic context. In the next section I try to extend this argument by illustrating the shortcomings of some important theistic theories of dignity.

4. Some Theistic Alternatives

As I noted at the outset, some claim that there is no plausible secular basis for human dignity whereas theism – in particular, Christian theism – can provide a solid foundation for human dignity. I think the view that Christian theism alone affords an adequate foundation for human dignity is mistaken. Part of my argument for that position is the secular account of dignity that I have developed. In this section I develop another part of my argument. Here I consider some theistic approaches to human dignity and human rights and argue that none of them is adequate. This discussion is of course not exhaustive – I do not attempt to discuss every theistic account of dignity. But it should serve to illustrate that explaining human dignity by appealing to God is not as straightforward is it may appear.

A natural thought from the perspective of Christian theism is that the fact that human beings are created in God's image explains the distinctive worth of human beings. So, Paul Copan writes:

> The strength of biblical theism is that it offers the requisite metaphysical foundation for human sanctity – 'the image of God'. This divinely bestowed worth is given to all participants in the

human race. It is not measured by functionalist standards routinely used by utilitarians – levels of social adeptness, rationality, or self-awareness. Moreover, this divine 'image' serves as the ground for universal human rights across all societies. (2013, 12)

But what *is* the image of God? As Nicholas Wolterstorff points out, 'There is probably no topic in Christian theology that has provoked more indecisive speculation and fruitless controversy than what constitutes the image of God' (2008, 342).[4] Furthermore, a number of prominent Christian thinkers have held that the *imago Dei* can be lost or damaged in humans and have rejected the view that being made in the image of God instils in humanity an ineradicable worth or dignity (see Kent 2017; and Kilner 2015). So Copan's proposal in the passage here is radically underdeveloped as it stands.

One way of understanding the *imago Dei* is that being in God's image is a matter of *resembling* God (see Linville 2009, 444–45). Robert Adams proposes that the ground of the 'distinction in value between human persons and [for example] sheep' (1999, 115) is resemblance (of a certain sort) to God. He suggests that finite things are valuable to the extent that they faithfully resemble the divine nature (49). He appeals to this theory of value to account for the distinctive value of human beings as follows:

> We may reasonably believe that human persons are more globally like God than sheep are, while resisting any attempt to rank individual persons on their global resemblance to God, since so many dimensions of comparison are relevant, and the resemblance is so distant, though still of the greatest importance [...] This grounds a qualitative superiority of the excellence of persons as such. (117–18)

Adams's proposal is that all human beings resemble God to a greater degree than any non-human creature does and we all resemble God to roughly the same degree; therefore, all human beings have roughly the same worth (or excellence, to use Adams's preferred terminology) and that worth surpasses the worth of any non-human creature. As he puts it, 'We are more excellent than dogs and daisies but one person is not more excellent than another' (117).

A straightforward weakness of Adams's account is that it is simply false that of any two human beings one is not clearly more God-like than the other. A thoroughly stupid, weak and evil human is clearly less God-like than a wise, powerful and good one. Martin Luther King Jr. is clearly more God-like than Stalin or Hitler. Furthermore, to return to an example from the previous section, it is hard to see what basis there is for claiming that

---

[4]   It seems to me that in some writings by theistic authors, talk of the *imago Dei* serves not to provide a purported explanation for human worth or rights but rather is simply a way of referring to or asserting the reality of human worth using religious terminology. This also seems to be true of Michael Perry's (1996) proposal that human beings are God's children and brothers and sisters to one another. As Perry seems to acknowledge, such talk is at best metaphorical since according to the Christian view human beings are not literally God's children nor are we all literally brothers and sisters to one another. Furthermore, Perry introduces his account by saying, 'I now want to present a *religious version of talk* about the inherent dignity of all human beings' (215, emphasis added).

a woman with severe dementia resembles the divine nature more than does a gorilla with roughly the same psychological capacities. So it appears that Adams's account is undone by the familiar challenge of human beings with impaired cognitive faculties.

A Lockean variation of Adams's approach is similarly undone. In his *Second Treatise of Government*, Locke (1980 [1690], 9) writes that human beings are 'all the workmanship of one omnipotent, and infinitely wise maker [...] sent into this world by his order and about his business' and are 'furnished with like faculties'. Consequently, 'there cannot be supposed any such *subordination* among us, that may authorize us to destroy one another, as if we were made for one another's uses, as the inferior ranks of creatures are for ours' (emphasis original). These remarks suggest a view according to which all human beings are endowed by God with similar faculties and assigned a common mission by God, part of which is to exercise dominion over the 'inferior ranks' of creatures. Wolterstorff interprets the Lockean view as implying that to be in the image of God is to possess the capacities necessary for exercising dominion over lesser beings. However, Wolterstorff points out that 'a good many human beings do not have the capacities necessary for exercising dominion. Those who are severely impaired mentally from birth never had them; Alzheimer's patients no longer possess them' (2008, 349).

Copan in one place seems to suggest a view along Lockean lines: 'Since we are created in the *imago Dei* as moral, volitional, and reasoning beings, we are capable of recognizing a self-evident *natural* law' (2012, 71, emphasis original). Copan adds that 'as beings created in God's image [...] we not only have dignity and worth but can recognize this fact in ourselves and others' (ibid.). These remarks suggest that a key element of being created in God's image is the possession of conscience. However, it is far from clear that all humans possess a conscience. To return to Wolterstorff's remarks, some who are severely mentally impaired from birth may never develop the ability to recognize the dignity and worth of others. Additionally, the existence of psychopaths seems to be at odds with Copan's position. The mainstream understanding of psychopaths has it that they lack a conscience. Psychologist Robert Hare explains that 'for psychopaths [...] the social experiences that normally build a conscience never take hold' (1999, 75). According to Eric Matthews, psychopaths 'do not really understand the concept of morality' (2014, 77). And Gwen Adshead writes that 'the predatory psychopath treats others as merely a means to an end and is puzzled at the suggestion that it could be otherwise' (2014, 117).[5] Neuroscientist Kent Kiehl has explored the neurological underpinnings of the psychopath's missing conscience, discovering that the brains of psychopaths have a distinctive pattern of deficits in the paralimbic system, which encompasses several regions of the brain (2014, 169). In Copan's view, it seems that psychopaths are not created in the image of God and hence lack dignity and worth.

So, it turns out that some natural ways of understanding the proposal that the source of human worth is that we have been created in God's image suffer from the same defect

---

[5] For a much fuller discussion of psychopaths and how their existence challenges certain theistic moral views, see Wielenberg (forthcoming).

that afflicts many secular approaches – they are unable to account for the worth of babies, those with dementia or the severely cognitively impaired.[6]

A different way of understanding what it is for humans to have been created in God's image is advanced by John Kilner. In Kilner's view, being created in God's image consists not in actually resembling God or having certain faculties but rather in being *destined* to become Christ-like:

> Humanity is profoundly connected with God by virtue of God's eternal purposes for humanity. God intends for people to reflect who God is and what God does, though they may fall short of actually doing so now. While they do not warrant the title of 'God's image' yet, they have dignity grounded in their destiny to become God's image – and so warrant that title once they are fully conformed to Christ. Until then, people are just 'in' or 'according to' God's image – always accountable to the standard of God's image, and developing toward that image as God enables and people endeavor. (2015, 123)

Speaking of 'people with special needs due to disabilities', Kilner declares that 'their glorious renewal according to God's image in Christ is sure if they are believers and still offered to them if they are not (yet)' (320–21). On Kilner's account, what gives human beings special worth is that they are destined to become Christ-like.

A simple problem with this account is that it is not clear why the fact that a being is destined to become Christ-like at some future time bestows rights on that being at the present time. Consider: a beautiful statue carved from marble may merit admiration and awe, but the block of marble that is destined to become that statue does not thereby merit admiration and awe. Perhaps the idea is that flawed humans destined to become Christ-like deserve protection so that they can become Christ-like later on. But that proposal seems flawed as well. Consider the right not to be tortured. Does being destined to become Christ-like give me this right? It is hard to see why it would, since if I am genuinely destined to become Christ-like, then being tortured will not prevent this from happening. Kilner's remarks about people with disabilities suggest that God will ultimately renew them 'according to God's image in Christ' (2015, 320). If that is true, then God can similarly renew anyone, regardless of what happens to them in this life. So, the fact that a given being is destined to become Christ-like does not seem to generate any sort of moral restriction on how that being should be treated in this life. To return to the marble statue example, Kilner's view seems to be that God is like a sculptor who will ultimately turn the marble block into a beautiful statue regardless of what happens to the block in the meantime.[7]

---

[6] For a discussion of how the idea that human worth is grounded in resemblance to God has been used to justify assorted bad behaviour throughout history, see Kilner (2015, 17–37).

[7] An important difference between being destined to become Christ-like and the concept of potential value that I discussed earlier is, in a word, *frailty*. In the marble block example, the block of marble will become a beautiful statue later regardless of what happens to it now. By contrast, consider an acorn, which must be protected and nurtured in various ways if it is to become a mighty oak later on. The potential value of human infants is more like the acorn than the block of marble.

Still another theistic account of dignity has been developed by Nicholas Wolterstorff. In fact, Wolterstorff has presented two slightly different accounts. The core idea of both accounts is that being loved by God in a particular way bestows dignity on a being and that God loves all (and only) human beings in the relevant way. In his initial account in *Justice: Rights and Wrongs*, Wolterstorff focuses on 'love as attachment' (2008, 359). However, in light of a certain type of objection to that view (e.g. see Weithman 2009), Wolterstorff later replaces love as attachment with love as desire for friendship (2012, 197). To motivate his theory, Wolterstorff considers a case of a good king who honours some of his subjects by choosing them to become his friends. According to Wolterstorff, 'To be honored is to have worth bestowed on one' (198). For the king to desire friendship with someone is for the king to honour that person, and to be honoured by the king is to have worth bestowed on one. Wolterstorff applies these ideas to God and humanity as follows:

> Suppose that one is chosen by God as someone with whom God desires to be a friend. This is to be honored by God. And to be honored by God is to have worth bestowed on one. Add now that every human being has the honor of being chosen by God as someone with whom God desires to be friends and that this desire endures. Then every human being has the ineradicable and equal worth that being so honored bestows on one. (198–99)

Jordan Wessling (2014) poses the following question about Wolterstorff's account: Is God's desire for friendship with all human beings necessary or contingent? That is, is it necessarily the case that God desires friendship with all humans, or is God's desire for friendship with all humans merely a contingent feature of our world? Wessling argues that the second option is unacceptable because it has a number of implausible moral implications. These implications arise from the fact that in Wolterstorff's view God's desire for friendship is essential for bolstering the worth of humans with greatly diminished psychological capacities, for example, those with severe dementia. If God's love for such human beings is merely contingent, then much of their worth is similarly contingent. Wessling points out that this implies that each of the following propositions is true in some possible world:

P1: Well-formed chimpanzees have greater inherent worth, coupled with weightier (or trumping) rights to life, than do humans with severe Alzheimer's disease. (293)

P2 One is morally required to treat all non-Caucasian infants with less respect than all Caucasian infants. (294)

P3 One is morally required to treat male dementia suffers with more respect than females with the same ailment. (Ibid.)

The problem is that it appears that these propositions are not merely false but necessarily false, whereas if God's desire for friendship with every human being is contingent, then Wolterstorff's account implies that P1, P2 and P3 are at best contingently false. Call this the 'contingency problem'.

A second worry about Wolterstorff's view is that it implies that it is not just human beings with whom God desires friendship. Wolterstorff declares that 'though God's desire for friendship with some human being does not presuppose that that human being presently have the capacities necessary for the satisfaction of that desire, it does presuppose that that human being *will some day* have those capacities, in this life or the next' (2012, 199, emphasis original). This is important because it allows Wolterstorff to include the severely mentally disabled in the category of those with whom God desires friendship. Although some in this category may be incapable of being friends with God in this life, God will give them that capacity in the next life. Wolterstorff also proposes the following explanation of why God desires friendship with all human beings:

> The explanation for God's wanting to be friends with us is presumably much like the explanation for why we want to be friends with some fellow human being. We desire to become friends with someone not because we think she merits it or because we think her worth requires it but because we anticipate that our friendship will be a significant good in the lives of both of us. So too for God's desire to be friends with us. (200)

Consider a human infant born with severe brain damage that quickly slips into a permanent vegetative state until death. In Wolterstorff's view, God desires friendship with this infant because He knows that in the next life the infant will become capable of such friendship and that the friendship will be a significant good for both God and the infant. God will have to bring about significant enhancements in the infant's cognitive abilities in the next life, but that is not a problem since God is omnipotent. Now consider a typical adult chimpanzee. It seems that, being omnipotent, God could bring it about that this chimpanzee exists in some sort of afterlife and acquires cognitive abilities that render it capable of friendship with God. At least, if God's omnipotence gives him the ability to do this for the vegetative human infant, it is hard to see why God could not do the same for the chimpanzee – and, indeed for many non-human animals. Trent Dougherty, in the course of defending a 'soul-making [...] theodicy for non-human animals' (2014, 135), draws a similar parallel between human infants and non-human animals. He claims that 'on the Christian conception of the world, [an infant that dies in infancy] [...] will get a chance to develop further in the afterlife [...] the same [...] goes for animals' (142).

If friendship with a cognitively enhanced human infant would be a significant good for God and the infant, then it is hard to see why friendship with a cognitively enhanced chimpanzee would not also be a significant good for God and the chimp. And so we are led to the result that Wolterstorff's view implies that many non-human animals possess the sort of worth that grounds human rights – an unwelcome result. Call this problem the 'animal problem'.

If Wolterstorff's account is to succeed, then it must avoid both the contingency problem and the animal problem. A natural way of handling the contingency problem is to suppose that necessarily, God desires friendship with x if and only if x is or will become capable of friendship with God. As for the animal problem, the following remarks by Wolterstorff suggest a way of addressing that problem:

Crocodiles lack the potential for being friends with God. Being friends with God is incompatible with crocodilian nature. To be a friend with God one has to have the nature of a person. Crocodiles at their best cannot be persons. Of all the animals, it's only human animals that can function as persons and can thus be friends with God. The worth bestowed on us by God's desire to be friends with us is both uniquely human and animal-transcending. (2012, 199)

Notice the distinction suggested in these remarks between *having the nature* of a person and *functioning as* a person. In Wolterstorff's view, to function as a person is not only to be a rational agent but also 'to be a center of trust and mistrust, of hope and despair, of love and hate, a center of emotions, of feelings, of beliefs, of intentions, of sensory perceptions, of plans, of private reveries' (190). According to Wolterstorff, not all human beings function as persons (191), but, as the crocodile passage suggests, all and only human beings have the nature of persons, which is to say that all and only human beings have the *capacity* to function as persons.

We are led, then, to the following understanding of Wolterstorff's position: among earthly creatures, all and only human beings essentially have the nature of persons (i.e. they have the nature of persons in every world in which they exist), whereas non-human animals are essentially non-persons (i.e. they lack the nature of persons in every world in which they exist). Furthermore, it is impossible for any person to be numerically identical with any non-person (for otherwise God could, for instance, turn a crocodile into a person in the afterlife and then become friends with that person). Necessarily, God desires friendship with all and only beings that have the nature of persons (to avoid the contingency problem), and the reason that God desires friendship with such beings is He anticipates the friendship will be a significant good in His life and the life of the being.

With this full picture of Wolterstorff's view in mind, let us revisit the case of the king and his subjects, the case to which Wolterstorff appeals to motivate the claim that for God to desire friendship with a being is for God to honour that being. Here is (part of) Wolterstorff's description of that case:

> Imagine a good monarch who is loved by all his subjects; he bestows on all of them the great good of a just political order that serves the common good. But he's rather lonely. So in addition to acting as a benefactor to all his subjects he decides to choose a few as those with whom he would like to be friends. This is an honor for the ones chosen. (2012, 197)

Notice Wolterstorff's remark that the king chooses 'a few' of his subjects to be his friends. Suppose that you are one of the chosen subjects and you feel honoured. But suppose we continue the story as follows. You discover that the king desires friendship with all subjects who could become capable of friendship with him. It seems to me that this discovery should lead you to realize that by desiring friendship with you, the king has not honoured you after all. If the king wants to be friends with anyone who could become capable of being friends with him, then where is the honour in being chosen for friendship? The alleged honour is more like a participation trophy. Similarly, if God necessarily desires friendship with all beings who could become capable of friendship with Him, it is hard to see how God's desiring friendship with such a being amounts to honouring that being. As the character Syndrome puts it in the film *The Incredibles*, 'When everyone's super, no one will be'.

Now, what *might* be true is that God's desire for friendship is a *sign* of worth that a creature already possesses in virtue of having the nature of a person. However, as Wessling points out, that suggests that it is having the nature of a person that bestows the worth rather than God's desire for friendship and so the worth would be present regardless of whether God exists at all (2014, 289). Ultimately, Wolterstorff's account founders on the fact that God's desire for friendship with a being may *reveal* value that being has but it does not *bestow* value on that being.[8]

5. Conclusion

'What a piece of work is man,' says Hamlet, 'How noble in reason, how infinite in faculty, In form and moving how express and admirable, In action how like an Angel, In apprehension how like a god, The beauty of the world, The paragon of animals' (*Hamlet*, Act II, Scene 2). Humans are far from perfect, but at our best we can come close to Hamlet's description. The intrinsic worth of such humans is the ultimate foundation for the dignity and human rights of all human beings. For each of us, psychological value, symbolic value and/or potential value add up to dignity and human rights, God or no God.[9]

References

Adams, Robert. 1999. *Finite and Infinite Goods: A Framework for Ethics*. Oxford: Oxford University Press.

Adshead, Gwen. 2014. 'The Words but Not the Music: Empathy, Language Deficits, and Psychopathy'. In *Being Amoral: Psychopathy and Moral Incapacity*, edited by T. Schramme, 115–36. Cambridge, MA: MIT Press.

Breeur, Roland, and Arnold Burms. 2008. 'Persons and Relics'. *Ratio* (new series) 21: 134–46.

Copan, Paul. 2012. 'A Protestant Perspective on Human Dignity'. In *Human Dignity and Bioethics: From Worldviews to the Public Square*, edited by Stephen Dilley and Nathan J. Palpant, 67–85. New York: Routledge.

———. 2013. 'Grounding Human Rights: Naturalism's Failure and Biblical Theism's Success'. In *Legitimizing Human Rights*, edited by Angus J. L. Menuge, 33–56. New York: Routledge.

---

[8] For a critique of Wolterstorff's account that reaches a similar conclusion via a different route, see Redmond (2017). Also, some readers may wonder whether an adequate theistic account of dignity could be developed by drawing on the concept of symbolic value discussed earlier. Perhaps, though I will leave it to theists to develop such an account. In any case, I do not claim that no adequate theistic account is possible; rather, I claim only that my secular account is plausible and that the theistic accounts discussed here are all inadequate.

[9] I am grateful to Jordan Wessling as well as the audience at the Special Workshop on the Inherence of Human Dignity at IVR 2019 in Lucerne, Switzerland, 8–9 July 2019, for helpful discussion of some of the ideas and arguments in this chapter.

Debes, Remy. 2017. 'Introduction'. In *Dignity: A History*, edited by Remy Debes, 1–17. Oxford: Oxford University Press.

Dougherty, Trent. 2014. *The Problem of Animal Pain: A Theodicy for All Creatures Great and Small*. New York: Palgrave Macmillan.

Feniger-Schaal, Rinat, and Tirsta Joels. 2018. 'Attachment Quality of Children with ID and Its Link to Maternal Sensitivity and Structuring'. *Research in Developmental Disabilities* 76: 56–64.

Gilabert, Pablo. 2018. *Human Dignity and Human Rights*. Oxford: Oxford University Press.

Hare, Robert D. 1999. *Without Conscience: The Disturbing World of the Psychopaths among Us*. New York: Guilford.

Kateb, George. 2011. *Human Dignity*. Cambridge, MA: Harvard University Press.

Kent, Bonnie. 2017. 'In the Image of God: Human Dignity after the Fall'. In *Dignity: A History*, edited by Remy Debes, 73–97. Oxford: Oxford University Press.

Kiehl, Kent. 2014. *The Psychopath Whisperer: The Science of Those without Conscience*. New York: Broadway Books.

Killmister, Suzy. 2017. 'Dignity: Personal, Social, Human'. *Philosophical Studies* 174: 2063–82.

Kilner, John F. 2015. *Dignity and Destiny: Humanity in the Image of God*. Grand Rapids, MI: Eerdmans.

Kittay, Eva Feder. 2008. 'At the Margins of Moral Personhood'. *Bioethical Inquiry* 5: 137–56.

———. 2009. 'The Personal Is Philosophical Is Political: A Philosopher and Mother of a Cognitively Disabled Person Sends Notes from the Battlefield'. *Metaphilosophy* 40, no. 3/4: 606–27.

Li, Yong. 2019. 'Virtue and Human Dignity: Confucianism and the Foundation of Human Rights'. *International Philosophical Quarterly* 59, no. 2: 175–92.

Linville, Mark D. 2009. 'The Moral Argument'. In *The Blackwell Companion to Natural Theology*, edited by William Lane Craig and J. P. Moreland, 391–448. Malden, MA: Blackwell.

Locke, John. 1980 [1690]. *Second Treatise of Government*. Edited by C. B. Macpherson. Indianapolis, IN: Hackett.

Matthews, Eric. 2014. 'Psychopathy and Moral Rationality'. In *Being Amoral: Psychopathy and Moral Incapacity*, edited by T. Schramme, 71–89. Cambridge, MA: MIT Press.

Mitchell, Adrian. 2004. 'Human Beings'. Poetry International Archives. https://www.poetryinternationalweb.net/pi/site/poem/item/13603.

Perry, Michael J. 1996. 'Is the Idea of Human Rights Ineliminably Religious?' In *Legal Rights: Historical and Philosophical Perspectives*, edited by A. Sarat and T. R. Kearns, 205–62. Ann Arbor: University of Michigan Press.

Redmond, David. 2017. 'Against Wolterstorff's Theistic Attempt to Ground Human Rights'. *Journal of Ethics and Social Philosophy* 12, no. 1: 127–34. https://doi.org/10.26556/jesp.v12i1.218.

Sallisbury, Christine L., and Christine G. Copeland. 2013. 'Progress of Infants/Toddlers with Severe Disabilities: Perceived and Measured Change'. *Topics in Early Childhood Special Education* 33, no. 2: 68–77.

Schroeder, Doris. 2012. 'Human Rights and Human Dignity: An Appeal to Separate the Conjoined Twins'. *Ethical Theory and Moral Practice* 15, no. 3: 323–35.

Singer, Peter. 2000. *Writings on an Ethical Life*. New York: HarperCollins.

———. 2009. 'Speciesism and Moral Status'. *Metaphilosophy* 40, no. 3/4: 567–81.

Stackhouse, Max L. 1998. 'The Intellectual Crisis of a Good Idea'. *Journal of Religious Ethics* 26, no. 2: 263–68.

Susman, Tina. 2014. 'Remains of Unidentified 9/11 Victims Moved to Ground Zero'. *Los Angeles Times*, 10 May. https://www.latimes.com/nation/nationnow/la-na-nn-911-remains-20140510-story.html.

'Universal Declaration of Human Rights'. 1948. https://www.un.org/en/universal-declaration-human-rights/index.html.

Weiss, J. A., V. Ting and A. Perry. 2016. 'Psychosocial Correlates of Psychiatric Diagnoses and Maladaptive Behavior in Youth with Severe Developmental Disability'. *Journal of Intellectual Disability Research* 60, no. 6: 583–93.

Weithman, Paul. 2009. 'God's Velveteen Rabbit'. *Journal of Religious Ethics* 37, no. 2: 243–60.

Wessling, Jordan. 2014. 'A Dilemma for Wolterstorff's Theistic Grounding of Human Dignity and Rights'. *International Journal for Philosophy of Religion* 76: 277–95.

Wielenberg, Erik J. 2018. 'Divine Command Theory and Psychopathy'. *Religious Studies*, 27 November. doi:10.1017/S0034412518000781.

Wolterstorff, Nicholas. 2008. *Justice: Rights and Wrongs*. Princeton, NJ: Princeton University Press.

———. 2012. 'On Secular and Theistic Groundings of Human Rights'. In *Understanding Liberal Democracy: Essays in Political Philosophy*, edited by N. Wolterstorff and T. Cuneo, 177–200. Oxford: Oxford University Press.

———. 2015. 'Would You Stomp on a Picture of Your Mother? Would You Kiss an Icon?' *Faith and Philosophy* 32, no. 1: 3–24.

Chapter Five

ATHEISM AND THEISM: A COMPARISON OF METAPHYSICAL FOUNDATIONS FOR HUMAN DIGNITY

Paul Copan

Introduction

Many of us are familiar with Bertrand Russell's bleak, despairing outlook of a world without God; he was convinced that such a stance was not only justified, but virtually guaranteed given an atheistic outlook. If we humans are simply 'accidental collocations of atoms' and our loves, beliefs, inspirations, labours and achievements are 'destined to extinction in the vast death of the solar system' (Russell 1963, 41), then such a depressing scenario ineluctably follows. He adds, 'All these things, if not quite beyond dispute, are yet so nearly certain that no philosophy which rejects them can hope to stand. Only within the scaffolding of these truths, only on the firm foundation of unyielding despair, can the soul's habitation, henceforth, be safely built' (ibid.).

The equally cheery Richard Dawkins puts it this way:

> If the universe were just electrons and selfish genes, meaningless tragedies [...] are exactly what we should expect, along with equally meaningless *good* fortune. Such a universe would be neither evil nor good in intention. [...] The universe we observe has precisely the properties we should expect if there is, at bottom, no design, no purpose, no evil and no good, nothing but blind pitiless indifference. [...] DNA neither knows nor cares. DNA just is. And we dance to its music. (1995, 132–33, emphasis original)

In this chapter, I aim to show that however interesting non-theistic or secular efforts to ground human dignity and rights may be, these accounts are invariably tenuous as well as fragmentary or partial, and they exhibit far greater optimism than their metaphysic warrants, as Russell and Dawkins rightly conclude. By contrast, a traditional theistic perspective is *considerably better* equipped to provide a more robust, comprehensive accounting of human dignity. In this view, valuable humans are made in the image of a supremely valuable God. To support this thesis, I will defend the following three main points.

First, many atheist thinkers, on pain of inconsistency, feel forced to acknowledge that a Godless (i.e. atheistic) world leaves them without confident metaphysical grounding for intrinsic human dignity, moral duties and moral facts. No doubt, many of them would be happy to have naturalistic grounds for affirming human dignity and worth. But not having any obvious grounds available, they take the bleak view. Yet Godless normative moral realists such as Erik Wielenberg strangely seem unmoved by this disconnect.

Second, though Wielenberg affirms human dignity without resorting to the image of God – a notion he finds confused and debatable – a concept like the image of God serves as an indicator or pointer to a source of objective value not found in an account like Wielenberg's. Theism clearly connects God to human worth and dignity, however vague or debated the definition of 'the image of God' may be. It is still a vast improvement over human value somehow emerging from valueless, mindless, deterministic, material processes. Wielenberg's secular account, which anchors human dignity in psychological, symbolic and/or potential worth, nevertheless fails to present an intelligible account for the emergence of objective worth from worthlessness.

Third, we examine more carefully Wielenberg's 'jolly' optimism that a secular account can actually deliver the metaphysic to ground human dignity – that somehow value and duties could emerge from valueless processes. And his view that the ontological status of his own brute moral facts is no worse off than the theist's equally brute fact is highly contestable. His cluster of brute facts required to arrive at human dignity is large indeed.

As we compare the resources of biblical theism and that of a Godless, secular worldview espoused by Wielenberg, the existence of a good God in whose image humans have been made offers a more robust, simpler, less ad hoc explanation of what all of us moral realists take for granted.

1. The Not-So-Jolly Implications of a Godless Universe

In addition to Russell and Dawkins, other atheists have offered similarly bleak assessments about objective moral values and human dignity. Jean-Paul Sartre confessed that it is 'very distressing that God does not exist, because all possibility of finding values in a heaven of ideas disappears along with Him. [...] As a result man is forlorn, because nei-ther within him nor without does he find anything to cling to' (1957, 22). No wonder the Oxford philosopher J. L. Mackie similarly acknowledged that if objective moral values exist, then this would be an argument for God. He observes an 'oddness' to morality in a naturalistic world; it is highly improbable that moral properties could have 'arisen in the ordinary course of events' – unless there was a God to bring this about (Mackie 1982, 115).

In his 'Amoral Manifesto' published in *Philosophy Now*, atheist philosopher Joel Marks calls those who think that objective moral values can exist without God 'softies'. He him-self confesses: 'this philosopher has long been laboring under an unexamined assumption, namely, that there is such a thing as right and wrong. I now believe there isn't' (Marks 2010). Why? Because atheism implies amorality. He admits that the fundamentalists are correct: 'without God, there is no morality' (ibid.).

> The long and the short of it is that I became convinced that atheism implies amorality; and since I am an atheist, I must therefore embrace amorality. I call the premise of this argu-ment 'hard atheism'. [...] [A] 'soft atheist' would hold that one could be an atheist and still

believe in morality. And indeed, the whole crop of 'New Atheists' are softies of this kind. So was I, until I experienced my shocking epiphany that the religious fundamentalists are correct: without God, there is no morality. But they are incorrect, I still believe, about there being a God. Hence, I believe, there is no morality. (Ibid.)

To this chorus of hard atheists, we could add many more resigned voices – though not without that stoical stiff upper lip – including the likes of Friedrich Nietzsche, John Searle, Daniel Dennett and Jaegwon Kim.

Philosopher Kai Nielsen confesses to his own depression about grounding moral realism for the atheist: 'We have not been able to show that reason requires the moral point of view or that all really rational persons, unhoodwinked by myth or ideology, need not be individual egoists or classical amoralists. Reason doesn't decide here'. He adds this: 'The picture I have painted for you is not a pleasant one. Reflection on it depresses me. [...] The point is this: pure practical reason, even with a good knowledge of the facts, will not take you to morality' (Nielsen 1984, 90).

In the same spirit, atheist Julian Baggini challenges the atheist's optimism that life *may* or *can* nevertheless be happy. (Compare Wielenberg's 'From valuelessness, value sometimes may come'; 2009, 40n). Baggini (2012) recognizes that atheism is powerless to secure objective moral values: 'And that means it can just as easily be meaningless, nihilistic and miserable'. The upbeat moral realist atheist may face harsh circumstances – a child commits suicide or becomes a rape victim – without the possibility of setting matters right in the end. Baggini asserts that this is the bedrock stance of atheism and that 'the jolly side' of atheism is unwarranted:

> The reason to be an atheist is not that it makes us feel better or gives us a more rewarding life. The reason to be an atheist is simply that there is no God and we would prefer to live in full recognition of that, accepting the consequences, even if it makes us less happy. The more brutal facts of life are harsher for us than they are for those who have a story to tell in which it all works out right in the end and even the most horrible suffering is part of a mystifying divine plan. If we don't freely admit this, then we've betrayed the commitment to the naked truth that atheism has traditionally embraced. (Ibid.)

Atheism's worldview exacts a high ontological price, raising the looming threat of moral nihilism:

> The British Humanist Association, for instance, claims that 'Right and wrong can be explained by human nature alone and do not require religious teaching'. But, just as with happiness, there is a need to distinguish the possibility of atheist morality from its inevitable actuality. Anyone who thinks it's easy to ground ethics either hasn't done much moral philosophy or wasn't concentrating when they did. (Ibid.)

Baggini points out a problem for the atheistic moral realist and why morality is better grounded in a theistic ('religious') world:

> Although morality is arguably just as murky for the religious, at least there is some bedrock belief that gives a reason to believe that morality is real and will prevail. In an atheist universe,

morality can be rejected without external sanction at any point, and without a clear, compelling reason to believe in its reality, that's exactly what will sometimes happen. (Ibid.)

Baggini continues with this not-so-jolly admonition:

So I think it's time we atheists 'fessed up and admitted that life without God can sometimes be pretty grim. Appropriating the label 'heathen' is part of this. Heathens are unredeemed outcasts from heaven who roam the planet without hope of surviving the deaths of their bodies. They may have values but they are not secured by any divine source. Yet we embrace this because we think it represents the truth. And so we don't just get on and enjoy life, we embark on our own intellectual pilgrimages, trying to make some progress in a universe on which no meaning has been writ. The journey can be wonderful but it can also be arduous and it may end horribly. But there is no other way, and anyone who urges you to follow a path that they promise leads to a bright future is either gravely mistaken or a charlatan. (Ibid.)

The naturalist philosopher of mind Jaegwon Kim captures what is at stake if one accepts the implications of naturalism: it is 'imperialistic; it demands "full coverage" […] and exacts a terribly high ontological price' (1993, 22–23).

Enter philosopher Erik Wielenberg. With undaunted confidence, he believes that, whatever the odds, a Godless, valueless, material, deterministic universe somehow produced robust value: 'From valuelessness, value sometimes comes' (Wielenberg 2009, 40n; see also Wielenberg 2005). According to Wielenberg's lights, however, it is 'terribly question-begging' to think that 'from valuelessness, valuelessness comes' (2009, 40n). But what is the *more likely* outcome given the backdrop of mindless, valueless matter – valuelessness or value? Plenty of atheists themselves challenge this 'jolly sided' picture of Wielenberg's, which seems too far-fetched to them. No doubt, many of these atheists would be happy with obvious metaphysical grounds for human dignity and worth – goods so familiar within a theistic framework. Such strict naturalists are simply attempting to be consistent with their rather Spartan metaphysical resources; they are doing the best they can with the metaphysical hand they have been dealt. Though Wielenberg believes he can somehow squeeze axiological water out of a metaphysical rock, these thinkers are persuaded that the emergence of human dignity and worth in a valueless universe is highly improbable. By contrast, theism leaves us with no such awkward question about the oddity of human dignity and value given the backdrop of a supremely valuable Creator God, who has made humans in his image.

2. Human Dignity, Human Rights and the Image of God

Human Dignity and Human Rights

Although various chapters in this volume address the topic of human dignity, perhaps it would be worth noting briefly what we generally mean by this concept and its connection to human rights.

George Kateb in his book *Human Dignity* (2011) – a secular account – presents what he means by 'human dignity'. At the heart of this idea is that on earth, humanity is the greatest type of being – or what we call species because we have learned to see humanity as one species in the animal kingdom, which is made up of many other species along with our own – and that every member deserves to be treated in a manner consonant with the high worth of the species. (3)

He emphasizes two components to this dignity: *status* and *stature*. In other words, 'all individuals are equal; no other species is equal to humanity' (6). In the first instance, while, say, Joe the Plumber may be far below Aristotle in reasoning abilities, the two nevertheless have equal worth; no human being is worth more than another (normative status). Second, out of all earthly species, humans are more important than any other (normative stature); a partial gap in nature exists between human beings and other animals.

While some of these claims could be nuanced and qualified (see Debes 2011), this view at least presents a general picture of human dignity that theists and many broad naturalists accept. As an aside, Muslims, though theists, reject the biblical doctrine of the image of God; they consider it blasphemous and demeaning to God. So when we refer to theism in connection with the divine image, we have the biblical version in mind.

Given this dignified status and stature, the question of rights naturally follows. What *is* a right? A right can be understood as a *title*. Yet the idea of a 'title' or 'entitlement' presumes a *source* or *justification* of the title in question. That is, a right is a relational title. It is not self-standing but is rooted in or springs from something else – a kind of authority or power that grants this status. So simply *defining* or *asserting* a right is inadequate. One needs to justify or provide a ground for this right. Human rights are not free-floating but anchored in a prior status of dignity or value that human beings have. Some metaphysical grounding is required to make sense of this entitlement (Montgomery 1986, 78–80; see Copan 2013b).

These are basic ideas that need teasing out, and other chapters herein will hone in on the topic of dignity in greater detail. Of course, one question that remains to be explored is whether theism or naturalism/atheism offers the more plausible context to make sense of human dignity and rights.

Naturalism, Brute Facts and Human Value

In his book *The Nature of Dignity* (2008), naturalistic philosopher Ronald Bontekoe admits that a Godless universe (i.e. naturalistic Darwinism) undercuts any presumed human dignity:

> In the light of [naturalistic] evolution, we are left with nothing but hypothetical imperatives. [...] Human beings cannot be deserving of a special measure of respect by virtue of their having been created 'in God's image' when they have not been *created* at all (and there is no God). Thus the traditional conception of human dignity is also undermined in the wake of Darwin. (15–16, emphasis original)

For Bontekoe, theism's dignity-conferring metaphysic (a good God making humans in his image) is not available within an atheistic/naturalistic worldview.

Of course, strict naturalism's metaphysical *materialism*, its etiological *determinism* and its epistemological *scientism* fundamentally threaten regions that are 'some of the most central in human life – the four Ms, for example: Morality, Modality, Meaning, and [the] Mental' (Price 1997, 247). These regions under threat include human dignity or worth, duties, free will/moral responsibility, beauty, intentionality and consciousness as objective realities.

In his chapter in this volume and his other writings, Wielenberg reveals a more optimistic or *broad* naturalism, which refuses to let go of these central features of human life. Wielenberg follows G. E. Moore in viewing morality as non-natural (morality is not reducible to natural facts) – a view that can be called non-natural non-theistic moral realism. He also argues that whether we are theists or non-theists, we must eventually arrive at a 'brute fact' stopping point, and neither can point to a deeper, more ultimate explanation than the other (Wielenberg 2009, 23). These facts include justice as giving a person what she deserves, pain as intrinsically bad, the wrongness of torturing persons for fun and so on. Theism's 'brute facts' are not 'better' or more fundamental or more basic than what Wielenberg proposes. But apart from this 'non-naturalistic' feature of his worldview, Wielenberg's approach to reality is essentially naturalistic. (For more on the two versions of naturalism and theistic responses to them, see Copan and Taliaferro (2018).)

In his chapter in this volume, Wielenberg wonders why a theistic metaphysic is the *only* basis for affirming human dignity. Why can a secular account not ground human dignity and human rights? For his part, Wielenberg states that, to varying degrees, each human has sufficient psychological, symbolic and/or potential worth to qualify as the possessor of human rights. He offers a 'pluralist' account:

> Although human beings are in many ways continuous with the rest of nature and, like all living things, products of unguided evolutionary forces, the ancient view that human beings have psychological capacities that set them well apart from all other living creatures is correct. In virtue of such capacities, any normal adult human has a special worth or value that cannot be possessed by any non-human creature that we know of. Let us call this particular sort of value 'psychological worth'. (65)

What of 'symbolic' worth? A person with dementia (or with 'diminished psychological capacities') or even a human corpse 'has symbolic worth because it stands for the person who did have psychological worth', and this can be 'quite substantial' (66). Wielenberg notes that the human adult with dementia, whose level of mental function might be lower than a healthy gorilla, nevertheless has greater overall worth than the primate. He thus concludes that given the 'virtue of this symbolic value (plus their remaining psychological value), human beings with dementia retain their human rights' (ibid.).

As for babies and children, Wielenberg speaks of 'potential' worth:

> As their psychological capacities grow, so does their psychological value. A newborn baby has a close material connection with its parents and so has a significant degree of symbolic value. Newborns also have a third sort of value which we may call 'potential value'. They possess value or worth *now* in virtue of being the sort of thing that, if it develops normally, will come to have a high degree of psychological worth. Foetuses have this sort of value as well but a

lesser degree of symbolic value; as a foetus develops and its psychological capacities emerge and expand, so does its psychological value. (67, emphasis original)

This is Wielenberg's perspective on human dignity. Now we explore why he rejects the image of God as a proper grounding for this dignity.

Wielenberg and the Imago Dei

Wielenberg considers the theistic basis for human dignity – the 'image of God' (*imago Dei*) – to be inadequate and flawed. He examines a number of theistic proposed definitions of the image of God, but these proposals stand in conflict with one another, and there is no unanimity on what this concept means for theologians and biblical scholars. For example, some theologians argue that this image has been obliterated by sin, yet, we can add that this kind of theological overreach repudiates what the Jewish-Christian scriptures in fact affirm (Gen. 9:6; Ps. 8; Jas 3:9). And, wonders Wielenberg, if human beings possess the dignity-conferring divine image – some suggest a kind of moral, relational and rational 'resemblance' to God – then what about humans who seem to lack this resemblance (e.g. the unborn or infants or the elderly with dementia)?

First, let us look at the various perspectives on the divine image that biblical theologians have generally adopted (see also Copan 2012; 2013a):

1. *Essentialist* (also, *structuralist* or *substantialist*): this view focuses on what humans essentially *are* – humans 'resemble' God in certain ways with their capacities of volition, rationality, spirituality, relationality, morality, self-awareness and the like.
2. *Functional*: this view focuses on what humans *do* – humans are commissioned to have dominion over creation, to be stewards or rulers over it. This functional emphasis is found in Gen. 1:28–30 and Ps. 8:5–6 (cf. Ps. 104:23).
3. *Relational*: this view focuses on the fact that humans *relate*. As suggested in Gen. 1:26–27, humans have the capacity for personal relationship with a relational God ('Let Us make humans in Our image') and with their fellow human beings (God made humans male and female).

We could add a fourth aspect to this 'image' – the *eschatological* (or teleological or dynamic), in which redeemed human beings become fully conformed to the moral image of Jesus Christ (e.g. Rom. 8:29; 2 Cor. 3:18, 4:4; Eph. 4:24; Col. 1:15). However, Scripture affirms a more fundamental image that is bestowed on all human beings, not simply those who are redeemed. So this fourth aspect need not concern us here.

As for the other three, one could see all of them as complementary rather than in conflict with each other. Yes, certain intrinsic or essential capacities enable human beings to carry out their task of being stewards of creation and of relating to God and others. But what if human beings are infants or suffer from dementia or act in evil ways? Do they lack the image of God? Not at all. The inherent capacities they have by virtue of their divinely bestowed nature may not be realized at present. For example, a human may be comatose due to a blunt trauma; a person with Asperger's syndrome may have physical blockages that prevent deep relationality or self-awareness, which could potentially be restored if the blockage were removed; or a properly functioning adult human being may even be sleeping and thus not exhibiting rationality or relationality at the moment. The relevant capacities or potentialities of the divine image rooted or bound up within human nature need not be functioning at a given moment in order for any human to possess fundamental dignity and worth. (For a defence of this view, see Moreland and Rae (2000).)

For our purposes, we need not quibble with Wielenberg concerning potential versus actual human worth (though see Moreland and Rae 2000). We can agree with Wielenberg, who has honed in on that unique significance far above other animals. To illustrate this vast gap, he uses an analogy: a range of high-priced wines (i.e. the sources or degrees of human worth) versus a range of very cheap wines (i.e. animals rank well below humans in worth, however intelligent or social the former may be). It is this worth that legitimately confers certain minimal, inviolable rights upon each human being.

Wielenberg rightly points out some notions of the divine image that are problematic, for example, that the divine image has been eradicated through the fall of humanity (again, an anti-biblical view) or John Locke's and Nicholas Wolterstorff's more function-alist versions discussed by Wielenberg (which display certain inconsistencies). Wielenberg claims that theistic attempts to define the divine image are at odds with each other, but, at their core, this is fundamentally not so. And, *contra* Wielenberg, even if one cannot pre-cisely specify what the divine image is, at minimum what *can* be said is that this divinely furnished status bestows special value upon human creatures and that there is an evident connection between God and human dignity. At bottom, both theism and Wielenberg's position affirm the essential worth of each human being, despite disagreement on the details.

The primary focus of this chapter is human dignity, more than the matter of pre-existing moral facts, though I touch on this later. The fundamental problem is whether Wielenberg's own metaphysical viewpoint can sustain such a hopeful version of human dignity and rights, to which we now turn.

3. Comparing Metaphysics: Are Theism's and Naturalism's Facts Equally Brute?

We have seen how plenty of naturalists feel metaphysically compelled to reject human dignity and worth – and objective morality as well – given our emergence from a value-less universe. And despite this dissonance, Wielenberg insists that objective value *may* still possibly emerge from valuelessness. And though we can dispute various details in Wielenberg's view of human worth, his view of human dignity has at its core something resembling the theistic view. What's more, his challenge to the coherence of the divine-image concept is not, in my estimation, substantive enough to undermine the coherence of human dignity being comfortably and organically rooted in a good, personal Creator.

This now brings us to the most fundamental question: Which perspective offers a more plausible metaphysical grounding for affirming human dignity and worth – theism or naturalism (which, for our purposes, includes Wielenberg's Godless normative realism)?

We could compare other views – Stoicism or Ramanuja's Eastern pantheism, say – but we'll limit ourselves to these two views. And we won't argue that theism is necessarily the *only* view that can legitimately account for human dignity, though I suspect it is.

Wielenberg contends that certain moral facts or truths exist independently of and prior to the eventual emergence of valuable human beings. These enduring moral *facts* are unchanging – eternal, as it were – whereas moral *value* emerged a finite time ago with the appearance of human beings on the scene (Wielenberg 2010). Wielenberg takes as inescapably brute both these moral *facts* and the moral *value* of the human being. Another naturalistic philosopher who makes a similar claim is Walter Sinnott-Armstrong. He insists that moral facts are on the same level as the laws of physics (e.g. e = mc^2) and mathematics (e.g. $2 + 2 = 4$). Before the emergence of valuable human beings, it was an enduring fact that 'free agents raping other free agents is wrong' (Sinnott-Armstrong 2009, 92–93). But just how stable are Wielenberg's brute givens? We'll explore the alleged parity of Wielenberg's brute facts and the resources of theism.

God and the Inference to the Best Explanation

Consider the following questions from naturalist John Searle:

> There is exactly one overriding question in contemporary philosophy [...]. How do we fit in? [...] How can we square this self-conception of ourselves as mindful, meaning-creating, free, rational, etc., agents with a universe that consists entirely of mindless, meaningless, unfree, nonrational, brute physical particles? (2007, 4)

Although he has entertained the possibility of libertarian free will (see Menuge 2013), Searle (as recently as 2016) continues to reaffirm determinism and even calls free will an illusion. The consistent answer to Searle's earlier questions is nicely captured by him in this quotation:

> Physical events can have only physical explanations, and consciousness is not physical, so consciousness plays no explanatory role whatsoever. If, for example, you think you ate because you were consciously hungry, or got married because you were consciously in love with your prospective spouse, or withdrew your hand from the flame because you consciously felt a pain, or spoke up at a meeting because you consciously disagreed with the main speaker, you are mistaken in every case. In each case the effect was a physical event and therefore must have an entirely physical explanation. (1997, 154)

While we believe that 'we could have done something else' and that human freedom is 'just a fact of experience', Searle claims that 'the scientific' approach to reality undermines the notion of a self that could potentially interfere with 'the causal order of nature' (1986, 87, 88, 92). Atheist philosopher Thomas Nagel says something similar regarding agency in a naturalistic world: 'There seems no room for agency in a world of neural impulses, chemical reactions, and bone and muscle movements'. Given naturalism, it is hard not to conclude that we are 'helpless' and 'not responsible' for our actions (Nagel 1986, 111, 113).

As we have seen with Searle and other naturalists, the emergence of consciousness, contra-causal freedom, and the like are 'odd' or 'queer', given the features of a naturalistic universe. Yet Wielenberg says that these are undeniable features of reality and that we must reject the stark implications of their strict naturalism; a rich array of phenomena – however fantastically improbable, surprising and 'unnatural' – somehow emerged from purposeless, non-conscious, impersonal, valueless, deterministic, materialistic processes.

Consider Table 5.1, which compares the greater plausibility or likelihood of an array of phenomena given the disparate backgrounds of biblical theism and naturalism. It would appear that, in general, theism is far better equipped – more 'natural', more at home, more organic – in making sense of these phenomena than the alternative of naturalism.

Theism and Wielenberg's Host of Brute Facts

Now, a broad naturalist like Wielenberg will affirm the reality of enduring moral facts over against strict naturalism. Even so, the background of biblical theism overall gives us a far richer, more highly probable context for affirming a bundle of goods – 'brute facts' – that Wielenberg and other broad naturalists take for granted. By contrast, as Alvin Plantinga puts it, these goods are 'not at all surprising or improbable on theism' since 'God presumably would want there to be life, and indeed intelligent life with which (whom) to communicate and share love; given atheism it is [surprising]; therefore theism is to be preferred to atheism' (2012, 199).

Consider below a number of human-related goods and other phenomena – 'brute facts' – that Wielenberg takes for granted. Note too that these features of existence are themselves highly contingent and improbable without God but highly probable if God exists. I can only briefly sketch out the scenario here, although I expound upon it elsewhere (Copan 2020; see also Copan and Taliaferro 2018).

Brute fact 1: Persons emerged from an impersonal universe

One of Wielenberg's 'brute facts' assumes that *personhood* somehow emerged from *impersonal* matter. Yet the very pre-existing, enduring moral facts to which Wielenberg is committed are themselves bound up with personhood – for example, justice as giving a person what she deserves, or the wrongness of inflicting pain on people for fun. Despite all odds, Wielenberg hopes that objectively valuable human persons somehow emerged from impersonal, valueless, material, non-conscious, deterministic processes. But the conditions for – and the highly contingent processes leading up to – personal human existence are stunningly improbable given naturalism. Placing one's metaphysical bets on a *personal God's* bringing about human persons is far more secure than betting on *unguided, impersonal processes* producing this result. The emergence of human personhood is a 'brute fact' for Wielenberg, but not for the theist.

Table 5.1 Theism versus atheism/naturalism

Phenomena We Observe, Assume or Recognize	Theistic Context	Atheistic/Naturalistic Context
Things exist. (Yet why does anything exist at all?)	God's very nature requires his existence. God necessarily exists.	Each of the physical universe's parts is contingent and thus cannot be self-existent. There is no necessity about the universe.
(Self-)consciousness exists.	God is supremely self-aware/self-conscious.	Consciousness was produced by mindless, non-conscious processes.
Personal beings exist.	God is a personal Being.	The universe was produced by impersonal processes.
We believe we make free personal decisions/choices, assuming humans are accountable for their actions.	God is spirit and a free Being, who can freely choose to act (e.g. to create or not).	We are products of material, deterministic processes beyond our control.
Secondary qualities (colours, smells, sounds, tastes, textures) exist throughout the world.	A personal God is a source of pleasure who gives capacities to his creatures to enjoy or take pleasure in his world.	The universe was produced from colourless, odourless, soundless, tasteless, textureless particles and processes.
We trust our senses and rational faculties as generally reliable in producing true beliefs. The world is knowable.	A God of truth and rationality exists.	Naturalistic evolution is only interested in survival and reproduction, not truth. So, many beliefs would help us survive (e.g. the belief that humans have dignity and worth) but would be completely false.
Human beings have intrinsic value/dignity and rights.	God is the supremely valuable Being.	Human beings were produced by valueless processes.
Objective moral values/duties exist.	God's character is the source of goodness/moral values.	The universe was produced by non-moral processes.
The universe began to exist a finite time ago – without previously existing matter, energy, space or time.	A powerful, previously existing God brought the universe into being without any pre-existing material. (Here, something emerges from something.)	The universe came into existence from nothing by nothing – or was, perhaps, self-caused. (Here, something comes from nothing.)
First life emerged.	God is a living, active Being.	Life somehow emerged from non-living matter.

(*continued*)

Table 5.1 (*cont.*)

Phenomena We Observe, Assume or Recognize	Theistic Context	Atheistic/Naturalistic Context
The universe is finely tuned for human life (known as 'the Goldilocks effect' – the universe is 'just right' for life).	God is a wise, intelligent Designer.	All the cosmic constants just happened to be right; given enough time and/or many possible worlds, a finely tuned world eventually emerged.
Beauty exists – not only in landscapes and sunsets but in 'elegant' or 'beautiful' scientific theories.	God is creative and capable of creating beautiful things according to His pleasure.	Beauty in the natural world is superabundant and in many cases superfluous (often not linked to survival).
We (tend to) believe that life has purpose and meaning. For most of us, life is worth living.	God has created/designed us for certain purposes (to love Him, others, etc.); when we live them out, our lives find meaning/enrichment.	There is no cosmic purpose, blueprint or goal for human existence.
Real evils – both moral and natural – exist/take place in the world.	Evil's definition assumes a kind of blueprint or design plan (how things ought to be, but are not) – a standard of goodness by which we judge something to be evil. A good God's existence supplies the crucial moral context to make sense of evil.	Atrocities, pain and suffering just happen. This is just how things *are*; given naturalism, there is no cosmic 'plan' or a standard of goodness to which things *ought* to conform.
We have deep longings for security (relationship), significance (purpose), forgiveness/relief from guilt, freedom from fear of death.	God has created us to find our satisfaction in him.	These longings are merely biological, being hardwired into us by naturalistic processes to enhance survival and reproduction.

Brute fact 2: A universe, which began a finite time ago, is necessary for valuable human beings

If valuable, though contingent, human beings are to exist, they must inhabit a universe. It will not do to say, as Bertrand Russell once did, that the universe is just there and that is all. No, it began to exist a finite time ago: the second law of thermodynamics as well as the universe's expansion and its cosmic microwave background radiation indicate that the universe is not eternal; it has been wound up and is now winding down.

Non-theists John D. Barrow and Joseph Silk acknowledge this: 'Our new picture is more akin to the traditional metaphysical picture of creation out of nothing, for it predicts a definite beginning to events in time, indeed a definite beginning to time itself' (1993, 38). They ask: 'What preceded the event called the "big bang"? [...] the answer to our question is simple: nothing' (209). Likewise, Tufts University cosmologist Alexander Vilenkin asks, 'Did the universe have a beginning?' His response is: 'It probably did'. And again: 'We have no viable models of an eternal universe' (Vilenkin 2018, 155). Though Vilenkin says the universe's cause is a mystery, the status of a finite universe leaves open a Creator God as a highly plausible explanation. And noted physicist Paul Davies says that when it comes to what caused the Big Bang, it seems that 'we don't have too much choice. Either [...] something outside of the physical world [...] or [...] an event without a cause' (1995, 8–9). It appears that the universe is ontologically haunted since it could not spring into existence without a cause. From nothing, nothing comes. Something exceedingly powerful – and *more fundamental* than the universe itself – brought it into existence. The finite universe's existence is a brute fact for Wielenberg, but not for the theist.

Brute fact 3: The life-permitting conditions of the universe's delicately balanced fine-tuning are necessary for valuable human beings

Just because a universe *exists*, this is no guarantee that it will have *life-permitting* conditions. This is another 'brute fact' that Wielenberg's worldview takes for granted. Consider biologist E. O. Wilson's perspective here. Despite his strict materialism, Wilson notes this staggering, 'tortuous' improbability: 'all tangible phenomena, from the birth of the stars to the workings of social institutions, are based on material processes that are ultimately reducible, however long and tortuous the sequences, to the laws of physics' (1998, 266). In the same spirit, naturalist Daniel Dennett writes of 'the exquisite sensitivity of the laws of nature': if any of the values of the laws of nature – the speed of light, the constant of gravitational attraction, strong and weak nuclear forces, Planck's constant – were altered 'by just the tiniest amount', no solids, no planets, no atmospheres would have emerged (2006, 143–44). Dennett concludes: 'So isn't it a wonderful fact that the laws are just right for us to exist? Indeed, one might want to add, we almost didn't make it!' (144). Even Wielenberg acknowledges that naturalistic moral realists concede that humans are 'accidental, evolved, mortal, and relatively short-lived' (2009, 35). This brute fact of fine-tuning – so massively improbable given a Godless universe – becomes highly explicable and probable given an intelligent Creator's existence.

Brute fact 4: Valuable human beings – along with all other living things – emerged from non-living matter

Another brute fact Wielenberg must take for granted is that non-living matter somehow produced life. To have valuable human beings, we need (1) a *universe* that is not just (2) *life-permitting* but also (3) *life-producing*. Consider what Nobel Prize–winning biologist Francis Crick observed about the many necessary conditions to produce biological life: 'the origin of life appears at the moment to be almost a miracle' (1981, 88). Other biologists have pointed out that it is 'virtually impossible to imagine how a cell's machines could have formed spontaneously as life first arose' (Ricardo and Szostak 2009, 54). This is no brute fact for the theist; a divine guiding hand to superintend this process is far more probable. As we will see in Table 5.2, getting from zero (no universe) to valuable *Homo sapiens* requires massive improbability upon massive improbability – brute facts for Wielenberg but not for the theist.

Brute fact 5: The existence of valuable human beings requires a life-sustaining universe under highly specified, 'tortuous' conditions

The existence of valuable human beings is one of those brute facts accepted by Wielenberg. But it is not enough for (1) a universe to *exist* – or for it to be (2) *finely tuned* (life-permitting), or even to be (3) life-*producing*. It must also be (4) life-*sustaining*, getting us from a single-celled organism to *Homo sapiens*. After all, even if life somehow emerged from non-living matter, the chances that it would be (nearly) immediately snuffed out – let alone the stunning eventual emergence of human beings – are immense. Again, if a good God exists, valuable human beings would be the kind of outcome we could expect – especially if there is a pre-existing set of moral facts that is rooted in God and thus corresponds to humans' moral nature. None of these four steps is a surprise or a brute fact for the theist.

Indeed, notice the kinds of calculations that knowledgeable philosophers and scientifically minded scholars assign to these stages. The existence of a theistic God removes all of these massive contingencies.

Brute fact 6: A massive cosmic coincidence exists between pre-existing moral facts and the highly contingent emergence of morally valuable human beings

Keep in mind that Wielenberg assumes the eternal pre-existence of moral *facts* exist independent of contingent moral *value* – namely the emergence of morally valuable human beings. Yet such a claim invokes a massive cosmic coincidence for Wielenberg, not the theist. The secular 'Platonic' moral realist in this case holds that (1) certain necessary (even timelessly true) *moral facts* exist and (2) *self-reflective, morally responsible and intrinsically valuable human beings* eventually appear on the scene (through unguided, highly contingent evolutionary steps) who both can recognize these pre-existing facts and are obligated to them. This remarkably ad hoc scenario begs for explanation. This Platonic-like moral realm – tailor-made for humans – appears to have been *anticipating* our emergence. This is a remarkable cosmic accident! A far simpler, less ad hoc explanation is available: a good God – the very locus of objective moral value – created human beings with dignity and worth. This scenario affords a far more elegant, smooth and natural explanation.

So we can say that theism simplifies matters here and renders Wielenberg's view superfluous. Why posit a set of moral facts independent of a good God, who can readily account for them? Anchoring such moral truths in a good God's character removes this stunning coincidence, and this God also accounts for the emergence of valuable human beings, his image-bearers. And as we have noted, Wielenberg's move into the non-natural realm of moral facts is a step closer to – indeed, *into* – the transcendent realm.

Brute fact 7: Consciousness somehow emerged from non-conscious matter

While we can have consciousness without having moral beings, we cannot have moral beings without consciousness. Finite moral beings must deliberate, make judgements, choose to do the right rather than the wrong (or vice versa). But the very existence of consciousness – let alone, self-consciousness – is something that seems wholly out of

Table 5.2 The increasing unlikelihood of naturalism

Stages to Consider	Calculated Odds
1. A *Universe* (or, Producing Something from Nothing in the Big Bang)	**Exactly 0** (Something cannot come into existence from literally nothing; there is not even the *potentiality* to produce anything.)
2. A Life-*Permitting* Universe	Roger Penrose (agnostic physicist/mathematician) notes the odds of a life-permitting universe – a figure requiring more zeroes than there are atoms in the universe: 'The Creator's aim must have been [precise] to an accuracy of one part in $10^{10^{(123)}}$' (1991, 334). What number are we talking about? It 'would be 1 followed by $10^{\wedge}123$ successive "0"s! Even if we were to write a "0" on each separate proton and on each separate neutron in the entire universe – and we could throw in all the other particles as well for good measure – we should fall far short of writing down the figure needed. [This is] the precision needed to set the universe on its course' (ibid.).
3. A Life-*Producing* Universe (Life from Non-life)	Stephen Meyer (citing Fred Hoyle) points out that the odds for *just one* of the necessary 250 proteins to sustain life coming about by chance are **1 in $10^{41,000}$** (in Meyer 2009, 213).
4. A Life-*Sustaining* Universe (Moving from the Bacterium to *Homo Sapiens*)	Astrophysicists Frank Tipler and John Barrow calculated that the chances of moving from a bacterium to *Homo sapiens* in 10 billion years or less is $10^{-24,000,000}$ (a decimal with 24 million zeroes; see Barrow and Tipler 1986, 557–66). Biologist Francisco Ayala independently calculated the odds of humans arising just once in the universe to be $10^{-1,000,000}$ (noted in Tipler 2003, 142). Tipler adds: 'This number is so tiny that the evolution of intelligent life is exceedingly unlikely to have occurred even once' (ibid.).

place in a strictly material universe. For example, philosopher of mind Colin McGinn points out: 'We know that brains are the *de facto* causal basis of consciousness, but we have, it seems, no understanding of how this can be so. It strikes us as miraculous, eerie, even faintly comic' (1990, 10–11). Geoffrey Maddell acknowledges: 'The emergence of consciousness, then is a mystery, and one to which materialism signally fails to provide an answer' (1988, 141). A brute fact Wielenberg takes for granted is that consciousness somehow emerged from non-conscious matter, and without consciousness, Wielenberg cannot have human dignity. The existence of a supremely self-aware divine being, who creates self-aware human beings, removes the bruteness.

Brute fact 8: Morally responsible free agents emerged from materialistic, deterministic, valueless material processes

In order to have moral agents who can make genuine personally responsible (moral) choices, they are presumably not the kind of beings that simply dance to the music of their DNA and of their environment; moral agents are not helpless organisms that are predetermined to act and to believe what they do by virtue of prior physical forces over which they have no control. In order for Wielenberg to sustain a robust notion of human dignity, he would have to recognize the place of agency, volition, responsibility, culpability, a significant measure of free choice. But why think that free choice should emerge in a naturalistic world of deterministic, valueless, material processes? This kind of freedom or agency is a brute fact for Wielenberg: humans can somehow rise above the deterministic forces at work in nature. But once more, theism has no such brute fact: we are made in the image of a free being who graciously chooses to create morally responsible, free-willing human agents.

Brute fact 9: Rationality somehow emerged from non-rational processes

Wielenberg must accept the emergence of objective human rationality from non-rational processes as a given – another brute fact. We have noted that human dignity or moral worth is connected to consciousness and free will, but it is also connected to rationality. Yet how do we arrive at rational thought if we are ultimately the products of non-rational processes? While we could allow for material processes to produce true beliefs, they would merely be accidentally true beliefs, not warranted or justified true beliefs. Evolution is interested in survival, not warranted true beliefs. We may believe *falsehoods* that enhance human survival and reproduction. For many naturalists, these falsehoods (or 'illusions') include beliefs like 'Humans have dignity and worth' or 'Humans ought to behave altruistically'.

For a number of naturalists, truth – and thus, knowledge – is elusive and accidental. According to Richard Rorty (1995), truth is 'un-Darwinian'. In the words of Patricia Churchland, 'Boiled down to its essentials, a nervous system enables the organism to succeed in the four F's: feeding, fleeing, fighting, and reproducing. […] Truth, whatever that is, definitely takes the hindmost' (1987, 548–49). By contrast, theism eliminates such problems facing the naturalist: the emergence of rational creatures is highly probable given the existence of a rational Creator who made us in his image.

Brute fact 10: Objective value emerged from valueless processes

We have already highlighted another brute fact of Wielenberg's: that valueless processes 'may sometimes produce value'. But we have also noted that such optimism is unwarranted given the naturalistic metaphysic he espouses. (Of course, Wielenberg makes a non-natural exception, as he believes in a kind of Platonic/transcendent realm of enduring moral facts.) Given the tortuous – indeed, questionable – steps of unguided evolution required to get to morally valuable, conscious, rational, free human beings, it seems that theism would be a welcome refuge to anchor human dignity and various other human goods.

Concluding Reflections: Isn't God a Brute Fact?

Wielenberg would, of course, offer that God himself is a 'brute given'. Well, if we mean a certain stopping point, fine. All of our explanations will require some kind of an endpoint to avoid an infinite regress of explanation. But we should ask: Which view – Wielenberg's or the theist's – is a *more adequate* stopping point? What view provides a sufficient reason for that stopping point? We have seen that Wielenberg's own naturalistic metaphysic is hard-pressed to extract a host of related, though distinct, emergent goods out of deterministic, valueless, non-conscious, material processes.

Of course, theists have argued that God is a necessary being that cannot *not* exist, a being that exists in all possible worlds. The universe, of which we are a part, is comprised entirely of contingent entities; the universe did not have to exist. Indeed, the universe began to exist a finite time ago. But as Paul Davies has reminded us, we do not have much choice: either the universe popped into existence uncaused out of nothing – *or* something independent of the universe brought it about. Put another way, unless we believe that being can pop into existence from non-being (literally, *no* thing), we must acknowledge that *something always had to exist*. We are pushed into the realm of the non-contingent. We find ourselves directed to something whose existence is not grounded in something outside itself (i.e. contingent), but grounded in its very nature (i.e. a necessary being). Indeed, two hundred years ago atheists argued that the universe was eternal, non-contingent and didn't need a cause. So why should this be a problem if God exists? Clearly, the contingent universe cannot adequately ground all of the brute givens Wielenberg wants to embrace.

If we utilize the inference to the best explanation (as suggested in Table 5.1), we see that something like the theistic God readily grounds all of these contingent goods. Indeed, this God presents a unifying explanation for all of the disparate goods to which Wielenberg adheres. These disparate goods include the very existence of a finely tuned, life-permitting, life-producing and life-sustaining universe – in addition to the emergence of consciousness, rationality and human dignity as well as the astonishing cosmic coincidence of the pre-existent moral facts and the eventual, highly contingent, accidentally emergent morally valuable human beings whose moral constitution corresponds with bullseye accuracy to those moral facts.

Is God a 'brute fact'? We can say that something like God satisfies the principle of sufficient reason – namely that for everything that exists, there is a sufficient reason for its existence, whether contingent or necessary (Copan 2020, 151–57). Wielenberg himself holds to the necessary existence of moral facts in a kind of Platonic/transcendent/non-natural realm – even though these facts concern *personal* beings that are themselves highly *contingent*. Why not anchor this transcendent realm in a *necessary personal being* that is also responsible for the emergence of those divine-image-bearing, morally valuable human beings that are actually profoundly and organically connected to the source of those moral facts? What's more, these eternal moral facts themselves can *do* nothing or *produce* nothing – unlike the personal God of theism whose agency and power can produce an intricate, habitable world for moral creatures.

Theism simplifies matters immensely. The reality of a personal God makes far greater room for a deep, organic connection between the transcendent realm of moral facts and morally valuable human creatures than what Wielenberg offers. His collection of moral facts just 'hangs' suspended, disconnected from all the naturalistic goings-on in the universe over billions of years that eventually – and astonishingly – led to morally valuable human beings. And we can add that a similar mistake has been made by a few theistic philosophers who create this needless chasm between moral facts independent of God and human beings that bear that divine image (see Copan 2020, 180–84).

So we can generally agree with Wielenberg that each human being has dignity and value above other animals. And though we could dispute some of the details, Wielenberg roughly articulates a secularized version of the value-bestowing image of God, though Wielenberg locates humans' dignity in their intrinsic *psychological, symbolic* and / or *potential* worth. But from a metaphysical vantage point, we find Wielenberg's view problematic. He ends up borrowing resources from theism (or a view strongly akin to it) to arrive at this threefold 'pluralist' account of human worth. But as we have seen, Wielenberg makes an astonishingly optimistic leap from a valueless universe to the emergence of deep value, which plenty of atheists we have quoted would consider irrational and utterly unjustified.

What is more, Wielenberg must assume at least 10 brute facts that move him from no universe at all to valuable *Homo sapiens*. Or, even if we grant the finite universe's existence, Wielenberg must move from the raw materials of a Godless universe – non-rational, valueless, non-conscious, deterministic, impersonal, material processes – to arrive at rational, valuable, conscious, free-willing/personally responsible, personal beings living in a finely tuned, life-permitting, life-producing and life-sustaining universe that eventually produces valuable human beings from valueless matter. But bring into the equation something like the personal God of theism, and the place of valuable human beings in the universe becomes unsurprising, highly probable, readily explained, simplified, non-ad hoc and even 'natural'.

References

Baggini, Julian. 2012. 'Yes Life without God Can Be Bleak'. *Guardian*, 9 March. Accessed 26 December 2019. http://www.theguardian.com/commentisfree/2012/mar/09/life-without-god-bleak-atheism.

Barrow, John D., and Joseph Silk. 1993. *The Left Hand of Creation*, 2nd ed. New York: Oxford University Press.

Barrow, John D., and Frank J. Tipler. 1986. *The Anthropic Cosmological Principle*. New York: Oxford University Press.

Bontekoe, Ronald. 2008. *The Nature of Dignity*. Lanham, MD: Rowman & Littlefield.

Churchland, Patricia. 1987. 'Epistemology in the Age of Neuroscience'. *Journal of Philosophy* 84 (October): 544–53.

Copan, Paul. 2012. 'Bioethics'. In *The Routledge Companion to Theism*, edited by Charles Taliaferro, Victoria Harrison and Stewart Goetz, 515–27. London: Routledge.

———. 2013a. 'A Protestant Perspective on Human Dignity'. In *Human Dignity in Bioethics: From Worldviews to the Public Square*, edited by Stephen C. Dilley and Nathan J. Palpant, 67–85. London: Routledge.

———. 2013b. 'Grounding Human Rights: Naturalism's Failure and Biblical Theism's Success'. In *Legitimizing Human Rights*, edited by Angus J. L. Menuge, 11–31. Applied Legal Philosophy Series. Aldershot, UK: Ashgate.

———. 2020. *Loving Wisdom: A Guide to Philosophy and Christian Faith*. Grand Rapids, MI: Eerdmans.

Copan, Paul, and Charles Taliaferro, eds. 2018. *The Naturalness of Belief: New Essays on Theism's Rationality*. Lanham, MD: Lexington.

Crick, Francis. 1981. *Life Itself: Its Nature and Origin*. New York: Simon & Schuster.

Davies, Paul. 1995. 'The Birth of the Cosmos'. In *God, Cosmos, Nature and Creativity*, edited by Jill Gready, 1–28. Edinburgh: Scottish Academic.

Dawkins, Richard. 1995. *River Out of Eden: A Darwinian View of Life*. New York: Basic Books.

Debes, Remy. 2011. 'Review of George Kateb, *Human Dignity*, Harvard University Press, 2011'. *Notre Dame Philosophical Reviews: An Electronic Journal*. Accessed 2 January 2020. https://ndpr.nd.edu/news/human-dignity/.

Dennett, Daniel C. 2006. 'Atheism and Evolution'. In *The Cambridge Companion to Atheism*, edited by Michael Martin, 135–48. Cambridge: Cambridge University Press.

Kateb, George. 2011. *Human Dignity*. Cambridge, MA: Harvard University Press.

Kim, Jaegwon. 1993. 'Mental Causation and Two Conceptions of Mental Properties'. Paper presented at the American Philosophical Association Eastern Division Meeting.

Mackie, J. L. 1982. *The Miracle of Theism*. Oxford: Clarendon.

Maddell, Geoffrey. 1988. *Mind and Materialism*. Edinburgh: Edinburgh University Press.

Marks, Joel. 2010. 'An Amoral Manifesto (Part 1)'. *Philosophy Now* 80 (August/September). Accessed 2 January 2020. https://philosophynow.org/issues/80/An_Amoral_Manifesto_Part_I.

McGinn, Colin. 1990. *The Problem of Consciousness*. Oxford: Basil Blackwell.

Menuge, Angus J. L. 2013. 'Neuroscience, Rationality, and Free Will: A Critique of John Searle's Libertarian Naturalism'. *Philosophia Christi* 15, no. 1: 45–60.

Meyer, Stephen. 2009. *Signature in the Cell*. New York: HarperOne.

Montgomery, J. W. 1986. *Human Rights and Human Dignity*. Grand Rapids, MI: Academie.

Moreland, J. P., and Scott B. Rae. 2000. *Body & Soul: Human Nature & the Crisis in Ethics*. Downers Grove, IL: IVP Academic.

Nagel, Thomas. 1986. *The View from Nowhere*. New York: Oxford University Press.

Nielsen, Kai. 1984. 'Why Should I Be Moral? Revisited'. *American Philosophical Quarterly* 21, no. 1 (January): 81–91.

Penrose, Roger. 1991. *The Emperor's New Mind*. New York: Bantam.

Plantinga, Alvin. 2012. *Where the Conflict Really Lies*. New York: Oxford University Press.

Price, Huw. 1997. 'Naturalism and the Fate of the M-Worlds'. *Proceedings of the Aristotelian Society* supp. 71: 247–67.

Ricardo, Alfonso, and Jack W. Szostak. 2009. 'Life on Earth'. *Scientific American* 301, no. 3 (September): 54–61.

Rorty, Richard. 1995. 'Untruth and Consequences'. *New Republic* (31 July): 32–36.

Russell, Bertrand. 1963. 'A Free Man's Worship'. In *Mysticism and Logic and Other Essays*. London: Allen & Unwin.

Sartre, Jean-Paul. 1957. *Existentialism and Human Emotions*. New York: Philosophical Library.

Searle, John. 1986. *Minds, Brains, and Science*. Cambridge, MA: Harvard University Press. Reprint.

———. 1997. *The Mystery of Consciousness*. New York: New York Review of Books.

———. 2007. *Freedom and Neurobiology*. New York: Columbia University Press.

Sinnott-Armstrong, Walter. 2009. *Morality without God?* Oxford: Oxford University Press.

Tipler, Frank J. 2003. 'Intelligent Life in Cosmology'. *International Journal of Astrobiology* 2, no. 2: 141–48.

Vilenkin, Alexander. 2018. 'The Beginning of the Universe'. In *The Kalām Cosmological Argument Vol. 2: Scientific Evidence for the Beginning of the Universe*, edited by Paul Copan and William Lane Craig, 150–58. New York: Bloomsbury.

Wielenberg, Erik J. 2009. 'In Defense of Non-natural, Non-theistic Moral Realism'. *Faith and Philosophy* 26, no. 1 (January): 23–41.

———. 2010. 'Objective Morality and the Nature of Reality'. *American Theological Inquiry* 13, no. 2: 77–84.

———. 2005. *Value and Virtue in a Godless Universe*. Cambridge: Cambridge University Press.

Wilson, Edward O. 1998. *Consilience: The Unity of Knowledge*. New York: Knopf.

Chapter Six

DIGNITY AND TOLERANCE: A TENSION AND A CHALLENGE

Claudia Mariéle Wulf

Die Würde ist antastbar.

Human dignity is supposed to be 'inalienable', in German: 'unantastbar', that is, not touchable. Playing with this word, Ferdinand von Schirach (2017) named his book *Die Würde ist antastbar* (Human dignity can be touched), by which he means 'destroyed'. He states that human dignity is permanently questioned, as human beings are often not treated in accordance with their dignity. Respect for a human being's value and dignity is not self-evident. The Universal Declaration of Human Rights just states that dignity *should be* 'intangibilis' – but in daily life this stays a *desideratum*.

Besides, we have to state that a discussion is ongoing as to whether the notion 'dignity' may still be used. Some theories compare human dignity to the dignity of animals[1] and try to gain a clearer concept of human dignity by doing so. Another tendency is to give human life into the hands of men at the beginning and at the very end of life (abortion and euthanasia). At the same time people claim that animals should not be at the disposal of human beings.

We are living in a pluralistic and relativistic context in which important values are questioned while other values seem to gain ground. One of the latter is *tolerance*. Political correctness pleads for accepting others and their opinions and attitudes without criticizing them.

Now we arrive at a difficult point: am I able or do I want to tolerate something which may destroy my dignity? This may be a kind of thinking that provokes an attitude towards others, a kind of speaking that expresses a conviction, or a kind of acting. In short: what makes tolerance impossible cannot be tolerated. Destroying dignity must not be tolerated as something dies down in human beings when their dignity is broken. In such moments human beings lose access to their inner value – what mostly affects their ability to estimate other people's value. Tolerance must be founded in respect for each other. Lacking respect and relativizing human dignity infects the social atmosphere. This becomes visible in political radical thinking, brutality in society, relationships breaking easily and increasing psychic diseases, for example, depression. Most of the time an

---

[1] This can be seen in the context of speciesism; cf. Ryder (2009).

important origin of these difficulties is forgotten: the lack of crucial values and among them, the *norma normans* ('the rule that rules'), dignity.

My thesis is that forgetting about the central values means forgetting about the human person. If persons are not respected in what they essentially are, namely human, a breakdown of dignity will result. In addition, this affects society in a very destructive way. This is the reason why tolerance must itself aim at guarding the central values.

Methodology

There are many ways to investigate the nature of human dignity. One can attempt to ground it in a traditional metaphysical analysis of human nature. One can offer an analysis of the ordinary language meaning of 'dignity'. Or one can attempt to discern the meaning of 'dignity' inductively, by studying examples in everyday life or in legal practice, to see what they have in common. But another approach, the one which will be taken here, is to use phenomenology to investigate the nature of dignity.

Broadly speaking, phenomenology seeks to provide an accurate description and analysis of phenomena or the world as it appears. Phenomenological thinking begins at scratch, leaving behind former scientific research on the subject, former experiences and even the particular, concrete experience at this very moment in order to find the essential characteristics of phenomena. The search for essential traits, which have to be distilled from experiences, is done in systematic research and in intersubjective dialogue. It is more than leaving behind prejudices or accumulating a set of empirical facts about one person's experience, which are common readings of 'phenomenology'. The goal of the approach to phenomenology taken here is to determine what is essential to human experience in general. This is achieved by identifying the features of an experience without which the experience is inconceivable. This method can be used to investigate what is essential to an experience of dignity and thus to intuit the nature of dignity itself.

In what follows, I proceed in this phenomenological way by means of an analysis of the essence of dignity. My phenomenology will be multidimensional and existential, which opens the possibility to see the problem in all its dimensions and in its existential effects.

By phenomenology I will here understand a method that deals with an object in order to describe its essence, the so-called eidetic phenomenology. Positive eidetic phenomenology enumerates all traits forming the essence and can separate them from arbitrary traits, so-called accidents. A negative phenomenology would try to find out whether a trait can be left out without changing the essence. If we apply this to the human being, it leads to the question: May a human being be deprived of this trait without losing his/her character as being human?

Phenomenologically speaking, the human being lives in different relations: the relation to him/herself, the relation to others, to the world and to meaning. Thanks to the research of Victor Frankl (1970), we cannot deny that striving for meaning is essential to the human being. If there is no access to meaning, human life seems to become impossible. This calls for a multidimensional phenomenology. Next to the basic needs (material needs representing the relation to the world) and social needs (relation to others), there is a need for adequate knowledge (rational truth) and a need for feeling values. Values reveal their character as values in the extensive horizon of meaning. Therefore, the phenomenological analysis of the human being cannot stick to just analyzing basic needs or experiences. It has to respect the dimension of rationality and meaning. These thoughts can be summarized in a multidimensional tetrahedron model.

The tetrahedron has four vertices: me (the self), you (the other), the surrounding world (our common environment) and the comprehensive meaning of it all. These vertices are the parameters that interact as people build their understanding of the nature and meaning of reality and of their lives. The content or filling of that quest is truth and value. This is because humans desire above all to know what is real (truth) and what can guide their life in the right direction (value). The tetrahedron can be seen as a layered hierarchy. At the foundational level, we see basic material and social needs, including the need for physical and economic security. With these in place, human beings are free to gain the relative truth that comes from experiencing the world and living their own lives. But they are not content to accept opinions: they strive to fulfil a higher need for rational truth and knowledge. Yet, even if this is achieved, it is still not enough: merely to know what is going on does not disclose whether the world or one's life has any ultimate meaning. Humans are driven by the need to make metaphysical and moral sense of reality, so that they see their lives as meaningful contributions to a meaningful whole. Humans are metaphysically open to, and hunger for, a transcendent or comprehensive meaning beyond the relative meanings of their self-chosen projects.

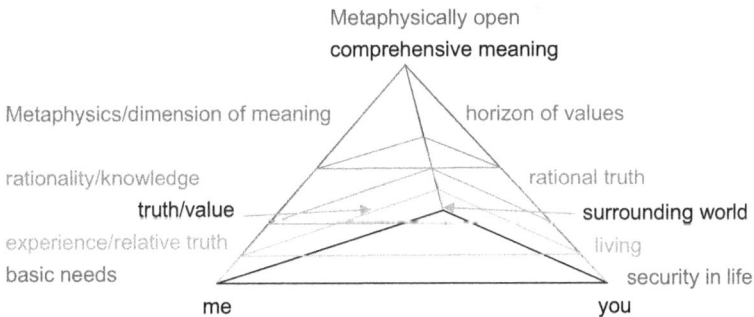

Here another form of phenomenology becomes visible: existential phenomenology. In an existential experience, a human being is totally confirmed or totally questioned. This can happen if a human being finds or loses an essential relationship, understands the truth or fails in doing so, when he/she experiences meaning or suffers from meaninglessness. When dignity is touched, it always ends up in a negative existential experience.

1. Dignity

Dignity is severely questioned by modern philosophy (Wulf 2017a). If the human being is reduced to an arbitrary construct or a neurological machine, human dignity becomes invisible.[2] The human being is more – but what makes him specifically human (freedom, spirit and the me) cannot be determined in an empirical setting. Empirical research reaches out to the basic level and can touch the human experience – but just in a superficial way. The higher levels of personhood become visible only if persons provide a testimony of their inner, lived experience about it. You cannot understand it by weighing or counting.

1.1 Philosophical Aspects of Dignity

In the first step I cite the most accepted vision on human dignity, the vision of Immanuel Kant. Kant's conclusion is that you must never treat the human being as a thing. Human beings do not have a *price*; they have *dignity*, as he states (cf. Kant 1983a, BA 78 and BA 85). All values which constitute meaning – the value of remembrance, relation, individuality and finally all values concerning the human being – cannot be transferred to monetary values. A price can be fixed for a thing which pleases or affects the human being positively; those values correlate with a desideratum (cf. BA 78). However, the human being him/herself does not exist for others but fixes the ultimate; this is why the dignity of the subject must be respected (cf. BA 85 and 78). Dignity consists in giving the law yourself; this is why dignity itself represents the highest value. If it is destroyed, the *holiness* of humankind is destroyed, as Kant says (cf. BA 78f).

According to Kant, the reason for the dignity of the human and each rational nature lies in autonomy (cf. BA 79) which makes it possible to act according to the realm of values (cf. BA 76). This presupposes that persons can refer to themselves (identity) and to the good. This double movement constitutes morality ('Sittlichkeit' as Kant calls it) which is the ultimate aim; this is the reason why the human being embodies an absolute value. The autonomous person is 'at the same time the source, the judge and the one obedient to well-founded and reasonable morals' (Ott 2001, 23).[3] Kant states that the human being understands dignity and freedom and is able to respect it in others as those persons are ultimate aims themselves (cf. 1983a, 74, 78f., 120 and 124).

1.2 Eidetic Phenomenological Analysis of Dignity

1.2.1 What belongs to the human being in an unconditional manner

Dignity is what belongs to the human being and cannot be taken from it. It must not be given to persons – they just possess it.

---

[2]   Here diverse schools of reductionism can be named.
[3]   Ott (2001) summarizes Kant this way. Translation by the author.

- Dignity is unconditional as it confirms the qualitative individuality, the peculiarity of each human being.
- The human being is a value *in se* – no price can be fixed for a human life; you have to desist from the attempt to do so forever (Ps. 49:7–9).
- In some situations, human beings may seem to lack dignity as they are not treated with, or did not act with, dignity. However, dignity as such, as an essential trait, is unconditional and stays. No condition can be named for it. Each condition would qualify it as an accident, as something which incidentally belongs to the person; this would debase human dignity.

Dignity is a metaphysical notion and as such it cannot be defined conclusively. This is why I just offer an open definition: Dignity is what protects the secret of the human being, the dignity of the individual and the dignity of humankind. It is the most common and the most personal trait. Someone destroying human dignity destroys the secret, the personality – though dignity as an essence is not touched.

Dignity is as incomprehensible as human spirit, freedom and individuality. Those metaphysical traits refer to transcendence. All living beings reach out to others or to the world; but we, human beings, are transcendent ourselves: we try to go beyond our human horizon in order to understand humanity. Though we cannot understand what our intellect, our me, our freedom is, and we do not know what continuously precludes us from getting the full concept, we keep trying. We long for full insight. But at this point psychology has to give up and philosophy touches its limits; just theology can cross this border.[4] The human being is, as a matter of principle, a secret. However, even if dignity cannot be proved and described by the intellect, it is existentially experienced: we get an idea of it when it is confirmed or questioned.

1.2.2 Anthropological aspects

If the essence of the human being is touched, trauma occurs. This happens when one of the essential traits is in danger. As human beings we have a conscious relationship to ourselves and to our existence; this is identity (1). This relationship makes *freedom* possible which entails responsibility, the two constituents of morality (2). The body (3) is our *living* but material dimension, constituting the relationship to space (4) and time (5). Individuality (6) is our most secret characteristic, directly linked to human dignity. Dignity is revealed by the level of our emotional (7) maturity; the 'feelings of value' testify to a certain objectivity, the all-embracing meaning. Values embody the moral truth which differs from rational *truth*, seized by the spirit (8) and expressed through language (9). The search for meaning testifies to another constitutive trait, namely transcendence (10) or religiosity. All constitutive, essential traits are experienced and developed in the most

---

[4] Cf. Ratzinger (2005, 110): Die grundsätzliche 'Transparenz des Subjekts für das Göttliche [konstituiert] die eigentliche Würde und Größe des Menschen' (The fundamental 'transparency of the subject for the divine [constitutes] the actual dignity and greatness of man').

basic characteristic, called sociality (11), which in its deepest and most existential form is *love*. In love, we experience what and who we are. This is why trauma in relationships affects the human being as a whole (Wulf 2014) and why love constitutes the experience of dignity.

1.2.3 Dignity and central values

The secret of the human being can be characterized by the four main values just mentioned: life, freedom, love and truth (Wulf 2017b). All these values are meta-physical which means that no empirical evidence can prove them, none of them. This is why reductionism, based on empirical methodology, does not touch them. Besides, the one who negates them already fully performs them: he lives, postulates to tell the truth and is free in it. Just love is performed in an indirect way: it aims at the value the person contributes to him/herself and to his/her statement. If we link the central values to the tetrahedron model already mentioned, the following results from it:

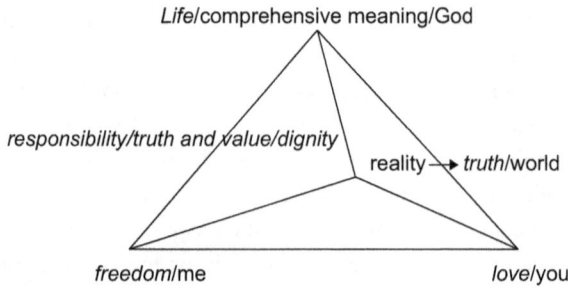

Life/comprehensive meaning/God

responsibility/truth and *value*/dignity

reality → *truth*/world

freedom/me

love/you

Each value is linked to the 'subject' governing it.

- Individuals control their freedom – nobody else may do that.
- The others freely control their love – nobody else may force them to love.
- The control of truth would mean the control of reality – which is not possible.
- Treating life as if it were under our control would destroy each possible meaning.

These basic values constitute dignity, and they warrant it. This is why nobody must give up even one of them. As dignity constitutes the deepest value a person can feel, it is the apex of emotional and moral orientation and must not be destroyed by: disordered love or deprivation of love; a lack of freedom, which causes powerlessness; arbitrariness and the rejection of truth; and life-threatening incidents. All these influences question human dignity; they can destroy the 'royal' or the 'divine spark' in the human being (Reddemann 2008, 29 and 46f.). Restoration of dignity is in the victim's own purpose ('Selbstzweck') and consists precisely in the restoration of love (41 and 43), freedom and truth (93; Wurmser 2007, 82ff.). The first step is regaining life by saying no to harming influences (Reddemann 2008, 41; Wulf 2014, 53ff., 120f., 156). Finally, everybody has a 'right to dignity' (Reddemann 2008, 58), which means that persons have the right that their dignity must be respected.

1.3 Existential Reasons for Dignity

Though dignity is an essential trait, it is possible that someone could try to take control of it or manipulate it. In this case human beings cannot experience their dignity anymore. The reason can be found in the different ways one can violate dignity. One way is taking away the possibility of living according to the human essence; another is invasive behaviour, that is, when someone tries to take control of what is withdrawn from anyone else's control. Human dignity should be confirmed by love and preserved even in the limited or handicapped person.

1.3.1 Violating dignity

If human beings are deprived of one of their *essential traits*, dignity is severely in danger: Maybe someone is withdrawn psychically from his identity (1) (in torturing or by drugs), so that he loses the fundament of freedom and morality (2). If the body (3) is tortured, no space (4) is given (in life-threatening circumstances or to asylum seekers), if no time (5) is given to develop personhood (to children, especially to unborn children), individuality (6) cannot develop and emotionality (7) cannot be unfolded. Under conditions of insecurity and arbitrariness, truth is forbidden or cannot be found; the spirit (8) dwindles and language (9) is lost. If the right to search for transcendent meaning (10) is taken away or the possibility to experience a community and personal love is denied (11), human beings are humiliated to such an extent that they lose the inner experience of dignity.

   Invasive behaviour can cause the same damage. Direct invasive behaviour is each touch or each word which (1) does not belong in this relation (e.g. incest) or (2) is not mutually agreed on. Someone is guilty of (3) indirect invasive behaviour if (a) he interprets the thoughts of another by his own absolute authority, (b) he interprets the feelings of others in his own way or (c) the freedom of the other is restricted without special reasons. It is also indirectly invasive (4) if someone says who the other is or has to be. By acting that way, the other seeks to rule over something he should not govern (spirit, freedom, emotions and individuality). The invasive behaviour destroys dignity. Taking control of another person's emotions is especially harmful as they are close to the personal core. If the emotions and deeper feelings become paralyzed, you finally lose yourself (Crastnopol 2015, 37ff.). If the access to the self is lost, the offender takes over and reigns over the soul of the victim who is dying internally. This causes a loss of trust in the world and in others and destroys hope. A feeling of deep powerlessness, insecurity and a death-threat can result from taking away the possibility of experiencing dignity. But even if dignity is hurt – if it cannot be experienced anymore – it persists. However, only love and unconditional acceptance can restore the experience of dignity.

1.3.2 Confirmation of dignity: Love

Thus, the positive existential experience of dignity consists in love: Love is the way by which you come close to the secret of a human being by deep respect. Love provides space for the secret of the human being and for its deployment in the different relationships in which human beings take over responsibility for each other.

Love means unconditionally respecting the other; this love sets us free as a *bonum* you must not dispose of. It accepts unconditionally our *boundaries* given by dignity. We experience this as a free space for the deployment of our individuality, our innermost secret, which then becomes visible gradually.

1.3.3 Limited human being: Persisting dignity

If you want to understand human dignity, you have to consider the dignity of the one who seems bare of dignity or whose dignity seems to be at risk. Dignity is not the dignity for or by somebody else; it is something existing in itself. This is why it has to be respected, even if it is not yet fully actualized or seems to vanish (an argument of potentiality) or is not visible in the actual situation. A limited, potentially developed, not-yet actualized being, depending on the situation, has its own value; in the case of the human being, it has dignity (Wulf 2011, chapter 13). Thus, especially at the borders, dignity becomes visible and stimulates the right action.

1.4 Dignity as a Benefit by Law

The idea of dignity is the foundation of human rights.[5] These rights were born from the existential experience in World War II and its extermination camps. Human beings are 'subjects of rights', embodying their own values (Ratzinger 2005, 38). The essential rights can be deduced from the essential traits of the human being: with the body the right to live (see: habeas corpus) is given; sociality needs a protected space for love; the spirit must get access to the truth, and individuality needs security to develop. The right to work is closely connected to material needs; the right to belong to a nation or a people warrants the space we need. A right to time should be added – for unborn and dying individuals – as in these periods this right is identical with the right to live and hand over your life (Rager 1998 and 2006). The right to practice your own religion goes along with transcendence. Dignity is the measure and the point of measuring of all those rights. If someone is deprived of one of these rights for a longer period and without free decision, his or her experience of dignity could seriously diminish or even die down.

1.5 What Constitutes Human Dignity in Theology

1.5.1 Being the image of God, redemption, social responsibility

Human dignity has to be respected in an unconditional way. This is also visible in the Jewish-Christian ethos, which is founded in creation. Human transcendence named

---

[5]   Internationale Erklärung der Menschenrechte, ratifiziert 1948. Cf. Ratzinger (2005, 87).

earlier already gives us a hint: the human being stays, metaphysically speaking, a secret which reveals its character in the wider horizon of meaning. Philosophically, this horizon stays abstract, but it has to give a conclusive answer to the metaphysical traits of personhood: the me, freedom and spirit. Therefore, it has to be a free and rational subject itself.[6] Theologically speaking, this horizon is a person responding to a person, a person constituting meaning: God (Wulf 2009, 54f.). The Bible postulates that the human being is created according to the image of God[7]; this is the centre of biblical anthropology (Dirscherl 2006, 17f.). Specifically, Christian theology adds another aspect: incarnation: God becoming a human being. Humanity is redeemed by Christ and will be perfected in God who wants us to have life in abundance.[8] The human being is in charge of the world; responsible for social ethics and for each single human being. Maybe these thoughts are 'outmoded' in a relativistic context. However, human nature is and stays an open question to which reductionism gives a reduced answer and relativism resists giving any commentary.

1.5.2 The God of love and the commandments of love

God is a God of love who has created human beings in their individuality and loves them for what they are. He gives eternal life to each person and loves the human being in each manner imaginable: as an obedient child,[9] a friend,[10] a bridegroom,[11] a father[12] and a teacher.[13] He freely meets the human being as free partner, setting this partner even more free.

According to these reflections, the commandments of love – loving the human being and loving God[14] – are not in human hands; they are the aim but also a minimum requirement. They are the sum of the Ten Commandments (Exod. 20:3–17) which – in their way – give an answer to human beings: reaching out for transcendence (Commandments 1–3), linking people to the time before (the 'parents' representing history and tradition) and promising future and space (living in one's own land, Commandment 4), protecting life (Commandment 5) and the secure room to love (Commandments 6 and 9), giving the right to material resources and work (Commandments 7 and 10) and the right to truth (Commandment 8). This is how dignity is preserved in a very basic way. Giving these rights is God's way of looking after his beloved people.

---

[6] The horizon in which all goods become visible is even according to the philosopher of Enlightenment, Immanuel Kant, a person, since the highest 'bonum' is free and spiritual. Cf. Wulf (2010, 95ff.). Cf. Kant (1983b, A225f).

[7] Cf. Gen. 1:27 and 5:1.

[8] Cf. Ju 10.10.

[9] Cf. Jn 5:30; 6:38; 7:17; 9:31; 10:18; Mk 3:35; we should follow him in this: Mt 7:21; 12:50; 21:31.

[10] Cf. Jn 15:15.

[11] Cf. Song of Solomon; Jas 61:10 and 62:5; Wis. 8:2; Jer. 2:2 and 32; 3; 11; Ezek. 16; Hos. 2:21f.; 14:5; Ps. 45; Mt 9:15 and Mt 25; Mk 2:19; Lk. 5:34 and 12:36; Jn 3:29; Rev. 19:7ff., 21.

[12] Cf. Mt 6:6; 11:27; 23:9; Jn 10:11ff.; 14 and 15 and so on.

[13] Cf. Mt 6:9, 23:10; Jn 3:2.

[14] Cf. Deut. 6:5; Lev. 19:18; Mk 12:29ff.

1.6 First Result: Dignity as a Unifying Item

The first result of this discussion is that dignity is a fundamental ethical element. It is a summary of all ethical requirements. It gives a trustworthy direction to it. Western culture after World War II is based on this basic value and cannot function without it.

2. Tolerance

Before I start the discussion about tolerance, I offer a small reflection regarding the first result: tolerance contributes to an attitude that does not mediate between different points of view which are incompatible. This is why tolerance finally leads to plurality – even if it would be important to mediate between the different positions.

2.1 The Essence of Tolerance

Tolerance lets others be what they are but does not totally accept them. In the *yes* of tolerance you always find a *no*; this is the essential difference between tolerance and acceptance (Forst 2003, 30ff.): you tolerate but you do not totally accept the otherness of the other. You can live with it – but need a distance. The danger may be that the different ideas do not communicate with each other anymore; each idea can be perverted into an ideology, into an idea which claims to be the whole truth. It may be considered as positive that tolerance gives space to others; but tolerance is not a unifying power, as the non-acceptance of others has to be tolerated even if you suffer from it.

However, one might not be able to choose between all the different ideas offered by different groups. In this case, truth becomes relative, namely relative to the group convinced of it. Tolerance contributes to *relativism*. Though this attitude belongs to the 'democratic ethos' (Mohrs 1997, 9), it must not be misunderstood as indifference. This would end up in *particularism*, which hinders integration (Nida-Rümelin 1997, 111; cf. Mohrs 1997, 8; and Forst 2003, 613). A 'liberal, tolerant attitude' (Macho 1999, 38) stimulates plurality which is as such an 'inherent appeal to tolerance' (Liessmann 2012, 11). Tolerance is not acceptance; it just tries to hinder conflicts (Mohrs 1997, 8).

If tolerance means to let different points of view exist without mediating between them or eliminating one of them, *pluralism* is established. Under these conditions, different kinds of thinking coexist without mediation. Each of them constructs a limited worldview, which in the pluralistic context just stands alongside the others. As all constructions seem to be valid or valuable, absolute statements are not possible anymore. This is why pluralism leads to relativism.

2.2 Tolerance in the Context of Ethics

In Kant we still find a strong image of humankind and, thus, a strong morality. In the postmodern context dignity cannot be linked to a concrete existing object

(Sikora 2000, 183); each relativistic or pluralistic worldview initiates another kind of ethics.

2.2.1 *Tolerated constructs: Relativizing in thinking*

In the context of relativism and pluralism, dignity cannot be warranted. It turns out to be nothing but a kind of interpretation, as one of those ideas constructed by human beings and thus only of relative importance.

The paradigm of tolerance means that you do not force your own culture on some-body else.[15] But if all 'cultures' are standing alongside each other without intermediation, this destabilizes culture as such. Meanwhile we arrive in a 'constructivistic deliberate confusion' as states Strasser (2008, 13), which relativizes the image of man and denies his essence. 'European culture is pluralistic, radically pluralistic. This is why it does not have a common image of man anymore' (Höffe 1995, 287). The human being is now seen as a product of evolution or of the subconscious motivations or as a compilation of predictable behaviour (Anzenbacher 1992, 200ff. and 214ff.). This would mean that human subjects are finally determined (18): they turn out depending on others bio-logically, psychologically and in their behaviour. However, without freedom, the human being is not the human being anymore and, as we saw before, the experience of dignity is lost.

Philosophers like Peter Singer do not see any significant difference between the human being and the animal anymore; he (like others) just enumerates functions of a 'being without consciousness', 'consciously perceiving beings' and 'persons' in the broader sense (Anzenbacher 1992, 259ff.). If the human being is restricted to some degree of con-sciousness, the concept 'person' collapses (260) and thus the notion of unconditional 'dignity' as well. Singer draws the conclusion that a baby, which is just a day old, may be treated like a slug and that 'killing, say, a chimpanzee is worse than the killing of a human being who, because of a congenital intellectual disability, [according to him] is not and never can be a person' (1993, 118). Of course, Singer's provocation became visible and famous in public. But he forgot about the persons whose dignity he denied and whom he hurt; he forgot about the existential experience of the handicapped who grasp the diffe-rence between themselves and animals. Singer hurt their dignity by his statements! The problem is: his view misses the phenomenological analysis of human essence, the meta-physical dimension and thus the dimension of meaning. In the face of the weakest, the unborn and the dying person, Singer's thoughts cannot be tolerated. If someone speaks about human dignity in the subjunctive or if the status of the person depends on con-sensus, human dignity is given up in fact since 'the recognition of the person's dignity will not be founded by a consensus depending on discourse, it has to be presupposed for the discourse' (Hertz et al. 1993, 6). Anzenbacher counters all relativisms with the argument

---

[15] Cf. Höffe (1995, 287): 'Selbst wenn sie noch ein einheitliches Menschenbild hätte, darf sie es nicht anderen Kulturen "aufzwingen"' (Even if she still had a unified human image, she shouldn't 'impose' it on other cultures).

that they have to rely on a certain notion of the person and human dignity.[16] Those who negate human nature forget that they all implicitly and explicitly assume it – at least if they want to be praised for their findings.

2.2.2 Effective constructs: Disposing over value and dignity

But, and this must not be ignored, constructs like those provided by Singer become effective. This is visible if the value and the dignity of the weakest – the unborn, for example – are not respected (Ratzinger 2005, 28). The right to live was described as the point of departure of all dignity ever possible; nobody must take control of it. The same is true for the basic values answering to spirit (truth), freedom and individuality (love), which make it possible to be a human being. Those values must never be sacrificed for practical or ideological means (Böckle 1966, 134). The attempt to seize control of human nature, to make humanity a means to an end, can result – which simply takes away human dignity.

2.3 The Limits of Tolerance: Destroying Dignity

As I stated before, dignity can be destroyed – especially by negating human nature or by transgressing personal boundaries. We saw that human beings must not be deprived of something which is part of their essence, of an essential relation or of an existential value: freedom (Kant calls it autonomy), truth, love and life. All goods sustaining life, social security, formation and education have to be preserved. We are back to human rights! Indeed, their core is dignity; this is the reason why they have to be guaranteed. This is what morality stands for: executing freedom in responsibility. For this reason, morality as such has to be seen as an essential feature, which is meant to protect mankind in yourself and the other. Freedom is not just arbitrariness; it is directed to a higher value, which has to be realized. Hence, articulating freedom in the right way is as such a moral duty. Acting in a responsible way helps the human being experience dignity.

---

[16] Cf. Anzenbacher (1996, 440):

> Es scheint, dass die gerechtigkeitsprinzipielle Normativität der universalistischen Moral letztlich von einem ontologisch bestimmten Begriff der Person abhängt. Sowohl die konstruktivistische (Rawls) als auch die prozedural-pragmatische (Habermas, Apel) Rekonstruktion der Moral verdanken ihre Plausibilität (trotz vielfältiger Versicherung ihrer Metaphysikfreiheit) letztlich doch der Überzeugung, dass der Mensch als Mensch ein Wesen ist, das auf Grund seiner ontologischen Verfasstheit Würde hat und Achtung verdient.

> (It seems that the principled normativity of universalist morality ultimately depends on an ontologically determined concept of the person. Both the constructivist (Rawls) and the procedural-pragmatic (Habermas, Apel) reconstruction of morality owe their plausibility (despite the multiple assurances of their freedom from metaphysics) ultimately to the conviction that man as a human being is a being who, on the basis of his ontological constitution, has dignity and deserves respect.)

3. Dignity Guaranteed by a Threefold Competence

We can see that dignity forms a common base. Tolerance, on the other hand, gives space to arbitrary value-constructs even if you cannot mediate between them. The question is how these two attitudes can be brought together.

The link can be found in the person him/herself, in an attitude he/she can take: *self-competence*. Self-competent persons know about their dignity: they are aware of their deep feelings of value; they can render an account in a rational way about this and transform what they understand into action. They decide to realize the good and by this combine all levels of the tetrahedron.

Persons with this attitude possess *social competence*, a social tolerance; they accept others under one condition: that their own dignity and the dignity of the other are not affected. Tolerance is in this case limited by a central value, the person as such.

This is how a *competence of meaning* is revealed: the concept of dignity was born from experience, especially from the existential experience of broken dignity. This means that the existential experience refers to the undeniable horizon of meaning in the individual life as in social, economic, ecological and even religious contexts. If dignity is respected, we experience meaning; if this is not the case, everything becomes meaningless indeed.

Tolerance is born from the will to accept other values, but it is also limited by the horizon of meaning. A person possessing a personal, a social and a meaning-competence shows moral courage and intervenes if human beings, institutions and social systems, even institutions meant to protect the law and rights of the person, offend against the horizon of meaning. The competence of yourself, of others and of the meaning is necessary in postmodern contexts in order to protect the inalienable dignity, which is the basis and aim of human rights.

References

Anzenbacher, Arno. 1992. *Einführung in die Ethik*. Düsseldorf: Patmos.

———. 1996. 'Christliche Ethik und kommunitaristische Liberalisierung'. In *Fundamente der Theologischen Ethik: Bilanz und Neuansätze*, edited by Adrian Holderegger, 431–49. Freiburg: Universitätsverlag.

Böckle, Franz. 1966. 'Naturrecht. Rückblick und Ausblick'. In *Das Naturrecht im Disput*, Drei Vorträge beim Kongress der deutschsprachigen Moraltheologen 1965 in Bensberg, edited by Franz Böckle, 121–50. Düsseldorf: Patmos.

Crastnopol, Margaret. 2015. *Micro-Trauma: A Psychoanalytic Understanding of Cumulative Psychic Injury*. New York: Routledge.

Dirscherl, Erwin. 2006. *Grundriss theologischer Anthropologie*. Die Entschiedenheit des Menschen angesichts des Anderen. Regensburg: Pustet.

Forst, Rainer. 2003. *Toleranz im Konflikt*. Geschichte, Gehalt und Gegenwart eines umstrittenen Begriffs. Frankfurt: Suhrkamp.

Frankl, Victor. 1970. *The Will to Meaning: Foundations and Applications of Logotherapy*. New York: Penguin.

Hertz, Anselm, Wilhelm Korff, Trutz Rendtorff and Hermann Ringeling, eds. 1993. 'Einleitung'. In *Handbuch der Christlichen Ethik*, vol. 1. S. 3–4. Freiburg: Herder.

Höffe, Otfried. 1995. 'Die Menschenrechte: europäisches Menschenbild oder interkultureller Diskurs?' In *Menschenbilder im Wandel – Menschenbilder im Dialog: fünfundzwanzigste Rechenschaft. Das*

Bild vom Menschen, wie ist es heute – wie soll es werden? edited by Engadiner Kollegium, 283–97. Zürich: NZN-Buchverlag.

Kant, Immanuel. 1983a. 'Grundlegung der Metaphysik der Sitten'. In *Kant's Werke in sechs Bänden*, edited by Wilhelm Weischedel, vol. IV. Darmstadt: Wissenschaftliche Buchgesellschaft.

———. 1983b. 'Kritik der praktischen Vernunft'. In *Kant's Werke in sechs Bänden*, edited by Wilhelm Weischedel, vol. IV. Darmstadt: Wissenschaftliche Buchgesellschaft.

Liessmann, Konrad Paul. 2012. 'Kultur ist alles. Aber nicht alles ist Kultur'. In *Zukunft. Kultur. Lebensqualität*, Schriftenreihe Zukunft: Lebensqualität, edited by Rheinhold Popp, Elisabeth Zechenter and Ulrich Reinhardt, 7–17. Wien: LIT.

Macho, Thomas. 1999. 'Säkularisierung und Multikulturalismus'. In *Perspektive Europa. Modelle für das 21. Jahrhundert*, edited by Konrad Paul Liessmann and Gerhard Wienberger, 37–50. Wien: Sonderzahl.

Mohrs, Thomas. 1997. 'Einleitung'. In *Eine Welt – eine Moral? Eine kontroverse Debatte*, edited by Wilhelm Lütterfelds and Thomas Mohrs, 1–17. Darmstadt: Wissenschaftliche Buchgesellschaft.

Nida-Rümelin, Julian. 1997. 'Über die Vereinbarkeit von Universalismus und Pluralismus in der Ethik'. In *Eine Welt – eine Moral? Eine kontroverse Debatte*, edited by Wilhelm Lütterfelds and Thomas Mohrs, 104–17. Darmstadt: Wissenschaftliche Buchgesellschaf.

Ott, Konrad. 2001. *Moralbegründungen. Zur Einführung.* Hamburg: Junius.

Rager, Günter, ed. 1998. *Beginn, Personalität und Würde des Menschen.* Freiburg: Alber.

———. 2006. *Die Person. Wege zu ihrem Verständnis.* Freiburg: Universitätsverlag.

Ratzinger, Josef. 2005. *Werte in Zeiten des Umbruchs. Die Herausforderungen der Zukunft bestehen.* Freiburg: Herder.

Reddemann, Luise. 2008. *Würde – Annäherung an einen vergessenen Wert in der Psychotherapie.* Stuttgart: Klett Cotta.

Ryder, Richard D. 2009. 'Speciesism'. In *Encyclopedia of Animal Rights and Animal Welfare*, edited by Marc Bekoff. Westport, CT: Greenwood.

Schirach, Ferdinand von. 2017. *Die Würde ist antastbar. Essays.* Munich: BTB Taschenbuch.

Sikora, Jürgen. 2000. 'Diskurs: Diskursethik versus Konstruktivismus – ein Streitgespräch'. In *Begründung von Moral. Diskursethik versus Konstruktivismus. Eine Streitschrift*, edited by Holger Burckhardy and Kersten Reich, 182–92. Würzburg: Könighausen und Neumann.

Singer, Peter. 1993. *Practical Ethics*, 2nd ed. Cambridge: Cambridge University Press.

Strasser, Peter. 2008. *Gut in allen möglichen Welten. Der ethische Horizont.* Paderborn: Ferdinand Schöningh.

Wulf, Claudia Mariéle. 2009. *Begegnung, die befreit. Christliche Erlösung als Beziehungsgeschehen.* Vallendar: Patris.

———. 2010. *Was ist gut? Eidetische Phänomenologie als Impuls zur moraltheologischen Erkenntnistheorie.* Vallendar: Patris.

———. 2011. *Der Mensch – ein Phänomen. Eine phänomenologische, theologische und ethische Anthropologie.* Vallendar: Patris.

———. 2014. *Wenn das Ich zerbricht. Gedanken zum Psychotrauma für Betroffene und ihre Begleiter.* Münster: LIT.

———. 2017a. *Phänomene des Menschseins. Zwischen Möglichkeit, Machbarkeit und Mut.* Philosophische Orientierungen vol. 6. Münster: LIT.

———. 2017b. 'Freiheit – individuell, relational, existentiell. Vorschläge zur Weiterarbeit mit Edith Steins origineller Anthropologie'. In *Edith Steins Herausforderungen heutiger Anthropologie*, vol. 3 der Schriftenreihe des EUPHRat Europäisches Institut für Philosophie und Religion, edited by Hanna-Barbara Gerl-Falkovitz and Mette Lebech, 87–105. Heiligenkreuz: BE&BE.

Wurmser, Léon. 2007. *Torment Me, but Don't Abandon Me: Psychoanalysis of the Severe Neuroses in a New Key.* Maryland: Rowman & Littlefield.

Chapter Seven

HUMAN DIGNITY: WHAT TO DO WITH IT? FROM FRUITLESS ABSTRACTION TO MEANINGFUL ACTION

Hendrik Kaptein

1. Human Dignity? Calm Down. You Can't Shoot Them All

Travelling through Germany by train may take extra time, or worse. Trying to get back to the Netherlands from Cologne (a wonderful city indeed) one late afternoon, this rail traveller received wonderful assistance from a counter clerk beleaguered by angry customers. On her desk was a mug with the words: 'Calm down. You can't shoot them all'. For this and other reasons (some self-interest among them) your up-to-then duly delayed present writer – and waiting again for some time for his turn at the desk – did his best to be as friendly as possible. This had a not completely surprising effect: the clerk's face cleared up, no doubt after a long day of being more or less continuously harassed. Her assistance was as wonderfully friendly as it was effective. So home was reached the same day after all, with a lesson on dignity learnt one more time. A fellow human being, however anonymous, was on the other side of the desk, not a foe responsible for the sometimes-disappointing failures of German rail transport. This is respecting human dignity in practice, to such good effect for all concerned.

The value of human dignity is not limited to its fragmentary realization in railway communication, of course. It must be something quite important and elevated in general. Still the concept is not clear and uncontested, thus lacking clear legal and moral implications as well. Human dignity cannot be some or other matter of fact anyway, 'out there' to be discovered by painstaking research. It is an evaluative and normative issue, thus lending itself to endless conflicts of more or less learned opinion rooted in conflicting views of man, the end or ends of life, the world and God(s).

So human dignity is an essentially practical notion, to be duly acted upon, here, now, whenever and wherever. So why not step down (for a while) from the high grounds or just thin air of philosophy and theology and ask what can be done to protect human dignity (whatever it may be in the end) in daily life? What can we do about it? This must seem a paradoxical or even contradictory enterprise, in deriving means to an unclear or even unknown end, or drawing a road map for a will-o'-the wisp.

Still it may be fairly clear what kind of everyday and not-so-everyday conduct is incompatible with any human dignity and how this may be worded in terms of practical rules. This may well result in a brief list of recommendations compatible with conflicting views of man, the world and God(s), given their formal and procedural nature. However, such recommendations may make sense only in a more or less decent legal order, in which respect for the law generally is respect for fellow human beings.

Here this will be further explained as follows. Section 2 offers a brief exposition of the ontological, epistemological and evaluative/normative elusiveness of human dignity and in fact of man himself. Must this lead to relativism, subjectivism, indifference and collective narcissism in a hopelessly divided world? Section 3 offers effective or simply practical rebuttal. Human dignity may still be respected in daily and not-so-daily life by adherence to nine basic formalities: (1) be polite and friendly, (2) respect the presumption of innocence, (3) *Audi et alteram partem*, (4) apply the principle of charity to all utterances, (5) respect facts, (6) be *ad rem* and not *ad hominem*, (7) be *fortiter in re suaviter in modo*, (8) care for due praise, blame and gratitude and (9) do not humiliate. Section 4 briefly explains 'the tenth commandment': more than self-respect is needed in order to really respect others' human dignity. Section 5 concludes with the compatibility of these dignified formalities with different and conflicting conceptions of man, the world and God(s). Living up to this free advice costs nothing and may even further enlightened self-interest. Formally respectful conduct instead of confrontation and worse may forestall so many deadly and less deadly but still saddening conflicts. So stop pondering, give it a try: start your dignification of daily and not-so-daily life right now and enjoy its manifold benefits for free. And remember, human dignity still need not be everything: 'without love there is nothing'.

The recommendations offered here may not be new, let alone really original. But then this ought not to distract from their practical importance, as long as human dignity is still so often violated even in the daily lives and times of so-called civilized societies.

2. So Many Concepts and Conceptions of Human Dignity: Will-o'-the-Wisps

Dignity: 1. Rank or elevation, 2. Grandeur of mien, elevation of aspect – Some men have a native *dignity*, which will procure them more regard by a look, than others can obtain by the most imperious commands, 3. Advancement, preferment, high place.

Thus reads Johnson's dictionary (1755), clearly expressing the comparative element or even essence of dignity. Native dignity was not for everyone yet, while today's legal and other solemn declarations of human dignity imply or even expressly state that nobody is exempt from it. So where is the comparative element in this new human dignity? Is man to be situated (just) below God – or Gods – and (just) above (other) animals, plants and the rest of nature, living or dead? What are the ranking criteria here? Leaving God or Gods out of account will not solve this problem.

Or: if everybody is entitled to or simply is in possession of the same human dignity, equality may be the real thing. Equality in and/or of what? Equal treatment? Treatment as equals? Just treatment for all? What is justice, retributive, distributive or whatever? Or does human dignity imply entitlement to equal and unconditional fundamental rights? Not much common ground here it well seems. Human dignity as a or even the common denominator of all human beings constituting mankind appears to be a rather empty notion, however solemnly it may be cited in order to justify some or other (dis)advantageous treatment of human beings.

Then next: who or what is a human being? What is the 'human' as supposedly essential for human dignity? This may not always be a practical problem, as sight, sound and sometimes even touch and smell may quickly lead to the conclusion that a more or less fellow human being is encountered – or at least some outward semblance of it. Human sciences such as biology, physiology, neurology, psychology and psychopathology try to get behind outward semblances, in order to more or less establish who and what human beings are and what moves them in directions right and wrong. Even apart from such more or less scientific knowledge human beings may have some or other form of self-consciousness and sometimes even self-knowledge. Self-consciousness may even be essential for being entitled to human dignity, in distinction to the rest of the world, living or dead.

Still this does not answer the question of who or what a human being really is, as long as human beings themselves only are to answer this question. There is no vantage point of view, enabling human beings to epistemologically completely separate them from themselves, in order to really look down at mankind and at last establish 'who they really are'.

But then even if what human beings really are, or what human life really is, remains unknown in principle, human life ought to have some or other meaning or value, if notions of human dignity are to be sensible at all. What is the meaning of life? '42' is one famous answer (according to Adams 1979), as meaningless as any answer to this mere semblance of a question. Indeed, the question itself is semantically meaningless, for at least two related reasons. First, meaning or value is a comparative concept, implying the possibility of comparing life with something else in principle. Life must be better than death! That would seem to be the obvious answer. But what is death, or what is it like to be dead? I cannot be dead in principle – though life may feel as if one is dead at times. Second, meaning or value implies some or other criterion or criteria in order to determine such meaning or value. Whence are such criteria to be derived, apart from life itself in whatever sense?

So let us leave the logical (and sometimes psychological or simply psychic) alienation of 'the meaning of life' alone. This semantic senselessness does not imply the impossibility of meaning in life and (thus) of the meaning of a human life, according to whatever standards. Most human beings set themselves goals in their lives, inspired by religion or other fundamental persuasions, however mundanely and even mindlessly so. This is meaning in life, detailed according to so many different life plans. Most human beings are not totally alone either. Human beings play more or less meaningful roles in each other's lives and in their societies. This of course contributes to meaning in and of their lives. For this and other reasons most human beings generally prefer life over death. As long as they are alive they probably prefer well-being over grief, sadness and pain and so on (see Nussbaum (1992) and her later work on human functioning and social justice).

Such basic and rather self-evident considerations may well furnish better starting points for realizing human dignity than any senselessly theoretical approaches. One more interesting fact of human beings is the difference in human reaction to wrongs done to them, compared with mishaps befalling them. Being hit by a sizeable hailstone hurts, being unduly wronged hurts all the more, as it rightfully evokes resentment (see Sacks 1984 and Kaptein 2004) as a consequence of not having been taken seriously.

So – and to end theorizing at last – how can we take each other seriously, respect each other's dignity here and now, whatever human dignity 'may really be' according to whatever fundamental persuasion? In order to – hopefully – forestall still more fruitless differences of opinion about the real material ends in life, here some basic and everyday formalities or even virtues are given pride of place.

Or: what are procedures fit for preserving and furthering human dignity? This is not trying to get hold of the 'real meaning of human dignity' or going after a theoretical will-o'-the wisp, but trying to be practical in protecting and furthering human dignity here and now. Again, this seems paradoxical or even contradictory in trying to devise means to an end unknown. How may this kind of know-how in respecting human dignity do without knowing that (human dignity is x, y, z, ...)? The answer to this is not logical but practical: give it a try and let us see. Then something about human dignity 'in itself' may be learned after all as well.

3. Dignified Formalities: The First Nine Rules

Here is the manual, more or less artificially and arbitrarily expressed in nine not really different rules. Though these recommendations for the protection and furthering of human dignity may be totally self-evident after all, a brief rehearsal may still make sense to further encourage action according to it.

1. As befits a paradoxical or even logically contradictory enterprise – in attempting to respect human dignity without knowing what it really is – this more or less arbitrary summary of formal recommendations starts with a lie, with the *pia fraus* (pious fraud) of **politeness** or good manners. Even most threatening competitors, debtors, (other) wrongdoers and other more or less hated and terrible foes may be best approached with friendly manners, according to the customs of the specific time, place and situation. Saying 'good day' to some or other imagined or even real enemy may not be a bona fide expression of any real intention towards the addressee. Still, it may not just contribute to a good social atmosphere and successful pursuit of any business, but also to mutual respect and thus to human dignity. Unexpected politeness may even 'disarm' opponents and elicit reciprocal politeness and even goodwill. This 'counterfactuality' of politeness is only part of the story. In fact, it may even be advantageous to be ignorant of the moral and other qualities of human beings concerned.

The same holds good for their social status and ranks. Their 'dignities' may lead to differences in styles of politeness, but not to different degrees of it. Higher rank ought not to deserve any higher degrees of politeness at all. It may well be the other way round: lower rank, however irrational as a social phenomenon, necessitates higher degrees of politeness – just because social rank is generally irrational. At least in this sense disrespect of any social status as higher or lower 'dignity' is a good thing indeed.

In fact, politeness need not be limited to casual and impersonal human encounters like those of passers-by in public space and people engaged in some or other common or not-so-common business. Personal and even most intimate relationships may profit from politeness or simply friendliness as well. Human dignity may not be the primary value for next of kin, but then politeness serves so many more humanly worthwhile purposes.

This is not equal treatment of human beings equally endowed with inalienable human dignity. Politeness implies treatment of fellow human beings as equals, according to historically and locally endlessly varying circumstances, customs and traditions. 'When in Rome, do as the Romans do'; but do not expect strangers (in whatever sense) to completely understand and act upon your own styles and manners of politeness.

Still one universal element of politeness may be the prohibition of publicly correcting people for any imagined or even real lack of manners. Also, any variety of good manners does not at all distract from the well-nigh universal cultural value and worth of politeness, not just as respect for human dignity but for furthering human understanding and communication as well.

And then of course simple friendliness may greatly add to different styles of politeness, in 'disarming' any potentially less friendly and less polite fellow human beings as well.

This may forestall or at least mitigate legal conflicts and their oftentimes harmful consequences. Remember, respect for civilized law is respect for your fellow human beings. So human beings involved in whatever superior or inferior role in whatever legal conflict are to be 'indifferently' treated with equal politeness and friendliness, whatever their legal and moral merits and demerits may be in the end.

2. Second, and in line with politeness, is the **presumption of innocence** (though there is no suggestion of any clear logical order here). Everybody is to be treated as innocent, unless there is authoritative proof of the contrary.

Nobody is to prove her or his own innocence (apart from special circumstances even in criminal procedure). As already noted concerning politeness, it may be a good thing to be ignorant of the moral and other qualities of fellow human beings. Still there may be endless varieties of circumstantial and sometimes rather direct evidence of somebody's misconduct and liability for it, leading to speculations against such 'suspects' and to due care in interaction with them. But then there ought to be no indictment, let alone sanction, against them unless there is certainty on some or other liability for misconduct, established by somebody or some body in charge of such issues.

Do not add to such sanctions yourself. There ought to be no private justice, unless the issue at hand is private in itself, as may be the case in personal relationships.

This is what Kant rightly coined as the fundamental right to be an 'unscolded human being' (1797, 237: *'das Recht ein unbescholtener Mensch zu sein'*). False charges are unjust in principle. This is a primary case in point of 'Nothing is more rightfully resented than injustice: all other harm is nothing compared to it' (36: '*Niemals empört etwas mehr als Ungerechtigkeit: alle andern Übel die wir ausstehen sind nichts dagegen*').

Falsely charging somebody is undeservedly and thus unjustly lowering this person's standing in comparison to and isolating her from supposedly innocent fellow human beings. Thus, adherence to the presumption of innocence is not just respecting human dignity but also an important 'cement' of society. Its formalism as a mere procedure ensures relative immunity from conflicts on material values and norms determining what is wrongful harm as a presupposition of liability.

Still not just human life but legal procedure in particular is oftentimes thwarted by violation of this principle. Two ever-recurring issues here are mistreatment of suspects and defendants awaiting trial and 'fact-finding' against defendants from wrongly verificationist perspectives. Treatment of anybody awaiting trial ought to be no punishment in any sense, as punishment is to be meted out only after fair trial and due conviction (as explained by Beccaria (1995) already in 1764 but even in so-called civilized criminal legal orders not respected at all). Also too many defendants are convicted on the basis of the probative value of the facts of the charge for the evidence at hand, whereas it ought to be the other way round of course. This prosecutor's fallacy is not just committed in criminal procedure of course but vitiates parts of less formal life and society as well (on the logic of the prosecutor's fallacy and related issues, see Kaptein et al. (2009)).

3. Next there is the overwhelming importance of ***audi et alteram partem*** (Hear the other side), not just in the establishment of any liability against anybody. Do not take for granted you know and know what to do unless everybody concerned had a proper say. This may not just lead to unexpected insights, acting upon which may do justice to everybody concerned. *Audi et alteram partem* also or even primarily is an expression of respect for everyone concerned. Everybody may have a say, thus being treated as an equal, though nobody's say may be decisive.

In fact, the awareness of properly being listened to is oftentimes considered more important than any adverse consequences of ensuing procedures, formal or informal. So many complaints against professionals like lawyers and medical doctors concern 'deafness' and general impoliteness and not so much professional incompetence per se (in as far as this may be judged by laypeople at all).

Attentively lending an ear to others in the first place may also ensure their respect for you. Letting others speak also acts against the common sin of talking too much yourself, leaving too little room for others and thus disrespecting their human dignity.

And if you still speak up, keep in mind that your words may not be the final say. Others may know better indeed, just as more or less maieutic conversation may lead to new or at least renewed insight. So do not be too sure in your utterances anyway, unless there is overwhelming evidence on your side. This leaves room for 'since we are a conversation – and can hear from each other', as Hölderlin so beautifully expressed it (around 1800: '*Seit ein Gespräch wir sind – Und hören können voneinander*').

So be really cautious with any testimonials *de auditu* (hearsay), and do not participate in gossip 'behind someone's back'. Any complaint against anybody ought to be discussed with the 'suspects' first and not in their absence at all, however unavoidable involvement of third parties or even authorities may be in order to solve the problem.

Still, duly listening to and discussing things with everybody concerned may not be enough. Any conduct burdening others ought to be justified in terms of all relevant facts and norms, having properly consulted all concerned however much they may disagree with measures to be taken after all. *Sic volo sic jubeo* (thus I will, thus I command) is incompatible not just with *audi et alteram partem* but with human dignity in general as well.

So the importance of this principle in legal procedure probably goes without any further saying. *Audi et alteram partem* may be no guarantee for truth on the facts of the matter by itself but surely it is a most important precondition for it. Parties involved in adversarial legal procedures may wrongly lose but may still live with the end result by experiencing the fairness and justice of having been able to adequately and fully represent their version of the conflict.

(In fact *audi et alteram partem* is not just a precondition for human dignity but also one more 'cement' of any decent society. On this, above all, see Hampshire (2000).)

4. Listen to others? Listen! Listen, look, use your senses. Again: do not talk, leave room for receptiveness as well. First impressions may well be as deceptive as they are wrongly decisive. If anything is at stake, it may well make sense to have a better look, in at least two senses. First, superficial observation may do no justice to the persons at hand and second, there may be different interpretations of outwardly identical features and utterances.

So be attentive and receptive and try to make the best of what comes to you. Linguistic and other interpretation of human utterances ought to be guided by **the principle of charity**. Interpret all human expression in the best possible light, such that everything expressed is as true or at least plausible as possible (see Wilson 1959).

Herman Melville's *Billy Budd* (1922–24) is a famous case in point. His stammer cost him his life, misunderstood as he was in his utterances – or absence of them – so imperfectly conveying his intentions and inner world. We are all stammering in a sense; we are all entitled to charity in interpretation of whatever we try to express and convey.

Somebody may appear to be angry or even aggressive and outwardly dangerous. Though due care may still make sense in such encounters with strangers or even with next of kin, such appearances may still be deceptive. Semblances of aggression may just hide fear of not being heard, driven by inferiority complexes or worse, just as outward serenity may sometimes hide inner turmoil and enmity. (And even if there is real anger or worse, it may be best to not 'pay back in kind': see also rule 8, on praise and blame.)

Undue generalization plays a major negative role here. False stereotypes may lead to misjudgements wronging fellow human beings not respected in their specific qualities and thus *qua* human beings. Somebody may look like a gang member, in style and general make-up and so on, but may in fact be a Good Samaritan. Outward appearances of race (whatever that may be), skin colour, ethnicity, religion, (other) political persuasion and so many more semblances of 'belonging to', 'being like' and thus 'behaving like' may be most misleading or worse.

Sure, respecting human dignity does not always presuppose specific personal knowledge of the fellow human beings concerned. But then still worse is the fallacious ignorance derived from false generalizations and other prejudices:

> Contrast is the only reality. Making somebody different from others is the most one can do for this person. This is because everything exists by being different from everything else. This holds good for human beings as well. They exist 'in' their material and spiritual differences with others.

Thus wrote Dutch novelist Carry van Bruggen (1919, 14: *ommis determinatio est negatio* (All determination is negation)).

This principle of charity is of utmost legal importance as well. No civilized law and right may be realized without due respect for the individual qualities and circumstances of all parties concerned. At least in this respect the principle of charity is a principle of relevance as well, however hard it may be to establish criteria of relevance transcending *ius in causa positum* ('the law is given in the unique facts of the case').

5. Not just human expressions but everything in the world of whatever human interest ought to be seen and interpreted 'in the best possible light'. This implies **respect for facts** as one more presupposition for respecting human dignity. Ignorance of facts implies ignorance of the consequences of human conduct, with possibly harmful consequences for everybody concerned. Sure enough, foreseeing everything ensuing from human conduct is not humanly feasible. Still respecting human dignity implies respecting facts common to (but for that reason alone not known by) all concerned. Different values and norms may be appealed to in order to do something with facts, but then without such facts nothing sensible by any standards can be done at all.

This totally excludes anything like: 'The world is how you see it so your world may be different from mine', or (still worse): 'My realities are not yours in principle so how can you contradict me' and so on. Such simplistic varieties of 'post-modern' subjectivism and relativism are at odds with human dignity in principle. Suppose such a post-modernist is bluntly told that he is talking nonsense, proving nothing more than his ignorance and plain stupidity. The post-modernist will probably not be so unintelligent as to miss the drift of such an insult (however truthful in its description). So he will protest, all the more so if he were insultingly addressed in public. To which the rather simple answer in his own terms may be: 'So this is how you experience things; we think and see things differently, so what are you talking about? You were not really insulted at all, it's just your experience of things; we're not responsible for that, thank you very much'.

Now of course many things are as we see them, hopefully in their best light, but there must be facts to be seen, interpreted and so on or there is no knowledge and thus no communication at all.

Thus lack of respect for the facts of the world (in as far as to be humanly established) does not just entail ignorance of the consequences of human conduct, it also leads to collective loneliness, certainly so if the basic given of a common life world is denied beforehand. This was poignantly expressed by Frankfurt:

Our recognition and our understanding of our own identity arises out of, and depends integrally on, our appreciation of a reality that is definitively independent of ourselves. In other words, it arises out of and depends on our recognition that there are facts and truths over which we cannot hope to exercise direct or immediate control. If there were no such facts or truths, if the world invariably and unresistingly became whatever we might like or wish it to be, we would be unable to distinguish ourselves from what is other than ourselves and we would have no sense of what in particular we ourselves are. It is only through our recognition of a world of stubbornly independent reality, fact, and truth that we come both to recognize ourselves as beings distinct from others and to articulate the specific nature of our own identities.

How, then, can we fail to take the importance of factuality and of reality seriously? How can we fail to care about truth?

We cannot. (2006, 100–101)

So take care with the truth, or simply: respect facts. This is respect for fellow human beings as well. Quine briefly expressed this as follows:

Unscientific man is beset by a deplorable desire to have been right. The scientist is distinguished by a desire to *be* right. (1987, 185, emphasis original)

Science is here to be taken in the broad sense of knowledge. So do not isolate and humiliate others by 'knowing better' against the facts of the matter – or even in accordance with them, certainly not so from positions of authority over these others. Duly inquire into everything relevant for your conduct towards others instead. Respecting individuals is respecting privacy but paying attention to shared mental, emotional and tactile realities as well.

You cannot always change for the better fellow human beings and the rest of the world but then at least look at everyone and everything in the best possible light. (Ethics and aesthetics are one, as remarked not just by Wittgenstein (1921).) This does not imply tolerating real wrongs of course, as this would be at odds with human dignity anyway.

The law may be appealed to redress wrongs real or imaginary. Then the facts of the matter are of utmost importance again. (Keep in mind that the great majority of legal conflicts is about contested facts and not contested law.) If facts are just 'what is made of the world', then there is no justice and right at all. *Da mihi facta dabo tibi ius* (Give me the facts and I will give you the law) is not just a heuristic principle but a fundamental truth as well. Thus in several civilized legal orders, parties ought to inform the court on all relevant information. (Lawyers may wrongly appeal to client confidentiality in order to hide facts not furthering their clients' cases and get away with it.)

6. The next precept stresses the importance of discourse **ad rem** (to the point) **not** to be confused with discourse **ad hominem** (against the person). The main significance of this may be explained as follows. Without respect for facts there is no respect for others. Still this does not imply that these others need to be known in every respect – insofar as such exhaustive human knowledge is possible at all. In fact, respect for fellow

human beings oftentimes implies 'leaving them out of account', at least in the sense of not unnecessarily personalizing discourse (see already rules 1 and 2). Discourse ought to be on the subject at hand in the first place, not on the persons involved in the discussion – unless these persons are the subjects of discussion themselves.

So do not look for who or even what somebody is as a possibly suspicious source of information, but look for good reasons behind statements made. Human beings may be moved by self- or even other-regarding motives to expression of whatever statements. Interesting or not in the end are these statements themselves and plausible arguments on their behalf. Only when such arguments are conspicuously absent, possibly mala fide (in bad faith), or simply uninformed by knowledge of relevant facts, may motives for making such statements become relevant. Therefore, 'Why do you state this?' if apposite at all ought to mean 'What are good reasons backing your statement?' in the first place and not 'What moves you to state this?'

Argumentation *ad verecundiam* (from authority) may be unavoidable at times. (Ask yourself how you know your date and place of birth: just the beginning of so much more 'second-hand knowledge'.) Such argumentation may not always do justice both to facts and to human beings. The treatment of the Turkish astronomer in *Le Petit Prince* is a moving case in point. His discoveries were taken seriously only after he changed his beautiful traditional dress for a business attire (according to De Saint-Exupéry 1943).

Be *ad rem* and *ad hominem* only if this is really relevant. So do not state 'You don't understand', but state something like 'This may be unclear' or even 'Excuse me for my unclarity'. This last statement is *ad hominem*, but self-related and thus not disrespecting others. And do not state 'You lie' unless there is overwhelming evidence for bad faith behind any demonstrably false statement. It is better to say: 'This may not be true, for this and that reason', or even 'I don't believe it but this may be my fault' and so on. Apart from such self-reference rightly motivated by modesty the ground rule is: *De nobis ipsis silemus* (On ourselves we are silent). Do not talk about yourself unless this is clearly *ad rem*, just as it is a good thing not to say too much in general (see already rule 3). Leave yourself out of the discussion unless you are the subject for good reasons.

Just as it is respectful to 'remove yourself' from any disagreement or even conflict not having to do with yourself and/or your personal relationships, so do not 'translate' any conflict on any business (*ad rem*) into deterioration of any politeness (wrongly *ad hominem*). This is not just respect for other human beings involved. It may also much facilitate fruitful solution of the conflict. This even applies to any discussion of personal qualities in any business-like context. You may be rightly or wrongly judged unfit for a job, however much you want it. But then in any discussion of it do not express negative emotions (and make good use of politeness as a shield against any such disturbing factors).

Do not take personally any impoliteness or even insult in any non-personal conflict. Others may vociferously express their disagreement with you against you. Do not react personally on it at all; try to solve the problem – which may be much helped by 'keeping yourself out of it' (see also Section 4).

If some or other conduct by some or other body is blameworthy, then address the body involved in the first place (again: *ad rem*) and not the person or persons representing the body (*ad hominem*). Thus state something like: 'The Public Prosecution Office in Amsterdam was mistaken in not prosecuting N.N. for cycling at the wrong side of the road at night'; and not 'Eelco De Bode again displayed his mistaken views on prosecution priorities in not having his Public Prosecution Office go after this misbehaving Hendrik Kaptein erring on his pushbike again' or something like it. Again: respecting somebody may imply 'leaving her or him out'.

Praise may still be bestowed on persons for their adequate or even supererogatory professional conduct – though they may be sufficiently dignified themselves to not look forward to that (see also rule 8).

All this relates to legal practice as well. Still, it is not fallaciously *ad hominem* to inquire into intellectual, mental and emotional qualities or even disorders of parties involved. One important issue here is examination of witnesses' credibility in court. Their statements cannot be fully verified independently (or their testimonies would be superfluous) so courts have to inquire into possible motives, intellectual, mental and emotional shortcomings and so on behind testimonies in order to (always unreliably) establish witnesses' credibility. (Try to do without them, as Hume (1963 [1777], section 10) famously explained.)

7. So 'the persons are better left out of the business and conflicts over it', however paradoxical this may sound. Still, sometimes something needs to be done about or even against the fellow human beings concerned, according to whatever values and norms are at hand. Then persons are to be respected according to the adage ***fortiter in re suaviter in modo***: be forceful and effective in the business itself but act on this as carefully as possible.

This may be translated in terms of the threefold imperative of priority, proportionality and subsidiarity. Or: first things first – again according to whatever are the norms and values at hand – 'no cannon against mosquitoes' and go for the least costly but still adequate means. In still simpler terms: do not overdo things against others if you do not really need to. Part of this respect for human dignity is expressed by: 'You can't control people unless you keep quiet yourself'. Winston Churchill endorsed a similar maxim (Arnavon 1944, 25): '*On ne règne sur les âmes que par le calme*' (We reign over hearts only by keeping calm).

Fortiter in re suaviter in modo is not just respectful and oftentimes a means of solving problems instead of aggravating them. It is also a practical expression of the truth of Kant's conception of man as an end in himself and never just a means. But then no more on this for now, as a practical guide on how to respect human dignity better shy away from too much ethical theory.

This principle is of overarching importance for any legal measures disadvantaging human beings concerned. Proportionality and subsidiarity have full priority here. Always try to realize law and right at the lowest possible cost for all concerned. This may be expensive but it is fully worth it.

8. One or even the most important application of *fortiter in re suaviter in modo* concerns **due apportionment of praise and blame**. As noted before (in Section 2), deliberate harm may be resented, while natural harm just hurts, however badly. So blame for wrongful harm may be unavoidable at times, but ought not to become something bad in itself – though this is too often the reality of irrational blame, as both a demonstration and a satisfaction of blamers' superiority, moral or otherwise.

Persons are no things in principle, in part because they may be praised and blamed for their conduct. This presupposes some or other autonomy, or at least the ability to do or not do something at will. (Kant one more time: nature happens according to laws; human beings act according to their conception of laws.) Praise and blame is respect for the human dignity of more or less autonomous persons, just as it is respect for persons to not blame them for any internally or externally unavoidable conduct or even bodily movement.

So praise fellow human beings for their good works, however near or far away they may be in social or whatever respects. Do not praise (or blame for that matter) human beings for their beauty or any other quality given to them, but praise them for their conduct. Great parts of the world thrive on supererogatory conduct furthering the common good but still more or less hidden from public and other views. Praise and reward may further such conduct, just as it is an important form of respect for actors concerned.

Endless varieties of harmful conduct, which may range from public crime to private misdemeanours, may still be better hidden from view, if only because perpetrators shun shame and sanctions. Still, evidence against ought to be conclusive, if any sanctions against them are to follow. Punishing (in whatever sense) somebody for something he did not do is a basic violation of human dignity. The same holds good for punishing anyone for conduct committed under some or other insuperable inward or outward compulsion – which may be more often the case than is oftentimes assumed.

Audi et alteram partem has pride of place here as well. Blaming somebody presupposes conclusive evidence on three issues: Who did it? What was done wrong? Was the actor liable for what he did? Results of properly hearing defendants (in a broad sense) may not at all be conclusive concerning evidence; still it is a basic presupposition of any measures against any suspects, defendants or even perpetrators.

So: *in dubio pro reo* (as already prescribed by the presumption of innocence: rule 2). But this may deeply disrespect victims (again in a broad sense), as they are entitled to recognition of harm done to them, just as they have rights to some or other compensation. So, go for other forms of solidarity with victims, among other things by trying to free them from their emotional (and sometimes material) dependence on wrongdoers against them.

Thus there is no human dignity without due praise and blame (for a fundamental explanation of this, see Strawson (1962 and 1983); see also Kaptein 2004). But always ask yourself whether you are the one to blame somebody else, and if so, what your blame really adds up to in terms of a better future. Unnecessary blaming easily degrades into humiliation by the false semblance of the blamers' superiority.

Your own conduct is to be the subject for rightful praise and blame as well of course. So do not go for any praise and do not occasion any blame as well as you can – whatever that may come down to according to the time and place – and by unconditionally offering apologies and reparation for anything done wrong 'as if nothing bad had happened after all': do not act as if nothing happened, but repair your own wrongs as if nothing happened. This is respect for victims, as well as it is self-respect in treating yourself as a responsible actor instead of as 'a tool of fate' or something like it. (On this, see Kaptein (2013 and 2018a), explaining the idea of compensation as restoration to the original unharmed position and its relationship to respect and self-respect.)

And do refrain from anything like tit for tat, however deeply engrained this resenting reaction may be in human nature. Though 'reacting in kind' may clarify misconduct for perpetrators by acting like a mirror in trivial cases, more often than not this tit for tat just adds to the already enormous amount of harm in the world (see Kaptein (2004) on issues of retribution and reparation).

And it probably goes without saying (again) that standards of right and wrong may not be and may not have been the same everywhere in the world. So praise and blame may follow upon different kinds and styles of conduct and misconduct as well, though praise and blame themselves may be well-nigh universal preconditions of human dignity.

Due expression of gratitude, at least so for supererogatory conduct towards yourself or to next of kin, is another important precondition for respecting human dignity. Indeed, in a sense gratitude is the counterpart to rightful resentment leading to blame and claims to compensation. (Discussion of interesting but complex relationships here is best left for another occasion.)

Last and whatever you do and do not do concerning praise, blame, gratitude and so on, go for a better future, here and now. So do not address the past at others' cost just for the past's sake, in terms of any so-called justice to be done. It does not make sense. This holds good for the 'backward-looking' retributive justice of compensation for harm as well. It ought to be directed to the undoing of harm, again here and now and for the future.

Offenders, however serious their crimes, remain human beings, entitled not just to politeness but to all conduct respecting their human dignity, certainly so if they made up for their wrongs.

9. Last – or better first and in fact implicit in all other precepts making up this manual – **do not humiliate**. Humiliation is a prime violation of human dignity, and this is more than mere tautology.

Humiliation is one of the great evils in the world, on a par with war, natural disasters, poverty, diseases and other inhumanities. These evils must be recognized as universal, whatever historical and local disagreements there may be on the ends of life, on morals, on God or gods or on whatever meaning and value in and outside human life – otherwise there is no basis for mutual respect and human dignity. (Thus 'universal' morality may not be merely procedural at all: on this, see Hampshire (2000) as well.)

So do not blame, shame and deride human beings for any lack of whatever qualities not completely in their own power. Do not at all disclose any personal knowledge of other people's potentially shameful qualities and circumstances, unless there is overriding need to do so in order to prevent really harmful wrong.

This is not at all limited to obvious physical and physiological shortcomings, of course. So many and oftentimes saddening mental and emotional defects are outside their subjects' control as well. Praise and blame ought to be strictly limited to products of free and deliberate conduct (as noted before, concerning rule 8).

Elevation by praise may be public or even ought to be. Blame ought to be private or at least limited to persons and bodies really concerned. So, for example, never blame subordinates in the presence of others having nothing to do with the issue at hand, as this is humiliation bereft of any sense of blame directed to a better future.

So, a fortiori, legal officials – and not just judges and not just because human beings are at their more or less full mercy in so many sometimes life-changing respects – ought never to humiliate anybody concerned, by addressing defendants 'as if they are already convicted' and thus blameworthy and in so many other ways wronging the relatively (sometimes absolutely) powerless.

Again: keep in mind that these nine rules are interrelated – interdependent in fact. They may be (and have been) expressed differently as well. Let this be no problem at all, as long as dignified conduct is still the result.

4. Guard Your Own Dignity (the Tenth Commandment)

So how do we realize this sound advice? Knowing that these nine basic rules are sensible precepts for respecting human dignity and knowing how to live up to them may not elicit dignified conduct by themselves. Even in relatively civilized societies populated by more or less civilized human beings so many external and internal factors may stand in the way. How do we still keep up this civilization, depending as it does in part on the dignity of our own conduct?

Externals first: remain undisturbed by – or at least do not express any disturbance upon – undignified behaviour by others. Staying calm and polite may even put an end to such misconduct. Why feel threatened and why act towards it in kind? Oftentimes impolite behaviour – or worse – is not meant against you personally at all, just as it is oftentimes motivated by fear more than by any real intention to hurt you in the first place. Unexpectedly polite and friendly reactions to any misconduct may well remove any remaining targets for insult and worse. At least in this sense, taking somebody seriously may imply not taking his adverse utterances seriously at all.

At least the gist of this has been stated here before (and elsewhere of course, incomparably so by Epictetus; see also Kaptein 2018b): remain undisturbedly polite in whatever circumstances, refrain from tit for tat and so on. Again: easier said than done. What kind of human beings are we to be, or to become, in order to be able to remain dignified in whatever circumstances, again apart from our personal and emotional lives?

What we need – not just as a precondition for dignified conduct – is something like Kant's 'self-esteem and inner dignity instead of dependence on others' opinions' (1803, 493: *Selbstschätzung und innere Würde statt der Meinung der Menschen*). Autonomy in this sense is not just insensitivity to others' impoliteness and worse, but independence from others' judgements of you – or of what you think others think of you. So do not brag in any sense. Be dignified by being 'outwardly undignified': no contradiction here. This is 'the internal secret of dignity' and not just of dignity of course but of being a human being.

This does not at all exclude openness to others' opinions and to the world of course. It may well be the other way round. The dignity of autonomy may lead to greater openness to others and to reality in general. Personal autonomy may also imply less fear for responsibility and thus to more adequate reactions to justified blame (and praise, see already rule 8).

This may not always be easily achievable. In fact, psychotherapy may here be more effective than any good hard thinking, philosophical or otherwise. This means accepting yourself for what you are and what you do, however much work on yourself still needs to be done, just as accepting others for who and what they are and do comes first, however much our and their conduct, as occasional passers-by or even as life-long next of kin, may be found wanting.

Too abstract? Ask yourself how you would like to be treated if you were that other person encountering you. This does not require mental and emotional identification with others. Quite to the contrary. I may treat others differently from what I might want from others, just because these other human beings are different (for more, and most interestingly, against psychological identification, see Camus (1951, 22)).

And – of course – have a good look in the mirror at times – not just because of 'what you do with others, you do with yourself'.

Quite a few legal conflicts may be avoided this way as well.

5. Conclusion: The Violet Smells to Him as It Doth to Me

So here are ten formal commandments hopefully still meaningful in a sometimes hopelessly divided world. These precepts are about how to live, about life. They do not depend on legal and other solemn declarations as impressive on paper as they are sterile or simply meaningless in the real world. We do not need to know what dignity 'really is', or what a human being 'really is' in the end – in as far as these are meaningful issues at all – in order to respect and further dignity in life. We even do not need to really know who a specific human being is in order to respect her. To the contrary: respect for somebody may imply abstaining from inquiry into anything personal.

Any positive or theoretical moral knowledge is not to be overestimated anyway: comprehending Kant's categorical imperative does not necessarily make one a better human being. (This holds good for this chapter as well, of course. So leave it behind, trying not to forget its message. Just regard it as an attempt to motivate you in right directions, not as any contribution to theoretical philosophy.)

As long as you do not generally respect your fellow human beings without further thought, there is still the minimal moral theory of the Golden Rule (already hinted at in Section 4): change positions and ask yourself 'What would you look forward to in terms of respecting your dignity?' Hobbes famously summarized all precepts for living together in 'Do not that to another, which thou wouldest not have done to thy self' (1651, part I, chapter 16), just as the same Golden Rule plays a main role in Rawls's theory of justice (as finally revised in 1999), however implicit.

In an academic setting (and in general education and upbringing), the example may be more important than any theory, at least concerning the realization of human dignity. This indeed is not the same as correcting fellow human beings in their supposed impoliteness or other trivial deviations from any ruling habits and customs.

In fact, this free (but far from cheap) enlightenment and advice on human dignity may require hard work at times but may still amply pay off. Setting the example may disarm potential opponents, elicit cooperation and heighten esteem for anybody displaying respect for others' dignity in the first place.

Just formal respect for dignity in terms of no more than our nine or in fact ten procedural commandments instead of confrontation may forestall so many deadly and not-so-deadly but still humanly costly conflicts. Humiliated human beings – or those just feeling humiliated – may go to any violent lengths in order to 'redress' their lost senses of self-respect.

Still these ten commandments are no more than fragments, however sensible of what is required for a really dignified human society or societies. These ten commandments are about what can be done here and now by ourselves, to immediate good effect. Really dignified society may require radical distribution of the good things in life worldwide, but that is another matter.

These ten commandments are no full manual for life anyway, let alone for (world) politics and public or not so public governance, though they are helpful in whatever circumstances. Still the ten formal commandments are compatible with different and conflicting views of the good life, of what society ought to be and of religion. Fanatics may not be convinced, but then they may not be convinced by any good reason. (Remember fanaticism's fertile ground in disrespect for human beings thus developing violent resentment against their oppressors, perceived or real.)

Issues of cultural relativism are not to be belittled, of course. But concerning human dignity in action the practical answer is: just give it a try, translating our practical recommendations into the languages of local customs and habits as well as you can, duly adapting your conduct in the process. The ten commandments need not be any expression of timeless wisdom in order to be humanly worthwhile here and now.

Rather more important than any more or less theoretical issues of cultural relativism is the really saddening fact that so many human beings do not live up to human dignity for others and for themselves, in so many different times and cultures, with so many dire consequences. Do not go along with this, even though it may feel like being an island of dignity in the turmoil of this world. On this island you are never alone.

The island of dignity may be expanded indefinitely at will, any time. This brings us back to the official behind the train counter in Cologne and the well-nigh universality of a friendly smile and ensuing politeness, eliciting a like reaction and supererogatory assistance and cooperation. It makes you less lonely, more happy and better equipped for any voyage in the world.

So stop reading and thinking for now. Further philosophy possibly behind these practical recommendations, to be developed in terms of reflective equilibrium or otherwise, is best left for another occasion. Here is the real summary for now (as already offered by Johnson in his 1755 dictionary quoted before):

> MAN: 1. Human being. The King is but a *man* as I am; the violet smells to him as it doth to me; the element shews to him as it doth to me, all his senses have but human conditions. *Shakespeare.*

Real dignity implies respecting no dignities at all.

References

Adams, Douglas. 1979. *The Hitchhiker's Guide to the Galaxy*. London: Pan Books.

Arnavon, Jacques. 1944. *W. Churchill ou ami de la France*. Paris: Les Éditions Universelles.

Beccaria, C. B. 1995 [1764]. *On Crimes and Punishments and Other Writings*. Edited by R. Bellamy. Translated by R. Davies, V. Cox and R. Bellamy. Cambridge: Cambridge University Press.

Camus, Albert. 1951. *L'Homme Révolté*. Paris: Editions Gallimard.

Epictetus, *Diatribai*. 1926 [± 100 AD]. *The Discourses as Reported by Arrian*. Edited by W. A. Oldfather. London: Loeb Classical Library, Heinemann.

Frankfurt, Harry G. 2006. *On Truth*. New York: Alfred A. Knopf.

Hampshire, Stuart. 2000. *Justice Is Conflict*. Princeton, NJ: Princeton University Press.

Hobbes, Thomas. 1651. *Leviathan, or the Matter, Forme, & Power of a Common-wealth Ecclesiasticall and Civill*. London: Andrew Crooke, at the Green Dragon in St. Pauls Churchyard.

Hölderlin, J. C. F. 1970 [± 1800]. 'Friedensfeier'. In *Sämtliche Werke*, vol. 2. Stuttgart: Kohlhammer.

Hume, David. 1963 [1777]. *Enquiries Concerning the Human Understanding and Concerning the Principles of Morals*, 2nd ed. Edited by L. A. Selby-Bigge. Oxford: Clarendon. Online Library of Liberty. https://oll.libertyfund.org/titles/341.

Johnson, Samuel. 1755. *A Dictionary Of The English Language: In Which The Words Are Deduced From Their Originals And Illustrated In Their Different Significations By Examples From The Best Writers. To Which Are Prefixed, A History Of The Language, And An English Grammar*. In two volumes. London: Printed by W. Strahan, for J. and P. Knapton; T. and T. Longman; C. Hitch and L. Hawes; A. Millar; and R. and J. Dodsley.

Kant, Immanuel. 1797. *Die Metaphysik der Sitten erster Teil: Metaphysische Anfangsgründe der Rechtslehre*. Königsberg: Friedrich Nicolovius. Also in *Kant's Werke*. 1907. Königlich Preussische Akademie der Wissenschaften, vol. VI. Berlin: Georg Reimer.

———. 1803. *Pädagogik*. In *Kant's Werke*, vol. IX.

Kaptein, Hendrik J. R. 2004. 'Against the Pain of Punishment: On Penal Servitude and Procedural Justice for All'. In *Crime, Victims and Justice: Essays on Principles and Practice*, edited by Hendrik J. R. Kaptein and Marijke Malsch, 80–111. Aldershot: Ashgate.

———. 2019. 'No Human Rights without Retribution: Plights and Promises of Redress As If Nothing Happened'. In *Legitimizing Human Rights: Secular and Religious Perspectives*, edited by Angus J. L. Menuge, 159–78. Farnham: Ashgate.

———. 2018a. 'Undoing Damage by Analogy: As If (Almost) Nothing Happened, with Notes on the Meaning of Everything'. In *Analogy and Exemplary Reasoning in Legal Discourse*, edited by Hendrik J. R. Kaptein and B. D. van der Velden, 137–64. Amsterdam: Amsterdam University Press.

———. 2018b. 'How to Make Room for God – in Man: Tracing Epictetus' Totality of Religious Freedom'. In *Religious Liberty and the Law: Theistic and Non-theistic Perspectives*, edited by Angus J. L. Menuge, 54–68. London: Routledge.

Kaptein, Hendrik J. R., H. Prakken and B. Verheij eds. 2009. *Legal Evidence and Proof: Statistics, Stories, Logic*. Farnham: Ashgate.

Melville, Herman. 1922–24. *Billy Budd, Foretopman* (before 1891). In H. Melville, *Works, Standard Edition*, Pequod ed., edited by R. M. Weaver. New York: A. & C. Boni.

Nussbaum, Martha. 1992. 'Human Functioning and Social Justice'. *Political Theory* 20, no. 2: 202–46.

Quine, Willard Van Orman. 1987. *Quiddities*. Cambridge, MA: Harvard University Press.

Rawls, John. 1999. *A Theory of Justice*, revised ed. Cambridge, MA: Belknap Press of Harvard University Press.

Sacks, Oliver W. 1984. *A Leg to Stand on*. New York: Simon & Schuster.

Saint-Exupéry, Antoine de. 1943. *Le Petit Prince*. New York: Harcourt, Brace & World.

Strawson, Peter F. 1962. 'Freedom and Resentment'. *Proceedings of the British Academy* 48: 1–25. Reprinted in Peter F. Strawson, *Freedom and Resentment, and Other Essays*. London: Methuen, 1974.

———. 1983. *Scepticism and Naturalism: Some Varieties*. The Woodbridge Lectures, no. 12. New York: Columbia University Press.

van Bruggen, Carry. 1919. *Prometheus*. Rotterdam: Nijgh en Van Ditmar's Uitgeversmaatschappij.

Wilson, N. L. 1959. 'Substances without Substrata'. *Review of Metaphysics* 12, no. 4: 521–39.

Wittgenstein, Ludwig J. 1921. 'Logisch-Philosophische Abhandlung'. *Annalen der Naturphilosophie* 14, 185–262.

Part II

COMPETING CONCEPTIONS OF HUMAN DIGNITY

Chapter Eight

TWO CONCEPTS OF DIGNITY: ON THE DECAY OF AGENCY IN LAW

Åsbjørn Melkevik and Bjarne Melkevik

1. Putting a Price on People's Lives and Getting a Good Bargain

In his book *What Money Can't Buy*, Michael Sandel (2012, 3–5) gave a number of compelling examples showing how, today, almost everything is up for sale. If one is so inclined, one can buy the right to immigrate to the United States ($500,000), the services of an Indian surrogate mother to carry a pregnancy ($6,250) or access to the carpool lane while driving solo ($8). Not only can one buy almost anything, but one can also make money in rather unusual ways. One can, for example, serve as a human guinea pig for a drug safety trial ($7,500), work for pay line-standing companies on Capitol Hill as some lobbyists are unwilling to queue up themselves ($15–25 per hour) or buy life insurances on the lives of strangers, and potentially make a fortune if one is lucky when betting on the misfortune of others.

Such an environment gives a whole new meaning to what the Roman dictator Appius Claudius Caecus once said, '*fabrum esse suae quemque fortunae*', that is, 'every man is the artisan of his own fortune' (Sallust 1921, 445). In fact, one can be the artisan of one's fortune by renting out space on one's forehead to display commercial advertising or by exhibiting oneself on some 'reality' television programmes. This is certainly not what any Roman meritocrat would have envisioned as an appropriate way to amass riches. Such phenomena are problematic, one could think, especially when we not only put a price on some unusual activities, but on human lives as well. This would be to go too far, one could argue. It would go against our understanding of human dignity following Kant.

Immanuel Kant (1993, 40) indeed told us that 'everything has either a price or a dignity. Whatever has a price can be replaced by something else as its equivalent; on the other hand, whatever is above all price, and therefore admits of no equivalent, has a dignity'. That one should be respected for one's own sake is a cornerstone of our modern societies, enshrined in our laws and constitutions. We can find such a conception of dignity, for example, in the Universal Declaration of Human Rights. Although we can distinguish between different interpretations of human dignity, the core idea following Kant is that people have some essential 'priceless' attributes, say their freedom, which are connected to duties, most important of which is a duty to oneself (Sensen 2015, 125).

The concept of dignity, therefore, has been, at least traditionally, an extension of the Enlightenment-era idea that people are the holders of inherent, inalienable rights. Yet that conclusion, we could think, contradicts how people operate in our market societies today. As Michael Jensen and William Meckling (1994, 10) noted, 'we all have a price', that is, 'Like it or not, individuals are willing to sacrifice a little of almost anything we care to name, even reputation or morality, for a sufficiently large quantity of other desired things; and these things do not have to be money or even material goods'. We therefore face a paradox – though enshrined in our modern constitutions, the Kantian concept of human dignity seems threatened by our modern way of life. In market societies, people put a price on what should otherwise be priceless, we may think – for example, their agency or their moral, physical or psychological integrity.

The present chapter explores this paradox, showing why it is not as problematic as one might think. The real problem, we argue, lies elsewhere. We should rather be concerned with how the supposed promotion of dignity has led to a certain decay of agency in law. To be more precise, we will examine two theories of dignity – namely the 'agency theory of dignity', which we can trace back to Kant, and the 'well-being theory of dignity', more recently championed by Alan Gewirth. The modern shift from the former to the latter, we argue, is problematic, first, inasmuch as it is an expression of the decay of agency in our legal systems, and, second, because the well-being theory of dignity is often self-defeating, hurting the well-being of the worst-off and lowering total welfare in society. In trying to reconcile market societies with human dignity, we have created a problem where none existed before. That is, we have taken away from the theoretical core of dignity, which was agency, to create the illusion of dignity as welfare, for example, in imposing some labour legislations restraining freedom.

We accordingly argue for two separate theses – first, we should go back to the agency theory of dignity, and, second, we should limit as much as possible the reach of the concept of dignity in our legal systems. That is, dignity should mainly be a philosophical concept, we argue, not a legal one. Inasmuch as legal philosophers want to make use of this concept, it should point towards a limit to the reach of public law in favour of private law. This is unfortunately the opposite of what we have witnessed in the past decades with the ever-increasing reach of public law. We begin (Section 2) by examining some problematic cases showing how markets regularly go against the value of dignity. Then, we distinguish four theories of dignity (Section 3). This will permit us to argue (in Section 4) for the agency theory of dignity and see how it connects to antinomianism, which makes people their own lawmakers. In the end (Section 5), we argue that the role of dignity should significantly be reduced in our legal systems.

2. Thank You for Smoking – How We Put a Price on People's Lives

Let us begin with some cases from the tobacco industry. A recent review, combining data from the World Health Organization, the United Nations Office on Drugs and Crime

Table 8.1 Public finance balance of smoking in the Philip Morris study

Positive Effects		Negative Effects
Direct	Indirect	
Excise tax	Healthcare cost savings	Increased healthcare costs
Value-added tax	Pensions savings	Lost income tax
Corporate income tax	Housing to elderly savings	Absenteeism-related costs
Customs duty		Smoke-induced fire costs
$522 million	$31 million	$403 million

and the Institute for Health Metrics and Evaluation, assessed the impact on human welfare of alcohol, tobacco and illicit drugs (Peacock et al. 2018). Following the World Health Organization, welfare was measured by calculating the loss of Disability-Adjusted Life Years (DALYs) – where one DALY can be thought as one lost year of 'healthy life'. Despite the high costs of illicit drugs in terms of human lives, tobacco and alcohol still came on top. In 2015, tobacco cost the world 170.9 million DALYs, alcohol 85 million DALYs and illicit drugs 27.8 million DALYs.

The methodology is straightforward – welfare is measured in terms of how much healthy life is lost without putting a monetary value on any specific person or condition. Of course, this is not how we usually proceed – it is common to ascribe different monetary values on various people with diverse conditions or social backgrounds. As troubling as it may be for our modern commitment to moral equality, some individuals are worth more. A common example would be the value insurance companies can put on people who travel by car or plane – it is much higher for the latter. This section shows how such differentiations in valuing life can be problematic inasmuch as we are committed to dignity in our legal systems. However, it is not as problematic as one might think.

Consider the study Philip Morris CR a.s. commissioned to Arthur D. Little in the Czech Republic (see Kmietowicz 2001, 126). After its leaking in 2001, it remains one of the most paradigmatic cases of a 'death benefit' argument. For every smoker, the study maintained, the state saves money (Table 8.1).

More precisely, smoking costs the Czech Republic budget 15,647 million CZK per year, that is, $403 million, while it brings in 20,270 million CZK in taxes ($522 million), as well as an additional 1,192 CZK ($31 million) in indirect savings. In the end, cigarette consumption benefits the Czech Republic, as the total public finance balance of smoking in 1999 amounted to 5,815 million CZK, or $150 million. Dying young is good for the budget. The 'Campaign for Tobacco-Free Kids' (2002) summarized well enough the argument of this report:

> The 'Death Benefit' Argument – i.e. governments should not invest in new efforts to reduce smoking and other tobacco use, since it is cheaper to let people die from smoking and other tobacco use than to pay the new costs caused by more people living longer because they quit using tobacco or because they never start.

Such an argument has been championed, for example, by William Kevin Viscusi (1997, 27): 'Some financial implications of smoking increase the costs to the states; other insurance effects decrease state budgetary costs. What matters is whether those net insurance consequences are positive or negative'. According to Viscusi, the consequences are positive. In the United States, if one ignores the excise taxes paid by smokers, every pack of cigarette brings a net cost saving of $0.32, and if one does not ignore the taxes, then that number jumps to $0.85. In other words, cigarettes are self-financing – since their benefits exceed the higher medical care costs they bring.

As one would expect, such an argument was met with overwhelming condemnation, and the many critics were quick to take apart the report on economic, political and ethical grounds. Economically, the core assumption of the study is flawed. If smokers would stop smoking, they would simply buy other goods with the money they would have spent on tobacco products. These other things would also be taxed, though, conceivably, they would not produce the same harmful effects. Rather than saving $150 million per year at the time of the study, some argued, smoking drained about $373 million from the annual budget of the Czech Republic (see Ross 2004; and Bates 2001).

Politically, this is a textbook case of the McNamara fallacy for which a given decision is justified solely by some quantitative observations, while ignoring all other relevant factors. The US Secretary of Defense Robert McNamara had already committed such a mistake when he measured success in the Vietnam War in terms of enemy body count, while ignoring some other factors equally relevant for winning a war.

Ethically, the study goes against our liberal values, especially dignity. Dianne Feinstein (2001), a US senator, noted how 'Philip Morris has stepped well-past the lines of decency and demonstrated, once again, that it conducts business in a manner completely disconnected from any sense of right and wrong'. Indeed, provided we care about dignity, this study illustrates what we should not do.

Yet it is easy to find similar cases in the construction industry or in the field of zoning regulation. For example, though some materials in houses may be harmful to people, even deadly, they are used because they are cheaper or easier to install than other materials. Our societies often tacitly accept such cases, since it is cheaper to let some people die. Pushed to its extreme, however, the argument becomes ludicrous. One could argue that we should not invest in research to cure some illnesses that disproportionally kill people at the end of their productive years. This cost-effectiveness method obviously misses quite a few things – for example, a society may consider the kinds of cost it is ready to shoulder, and it is far from obvious that we should prefer healthcare costs to costs associated with people living longer and healthier lives, such as social security payments.

But these cases should remind us of one thing – we do indeed put a price on people's lives. As much as dignity may be a core feature of our modern liberal democracies, the fact remains that we put a price on people's lives. This can be observed in all areas of society. Different people are ascribed different values, depending on the kind of activities they engage in. This is a common practice. A brief look at the literature is enough to see

Table 8.2 Different values of a statistical life in different studies

Year of Study and Article	Value of a Statistical Life (in 2012$)
1997 – C. R. Scotton and L. O. Taylor. 2011. 'Valuing Risk Reductions: Incorporating Risk Heterogeneity into a Revealed Preference Framework'. *Resource and Energy Economics* 33, no. 2: 381–97.	8.04M
2002 – J. D. Leeth and J. Ruser. 2003. 'Compensating Wage Differentials for Fatal and Nonfatal Injury Risks by Gender and Race'. *Journal of Risk and Uncertainty* 27, no. 3: 257–77.	8.90M
1998 – M. F. Evans and G. Schaur. 2010. 'A Quantile Estimation Approach to Identify Income and Age Variation in the Value of a Statistical Life'. *Journal of Environmental Economics and Management* 59, no. 3: 260–70.	9.85M
2000 – W. K. Viscusi and J. Hersch. 2008. 'The Mortality Cost to Smokers'. *Journal of Health Economics* 27, no. 4: 943–58.	9.86M
1997 – W. K. Viscusi. 2003. 'Racial Differences in Labor Market Values of a Statistical Life'. *Journal of Risk and Uncertainty* 27, no. 3: 239–56.	21.65M
1997 – T. J. Kniesner, W. K. Viscusi and J. P. Ziliak. 2006. 'Life-Cycle Consumption and the Age-Adjusted Value of Life'. *Contributions to Economic Analysis and Policy* 5, no. 1: 1–34.	36.17M

how the Value of a Statistical Life (VSL)[1] differs when we use different criteria, such as smoking, race or gender (Table 8.2). It is not the case, therefore, that a human life 'admits of no equivalent'.

One may think this trend deeply troubling, but one should not. Governments, courts and businesses regularly put a price on people's lives, and, in the process, they consider them as means. Valuing life is an important part of public decision-making today, as utilitarian considerations now occupy a large space in the public sphere. One may notice an additional point – people themselves put different values on their lives, at least implicitly. This can be observed, for instance, in their willingness to pay for reductions in mortality risks.

With the Kantian theory of dignity, we may remember, comes duties towards others and to oneself. Smoking itself could be understood as a failure of one's duty to oneself, as one must know that such an activity is likely to cripple oneself. The same goes for people who work jobs with a likelihood of long-term physical degeneration. These could be understood as going against human dignity, inasmuch as they fail to properly respect persons' inherent worth, and they may cripple their long-term decision-making ability. If we are committed to upholding dignity, we could think, it may then be important to

---

[1]   The Value of a Statistical Life is not the price a given individual would pay to avoid dying, nor the actual value of a human life, but rather an estimate of willingness to pay for small reductions in mortality risks.

legislate in those areas where dignity is lost. This has been the recurring argument of our modernity, though, as the next sections show, it is also a dangerous approach.

3. Four Theories of Dignity – On Value, Honour, Agency and Welfare

The examples we gave about what appears to be a coordinated assault on dignity in our market societies could be complemented with many more. We should not underestimate the extent to which, for example, the labour market today is encroaching on human dignity. We must nonetheless, this section argues, resist the modern call to legislate on everything dignity related. In fact, we should not legislate to preserve people's dignity. Ever. One may think such a proposition radical, especially as we remember how dignity is constitutive of our modernity, say through the Universal Declaration of Human Rights. But the proposal becomes much less extreme once we consider how we can establish a distinction between different conceptions of dignity. The problem, we argue, is that these conceptions have been confused with one another, though they lead us to different policy conclusions. Let us distinguish four theories, without any claim to exclusivity – three are from Kant, the fourth is from Gewirth.

1. The Value beyond Price Theory of Dignity – that is, according to Kant, there is an intrinsic non-negotiable non-fungible worth that inheres in every human being by virtue of his or her moral capacity (see Waldron 2012, 24; and Dworkin 2006, 9).
2. The Honour Theory of Dignity – that is, a man of honour, says Kant, will treat his independence and self-esteem as being above any price, such that it cannot be traded for the sake of any material interest (see Anderson 2008). Such a theory can be traced back to Aristotle for whom dignity referred to the respect due to those of high rank as well as the duties of holding a higher-ranking role (see Sangiovanni 2017, 16).
3. The Agency Theory of Dignity – that is, based on their capacity for free will, Kant argues, people possess dignity, and they are therefore to be regarded as ends in themselves, never as means. Such dignity means that we should endorse strong negative duties, such as 'do not kill', but not positive duties, such as duties of welfare (see White 2009, 84f.).
4. The Well-Being Theory of Dignity – that is, dignity, says Gewirth (1992, 12), is 'a kind of intrinsic worth that belongs equally to all human beings as such, constituted by certain intrinsically valuable aspects of being human'. From this dignity, in turn, we can derive rights not only of negative freedom, but also duties of well-being towards others that all people and the state must equally recognize and support (Lutz 1999, 471f.).

The first three theories can all be found in Kant's works, and therefore they are not to be understood as necessarily inimical to one another. Yet the third definition, we maintain, is the most interesting one. The other theories, in the end, are not entirely satisfying to understand the relation between law and dignity.

First, the value beyond price theory goes against the very act of legislating. There must be some negotiable value to human life, without which we simply could not legislate. In zoning regulation, for instance, we must always consider the possibility of externalities, some of which may be deadly – say for industrial equipment. As *Powell v. Fall* (5 Q.B. 597 (1880)) established, 'It is just and reasonable that if a person uses a dangerous machine, he should have to pay for the damage which it occasions; if the reward which he gains for the use of the machine will not pay for the damage, it is mischievous to the public and ought to be suppressed'. In other words, though we may want to limit the number of accidents as much as possible, the legislator will have to pay special attention to inefficient accidents. Those will be the accidents that cost less to prevent than preventing them is worth, as David Friedman (2000, 197f.) explains. For such a determination to be made, we must be able to establish a value for the life of the people. The same goes for budgetary considerations – for example, whether a hospital should buy a new and expensive device that can save a very limited number of lives. The value beyond price theory of dignity does not permit us to do that, and accordingly it is more a philosophical theory than something legislators or lawyers can use in their daily practice.

Second, as appealing as a universalizing theory of honour may be, it fails to capture the reality of many people, especially those who are more disadvantaged. The labour market often requires of employees to let go of their self-esteem in exchange for remuneration. They can, for example, be forbidden to pee, as they must work long hours without interruption, or commanded to pee, like athletes, or asked to dress in some unusual ways. That people consent to such agreements should not necessarily be understood as undignified, as it may be essential for feeding their family. Nor is it always undignified for employers to ask for such things. This theory is accordingly unsatisfactory, if only because it cannot be used in a modern market society. Honour is a moral ideal, and it is not appropriate as a constitutive principle of law. It also fails to grasp the challenges of pursuing one's understanding of the good life, especially for underprivileged people who may put subsistence before their honour.

Third, and more interestingly for our purpose, Kant's (1993, 36) theory of dignity as agency is intimately connected to the version of his categorical imperative which goes as follows: 'Act in such a way that you treat humanity, whether in your own person or in the person of another, always at the same time as an end and never simply as a means'. Free will, that is, the capacity for self-determination or autonomy, implies that people have a right to act free of interference or domination, and therefore such a theory falls in with classical liberalism in defending a more modest, if not minimal, function for the state. Of course, different readings of Kant can lead one to different theories. It can lead, for instance, to giving a greater role to the state, which is what Gewirth did. But the traditional reading of Kant is that negative duties derive from dignity – not positive ones.

The key premise, free will, must be read in relation to the 'positive' conception of freedom Kant defended – not to be confused with the similar notion put forward by Isaiah Berlin. With this concept of freedom, Kant reminds us that people are to live by rules which are their own. 'What else, then,' wrote Kant (1993, 49), 'can freedom of the will be but autonomy, i.e., the property that the will has of being a law to itself?' Kant thus understood the will as being 'in every action a law to itself', which implied the above categorical imperative.

From such a premise, Kant derived human rights as well as interpersonal and personal duties. Once we get there, however, it is easy to forget the core intuition behind dignity – namely that rational people are to be their own lawmaker. Their rationality should lead them to subject themselves to the moral laws, or so Kant argues. But within such an understanding of morality, it is for the people themselves to pursue their endogenous preferences and values. 'Reduced to its essentials', said Timothy Roth (2002, 74) on the Kantian enterprise, 'individuals should be free to pursue their objectives – whatever they may be – subject to the constraints imposed by respect for rights and by just or impartial institutions'. To leave individuals free to pursue their own ends and values, therefore, is a requirement of that understanding of human dignity. We will come back to this idea of agency in the next section to explore its consequences.

Fourth, as it has been noticed before, Gewirth's theory may be Kantian in inspiration, but not in execution (White 2009, 85). The theory also takes human agency as its starting point, such that rights arise from dignity because people possess a capacity for self-determination. But it is generally more focused on positive obligations that both individuals and the state have towards the well-being of everyone else. It is such a theory that now animates most of the discussions around dignity and human rights.

Article 23.1 of the Universal Declaration of Human Rights, as well as article 6 of the International Covenant on Economic, Social and Cultural Rights, for example, both recognize a 'right to work', which includes, among others, a right for people to choose whether they want to work, where they want to work and to join a work union. Article 24, moreover, assumes a 'right to rest and leisure' on grounds of human dignity. For some scholars, say Mark Lutz (1999) or David Ellerman (1990), such a theory is also used to question the morality of the current labour system because labour is supposedly used as a means for capital (in contrast, see White 2008). It is also used to criticize welfare economics and the rational economic man, both of which are in theory characterized by instrumentality.

Policymakers have generally followed this fourth theory of dignity to shape or reshape our modern societies. We now often assume that upholding people's dignity involves positive duties, not just from the state, but also from individuals. The International Covenant on Economic, Social and Cultural Rights, for instance, assumes that people have a collective positive duty to help other members of their society secure job opportunities. We are then quite far from Kant's theory of agency. It is now assumed that to properly respect others we must assist them. But the equivalence between respect and assistance, we argue, is dangerous from a legal point of view.

Though we may agree that respect is a moral requirement, it is much less clear that we should equally offer assistance to others. In fact, as much as laws and constitutions are eager to recognize the value of dignity, they have been much less inclined to recognize a duty of assistance. The House of Lords, for example, ruled that 'when a person has done nothing to put himself in any relationship with another person in distress or with his property mere accidental propinquity does not require him to go to that person's assistance. There may be a moral duty to do so, but it is not practical to make it a legal duty' (*Home Office v. Dorset Yacht Co.*, [1970] AC 1004, [1970] UKHL 2). Changing the meaning of dignity, then, may be a way to sneak in some positive duties in the law that were otherwise repudiated. The problem is that in so doing we further the decay of the concept of agency in law.

4. Inasmuch as Dignity Is Autonomy, It Cannot Be a Principle of Law

Now that we have established a distinction between four understandings of dignity, we must explain how radical Kant's theory of agency really is, and how it can lead us to an antinomian legal philosophy. Rational people are to be their own lawmaker, not just in a metaphorical way, we argue. The scope of legislative activity should be limited as a matter of dignity. This section will then disagree with Jeremy Waldron (2012, 13ff), who made dignity 'a principle of law'. Inasmuch as dignity is autonomy (see Macklin 2003), it cannot be a principle of law. It is rather a principle to restrain law. In fact, the definition of dignity Kant gave in the *Grounding for the Metaphysics of Morals* must be read in relation to the provocative passage 'On Servility' in 'The Metaphysics of Morals' (1999, 558f). In this section, Kant gives the following examples for our 'duty with reference to the dignity of humanity within us':

> Be no man's lackey. – Do not let others tread with impunity on your rights. – Contract no debt for which you cannot give full security. [...] – Kneeling down or prostrating oneself on the ground, even to show your veneration for heavenly objects, is contrary to the dignity of humanity, as is invoking them in actual images; for you then humble yourself, not before an ideal represented to you by your own reason, but before an idol of your own making. (558–59)

The first line is especially interesting. It shows that the autonomy at the heart of human dignity provides people with rights. Because people are autonomous, their standing with regard to any system of law must be premised upon their inalienable rights. They are not to be anyone's lackey, nor are they to bow or kneel down before others. The lawmaker's authority to legislate is often incompatible with this idea of self-determination.

Here, we are building on Kant's theory, not simply repeating it. But the intuition remains nonetheless Kantian – 'Bowing and scraping before a human being seems in any case to be unworthy of a human being' (Kant 1999, 559). Taking seriously the idea of dignity in law, therefore, may point towards a certain emancipation of the individual capacity for judgement. Against the 'propensity to servility' we can find in human beings, as Kant noted, the concept of dignity should lead us to a certain antinomian legal philosophy.[2]

Antinomianism, from the Greek αντι and νομος, meaning 'against the law', is a form of individualist anarchism that puts people above the law. It was first a theological

---

[2] Autonomy must be reconciled with other values, say with efficiency in business organizations or the military. We accordingly do not argue for antinomianism tout court. Such a philosophy is to be valued only to the extent that autonomy is as well, as opposed to other commitments we may have.

doctrine pejoratively named for its rejection of the requirement of obedience to the Law of Moses. In legal philosophy, however, it now refers to a theory for which one will not obey any set of rules with which one disagrees. Such a view is commonly opposed to 'legalism', which overemphasizes the requirement of obedience to the letter of the law.

In Christian theology, legalism and antinomianism were respectively an accusation of overzealous adherence to the Mosaic Law or an accusation of lawlessness. Two famous antinomian controversies defined the latter view – one in Wittenberg, in 1538, which opposed Martin Luther to Johannes Agricola, and a second one, exactly a century later, in the Massachusetts Bay Colony, which led to the banishment of Anne Hutchinson from Boston. Both incidents were prompted by Christians who believed that moral laws were not inevitably binding.

For Agricola of Eisleben, for example, salvation was to be achieved through faith, not compliance with the law. As Saint Paul said, 'For as many as are of the works of the law are under the curse' (Gal. 3:10) and 'the law entered, that the offence might abound' (Rom. 5:20; see also Waldron 2006). Luther condemned the antinomian reading of the Scriptures, even though his own teachings also bolstered the ideal of self-governance, which antinomians championed. 'Thus you are your own Bible, your own teacher, your own theologian, and your own preacher', wrote Luther (1958, 236f.). 'Just guide yourself by this, and you will be more wise and learned than all the skill and all the books of the lawyers' (ibid.). The Protestant doctrine of justification by faith alone, *sola fide*, has also been charged with antinomianism for its hostility towards the Law and its defiance of arbitrary moral rules.

Beyond these theological controversies, antinomianism is now a secular theory as well, popularized, for example, by George Orwell or Eric Hobsbawm. The latter wrote that the twentieth century was epitomized by an 'antinomian rebellion' (1995, 16). To the question 'should we obey the law?', antinomianism firmly answers 'no'. One should never obey anything but one's own conscience. Antinomians believe in the justification of any conformity to the law, such that any compliance is to be motivated by individual deliberation, not by the authority of the law. Although they will often comply with the law, antinomians think that they are fundamentally free from it. No one can be made to obey any law. It is a matter of private conscience. Therefore, antinomianism challenges the Latin dictum '*omnes legum servi sumus ut liberi esse possumus*', that is, 'we are all servants of the laws in order that we may be free'. Freedom precedes and supersedes the law, according to antinomianism, and for that reason it can never be defined by legalistic righteousness.

Kant's theory of dignity as autonomy resonates with this legal philosophy. 'But one who makes himself a worm,' said Kant (1999, 559), 'cannot complain afterwards if people step on him'. The point of both Kant's theory and antinomianism is that one should never make oneself a mere servant. One should remain one's own lawmaker and comply with others' laws only to the extent that one can justify those laws to oneself. Dignity is then a matter of self-determination. To properly respect oneself, one should follow one's conscience and not blindly follow the commandments of others. In a way, this theory of dignity is also a plea to believe in the responsibility of people to manage their own lives.

'The less the state interferes with industry', said the Supreme Court of Maine (1871) 'the less it directs and selects the channels of enterprise, the better. There is no safer rule than to leave to individuals the management of their own affairs'. People know how to pursue their own objectives better than the state does. Though that may not always be the case, since, after all, some people smoke until they kill themselves, it is generally a good principle for the law to pursue – both for self-determination and for efficiency purposes. To make people responsible for their own actions is then a way to respect their dignity. Thomas Hill Jr. (1992) indeed argued that to uphold Kantian dignity, people must be able to develop their capacity to act on reason and on the basis of prudence or efficiency and their capacity to develop their own goals. Dignity then becomes an ethics of personal responsibility. Antinomianism furthers such an ethics as it asks everyone to be their own lawmaker. In this case, no deference is given to the law, and the question of obedience is reformulated in terms of acquiescence.

The process of following the rules is then governed by individual rationality. The advantage is that people are made responsible for their own life story. This is the second principle of dignity Ronald Dworkin discussed in his book *Is Democracy Possible Here?* (2006) – the first being the value beyond price theory of dignity. The 'principle of personal responsibility', said Dworkin 'holds that each person has a special responsibility for realizing the success of his own life, a responsibility that includes exercising his judgment about what kind of life would be successful for him. He must not accept that anyone else has the right to dictate those personal values to him or impose them on him without his endorsement' (10). In other words, people have a 'sovereign responsibility' over their own life story, which can never be taken away from them, nor should it be given to anyone. A subordinated life, it is argued, is undignified.

Nothing that has been said, however, means that we should reject any legislative activity coming from the state, nor that we should remain indifferent to the plight of others. There are other important values on which our societies are built, and therefore we will have to balance our commitments to dignity with, for example, the values of liberty, equality and efficiency. These values will most likely make us endorse some form of liberalism because of liberty; some market institutional design, because of Marshall efficiency; and a certain welfare state, because of equality. Dignity itself, though, we argue, points towards a limit to the reach of public law. Yet, as we noted before, this is the opposite of what we have witnessed in the past decades. The ever-increasing reach of public law is a problem inasmuch as it goes against Kantian positive freedom – people must act from laws that they made themselves. Acting autonomously, guided by one's own conscience, is a demonstration of our capacity to act with dignity, Denis Arnold and Norman Bowie noted (2003, 229). Do we, for example, need laws prohibiting 'super-size' sodas? Probably not.

Acting with dignity is also about being responsible for one's own failures. If one smokes, it may lead to an early death. Owning such failures is as important as the ability to define how one wants to succeed in life. It is true that the state should provide some autonomy-enhancing laws, for example, to deal with problems of addiction. But save for such cases in which autonomy is compromised, the law must respect individual autonomy.

As Dworkin (2006, 18) said, Americans often 'take pride in marching to the beat of their own drum, of following no one else's lead, of doing it their way'. Many will fail, that is, they will not live their most fulfilling lives. Our commitment to equality should then incite us to have welfare institutions, which may include a floor below which nobody needs to descend. Yet dignity requires that people might fail. Not being subordinated to others means owning your successes as much as your failures.

We can now see why the concept of dignity cannot be a principle of law at large, contrary to what Waldron argued. The ethics of dignity, namely of people exercising their own capacity for self-determination, their agency if you will, is an ethics of responsibility. Individuals are responsible for their own life choices. They are responsible for the contracts they draft or for the loans they take. Catholics may recognize the pope as having some authority over their religious beliefs, and citizens may recognize some authority for the state to legislate over some matters. The authority given in those cases, however, will only be epistemic, as Dworkin (2006, 19) noted, or maybe prudential. People remain their own masters, and therefore they do not give anyone the authority to compel deference.

This agency theory of dignity cannot be a principle of law as a whole. If we follow it, we should rather limit the scope of public law to provide individuals with more opportunities to exercise their autonomy, say through private law. Of course, people cannot decide everything on their own, and therefore we still need some laws, if only a minimal legal framework. For example, one cannot unilaterally decide what one owns or whether one can kill people. Other important values for our societies make those choices fall outside the scope of personal responsibility. Antinomianism is not anarchism. Yet it is nonetheless important to understand how the concept of dignity should be used, and in which direction it should be taking our institutions. As the law compels deference, dignity cannot be a principle of law since it rather requires of people to be their own sovereign lawmaker and write their own story.

5. A Liberal Society Must Be Built around the Agency Theory of Dignity

It is rather common to engage in a budgetary line of questioning that would ask how much money we are ready to spend to save a certain group of people, such as smokers, diabetics or people who need dialysis. It is easy to think that therein lies the problem for autonomy in our societies. John Stuart Mill (1936, 8), for instance, reminded us that 'in propriety of classification the people of a country are not to be counted in its wealth. They are that for the sake of which wealth exists. The term "wealth" is wanted to denote the desirable objects which they possess, not inclusive of, but in contradiction to, their own persons'. In other words, according to Mill, it would be a category mistake to ascribe value to a life, because value can only measure that which is owned by some people. One could then argue, along with Gewirth, that people have a duty to support others who have no such wealth. Provided the law takes such an ideal of dignity seriously, we would have to give a proper legal form to some duties of well-being towards others. We have defended a fundamentally different understanding of dignity.

The best way to pursue dignity as agency is often to not legislate – let the people be their own masters. '*Cessante ratione legis cessat ipsa lex*', that is, 'when the reason for the law ceases, the law itself ceases'. Antinomianism is an individualistic understanding of such a Roman maxim according to which the only valid reasons for any law are those individuals come up with themselves. Unlike most anarchists, however, antinomians will not advocate for the abolition of the state. Inasmuch as the rules are agreeable to most people, they will generally be respected. A Kantian understanding of such a philosophy, we argued, challenges the common discourse on dignity. Dignity is a philosophical concept. It begins with the idea of free will from which it then derives an ethics of responsibility.

On the other hand, the current uses of dignity we can find characteristically defended by the International Covenant on Economic, Social and Cultural Rights, which emphasizes positive duties, for example, 'in assisting persons to have freedom and well-being when they cannot attain these by their own efforts' (Gewirth 1986, 33). Whether such duties are worthwhile objectives for our societies is an open question. We should not, however, try to sneak in some duties by artificially linking them to the concept of dignity. One may think such a scheme praiseworthy, but it is probably a mistake. In the end, it weakens both the concept of dignity, which then justifies too many duties to be taken seriously, and those duties themselves, which now have a puzzling justificatory story linking them to dignity.

One does not help the dignity of others by preventing them from working in a tough but fair job. Quite the opposite, it takes away their ability to define their understanding of the good life and to pursue it. Many so-called problems of dignity are more appropriately understood as problems, say, of equality or fairness. Perhaps it is a sign of our times that the value of dignity is now used to justify them. The concept may be more popular. We should nonetheless be careful, especially now that the concept of dignity is enshrined in so many constitutions and global declarations. Of course, we do not want to live in a world full of indignities. But we should not take it upon ourselves to create imaginary indignities.

It is true that some people can make the wrong choices – say, smoking. We know that smoking can lead to an early death and to serious health problems, many of which will considerably lower one's quality of life, and maybe even compromise one's ability to plan rationally in the future. We believe, however, that as the concept of dignity leads us to an ethics of responsibility, it is important for people to own their failures. At least, people should be able to fail, that is, able to try to pursue their good life. Over-legislating in the name of dignity could make this pursuit harder for some people, for example, poorer people. As for problems of discrimination, inequality or exploitation, they should be solved by using the appropriate reference point – which is not dignity, but rather such values as equality, equity or fairness. The way we arrive at some conclusion matters.

In conclusion, we argued that we should go back to the agency theory of dignity. Using an antinomian reading of Kant's theory, we maintained that rational people are to be their own lawmakers. That is, they have to act from laws they themselves made. The scope of any legislative activity should accordingly be limited as a matter of dignity. On the other hand, we also argued that the role of dignity should be reduced in our laws. Dignity cannot be a principle of law, as it is rather a principle of responsibility.

References

Anderson, Elizabeth. 2008. 'Emotions in Kant's Later Moral Philosophy: Honor and the Phenomenology of Moral Value'. In *Kant's Ethics of Virtue*, edited by Monika Betzler, 123–46. New York: de Gruyter.

Arnold, Denis G., and Norman E. Bowie. 2003. 'Sweatshops and Respect for Persons'. *Business Ethics Quarterly* 13, no. 2: 221–42.

Arthur D. Little International, Inc. 2000. 'Public Finance Balance of Smoking in the Czech Republic'. Commissioned by Philip Morris CR a.s.

Bates, Clive. 2001. 'Study Shows That Smoking Costs 13 Times More Than It Saves'. *British Medical Journal* 323, no. 7319: 1003.

Campaign for Tobacco-Free Kids. 2002. 'Immorality and Inaccuracy of the Death Benefit Argument', 28 October. Archived at: https://web.archive.org/web/20110725101846/http://www.tobaccofreekids.org/research/factsheets/pdf/0036.pdf.

Dworkin, Ronald. 2006. *Is Democracy Possible Here?* Princeton, NJ: Princeton University Press.

Ellerman, David. 1990. *The Democratic Worker-Owned Firm*. Boston, MA: Unwin Hyman.

Feinstein, Dianne. 2001. 'Letter to Geoffrey Bible, Chief Executive Officer of Philip Morris Companies, Inc.' In *Truth Tobacco Industry Documents*. University of California San Francisco.

Friedman, David. 2000. *Law's Order*. Princeton, NJ: Princeton University Press.

Gewirth, Alan. 1986. 'Human Rights and the Workplace'. *American Journal of Industrial Medicine* 9: 31–40.

———. 1992. 'Human Dignity as the Basis of Rights'. In *The Constitution of Rights: Human Dignity and American Values*, edited by Michael J. Meyer and W. A. Parent, 10–28. Ithaca, NY: Cornell University Press.

Hill, Thomas Jr. 1992. *Dignity and Practical Reason in Kant's Moral Theory*. Ithaca, NY: Cornell University Press.

Hobsbawm, Eric. 1995. *Age of Extremes: The Short Twentieth Century*. London: Abacus.

Jensen, Michael, and William Meckling. 1994. 'The Nature of Man'. *Journal of Applied Corporate Finance* 7, no. 2: 4–19.

Kant, Immanuel. 1993. *Grounding for the Metaphysics of Morals*. Translated by James W. Ellington. Indianapolis, IN: Hackett.

———. 1999. 'The Metaphysics of Morals'. In *Practical Philosophy*, translated by Mary J. Gregor, 353–604. Cambridge: Cambridge University Press.

Kmietowicz, Zosia. 2001. 'Tobacco Company Claims That Smokers Help the Economy'. *British Medical Journal* 323, no. 7305: 126.

Luther, Martin. 1958. *Works*, vol. 21. St. Louis, MO: Concordia.

Lutz, Mark A. 1999. 'Human Dignity'. In *Encyclopedia of Political Economy*, edited by Phillip Anthony O'Hara, 471–72. London: Routledge.

Macklin, Ruth. 2003. 'Dignity Is a Useless Concept'. *British Medical Journal* 327, no. 7429: 1419–20.

Mill, John Stuart. 1936. *Principles of Political Economy*. London: Longmans, Green.

Peacock, Amy, Janni Leung, Sarah Larney, Samantha Colledge, Matthew Hickman, Jürgen Rehm, Gary A. Giovino, Robert West, Wayne Hall, Paul Griffiths, Robert Ali, Linda Gowing, John

Marsden, Alize J. Ferrari, Jason Grebely, Michael Farrell and Louisa Degenhardt. 2018. 'Global Statistics on Alcohol, Tobacco, and Illicit Drugs Use: 2017 Status Report'. *Addiction* 113: 1905–26.

Ross, Hana. 2004. 'Critique of the Philip Morris Study of the Cost of Smoking in the Czech Republic'. *Nicotine & Tobacco Research* 6, no. 1: 181–89.

Roth, Timothy. 2002. *The Ethics and the Economics of the Minimalist Government.* Cheltenham: Edward Elgar.

Sallust. 1921. *Ad Caesarem Senem de Re Publica Oration (Speech to Caesar, In His Old Age, on the State).* London: William Heinemann.

Sandel, Michael. 2012. *What Money Can't Buy.* New York: Farrar, Straus and Giroux.

Sangiovanni, Andrea. 2017. *Humanity without Dignity: Moral Equality, Respect, and Human Rights.* Cambridge, MA: Harvard University Press.

Sensen, Oliver. 2015. 'Kant on Human Dignity Reconsidered'. *Kant-Studien* 106, no. 1: 107–29.

Supreme Court of Maine. 1871. *Opinion of the Justices,* 58 Me. 598 (1871).

Viscusi, William Kevin. 1997. 'From Cash Crop to Cash Cow: How Tobacco Profits State Governments'. *Regulation* 20, no. 3: 27–32.

Waldron, Jeremy. 2006. 'Dead to the Law: Paul's Antinomianism'. *Cardozo Law Review* 28, no. 1: 301–32.

———. 2012. *Dignity, Ranks, and Rights.* Oxford: Oxford University Press.

White, Mark D. 2008. 'Social Law and Economics and the Quest for Dignity and Rights'. In *The Elgar Companion to Social Economics,* edited by John Davis and Wilfred Dolfsma, 575–94. Cheltenham: Edward Elgar.

———. 2009. 'Dignity'. In *Handbook of Economics and Ethics,* edited by Jan Peil and Irene van Staveren, 84–90. Cheltenham: Edward Elgar.

Chapter Nine

HUMAN DIGNITY AS LAW'S FOUNDATION: AN OUTLINE FOR A PERSONALIST JURISPRUDENCE

Michał Rupniewski

Introduction

Numerous appeals to human dignity in legal texts and jurisprudence, strongly marking the global development of law after the Universal Declaration of Human Rights from 1948 (hereinafter the UDHR), are an evident fact.[1] However, the manifold context in which the law calls forth dignity, as well as different legal effects that human dignity is considered to have, may appear puzzling indeed. To make a terribly long story terribly short: in certain cases, human dignity is considered the source of rights (e.g. Article 30 in the Constitution of the Republic of Poland); in others, it is proclaimed explicitly as a separate right itself (as in Article 5 of the African Charter on Human and Peoples' Rights). The normative content of this right, however, is ambiguous. Whereas sometimes it protects the individual against the interference of the state such as degrading treatment or infringements of privacy, under certain conditions it *obliges* the state not only for restraint but for certain actions to sustain the dignity of its citizens, in the context of social law (Daly 2013, 54–65). As a regulative principle, sometimes it is used to justify extending individual freedom and autonomy, on other occasions, it restricts the sphere of choices concerning one's occupation, for example. The panorama becomes even more complex if we recall that dignity appears also in torts, or labour law, as a protected private interest.[2] All this calls for sorting out, but perhaps before any sorting out

---

[1]   This chapter presents research supported by the NCN (Poland), under the project no. 2016/23/D/HS5/02400. An earlier version of the chapter was discussed at seminars at the University of Warsaw and the University of Wrocław, as well as at the IVR 2019 workshop on 'The inherence of human dignity'. I am grateful for all the helpful criticism I received there, which was possible thanks to Marcin Romanowicz (Warsaw), Tatiana Chauvin (Warsaw), Paweł Jabłoński (Wrocław), Andrzej Bator (Wrocław), as well as Barry W. Bussey and Angus J. L. Menuge, who organized the IVR workshop.

[2]   In the Polish Labor Code, Article 11, one finds a provision that clearly identifies dignity of the employee as a fundamental interest to be protected by labour law. Another interesting example is Article 16 of the French Civil Code stating that the law is supposed to protect the primacy of the person and her dignity. Common law identifies a class of 'dignitary torts' which could

can be attempted, one should ask a more fundamental question: is human dignity something real and legally relevant? In other words: is there one common point of reference that matters for different legal applications, within and across jurisdictions? Is it possible to unify contingent legal discourses in reference to one ideal or principle? This chapter addresses these questions and provides grounds for answering them in the affirmative.

We should bear in mind, however, that the opposite answer is also widely represented: according to some, the best solution for the puzzles of dignity would be to abandon interpreting it as legally relevant, especially as bearing a concrete legal effect. Those scholars seem to suggest that while the appeal to human dignity might express some of our ethical aspirations, it does not bear much more than blurry, inconsistent intuitions when applied to the legal sphere (Hennette-Vauchez 2007). Others express a worry that human dignity is merely 'providing a language in which judges can appear to justify how they deal with issues' rather than really justifying anything in a principled and intelligible manner (McCrudden 2008).

Taking this criticism into consideration, but at the same time assuming that the recurring appeal to dignity should be explained and sorted out rather than ignored or disparaged, the goal of this chapter is to provide a principled explication of human dignity as a legally useful term.[3] In my view, an internally consistent, empirically relevant and legally useful conception of human dignity can be achieved by re-engaging with the personalist conception of human dignity, or more precisely with the jurisprudential implications of this conception. As the term 'personalism' is quite fuzzy, for purposes of this chapter, I propose to understand 'personalism' as a philosophical reflection on the internal structure, efficacy and ethical status of the person (understood as a real, dynamic being). A personalist conception of human dignity in the law would amount to a juridical interpretation of the legal status, and the internal structure, of the person. The most important classical patron here is, of course, St Thomas Aquinas, alongside phenomenologists such as Max Scheler. Although the tradition is, again, rich and multi-layered, my focus here is the work of philosophers Karol Wojtyła and Tadeusz Styczeń (Wojtyła's disciple), whose work (which could be labelled as 'The Lublin School')[4] strikes me as both extremely relevant for the law and underexplored within legal philosophy.

An important desideratum is that the personalist conception of human dignity should be able to embrace different uses of dignity which have just been mentioned, and as such, include human rights law, but also go beyond, towards private law, for example. A reductionist theorizing would simply go against the law that it is supposed to interpret. This can be called 'the wide-view' criterion. Another important preliminary assumption is connected to the fact that, despite some criticism, there is a good deal of consensus with

---

be understood as protecting the personal, dignitary interest. The latter, however, is deemed heavily undertheorized (Abraham and White 2019).

[3] To be sure, there has already been a lot of effort to grasp the meaning and functions of dignity in legal-philosophical literature (e.g. Tiedemann 2012; Rosen 2012; McCrudden 2013; Riley 2017).

[4] Both Karol Wojtyła and Tadeusz Styczeń worked at the Catholic University of Lublin (respectively in the periods of 1954–78, and 1963–2010).

regards to the foundational role that human dignity plays in the law. This recognition is not a mark of a particular school of legal theorizing: it is present not only among natural law or non-positivism theorists (Jovanović 2013), but also among some legal positivists (Raz 1979, 221), as well as within critical legal studies.[5] Although it may be impossible to reconcile those different legal theories in one conception of human dignity, it seems that its foundational role in the law should be conceptualized in a manner that does not directly presuppose a particular commitment in legal theory. This can be called the 'free-standingness' criterion.

In my attempt to demonstrate that the personalist conception is relevant for the law, and is meeting the aforementioned criteria, I will first explain why human dignity is indeed indispensable for the law, as its foundation, and not merely a rhetorical decoration. The indispensability of human dignity has been identified by legal scholars outside the personalist movement (particularly Jeremy Waldron, Stephen Riley and Stephan Kirste). I will summarize their results in Section 1. Sections 2 will be devoted to presenting the crucial aspects of the personalist conception and defending it against most common charges. Section 3 will argue for the relevance of the personalist conception in the legal context.

One may identify two main problems with the personalist conception, if it is to be considered a legal doctrine. The first is its alleged dependence on Christian religious truth, or if not that, at least on a metaphysical speculation of the objective order of the world and the entirety of human nature. In Section 2, I will provide the characteristics of the personalist conception offered by Wojtyła and Styczeń which allows us to understand it as independent of religion or metaphysics, although in a limited sense of independence. The second problem is that the personalist conception has not been yet systematically applied to jurisprudence. It is therefore not clear whether it has anything relevant to say about the law, and if it has, if it tells us something about the positive law, or about natural law, or about both? In Section 3, I will provide an outline of such an application, alongside the argument that the personalist conception (as a free-standing and wide view) is needed to explain and interpret the indispensability of human dignity as identified in Section 1.

1. The Indispensability of Human Dignity in Modern Law

According to Jeremy Waldron, the development of human dignity as a *moral* idea of absolute human worth (most famously expressed by Kant in the *Groundwork for the Metaphysics of Morals* (1997)) has been preceded by the *legal* construction of dignity as rank and status. *Dignitas*, as a special standing and honour, used to be exclusively bestowed upon some distinguished groups of society, such as those holding high offices (Waldron 2009, 225). As Waldron argues, modern law ascribes a similar special standing to all humans equally, as a result of historical development that led from aristocratic towards egalitarian

---

[5] Although the CLS movement is famous for having a rather deconstructive attitude, there some positive projects engaged with the idea of human dignity; see, for example, McManus (2019).

society (229–32). Consequently, everyone is treated as an autonomous agent who is due at least the minimum conditions of self-possession and self-control. Human dignity can therefore be regarded as inherently legal; that is, something explainable from within the law itself. As a consequence, one does not necessarily need morality in order to answer the question of what dignity consists in, as the very roots thereof are embedded in the law itself. Although dignity so understood is perhaps never fully secured (Waldron 2011, 25), legal systems generally do treat human beings as rational, autonomous and respon-sive agents, which is easily distinguishable from treating them as mere objects of legal regulation. The particular institutions and features of law discussed by Waldron are the following: law's reliance on self-application, the use of legal standards (as opposed to strictly determined rules), the special position of the individual in the trial, the argumen-tative structure of law, the importance of legal representation and the dignified use of coercion (Waldron 2009, 237–49). We do not have to discuss them here in detail. The general conclusion is, however, extremely important for this chapter. The law, at least in Western legal culture, respects human beings as persons in the law, which is not an extra-ordinary legislative fiat, but rather a result of the way in which law works on a daily basis. As Waldron strongly claims, 'There is an implicit commitment to dignity in the tissues and sinews of law – in the character of its normativity and in its procedures' (2011, 25). In this sense, human dignity, as a founding idea of law, appeared long before the UDHR, and, on the other hand, is still a task to pursue. The protection of human dignity *equally to all persons* is a fundamental commitment of legal systems to the extent that jurisdictions abandoning this idea overall can hardly be called 'systems of law' (17).

Although Waldron represents the positivist tradition, his conclusions concerning the indispensability of human dignity in the law can be well accepted (although differ-ently grounded) by representatives of other jurisprudential orientations. In a recent work Stephen Riley develops an account of human dignity as an 'interstitial' concept, that is, the concept that resides somewhere *in between* the moral, the political and the legal, governing the limitations of each by the others, and providing guidance for their harmonization (2017, 68). As such, this theory is much closer to natural law than to legal positivism. In Riley's view, human dignity should be understood as providing standards governing authority, including the authority of, and the rule of, law (8–14). The dignitarian implications for the rule of law are, according to Riley, those connected to human agency. As he puts it: 'Laws should address agents as rational actors; it should be coordinating and not simply controlling; it should rely upon, and not simply bypass, rational individual agency' (178). Along these lines, Stephan Kirste develops a purely legal conception of human dignity as 'a right to be recognized as a person in law' (2013, 73). Again, according to Kirste, dignity is a kind of standing that law recognizes, and makes the legal person distinguished as subject, and not mere object, of legal regulation. Everyone is entitled to have their legal personhood recognized, which 'is the founda-tion for all other rights' (81). Although those three theories differ with regards to the scope they envisage for human dignity in the law, as well as to particular methodological commitments, they all acknowledge the fact that (at least the modern) law is grounded in human dignity, in the sense of expressing respect to human agency, at least at the basic level.

Another important common denominator of the aforementioned theories – one that is more general and not limited to those three – is that alongside recognizing the indispensability of human dignity in the law, they explicitly refuse to address the extra-legal conception of the human person. The underlying worry seems to be that once one engages with the issues of human ontology, one inevitably falls into metaphysics that is both methodologically unnecessary and substantially dubious (i.e. vulnerable and open to disagreement more than any other field of rational inquiry; see Tiedemann 2013, 29). This is precisely the position I intend to challenge. In my view, the denial of human ontology is methodologically unsound, since it has always been present in the law (Chauvin 2014), and the implicit engagement with different conceptions of the person determines the structure and workings of law even today. It seems particularly obvious in dignity jurisprudence – courts, and legislators, find themselves in a position of determining *what elements of the open-ended human reality are worthy of protection and respect* (e.g. see Daly 2013). So, instead of escaping or bypassing the problem,[6] I propose to tackle it directly – to ask what conception of human agency is in equilibrium with the legal status of every human individual that modern law is bound to acknowledge.

This is when the personalist conception enters into play. I will argue that the personalist insights may contribute to our understanding of human dignity, as an indispensable commitment of modern legal orders. The usefulness of the conception, however, requires a justification meeting the free-standingness and the wide-view criteria, as set forth at the beginning of this chapter. Also, the issue of usefulness in legal interpretation should be reviewed. These are not addressed in the current literature. The following sections are my attempt to remedy this need.

2 Personalism: The Independence of Practical Reasoning and 'Axiomatic' Human Dignity

As stated earlier, an important insight into the issue of human dignity in the legal sphere can be obtained through examination of personalism, particularly the approaches offered by Karol Wojtyła and Tadeusz Styczeń (in the broad context of personalist-Thomist philosophy).[7] This approach has been neglected in the jurisprudence, and it is not a goal of this chapter to examine the reasons in detail. However, one reason is the alleged

---

[6]   What I mean by bypassing can be well illustrated by the example of Kirste (2013, 75–78). He argues – following famous patrons such as Friedrich Carl von Savigny – that jurisprudence should be interested only in the legal person, leaving the extralegal notion of the moral person aside. A closer examination of the work that dignity is doing in legal reality (e.g. see Daly 2013) shows that judges cannot escape asking the pressing question of what it means to be human.

[7]   An important reservation to be made is that the Catholic Social Teaching, to which Karol Wojtyła himself as Pope John Paul II made important contributions, and to which Tadeusz Styczeń as a Roman Catholic priest and a Salvatorian was committed, is not a direct focus of this chapter. Regardless of my personal reverence towards that doctrine, I work here with the personalist conception of human dignity as a purely philosophical conception, and I interpret only the purely philosophical (not theological or ecclesiastical) works of the Lublin School personalist.

'particularism' of personalism. Namely the personalist conception is deeply rooted in the Catholic religion, and as such, it seems to depend on a particular belief in God, and a certain metaphysical worldview about the world's structure and the ultimate human fate. This is considered problematic, as human dignity is supposed to be theorized as a universal ground for law in *pluralistic* societies. This way of thinking, omnipresent in human dignity literature, strikes me as a mistaken simplification. While personalism is, of course, a worldview that is well sustainable with Catholic faith, it is at the same time a *philosophical*, not *religious* worldview. Therefore, it constitutes a theory that may claim to be universal in a way that any other theory can: it does not depend on a religious confession. Moreover, the Catholic tradition itself has affirmed human dignity as grounded in experience and practical reason as much as in metaphysical speculation and theological truths (Hollenbach 2013).[8] In what follows, I will outline the personalist conception of human dignity in this 'independent' and 'universalist' manner, that is, with a view to providing a basis for modern law, in the context of a pluralistic legal community.

An explanation of how a philosophical theory may be independent of the broader religious or theological context in which this very theory is embedded comes from Aquinas. In *Summa Contra Gentiles*, he argues that human reason can grasp certain truths in a demonstrative way, based on first principles that are known to all naturally, with no divine revelation working as a mediator (63–77). In this perspective, although the most important truth about the human being is that of the Divine creation of humans as *imago Dei* and the ultimate destiny of salvation (contemplation of God in eternity), at the same time certain practical truths about the human good and principles of social life can be grasped without recourse to theological truths and revelation, as accessible to natural reason common to all.

Of course, Aquinas's agenda was different than mine in this chapter: he aimed at demonstrating congruence between revelation and natural reason in order to defend the Christian faith rather than to praise natural reason in itself. However, contemporary Aquinas-inspired accounts emphasize the independence of moral theory. For instance, John Finnis has compellingly argued that Aquinas's conception of natural law does not rest upon metaphysical speculation (2011, 33–50). According to Finnis, both with regards to his own theory of natural law and to his reconstruction of Aquinas, practical reasoning (reasoning about human aims, duties and entitlements) is *autonomous* – it can be conducted within its own terms, starting with its own axioms that are not conjured from elsewhere. The metaphysical system may offer the *ultimate grounding* for morality or politics, but the *justification* of moral or political claims is not simply derivative of a particular metaphysical doctrine (see Rupniewski 2019). Quite to the contrary: basic practical principles are per se *notae* (self-evident) propositions. As Finnis writes:

---

8   Although the wording 'human dignity' has been used only after the Second Vatican Council, similar ideas are deeply embedded in the Catholic tradition. For example, a Polish legal scholar Paweł Włodkowic (Paulus Vladimiri) argued at the Council of Constance, in 1416, that *ius gentium* and natural law authorize pagans to have their own states and enjoy property. According to Vladimiri, moral status does not depend on confession (see Tulejski, forthcoming).

A basic practical principle serves to orient one's practical reasoning, and can be instantiated (rather than 'applied') in indefinitely many, more specific, practical principles and premises. [...] In this respect, practical reasoning is like 'theoretical' reasoning, which has its own basic and usually tacit presuppositions and principles. We often say 'Too late!'; but how often do we formulate the presupposition on which our conclusion rests – the guiding presupposition that time cannot be reversed? (2011, 63–64)

For Finnis, those basic practical principles are necessary preconditions in 'trying to make sense of someone's commitments, projects, and actions over a period' (64). And those principles provide an autonomous basis for ethics and jurisprudence. To use an example analogous to one Finnis gives: reading this chapter (if it results from a genuine commitment) is sufficiently explained only if we assume that the reader engages his or her time and capacity in order to participate in a value; the value in this case is knowledge. The proposition 'knowledge is good' is therefore not derived from a theoretical claim that, say, God has endowed us with reason that we are obliged to cultivate. Rather, it is a tacit principle, adoption of which makes human actions that pursue knowledge *intelligible* (and not just a result of a contingent determination by external or internal forces). So, even if it is true that God created humans as reasonable, and commanded them to use their reason, this truth is not directly involved in the practical reasoning concerning what is good, right or worth pursuing.

I appeal here to Finnis only to emphasize that the commonly adopted picture of the Aquinian tradition in ethics and politics as dependent on theological or general-metaphysical premises is false. Although I doubt if Finnis could be rightly labelled 'personalist', and the conception of human dignity is not foundational for his own theory of natural law, his refutation of the false image of Aquinas seems both correct and of great use here, as this false image is adopted also in considerations of the personalist conception of human dignity. Michael Rosen, for instance, claims that according to Aquinas (and, allegedly, all Aquinian-inspired views) dignity of humans (or other beings, for that matter) is that of 'the value something else has in virtue of occupying its proper place within a divine order' (2012, 47–48).[9] If this were true, the personalist conception of dignity would be indeed context-dependent and as such not eligible for universalization. If the basis of an ethical or political judgement within the Aquinian framework is autonomous, accessible to practical reason within its own terms, and if one can demonstrate the same obtains in the case of human dignity, then it might serve the purpose we seek, that is, serve as foundation of modern law.

The autonomy of ethics was the leading theme in the thought of Tadeusz Styczeń (2012a). Comparing him to Finnis (which is only of expository value, since to my knowledge the two philosophers never exchanged thoughts), one can say the conception of Styczeń is minimalistic. As commonly known, Finnis adopts a set of basic forms of good – practical principles – as the foundation of practical reasoning (including but not limited

---

[9] For a refutation of this, see Piechowiak (2016), who argues that dignity for Aquinas is a mode of being (a way in which a personal being exists) rather than a result of place in the hierarchy of beings.

to morals). These are life, knowledge, play, aesthetic experience, sociability, practical rea-
sonableness and religion (Finnis 2011, 65–97). To the contrary, Styczeń argues that ethics
should be based on one practical principle, that is, the dignity of the person. Dignity, in
his view, is an inalienable condition of every individual, and at the same time an obligation of all other persons to affirm that individual, for her own sake, in their actions. For
Styczeń (which is clearly a Kantian stance), ethics should be based on moral duty towards
other persons rather than on flourishing or happiness of the agent performing moral
actions. The most synthetic expression of the moral duty is: 'a person unconditionally
owes love to other persons' (Styczeń 2012b, 216). Methodologically speaking, dignity of
the person is a non-derivative practical principle, but it is also an object of a peculiar kind
of experience – the moral experience. As Styczeń writes:

> So, what is this duty-bearing 'thing' that serves both as subject and grounding of the duty
> judgment? What can be the adequate reason to 'transcend oneself', which is the underlying
> commitment in every moral judgement? This *par excellence* duty-bearing 'thing' is the dignity
> of the person. One does not need to look elsewhere, in order to take notice of a moral obli-
> gation, and the very same dignity of the person contains everything that constitutes the moral
> duty, and gives it a mark of unconditionality. The person, by the very fact of being what she
> is, is the one that should be affirmed for her own sake. (2012a, 312; translation by the author)

It is important to put this quotation into context. Styczeń (2012c) was well aware of the
famous Humean charge of illicit derivation of norms from facts and the extensive literature on the topic. The affirmation of the intrinsic worth of the person is therefore
first and foremost *an intuited practical truth rather than an ontological claim*. Styczeń, unlike
Finnis, was heavily influenced by *phenomenology*, with its wide conception of experience
that rejects empiricism (say, empiricism associated with the British analytical tradition or
with the Vienna Circle), as an instantiation of unjustified reductionism. A wide concept
of what constitutes experience allows Styczeń to say that human dignity, and thus morality, has an empirical foundation (2012b, 153–84).

Karol Wojtyła – who was Styczeń's teacher, and thus their doctrines may be treated as
complementing one another – develops his conception of the human person on a slightly
different level. Analyzing human action, he 'factors out' the moral dimension thereof.
This is, however, only a methodological move, in order to give more focus to human
agency itself (Wojtyła 1979, 14). Human agency, and the human person as a whole, can
be recognized through the action. As he writes:

> For our position is that *action serves as a particular moment given in an intuition – that is, in experien-
> cing – the person.* Undoubtedly, this experience yields at the same a substantively determined
> understanding, which consists, as already mentioned, in an intellectual apprehension
> grounded on the fact that man acts in its innumerable recurrences. The datum 'man-acts',
> with its full experiential content, now opens itself to be understood as a person's action. (10,
> emphasis original, translation modified)

The structure of human action is characterized by two fundamental moments: transcendence and integration. Those complicated technical terms must be left with no closer

explanation for now. It is sufficient to say that, according to Wojtyła, the human being determines herself in action: she is capable of reasonable choice and peculiar ordering of bodily movements, emotions and cognition of truth – all in one act or action (*actus humanus*). This structure should be strictly opposed to processes that merely *happen in* man which could be called 'activations' (61–70). In these latter structures, the human being is subject to processes that come from her internal dynamism, but do not involve efficacy, and are marks of passiveness, rather than action. According to Wojtyła, by examining the complex structure of genuine actions – that which contain efficacious moments – one is able to capture the truth about their value. In this sense, morality remains the crucial aspect of human action. Indirectly, the person has special value or status. In the next section, I will examine the latter dichotomy in more detail.

In my view, however, the emphasis the Lublin personalists put on the experience (understood in phenomenological terms) may be somewhat misleading. Arguably, human dignity in the personalist conception is *axiomatic* in a way similar to Finnis's first practical principles. Alongside the empirical component (the intuition of the person and her value), human dignity is inevitably and tacitly assumed in the way we interact with other persons, when participating in common projects or social unions. Wojtyła's theory of participation, for example, shows that working with others (genuine common action) can be intelligible and possible only if mutual recognition of the personal status is assumed (1979, 266–71). On the other hand – what might seem paradoxical – wrongdoing, or even atrocity, is unintelligible should human dignity be removed from the equation (Styczeń 2012a, 257). Another important argument coming from the work of Styczeń is that *moral disagreement* with regard to particular issues (such as, say, admissibility of euthanasia, or standards of education) can take place only with a simultaneous affirmation of the person – in normal circumstances the debate regards the issue of what constitutes human good or human rights, and it is at the same time beyond question that human good or rights should be pursued (328–30). As he writes:

> Is D [someone – M.R.] affirmed when we take good care of his religious formation, or, quite to the contrary, when we discourage him from religion? In both cases it is indisputable that we should affirm him – the object of the controversy is what action towards D effectively affirms D. [...] In order to determine the latter one needs the closer and more specific knowledge [about D] to whom we owe affirmation: the knowledge about his structure and position in reality. (341; translation by the author)

Human dignity, in this perspective, has a non-derivative basis and 'shows itself' in the ways we work with, deliberate about or debate with others. Particular moral judgements (as opposed to the general moral judgement affirming human dignity) must be informed by a more detailed knowledge. In this sense, human dignity alone is not supposed to yield all particular practical principles or all particular moral judgements. It needs information taken from elsewhere. The necessary cognitive supplement may come from empirical observation, common sense, natural or social science, philosophical anthropology, religion – everything depending on the context and particular issue to be decided. In this mode, the personalist conception of human dignity is not dogmatic and is left open for an interdisciplinary discourse, as far as particular judgements are concerned.

Granted this, one comes to a conclusion that human dignity claims are justified independently from the *metaphysical* speculation. To be sure, this conception assumes certain *ontology*, namely the ontology allowing the existence of persons (free, conscious and self-constituting beings), but this is not tantamount to speculation about either the complete structure of the world or human nature in its entirety. The personalist conception shows only some important, perhaps crucial, aspects of human life – but still, *only aspects, not the human life as a whole*. It identifies certain goods, such as the good of genuine action, but is not aimed at finding an exhaustive list of human goods (let alone the ways they should be pursued). Therefore, the personalist conception is not vulnerable to arguments conventionally used against philosophical anthropology in legal considerations, namely that it should be rejected as fixing human nature and thus impeding individual self-constitution understood as 'a special *dynamic* relationship between each individual and the human condition' (Riley 2017, 33). Quite to the contrary, the personalist conception prioritizes this aspect of human existence. According to Wojtyła, the acting person must engage with her own condition in all its aspects, in order to constitute herself in the action, or rather, in the series of actions (the complexities are discussed in Wojtyła 1979, 105–48).

On the other hand, the independence of the personalist conception does not mean that it is in any sense at odds with metaphysics, and more generally with the truth about the world in general or the human being in particular. The category of truth remains in the equation as the crucial aspect – one of the important characteristics of the way the person exists is her orientation towards finding the truth (Wojtyła 1979, 136–39). However, the commonly overlooked feature of the conception in this regard is that it does not presuppose *what the truth is*. The individual will respond to truth, but the content of the truth is left to personal, individual inquiry, deliberation and discovery. This is not to be conflated with merely an individual decision or contract in a Hobbesian or Humean sense. According to the Lublin School, the objective truth does exist, despite being difficult to grasp.

The image of the person that is found in the personalist conception is therefore that of an active, self-conscious and self-constituting agent, responding to truth and objective values in the state of inner freedom. At the same time, the only proper way one can refer to such an agent is respecting her agency and affirming her for her own sake. All this is inscribed into the experience of the person and interacting with persons, and hence independent from metaphysics.

3 Human Dignity: Value or Status of the Person?

The previous section was devoted to identifying the central points of the personalist conception of human dignity, showing its autonomy and methodological specificity. However, I have not yet considered the second (perhaps more troubling) problem: the Lublin personalists were not lawyers. This section is aimed at providing the main lines of a juridical application of the personalist conception to human dignity in the law, bearing in mind its indispensability, as discussed in Section 1.

The primary focus of Styczeń is meta-ethics, and it is by no means clear how (and whether or not in the first place) his conception of dignity may be applied to jurisprudence, as it seems to depend on a particular vision of the relations of law and morals, namely on a natural law vision. As I emphasized at the beginning of this chapter, the quest is to find a free-standing theory. The case of Wojtyła is a little bit different in this regard – in his fundamental work *The Acting Person* (1979), he discusses action in general which is not limited to *moral* action. Thus, his work has some overlap with *praxeology*, in the sense adopted by Tadeusz Kotarbiński (1965) or Ludwig von Mises (1996). In the case of Wojtyła, then, a free-standing link to jurisprudence would be easier to demonstrate, insofar as making, interpreting and applying law instantiate human action. In what follows, however, I am going to take a slightly different path – instead of sticking to the personalist conception of human dignity and trying to make a way out into jurisprudence from there, I will identify what I consider the most sensible conception of human dignity in non-personalist literature and then see whether the personalist conception complements or contradicts it.

To do this, we should recall the ongoing debate in legal philosophy concerning the issue of whether human dignity should be understood as a certain *value* (intrinsic/absolute worth) of the human being or her special *status* (Waldron 2009). In my view, this distinction is not particularly clear and might even be misleading – many philosophers, as well as lawyers or judges, have talked about some mix of value and status at the same time, and perhaps it is not due to them being not careful enough, but simply because value and status indeed go hand in hand and are dialectically bound with one another (Mahlman 2012). Despite this, the status-value opposition might help us in grasping something important about human dignity *in the law*. Human dignity as intrinsic worth is most commonly associated with Kant's *Groundwork for the Metaphysics of Morals* where he famously described the person (or more precisely the moral law within each rational being) as 'what [...] is raised above all price and therefore admits of no equivalent has a dignity' (1997, 42). However, dignity as value beyond price, according to Kant, does not constitute a foundation of law – it is not to be found as a law-grounding principle in his later philosophy contained in the *Metaphysics of Morals* (1996). The reason for this might be that Kant distinguishes law from morality, human dignity pertaining to the latter. In his subsequent works, Kant (1996) discusses dignity as a virtue, but neither as a foundation of law nor rights, which is *freedom* rather than dignity. Paradoxically, then, the category of absolute worth has a doubtful application to law even for Kant, who has been the crucial inspiration for it.

A similar, positivistic scepticism with regards to moral standards as directly applicable to law has drawn Jeremy Waldron (2009) to defend a status account of human dignity, understood as an inherently legal (and not primarily moral) idea. He distinguishes status and value in the following way:

> The thing to do with something of value is to promote it or protect it, perhaps maximize things of that kind, at any rate to treasure it. The thing to do with a ranking status is to respect and defer to the person who bears it. (218)

Waldron seems to claim that if human dignity in law was understood primarily as value of the human person, then the law would have to 'treasure' and 'promote' humanity, but the idea of the foundational role of dignity, and its non-contingent relation to the law, would not be sufficiently explained. In other words, human dignity would be one of the moral postulates with regard to the law, but not something that is deeply embedded in law's 'tissues and sinews'. The notion of status fulfils the latter requirement, since it embodies respect for the agency of the human person by respecting his basic standing towards the law, such that he is never treated as a mere object when interacting with the law or legal enforcement authorities.

Now, perhaps a natural response from the personalist perspective would be to refute the status account and argue for a conception of human dignity as intrinsic value above all price. In *The Acting Person*, Wojtyła does not use the term 'human dignity': as noted before, the book does not directly concern morals (or other normative order). However, at the end of the book, he speaks of the worth of the human being. According to Wojtyła,

> The performance itself of an action by the person is a fundamental value, which we may call the *personalistic* – personalistic or personal – value of the action. Such a value differs from all moral values, which *belong* to the nature of the performed action and issue from their reference to a norm. The personalistic value, on the other hand, inheres in the performance itself of the action by the person, in the very fact that man acts in a manner appropriate to him [...]
>
> The 'personalistic' value of the human action – that is, the personal value – is a special and probably the most fundamental manifestation of the worth of the person himself. (1979, 264, emphasis original)

As paradoxical as it might seem at first glance, however, I argue that the personalist conception, *when applied into the law*, yields a status account of human dignity. Perhaps a good way to explain this would be to introduce some more detail of the structure of human action, particularly to the aspect Wojtyła calls 'the transcendence of the person in action'. According to Wojtyła, the human being *transcends himself in action*, by virtue of exercising self-possession and self-determination. The genuine human action consists therefore in a free act of the will, governing the person as a whole:

> Every actual act of self-determination makes real the agency, in self-governance and self-possession. In each of these structures that are inherent to the person, the person-as-agent (as the one who governs and owns) obtains the insight into his own person as the object: as one that is governed and owned. This objectiveness is, as may be seen, the correlate of the person's agency, and moreover, seems to bring out the agency itself in a particularly strong way.
>
> [...] In this sense, we may speak of an 'objectification' that is introduced together with self-determination into the dynamism that is peculiar to the person. The objectification means that in every actual self-determination (that is, in every act of 'I will') your own 'I' is the object, indeed the primary and nearest object. This is contained in the very notion of self-determination, and in the term expressing it – 'self-determination' means that someone is determined by oneself. The subject and object are simultaneously and correlatively evoked. And both of them are your own 'I'. (108–9; translation modified)

If we consider this passage in the light of the status-value controversy, the specific kind of *worth* of the person revealed through the structure of action is hardly distinguishable from her *status*. The person is the being capable of valuing, responding to values (but never creating values out of nothing; see Wojtyła 1979, 135–39), and, as such, has a special self-governing status that situates her, in a specific sense, above value. Of course, the objective and apodictic value of all persons (whether human or Divine) is unquestioned and inalienable.

In my interpretation, however, in the personalist conception – as far as the juridical sphere is concerned – one is obliged in the first place to *respect* each individual person, in a sense of taking him into account as a self-authenticating source of claims, valuing acts and practical propositions (which amounts to human dignity as status); and only subsequently promoting or protecting her good (which amounts to human dignity as value). Insofar as the law realizes the common good, it must take the good of individual persons as its basis (this is where dignity as worth comes into play). However, the necessary prerequisite of the pursuit of the common good is securing basic status that everyone should enjoy as member of the legal community – and in this sense human dignity as status prerequisites human dignity as worth. The law, strictly speaking, is founded on the former.

As already mentioned, for Styczeń the respect for the person (as a whole) is the necessary prerequisite of any moral discussion and action striving towards the good of that person (2012a, 328–32). On the other hand, this discussion is genuine, and one is always engaged in a complex argumentative endeavour when deliberating on the issue of what effectively affirms a particular person in particular circumstances. Therefore, *morally* speaking, one is bound to help, promote and foster the good of all persons he is able to, according to his own apprehension of their good. However, one is not entitled to impose one's own view of the good of a person he strives to affirm. This is particularly obvious in the sphere of (coercive) laws. If the personalist value of the action is taken for granted, then the agency of every person should be respected. Therefore, *juridically* speaking, one is obliged (as a citizen or public officer) to strive towards a legal order that respects the status of each person as an acting agent capable of genuine efficacy rather than a passive unit subject to legal incentives and sanctions. I think this is precisely what the personalist conception demands, underlies and explains. The person's efficacy, self-determination and self-possession, as well as the obligation to affirm and respect the person as such, are in equilibrium with the legal status of the person as the legal agent. In this particular respect, phenomenological analysis of experience goes hand in hand with legal interpretation.

One important issue that makes the standard account of status different from the one presented in this chapter is the issue of *contingency*. The legal construction of status refers to something that is conferred upon someone in a conventional manner, or something that is attached to holding certain office – certainly something that can be lost. The personalist conception goes against this intuitive understanding and claims that basic status is inherent to the person as such. Or, in other words, that law confers basic status on all persons in a transcendental, and not merely conventional or contingent, way. The basic status of dignity is also not conditioned on factual enjoyment or exercise of the capacities peculiar to the person. Rather, the structure of the human action is considered to be central to the human condition as such, and therefore also humans beings as only potentially capable of action, or those who enjoyed this capacity in the past but no longer do, have equal basic status. The respect and affirmation, as moral experience teaches us, is not conditional. In this sense, the basic status is not something inevitably attached to a particular branch of law. Quite to the contrary: it is something that constitutes a common point of reference to laws as distant from each other as the Universal Declaration of Human Rights and a code of civil procedure regulating the status of the defendant.

Conclusion: A Further Road to Come

The considerations in this chapter constituted an attempt to introduce a new, although eclectic, conception of human dignity. The argument was aimed at integrating the structure of human action, the ultimate value of the human being and her legal right to be recognized as an acting agent. So conceived, commitment to dignity is indispensable for law and shapes modern legal ideas and practices. As I sought to demonstrate, the personalist conception of human dignity is a necessary component providing explanatory power to the law evoking human dignity and allowing us to analyze divergent uses of dignity that appeal to different aspects of personal existence, by referring to the structure of human action and respect that is due to the human person.

At the present stage, the latter is merely a desideratum: the conception, as outlined in this chapter, still awaits its 'baptism of fire', that is, application in legal interpretation of some particular instances of human dignity present in the law. The fact that dignity can be observed not only in human rights or constitutional law, but also in penal law codes, procedural law, as well as in private law, making it a common element of many jurisdictions (and within different cultural backgrounds), should be the starting point of any such interpretation. Further research should then sort out the multitude of dignitarian principles and doctrines within law by reference to the personalist conception in a comparative legal interpretation. This is, however, a separate task and the next step to be made.

References

Abraham, Kenneth S., and G. Edward White. 2019. 'The Puzzle of the Dignitary Torts'. *Cornell Law Review* 104, no. 2: 317–80. https://scholarship.law.cornell.edu/clr/vol104/iss2/2.

Aquinas, Thomas. 1955. *Summa Contra Gentiles: Book One*. Translated by Anton C. Pegis. New York: Image Books.

Chauvin, Tatiana. 2014. *Homo Iuridicus. Człowiek jako podmiot prawa publicznego* [Homo Iuridicus. The Image of Man in the Public Law]. Warsaw: C.H. Beck.

Daly, Erin. 2013. *Dignity Rights*. Philadelphia: University of Pennsylvania Press.

Finnis, John. 2011. *Natural Law and Natural Rights*. Oxford: Oxford University Press.

Hennette-Vauchez, Stephanie. 2007. 'When Ambivalent Principles Prevail: Leads for Explaining Western Legal Orders' Infatuation with the Human Dignity Principle'. *EUI Working Papers Law*. https://cadmus.eui.eu/bitstream/handle/1814/7664/LAW-2007–37.pdf;sequence=1.

Hollenbach, David. 2013. 'Human Dignity: Experience and History, Practical Reason and Faith'. In *Understanding Human Dignity*, edited by Christopher McCrudden, 123–39. Oxford: Oxford University Press.

Jovanović, Miodrag. 2013. 'Legal Validity and Human Dignity – On Radbruch's Formula'. In *Human Dignity as a Foundation of Law*, edited by Winfried Brugger and Stephan Kirste, 145–69. Stuttgart: Franz Steiner Verlag.

Kant, Immanuel. 1996. *The Metaphysics of Morals*. Translated and edited by Mary Gregor. Cambridge: Cambridge University Press.

———. 1997. *Groundwork for the Metaphysics of Morals*. Translated and edited by Mary Gregor. Cambridge: Cambridge University Press.

Kirste, Stephan. 2013. 'A Legal Concept of Dignity as a Foundation of Law'. In *Human Dignity as a Foundation of Law*, edited by Winfried Brugger and Stephan Kirste, 63–83. Stuttgart: Franz Steiner Verlag.

Mahlman, Matthias. 2012. 'Human Dignity and Human Autonomy in Modern Constitutional Orders'. In *The Oxford Handbook of Comparative Constitutional Law*, edited by Michael Rosenfeld and Adrás Sajó, 370–97. Oxford: Oxford University Press.

McCrudden, Christopher. 2008. 'Human Dignity and Judicial Interpretation of Human Rights'. *European Journal of International Law* 18, no. 4: 655–724.

———, ed. 2013. *Understanding Human Dignity*. Oxford: Oxford University Press.

McManus, Matthew. 2019. *Making Human Dignity Central to International Human Rights Law: A Critical Legal Argument*. Cardiff: University of Wales Press.

Piechowiak, Marek. 2016. 'Thomas Aquinas – Human Dignity and Conscience as a Basis for Restricting Legal Obligations'. *Diametros* 47: 64–83.

Raz, Joseph. 1979. *The Authority of Law*. Oxford: Oxford University Press.

Riley, Stephen. 2017. *Human Dignity and Law*. London: Routledge.

Rosen, Michael. 2012. *Dignity: Its History and Meaning*. Cambridge, MA: Harvard University Press.

Rupniewski, Michał. 2019. 'Natural Law Ethics and the Issue of Legal Change'. In *The Philosophy of Legal Change*, edited by Maciej Chmieliński and Michał Rupniewski. London: Routledge.

Styczeń, Tadeusz. 2012a. 'Etyka niezależna?' [Independent Ethics?]. In *Dzieła zebrane, T.2. [Collected Works, V. 2]*, edited by K. Krajewski, 247–373. Lublin: Towarzystwo Naukowe KUL.

———. 2012b. 'Problem możliwości etyki jako empirycznie uprawomocnionej i ogólnie ważnej teorii moralności' [The Problem of the Possibility of Ethics as an Empirically Justified and Universal Moral Theory]. In *Dzieła zebrane, T.2. [Collected Works, V. 2]*, edited by K. Krajewski, 17–246. Lublin: Towarzystwo Naukowe KUL.

———. 2012c. 'W sprawie przejścia od zdań orzekających do zdań powinnościowych' [On the Issue of Deriving the Normative from Descriptive Sentences]. In *Dzieła zebrane, T.2. [Collected Works, V. 2]*, edited by K. Krajewski, 401–19. Lublin: Towarzystwo Naukowe KUL.

Tiedemann, Paul. 2012. *Menschenwürde als Rechtsbegriff*. Berlin: Berliner Wissenschafts-Verlag.

———. 2013. 'Human Dignity as an Absolute Value'. In *Human Dignity as a Foundation of Law*, edited by Winfried Brugger and Stephan Kirste, 25–40. Stuttgart: Franz Steiner Verlag.

Tulejski, Tomasz. Forthcoming. 'Paulus Vladimiri and His Forgotten Concept of the Just War'. *Archiwum Filozofii Prawa i Filozofii Społecznej* 2, no. 20: 39–50. doi:https://doi.org/10.36280/AFPiFS.2019.2.39.

Waldron, Jeremy. 2009. 'Dignity, Rights, and Rank'. The Tanner Lectures on Human Values, 209–53. Delivered at the University of California, Berkeley. https://tannerlectures.utah.edu/_documents/a-to-z/w/Waldron_09.pdf.

———. 2011. 'How Law Protects Dignity'. https://papers.ssrn.com/sol3/papers.cfm?abstract_id=1973341.

Wojtyła, Karol. 1979. *The Acting Person*. Translated by Andrzej Potocki. Dordrecht: D. Riedel.

Chapter Ten

THE SOCIAL ONTOLOGY OF HUMAN DIGNITY

Nicholas Aroney

Introduction

The 1948 Universal Declaration on Human Rights (UDHR) begins with the striking claim that the 'recognition of the inherent dignity and of the equal and inalienable rights of all members of the human family is the foundation of freedom, justice and peace in the world'.[1] According to Johnson and Symonides, the Declaration 'recognizes the fundamental unity of all members of the human family and their inherent dignity and diversity, and proclaims that the human genome is, symbolically, the heritage of humanity' (1998, 84). Mary Ann Glendon (2001) has similarly spoken of 'the spirit of the preamble, the spirit with which the document opens, the affirmation of the unity of the human family' (qtd in Ramcharan and Ramcharan 2019, 223). The term 'human family' deliberately evokes images of the most intimate of human relationships: bonds of marriage, nurture of children, ties of kinship. Rather than use words that individualise and universalise in abstract terms (e.g. 'human beings', 'humanity', 'homo sapiens'),[2] the Declaration describes humanity as an extended family, knit together by ties that are personal, natural and communal.

Despite this language, the rights enshrined within the Declaration and other international instruments, such as the 1966 International Covenant on Civil and Political Rights (ICCPR), have generally been understood in a way that prioritises the rights of individuals.[3] This is not only the case in relation to the liberty rights affirmed by the UDHR and the ICCPR, but is also affirmed through increasingly influential

---

[1] The International Covenant on Civil and Political Rights (1966) and the International Covenant on Economic, Cultural and Social Rights (1966) begin with the same remarkable statement.

[2] Compare the Charter of the United Nations (1945) which recites the intention of 'We the Peoples of the United Nations […] to reaffirm faith in fundamental human rights, in the dignity and worth of the human person, in the equal rights of men and women and of nations large and small'.

[3] Human Rights Committee, *General comment No. 31: The Nature of the General Legal Obligation Imposed on States Parties to the Covenant* (2004) [9]. See also Sarah Joseph and Melissa Castan (2013, [1.18], [1.20]–[1.21]).

understandings of equality rights to non-discrimination as protecting individual self-identity.[4] In such analyses, the concept of human dignity is often cited as fundamental, but in a way that connects it immediately with individual autonomy.[5] This emphasis on individual autonomy underplays the familial, societal and communal framing of the leading international human rights instruments. A close examination of these instruments shows them to presuppose a social ontology in which human beings are not merely isolated individuals, but constituted as members of communities at familial, local, regional, national and global scales.

An exploration of this communal embedding of the dignity of all members of the human family has implications for how international human rights are understood, particularly in controversial cases where the rights of human beings conceived as individuals have to be harmonised with the rights of human beings living in community with others. For example, the rights of individuals not to be discriminated against on the basis of protected attributes (Articles 2 and 26 of the ICCPR) have to be harmonised with the rights of human beings to manifest their religious beliefs, enjoy their own culture and use their own language in community with others (Articles 18 and 27 of the ICCPR). A better understanding of the social ontology presupposed by international human rights law is a prerequisite for addressing problems of harmonisation of this kind.

This chapter is divided into five substantive parts. The first of these explores the social ontology presented and presupposed by key international human rights instruments, in particular the UDHR and the ICCPR.[6] It is shown that although most of the human rights protected by these international instruments are often framed in primarily individual terms, there are also important and ineradicable associational and communal dimensions to these ideas, and that this social ontology is also predicated on human dignity. Noting that the individualistic aspects of human rights law is often said to reflect Western influence, the second, third, fourth and fifth parts of the chapter trace the historical development of the idea of human dignity in classical, patristic, medieval, reformed and modern Western thought. Three issues are identified. First, there is the question whether dignity is conceived as an attribute of certain privileged classes of human beings or an attribute of all human beings without distinction. Second, there is the question whether human dignity is necessarily associated with the possession or exhibition of certain virtues or qualities of character. Third, there is the related question of the extent to which dignity is an attribute of human persons conceived as autonomous and atomised individuals or as persons embedded in an array of associations and communities. This last question concerns the social ontology of human dignity.

It is argued that while the older classical conception of *dignitas* understood it to be an attribute that set some classes or groups of human beings apart from others, the idea was

---

[4]   *Obergefell v. Hodges*, 576 US ___ (2015) 10, referring to 'personal choices central to individual dignity and autonomy'.

[5]   For example, *Coleman v. Attridge Law and Steve Law* (2008) ECR I-5603, Opinion of AG Poiares Maduro at [11], cited in Nicholas Hatzis (2011, 293).

[6]   A similar analysis could be applied to the International Covenant on Economic, Social and Cultural Rights.

transformed under the influence of Stoic philosophy and especially Christian theology into an attribute possessed by all human beings by virtue of their created nature. In the patristic, medieval and reformed perspectives, human dignity is an attribute of all human persons, conceived not as autonomous and atomised individuals, but as embedded in a great variety of associations and communities. However, in the classical, patristic, medieval and reformed conceptions alike, dignity is something that can never be separated from one's moral responsibilities as a human being called upon to perform the duties associated with one's particular callings and stations in life. It is only in certain modern conceptions that human dignity becomes disassociated from the qualities of one's character and from the associations and communities in which human beings are naturally embedded. It follows that international human rights law, insofar as it recognises a social ontology which is simultaneously individualistic, associational and communal, is not entirely oriented to modern Western atomising conceptions of human dignity, but embraces older Western and possibly wider non-Western conceptions as well.

I. International Human Rights Law

Much of the language of international human rights law is framed around the rights of the individual human person. The UDHR, for example, opens by reciting 'the dignity and worth of the human person' as one of its most fundamental principles and proceeds to catalogue the fundamental rights that inhere in each individual, including the right 'to life, liberty and security of person' and the right to 'recognition everywhere as a person before the law' (Articles 3, 6). In similar language, the ICCPR affirms that the rights acknowledged in the Covenant 'derive from the inherent dignity of the human person' and that these rights must be respected and ensured for 'all individuals' within the territory of each state party to the Covenant 'without distinction of any kind' (Article 2). The ICCPR accordingly requires that 'everyone' shall have the right to 'freedom of thought, conscience and religion', 'freedom of expression' and 'freedom of association' (Articles 18, 19, 22), that 'all persons' are 'equal before the law' and that the law should therefore 'guarantee to all persons equal and effective protection against discrimination on any ground' (Article 26).

Although these rights appear to inhere, fundamentally, in individual persons, several of them have explicit or implicit social, collective, corporate or communal dimensions. As Mary Ann Glendon has observed, while the rights contained in the UDHR are enjoyed by 'everyone', all such persons are 'portrayed as situated in families, communities, workplaces, associations, societies, cultures, nations, and an emerging international order' (1999, 1172). Both the UDHR and the ICCPR make clear that the right to freedom of religion, for example, although a right of 'everyone', may be exercised both 'individually' and 'in community with others' (Article 18).[7]

---

[7]   Much of this might not have been the case. The prime author of the UDHR, René Cassin, had originally framed the right to freedom of religion, for example, as an individual right. It was Charles Malik who advocated for changes to Article 18 so that it affirms the right to manifest one's religion or belief not only individually, but in community with others. See Glendon (1999,

Freedom of association also has an obvious individual and collective dimension, for it embraces both the right of an individual to join an association and the right of that association to exist and operate freely (UDHR Article 20; ICCPR Article 22).[8] Similarly, while freedom of expression is a right enjoyed by 'everyone' (UDHR Article 19; ICCPR Article 19), it is recognised that newspapers and other media outlets are typically organised in corporate form, and the right to freedom of expression includes the rights of media organisations to exist and operate under state licencing regimes.[9] Moreover, some rights in the ICCPR are expressly collective or communal in nature and content. Article 1, for example, states that 'all peoples have the right of self-determination' and that 'by virtue of that right they freely determine their political status and freely pursue their economic, social and cultural development'. Article 27 similarly recognises the rights of ethnic, religious and linguistic minorities to enjoy their own culture, profess and practise their own religion and use their own language in community with the other members of their group. Likewise, Article 23 states that 'the family is the natural and fundamental group unit of society and is entitled to protection by society and the State'. These Articles demonstrate that in the ICCPR, families, religious communities and ethnic groups are seen as part of the social and institutional infrastructure of a rights-respecting society. Article 29 of the UDHR goes further: it says that 'everyone has duties to the community in which alone the free and full development of his personality is possible', language which is taken up by one of the recitals of the ICCPR, which affirms that 'the individual' has 'duties to other individuals and to the community to which he belongs'.

The provisions relating to family and marriage in the UDHR and ICCPR are instructive. Notably, they affirm the equal rights of men and women 'as to marriage, during marriage and at its dissolution' and stipulate that marriage 'shall be entered into only with the free and full consent of the intending spouses' (UDHR Article 16; see similarly ICCPR Article 23). Reflecting on the UDHR provisions, Glen Johnson and Janusz Symonides have observed that 'few customs are as central to the maintenance and perpetuation of a given culture as those surrounding the institution of marriage' (1998, 52). These provisions of the UDHR contradict some of the deeply rooted cultural

---

1166), citing Philippe de la Chapelle (1967, 151). Johnson and Symonides (1998, 53) also note that the right to freedom of religion guaranteed by the UDHR was a 'reworking and expansion of a right to worship which it appeared in some earlier drafts'.

[8] Manfred Nowak has explained that freedom of association includes the right to found an association with like-minded people; the right of a group of people to a legal framework making possible the creation of juridical persons; the collective right of an existing association to represent the common interests of its members; the individual negative freedom to leave freely, or not to join an association; and the collective negative freedom of an association to expel a member who has breached the terms of association. See Nowak (1993, 386–89), cited in Julian Rivers (2010, 39).

[9] UN Human Rights Committee, *CCPR General Comment No. 34 Article 19: Freedoms of Opinion and Expression*, UN Doc CCPR/C/GC/34 (12 September 2011) [13]-[14], [39]. See also *Mavlonov and Sa'di v Uzbekistan*, Comm. 1334/2004, UN Doc CCPR/C/95/D/1334/2004 (19 March 2009).

beliefs and practices of many particular societies, such as racial or religious constraints on the choice of marriage partner and arranged marriages in which the consent of the intended spouses is limited or eliminated (52). However, the relevant articles are nonetheless premised, as noted, on the proposition that the family is the natural and fundamental group unit of society and, further, that everyone has the right to 'found a family' (UDHR Article 16.1; ICCPR Article 23.1). Likewise, the right to education (UDHR Article 26.1) and the requirement that state parties must respect the liberty of parents to ensure the religious and moral education of their children (ICCPR Article 18.4) are premised on the proposition that parents have the 'prior right' to choose the kind of education that shall be given to their children (UDHR Article 26.3). Similarly, the right to work and the right to an adequate standard of living (UDHR Articles 23.1, 25.1) is oriented to the needs of families (UDHR Articles 23.3, 25.1). As Glendon has observed, the UDHR's treatment of the right to marriage 'is a blend of old and new ideas with varying genealogies' (1999, 1166). Its provisions reflect, among other things, the Preamble to the 1946 French Constitution, which stated that 'the nation ensures to the individual and the family the conditions necessary to their development', and Article 6.1 of the German Basic Law, which provides that 'marriage and family shall enjoy the special protection of the state' (1166; see also Italian Constitution, Articles 29–31).

Underlying these human rights provisions are deep philosophical waters. Do we conceive of the relationship between individuals and groups as constitutively independent, interdependent or dependent (Gould 2015, 177)? Some of the provisions seem to suggest relationships of original independence: marriages are formed only through the consent of the intended spouses, associations are formed through the consent of their members and each individual has the right to manifest his or her religion both individually and in community with others. But other provisions seem to suggest relations of original dependence: children are born into families, and their birth within the territorial borders of a particular state or to parents who are citizens of a particular state usually makes them citizens and therefore subjects of that state, just as their birth or upbringing makes them members of a particular ethnic, religious or linguistic community.

The founding international human rights instruments thus presuppose that human beings are not only individual rights-bearers, but also born into families, adherents of religions, members of associations and citizens of states. Mary Ann Glendon has concluded that the Declaration was in fact 'ahead of its time in recognising the importance for human freedom of a wide range of social groups, beginning with families, and extending through the institutions of civil society, nation states, and international organizations' (1999, 1170). Even though the UHDR and ICCPR are in the form of agreements among states, René Cassin considered that it would be wrong to regard the state as the 'permanent and only agency' for the protection and regulation of human rights. As Cassin put it, 'Man must be envisaged not only in his relations with the State, but with the social groups of all sorts to which he belongs: family, tribe, city, profession, confession, and more broadly the global human community' (Glendon 1999, 1169, citing Cassin 1972, 10).

If the leading international human rights instruments present an understanding of the rights of human beings as embedded within a complex social context in the sense described, can the same be said of human dignity? Does it also presuppose a corresponding social ontology? The UDHR and ICCPR offer only a minimal account of human dignity in particular. Dignity is said to be 'inherent' and enjoyed by 'all members of the human family' and, alongside equal and inalienable rights, it is the 'foundation of freedom, justice and peace in the world' (UDHR and ICCPR Preambles). Dignity is associated with the 'worth of the human person', and it is a quality that all human beings are born with: each person is 'born free and equal in dignity and rights', 'endowed with reason and conscience' and should act towards others 'in a spirit of brotherhood' (UDHR Preamble and Article 1). Human dignity is the reason why all persons should be 'treated with humanity and with respect' (ICCPR Article 10.1). Moreover, some rights – especially economic, social and cultural rights – are 'indispensable' for the securing of each person's 'dignity and the free development of his personality' (UDHR Article 22). The right to work and fair remuneration, for example, is necessary to ensure 'an existence worthy of human dignity' – not only for each person, but also for 'his family' (UDHR Article 23.3). Thus, while such an account of dignity is relatively thin, it appears that human dignity, like human rights, has individual, associational and communal dimensions.

II. Classical and Patristic Conceptions

In classical Rome, *dignitas* was closely associated with a person's social standing and with the duties that particularly pertained to that status. In the prevailing Roman view, 'human beings [...] do not have an automatic and inalienable dignity. Nature gives them a role to play, and they must strive to play that role' (Griffin 2017, 55). Dignity therefore meant 'worthiness', the respect or honour due to someone on account of their office or rank (Cancik 2002). Moreover, dignity was an attribute that attached, not only to individuals in their particular duties and offices, but also to entire institutions and groups. As Miriam Griffin explains, the *dignitas* of a *gens* implied a family's superiority over other families, just as the *dignitas* of the equestrian order implied its superiority over the rest of the citizenry and the *dignitas* of the Roman people implied its superiority over other peoples (2017, 50). *Dignitas* was therefore inherently comparative. The treatment to which a person was entitled depended on that person's social standing. Honours were distributed, freedoms conferred and punishments executed in a manner that was proportionate to a person's status within society. Moreover, each person was expected to live up to that social status or lose the marks of respect that went with it. Human dignity was therefore more about the privileges and duties associated with a particular position in society than it was about the rights inhering in all human beings.

There were some Roman writers who came close to affirming a universal dignity possessed by all human beings. Marcus Tullius Cicero, for example, considered that it was unworthy of the superior qualities of human nature (*dignam hominis praestantia*) for us to be controlled, like brute animals, by desires for sensual gratification (Cicero, *On*

Duties 1.106).[10] Cicero's argument was premised on the qualities of excellence and dignity (*natura excellentia et dignitas*) which he appeared to attribute to all human beings (but see Harper 2016, 127–28). However, his concern was with the duties, and not only the rights or liberties, that this implied. Thus, he noted that some human beings are so controlled by their desires that they live like beasts, while others conceal their appetite for such pleasures so as to avoid the shame (Cicero, *On Duties* 1.105). For Cicero, like Seneca, *dignitas* was still very much conceived as a 'sliding scale of worthiness' (Harper 2016, 129), in which there ought to be a 'proportion between persons and their dignities' (Seneca, *De beneficiis* 2.16, cited in Harper (2016, 129)). Accordingly, there were special dignities, inhering in certain offices, which ought also to be recognised and preserved. Thus, it was the special office of the magistrate to represent the state, to uphold its honour and dignity, to enforce the law and to dispense to all their rights, remembering that this was committed to him as a sacred trust (Cicero, *On Duties* 1.124). For Cicero, the individual is always situated within a system of many concentric circles consisting of families, kinship groups, neighbourhoods, cities, nations, allies and the human race as a whole (*totius gentis humanae complexus*) (Cicero, *On Ends* 5.65; see also Cicero, *On Duties* 1:50–55; 3.69) So, although there is an important sense in which every individual could therefore be regarded 'a citizen of the universe as if it were one city' (Cicero, *On the Laws* 1.61), Cicero's concern was to emphasise the moral duties that attach to one's place in the world, rather than the rights or freedoms that one is entitled to exercise.

According to John Milbank, Cicero's conception of cosmopolitan citizenship remained abstracted from local political realities. Cicero proposed a conception of humanity that was universal, but the conditions of his time, and his own views about citizenship prevented its political realisation (Milbank 2013, 198). There could be no way of bringing the principle of the universal dignity of all human beings to bear on the particular civic identity of each person, for there was no political community which was understood to be intrinsically cosmopolitan. Milbank argues that a universal yet concrete polity of this kind only came into being with the advent of the church (199). In his account, the church represented a kind of 'alternative polity' (*ecclesia*) that was both concrete and universal in the sense that it was open to all human beings without any distinction on the basis of nationality, language, status or sex.

This did not mean that human dignity came to be conceived only or merely as an abstract property possessed equally by all. The biblical teaching that all human beings are made in the image and likeness of God (Gen. 1:27) became a mainstay of Christian reflection on human nature, but this was framed within the specifically Christian doctrines

---

[10] The full passage reads: 'Ex quo intellegitur corporis voluptatem non satis esse dignam hominis praestantia, eamque contemni et reici oportere; sin sit quispiam, qui aliquid tribuat voluptati, diligenter ei tenendum esse eius fruendae modum. Itaque victus cultusque corporis ad valetudinem referatur et ad vires, non ad voluptatem. Atque etiam si considerare volumus, quae sit in natura excellentia et dignitas, intellegemus, quam sit turpe diffluere luxuria et delicate ac molliter vivere quamque honestum parce, continenter, severe, sobrie'.

of creation, fall and redemption. Gregory of Nyssa, in his treatise *On the Making of Man*, taught that human beings were created in the likeness of 'the King of all' and were therefore made to exercise beneficent rule over the creation: 'clothed in virtue', 'decked with the crown of righteousness' and bearing the 'dignity of royalty' (τῆς βασιλείας ἀξιώματι) (Gregory of Nyssa, *On the Making of Man* IV.1).[11] As a consequence of the fall from the state of innocence, however, the divine image was distorted and could only be fully restored by being remade by the grace of God into the likeness of Christ (Kent 2017).[12] For Gregory of Nyssa, this restoration of the 'grace of the image' meant a restoration of the 'dignity of rule' (τῆς ἀρχῆς ἀξία) (Gregory of Nyssa, *On the Making of Man* XXI.4). As Leo the Great put it in one of his sermons:

> Wake up, human being, and recognize the dignity of your nature. Recall that you have been made according to the image of God, which, although it has been corrupted in Adam, has nevertheless been reformed in Christ. (Leo the Great, *Tractatus septem et nonaginta* 27.137, quoted in Kent (2017, 91))

III. Medieval Conceptions

In the medieval Latin West the term *dignitas* retained much of the semantic sense and range that it had in classical times, but in a way that was shaped by Christian doctrine (Kent 2017, 78). While many medieval works discussed 'the dignity of God or Christ, the angels, Christ's followers, or kings, bishops, priests, and other people with special offices', several important texts also expanded on the dignity that all people have because they are created in the divine image (73–74).[13]

In his treatise *On Loving God*, Bernard of Clairvaux understood dignity, alongside knowledge and virtue, to be the first of the three attributes of our 'higher nature' (*dignitatum, scientia, virtus*), the quality that distinguishes human beings from non-sentient animals. Dignity, for Bernard, meant free will (*liberum arbitrium*), the attribute by which human beings excel when compared with all other earthly creatures and the reason why they have dominion over them. Knowledge he considered to be the capacity to recognise the dignity possessed by all human beings and to understand that it is in its nature a gift rather than an accomplishment. Virtue, in turn, is the quality that impels man to seek for and adhere to the divine source and author of these good gifts. Bernard emphasised that all three qualities are vital. Dignity, although a 'peculiar eminence' naturally enjoyed by all human beings, is worthless without knowledge and harmful without virtue. When

---

[11] See also XVI.16, making clear that this dignity applies to 'all mankind', for all 'equally bear in themselves the Divine image'.

[12] Indeed, as Kent observes, everything has dignity by virtue of its creation by God, from the angels in heaven to the lowest earthly things (2017, 78).

[13] *Dignitas* obtained a highly technical meaning in medieval jurisprudence in which it designated a quality that attached to high offices such as king and bishop. See Kantorowicz (1957, 383–450).

men lack wisdom they are prone to two errors, one which leads them captive to merely sensual things and makes them comparable to irrational beasts, the other which causes them to glory in their dignity, forgetting that it is a gift given to them by God and usurping the glory that is alone due to Him. For this reason, Bernard stressed the importance of adding virtue to dignity and knowledge. He put it this way:

> Who is so impious as to attribute the splendour in the soul to another author of human dignity than the one who says in Genesis, 'Let us make man in our image, after Our likeness'? (Genesis 1:26). Who else would he esteem as the giver of knowledge except him 'who teaches man knowledge'? (Psalm 94:10). Who would he think had given him virtue, or from whom would he hope for virtue, except from the Lord of virtue? Therefore even the unbeliever who does not know Christ, but knows himself, ought to love God for God's own sake. He is therefore unpardonable if he does not love the Lord his God with all his heart, and with all his soul, and with all his strength; for the justice innate in him, and not unknown to reason, cries out that with his whole self he should love him, to whom he knows he owes his whole self.[14]

In this discussion, Bernard gave expression to the prevailing medieval understanding of the *imago Dei* as involving both intellectual capacities and moral dispositions. All people have the inner knowledge that they are bound wholly to love God, but achieving this is difficult to the point of impossibility for 'man by his own strength' and 'in the power of his free will'. The fall has disordered our natural dispositions and capacities, and they can only fully be restored by the grace of God.

Thomas Aquinas took these themes further. Like Bernard, he considered the image of God to consist in our creation as intelligent beings endowed with free will and self-movement.[15] Free will, in his view, is simultaneously a faculty of reason and a faculty of will which is properly directed towards truth, goodness and, ultimately, beatitude. Following Peter Lombard, it is a 'faculty of reason and will, through which good is chosen with grace assisting, or evil with grace desisting' (Peter Lombard, *In Sent.* II.24.3). Accordingly, it is also 'a power, progressively formed in us, to produce moral acts of excellence' (Pinckaers 2005, 138). Bad choices are not fully acts of freedom, for they involve a kind of bondage to sensual cravings rather than decisions directed by reason and oriented to that which is truly good.

---

[14] See https://www.pathsoflove.com/bernard/on-loving-god.html.

[15] As Servais Pinckaers points out, Aquinas's discussion of the image of God was positioned at the pivotal point in the *Summa Theologiae* where he turned from theology to anthropology. See Pinckaers (2005, 130, 132–33). See also *ST* I–II, prologue:

> Since, as Damascene states (*De Fide Orthod.* II, 12), man is said to be made to God's image, insofar as the image implies an intelligent being endowed with free will and self-movement: now that we have treated of the exemplar, i.e., God, and of those things which came forth from the power of God in accordance with His will; it remains for us to treat of His image, i.e., man, inasmuch as he too is the principle of his actions, as having free will and control of his actions.

Many of the hundreds of Aquinas's references to *dignitas* reflect the diverse senses of the term derived from classical usage (Pinckaers 2005, 146). His most consequential discussions of the matter appear, however, in connection with his consideration of what it means to be a 'person', especially in relation to the Christian doctrines of the Trinity and the Incarnation. Following Boethius, Aquinas defined 'person' as an 'individual substance of a rational nature' (*ST* I.29.1). Noting that the term 'persona' had been used to designate the theatrical portrayal of prominent city dignitaries, he considered it fitting to use the term to designate even the divine persons of the Trinity. Observing that 'subsistence in a rational nature' is itself a status 'of high dignity', Aquinas extended the same honour of 'personhood' to every individual who possesses a rational nature (*ST* I.29.3 ad 2). As Pinckaers has observed, this enabled Aquinas to continue to use the term *dignitas* to designate the high personages of medieval civil and ecclesiastical society, but also to use the term 'persona' to designate every human being, since everyone possesses the dignity of human nature (Pinckaers 2005, 151). As a consequence, all human beings were considered to have *dignitas* in this basic sense, but they may become more dignified to the extent that they better come to resemble the divine personality (152).

According to Aquinas, it was due to both the dignity and the fallenness of human nature that it was a fitting or suitable candidate for union with the divine nature in the Incarnation (*ST* III.4.1). Here, recall that, for Aquinas, the dignity of human nature consisted in its rationality and its capacity to know and love God, whereas the fallenness of human nature consisted in its defection from the divine image in which it had been created. It followed, remarkably, that the union of human nature with the divine elevated it to an even higher dignity than could be grasped if humanity were conceived merely in itself, let alone in its fallen nature, without any relationship to God. Thus, Aquinas observed that one of the reasons for the Incarnation was 'to teach us about the great dignity of human nature, so that we will avoid marring it by sin' (*ST* III.1.2; *Summa Contra Gentiles* IV.54).

In this way the whole point of human dignity was, for Aquinas, entirely moral and theological. As Pinckaers has pointed out, the result was a threefold conception: first, the basic and ineradicable dignity possessed by all human beings due to their rational capacity to know and love God; second, the inherent potential for growth and development in virtue through the course of a life lived under the influence of divine grace; and third, the perfect knowledge and love of God that may be secured in the heavenly beatitude, the ultimate human destiny (2005, 158). In this theological context, while sin can never destroy the inherent dignity of the human person, it does diminish our natural inclination to virtue, truth and goodness, and therefore causes us to 'fall away' from our original created dignity and to 'fall into' the 'slavish state of the beasts' (*ST* II.II, Q 64, Article 2, ad 3). Sinful human beings are therefore deserving of punishment for their sins: not because they have become irrational animals in their essential nature, but because they have the high dignity of human nature and therefore possess the capacity to choose between good and evil. Given the extraordinary powers of human beings to use their rational capacities rightly or wrongly, Aquinas's observation was blunt and to the point: 'a bad man is worse than a beast, and is more harmful' (*ST* II.II, Q 64, Article 2, ad 3; see Budziszewski (2014, 160–66)).

IV. Reformation Conceptions

In his *Politica Methodice Digesta*, first published in 1603, Johannes Althusius developed the concept of *dignitas* in a further direction.[16] A jurist and syndic of the Calvinist city of Herborn, Althusius adhered to the Protestant tendency to emphasise the Ten Commandments as setting forth the organising principles of a Reformed Christian polity (Witte 2002, 2007). Following the traditional method of exegesis, Althusius distinguished between the 'First Table' of the Decalogue as setting out the duties that human beings owe to God and the 'Second Table' as setting out the duties that they owe to each other. He accepted that the duties contained in the Second Table implied the existence of correlative rights (Althusius, *Politica* X.6). Thus, the duty not to steal the property belonging to one's neighbour necessarily entailed the right of the neighbour to the possession of his lawful property. Reflecting on the principle underlying the duties and rights contained in the Second Table, Althusius strikingly observed that they were especially concerned with the 'preservation of human dignity' (*conservanda dignitate hominis*) (Althusius, *Politica* 1603 ed. XVI, 206). He put it this way:

> Thus we render to him honour, authority, dignity, pre-eminence, and, indeed, the right of family; nor do we, on the contrary, despise him or hold him in contempt, the fifth precept of the Decalogue. His life is to be defended and conserved, and his body may not be injured, hurt, struck, or treated in any inhumane way whatever, nor may the liberty and use of his body be diminished or taken away, the sixth precept. His chastity is to be left intact, free from fornication, and may not be taken away in any manner whatever, the seventh precept. His goods and their possession, use, and ownership are to be conserved, and they may not be injured, diminished, or taken away, the eighth precept. His reputation and good name are to be protected, and they may not be taken away, injured, or reduced by insults, lies, or slander, the ninth precept. And so one may not covet those things that belong to another, either by deliberation or by passion, but everything our neighbour possesses he is to use and enjoy free from the passion of our concupiscence and perverse desire. (X.7)

Notably, in Althusius's analysis, the ninth precept was particularly directed to the preservation of the reputation and good name of one's neighbour. Elsewhere he observed that the rights enjoyed by one's neighbour included the following:

> First, his natural life, including the liberty and safety of his own body. The opposite of these are terror, murder, injury, wounds, beatings, compulsion, slavery, fetters, and coercion. Secondly, the neighbour possesses his reputation, good name, honour, and dignity, which are called the 'second self' of man. (Opposed to them are insult, ill repute, and contempt.) Also pertaining to this category are the right of family, and the right of citizenship that belongs to some. Thirdly, a man has external goods that he uses and enjoys, opposed to which are the corruption, damage, and impairing of his goods in any form, as well as their plundering or robbery, and any violation of their possession or artificial impediment to their use. (X.6)

---

[16] Unless otherwise indicated, references are to the abridged translation by Frederick Carney (1995).

In this discussion, dignity is something both rightly possessed by and properly accorded to one's neighbour, alongside honour, authority and even a kind of pre-eminence, and this duty to uphold the dignity of our neighbour is indissolubly associated with the full ensemble of rights possessed by our neighbour, consistently with Christian teachings.

Althusius presented much of this material in the context of his discussion of what he called the 'commonwealth' or 'universal association'. The commonwealth, he said, provides the political context in which 'the necessary and convenient means for carrying on a common life of justice together are communicated' among the 'members' of the society (X.1). However, for Althusius, the members of the commonwealth are not merely individuals. The commonwealth is properly understood to be a 'mixed society' consisting of 'many symbiotic associations and particular bodies [...] brought together under one right' (IX.1). These associations and bodies are 'variously private, natural, necessary, and voluntary' as well as 'public', and they include 'families, cities, and provinces' (IX.1). Accordingly, human society develops 'by the definite steps and progressions of small societies' (V.1), for families, cities and provinces 'existed by nature prior to realms, and gave birth to them' (IX.1).

According to Althusius, our first associations are, fundamentally, the families into which we are born and within which we are nurtured. The deep personal bonds of this 'most intense' form of 'society, friendship, relationship, and union' constitute 'the seedbed of every other symbiotic association' (II.14). It follows that husband and wife will share the same family name, the same rank (*dignitatum*), the same status and the same condition (II.12). Next, and beyond the natural and necessary bonds of families and kinship groups, the second important category of human association are the civil and voluntary associations which Althusius called *collegia* (IV). He considered this category of human sociability to be very various and extensive:

> Collegia of bakers, tailors, builders, merchants, coiners of money, as well as philosophers, theologians, government officials, and others that every city needs for the proper functioning of its social life. Some of these collegia are ecclesiastical and sacred, instituted for the sake of divine things; others are secular and profane, instituted for the sake of human things. The first are collegia of theologians and philosophers. The second are collegia of magistrates and judges, and of various craftsmen, merchants, and rural folk. (IV.30)

These associations, although voluntary, constitute the building blocks of every political community. The first of the specifically political associations, for Althusius, is the city, which he observed is 'an association formed by fixed laws and composed of many families and collegia living in the same place' (V.7–8). Here there is again variety, and a progression from small and local to relatively larger and more extended, in a succession of nested distinctions between hamlets, villages, towns and cities (V.28–41), for even the fully developed city is conceived as an association of hamlets and villages (V.40–41). Next, there is the province, which 'contains within its territory many villages, towns, outposts, and cities united under the communion and administration of one right (*ius*)' (VII.1). And finally, there is the 'universal and major public association', which is formed when 'many cities and provinces obligate themselves to hold, organize, use, and defend, through their common energies and expenditures, the right of the realm (*ius regni*) in the mutual communication of things and services' (IX.1).

All of these associations, from the private and voluntary to the public and compulsory, despite their diversity, are subject to the same principle of 'symbiosis', which is an organic-like relationship involving 'mutual communication of whatever is useful and necessary for the harmonious exercise of social life' (I.2). Thus: 'communication among citizens of the same community for the purpose of self-sufficiency and symbiosis pertains to things, services, right, and mutual concord' (IV.15). Nonetheless:

> Concord is fostered and protected by fairness (*aequabilitas*) when right, liberty, and honour are extended to each citizen according to the order and distinction of his worth and status. For it behooves the citizen to live by fair and suitable right with his neighbour, displaying neither arrogance nor servility, and thus to will whatever is tranquil and honest in the city. Contrary to this fairness is equality (*aequalitas*), by which individual citizens are levelled among themselves. (VI.47)

In this complex way, Althusius considered *dignitas* to be foundational to the rights of all human beings – a quality enjoyed by all equally – and yet it was also, in another sense, a quality that might be variously distributed within a society in proportion to the specific roles and offices held by each member. Dignity and honour are owed to everyone within the commonwealth, but there are also degrees of authority, dignity and honour distributed among citizens in order to preserve proper order. The term *dignitas* thus continued to retain much of the varied and relative meaning it had in classical Latin, but it was also used to designate what today might be called the special 'honours' that are accorded to individuals in view of their particular roles or contributions to the good of the community. Also, importantly, Althusius understood the concept of dignity in the context of rich social ontology in which not only individuals, but also families, *collegia*, cities and provinces, are the constituent members of the political order as a whole. Those who hold office within the commonwealth are therefore bound to exercise their powers in accordance with their particular vocations and duties (XVIII.43). The due performance of these responsibilities (*munera*) are the 'bonds and nerves', he explains, 'by which so great a conjunction of diverse bodies is held together and conserved' (XIV.1–2).

Russell Hittinger has drawn attention to similar themes in contemporary Catholic social teaching, particularly in relation to what has become known as the *munus regale* – the function, mission, gift or vocation of ruling. The *munus regale*, Hittinger explains, originated in theological reflection on the offices of Christ as prophet, priest and king, and the recognition that all Christians participate in these *munera* by virtue of their baptism.[17] All individual human beings are the recipients of manifold divine gifts or talents which constitute their calling or vocation, and they exercise these *munera* in all of the diverse spheres of life, such that even the associations themselves – families, corporations,

---

[17] See Russell Hittinger (2002, 385, 388–89, 390, 405, 407), citing John Paul II, *Lumen gentium* (1964) §§ 31, 36; *Catechism of the Catholic Church* (1997) §§ 436, 783–86; John Paul II, *Christifidelis Laici* (1988) § 14. See also Kantorowicz (1957, 489–91).

churches, states – are said to have *munera*, together with the rights (*ius*) necessary to fulfil their distinctive callings (Hittinger 2002, 390–91). As a consequence, human rights find their rationale in the *munera* and are expressed through a plurality of social forms (391).

It was these societies – families, unions, religious orders – that the totalitarian regimes of the twentieth century had attempted to deprive of their legal personality and independence. Pius XI (1922–39) responded by making clear, as Hittinger explains, that rights are not derived from human nature 'abstractly considered' but rather flow from a human nature already bearing and exhibiting a social ontology. Accordingly, negative rights (*immunities*) are not the logical starting point of rights, but rather exist in order to safeguard antecedent *munera*. The common good thus has a 'manifold organicity' (Hittinger 2002, 393). In this view, the role of the state is not primarily distributive, but rather facilitative and supportive. The state recognises and supports an existing distribution of *munera* that is already contributing to the common good in manifold ways – through families, schools, hospitals, charities and so on. It is with this understanding in mind that the principle of subsidiarity must be understood (*Catechism of the Catholic Church* 1997, sections 1883–5). Every human being – as a person created in the *imago Dei* – has been given a unique set of gifts and is called to a particular vocation which is inherently relational and social. It is in this that human dignity consists. As Benedict XVI (2009) put it in *Caritas in Veritate*, 'Subsidiarity respects personal dignity by recognizing in the person a subject who is always capable of giving something to others'.[18] And as the Second Vatican Council taught, the human dignity that is the foundation of all human rights is a quality that reflects the social and communal nature of human beings (Paul VI 1965).

V. Modern Western Conceptions

Many modern conceptions of human rights downplay the social embeddedness of the human person. Immanuel Kant's conception of human dignity is an important part of this development, although in some ways, it is possible to discern the imprint of older, medieval ideas on his thought (Insole 2015). In particular, his focus on practical reason – even if for the purpose of engaging in a critique of it – recalls the long tradition, reflected in Gregory of Nyssa, Bernard of Clairvaux and Thomas Aquinas, that human dignity is intimately associated with our rational nature and capacity to make moral choices.[19] Moreover, despite Kant's far-reaching criticisms of metaphysics generally (1999 [1781, 1782]), he developed what he was prepared to call a 'groundwork' for a 'metaphysics of morals' (2011 [1785], 10–11 (4.391)).[20] However, what he meant

---

[18] Benedict XVI (2009): 'The contribution of disciplines such as metaphysics and theology is needed if man's *transcendent dignity* is to be properly understood' (emphasis added).

[19] To be more precise, Kant proposed a critique of *pure* practical reason: see Kant (2011 [1785], 10–11 (4.391)).

[20] See also Kant (2011, 80–81 (4.426)): 'One must, however reluctantly, take a step outside, namely into metaphysics, if into a region of it that differs from that of speculative philosophy, namely into the metaphysics of morals'. On the various senses in which Kant used the term, see Schönecker and Wood (2015, 3–4, 14–25).

by metaphysics in this context was not what it had meant in medieval philosophy. Kant was insistent that the principles of morality are not to be derived from our knowledge of human nature, let alone divine revelation, but are rather to be found in 'purely rational concepts' known a priori without any resort to anthropology or theology (Kant 2011, 48–49 (4.410)).[21] This metaphysics of morality entailed an individualisation of human dignity in two correlative ways: first, in his concept of each human being as a 'moral self-legislator' (94–105 (4.433–438)), and second, in his understanding of each human being as an 'end in itself' (84–87 (4.428–9)). For Kant, human freedom is 'the key to the definition of the autonomy of the will', and this 'autonomy' is 'the ground of the dignity of human nature' (100–101 (4.436); 120–21 (4.446)). For 'the dignity of a rational being' consists in its obeying 'no law other than that which at the same time it itself gives' (96–97 (4.434); 108–9 (4.440)).[22]

Kant's theory should not be seen as specifically endorsing the view that each individual is free to make up their own morality in some radically subjective sense (Schönecker and Wood 2015, 17–18). In his account, the individual does not have the right simply 'to do as one chooses' (Rosen 2013, 150), for the categorical imperative imposes a duty that binds the rational will to act only in a way that treats humanity – in one's own person as well as in the person of any other – as an end and never as a means to some other end.[23] Such a conception of human autonomy has, however, become increasingly common in many contemporary Western societies. Such a view was articulated, for example, by the US Supreme Court when it referred to the 'right of the individual' to make personal choices 'central to personal dignity and autonomy', a conception of liberty which at its heart involved 'the right to define one's own concept of existence, of meaning, of the universe, and of the mystery of human life'.[24] Likewise, a leading judgement of the Canadian Supreme Court adopted, under the guise of 'the inherent dignity and inviolable rights of the human person', a conception of freedom of religion described to be 'personal' and 'subjective', and therefore 'integrally linked with an individual's self-definition and fulfilment' and 'a function of personal autonomy and choice'.[25] Aharon Barak, summarising a line of decisions of the Supreme Court of Israel, has similarly written that human dignity 'extends to all those activities in which human beings must be recognized as free agents, developing their body and mind according their own free will' (2013, 368). Observing, moreover, that individuals must also live within society, he went on to characterise the social context as involving 'mutual relationships between the

---

[21]   See also Kant (2011, 110–15 (4.441–443)).

[22]   The opposite of autonomy is heteronomy, which exists whenever the will is subjected to something outside the will, even some 'good' property of an object external to the will. In such a case, 'the will in that case does not give itself the law; instead the object, by means of its relation to the will, gives the law to it' (Kant 2011, 110–11 (4.441)).

[23]   Kant (2011, 86–87 (4.429)). Kant said that 'rational beings are called *persons*, because their nature already marks them out as ends in themselves'; he also explained that they are called this because all rational beings are universal legislators: cf. 84–85 (4.428)) and 104–5 (4.438)).

[24]   *Planned Parenthood v. Casey*, 505 US 833, 851 (1992).

[25]   *Syndicat Northcrest v. Amselem*, [2004] 2 SCR 551, 577.

individual and other individuals, and between them and the state' (369). Notably, however, he made no mention of intermediate groups or associations between the individual and the state.

Taken to their logical conclusions, such conceptions of individual autonomy have four important implications for the concept of human dignity. First, conceiving human rights as abstract *liberty* rights tends to hollow out the concept of dignity. Dignity comes to be seen as autonomy, meaning nothing more than the right to exercise an array of freedoms in any manner and in pursuit of any goals, provided this does not interfere with the rights of others. In this view, the concept of dignity is hollowed out because it is divested of any essential connection to duty, virtue or teleology, except the duty not to interfere with the rights of others. Second, conceiving human rights as abstract *equality* rights tends to flatten the concept of dignity. Dignity comes to be seen as equality, meaning nothing more than a right to equal treatment, without discrimination, understood in both formal and substantive terms. In this view there can be no gradations of dignity, no distinctions of honour, deference or moral expectation accorded to persons on the basis of their character, office or role. Third, conceiving of human rights as abstract *individual* rights tends to atomise the concept of dignity. Dignity comes to be seen as nothing more than the liberty and equality of the individual considered in abstraction from the associations, communities and groups in which each individual is situated. Such groups and associations are nothing more than constructs of individual human choices. Fourth, and most radically, grounding human rights in individual choices threatens to explode them into expressions of individual *will* unlimited by the rights of others. For when the individual will is absolutised, the endpoint is Friedrich Nietzsche's will to power, a world in which 'man in himself [...] possesses neither dignity, nor rights, nor duties' (1911, 17).

All four of these implications have a tendency, collectively, to undermine the social ontology of human rights and human dignity (Glendon 1999). Freedom of religion, in particular, is liable under such conceptions to be individualised, flattened and hollowed out, with the effect of undermining the collective capacity of religious believers to live in committed relationships in which duties are owed, the virtuous are especially esteemed and personal rights are set aside in favour of the good of the whole.[26] Human dignity, under the influence of such conceptions, becomes a basis on which religious freedom is limited rather than protected (McCrudden 2013). For when religious freedom is 'integrally linked with an individual's self-definition and fulfilment' and 'a function of personal autonomy and choice', the whole concept of 'communal religion' is undermined in its very foundation.[27]

---

[26] As Julian Rivers has put it, 'In a postmodern context which idolizes self-constructed identities, religions can only be valuable as personal ideologies' or as 'the projections of individuals' (2013, 419).

[27] See Trigg (2012, 104–5), discussing *Syndicat Northcrest v. Amselem*, [2004] 2 SCR 551.

Conclusions

It is recognised that the international human rights instruments of the post-war era were shaped by diverse influences, including the Catholic personalism effectively promoted by Jacques Maritain. Samuel Moyn has gone so far as to argue that this kind of personalism was the conceptual means through which post-war continental Europe first embraced human rights (Moyn 2010, 2011). The language of the UDHR and the later ICCPR owes much to this, although it also displays other significant influences (Morsink 2009, chapter 1). As argued in this chapter, while many of the rights protected in international instruments are framed as rights of the individual, many also have important and ineradicable social, collective, corporate or communal dimensions. As Charles Malik, one of the founders of international human rights, put it, the relationship between the individual and the state must always be understood in the context of the 'innumerable other intermediate loyalties which the individual must respect', such as families, professions, associations and so on. 'Real freedom', he said, 'must spring from the loyalty of the individual not to the state but to these intermediate forms', and these forms must therefore 'find their place in the general social picture' (cited in Morsink 2010, 242).

Recognising the social dimensions of human dignity may help to clarify the relationship between older classical, medieval and reformed conceptions of *dignitas* and modern conceptions of dignity. Modern conceptions tend to regard dignity as an attribute of all individuals, possessed equally by all, unaffected by a person's social or economic class or status within a society and unrelated to one's virtue or character. On the other hand, classical conceptions tended to regard *dignitas* as a relative and merited attribute, determined largely by a person's status in society and dependent on the virtuous performance of the obligations associated with that person's position and office. Between these two views, Christian medieval and reformed views emphasised that dignity is a quality possessed by all human beings by virtue of their creation in the image of God. This means that all human persons enjoy the same fundamental rights and are all held to the same fundamental standards of behaviour. However, each person is also embedded in a social and communal context in which he or she is expected not only to respect the rights of others, but also to perform his or her own duties towards others and pursue the common welfare of all (Paul VI 1965, [7]).

This social ontology of human rights and human dignity is fundamental to the Western tradition. It is only in certain modern conceptions that human dignity has become disassociated from the qualities of one's character and from the associations and communities in which human beings are naturally embedded. It follows that international human rights law, insofar as it recognises a social ontology which is simultaneously individualistic, associational and communal, is not entirely oriented to modern Western atomising conceptions of human dignity, but embraces older Western and possibly wider non-Western conceptions as well.

References

Althusius. 1603. *Politica Methodice digesta et exemplis sacris et profanes illustra*, 1st ed. Herborn: Christophorous Corvinus.

Barak, Aharon. 2013. 'Human Dignity: The Constitutional Value and the Constitutional Right'. In *Understanding Human Dignity*, edited by Christopher McCrudden, 361–80. Oxford: British Academy.

Benedict XVI. 2009. *Caritas in Veritate*. Libreria Editrice Vaticana. http://www.vatican.va/content/benedict-xvi/en/encyclicals/documents/hf_ben-xvi_enc_20090629_caritas-in-veritate.html.

Budziszewski, Jay. 2014. *Companion to the Commentary on Thomas Aquinas's Treatise on Law*. New York: Cambridge University Press.

Cancik, Hubert. 2002. '"Dignity of Man" and "Persona" in Stoic Anthropology: Some Remarks on Cicero, De Officiis I 105–107'. In *The Concept of Human Dignity in Human Rights Discourse*, edited by David Kretzmer and Eckart Klein, 19–40. The Hague: Kluwer Law International.

Carney, Frederick. 1995. *Politica: An Abridged Translation of Politics Methodically Set Forth and Illustrated with Sacred and Profane Examples*. Indianapolis, IN: Liberty Fund.

Cassin, René. 1972. *La Pensée at l'Action*. Boulogne-sur-Seine: F. Lalou.

Catechism of the Catholic Church. 1997. Libreria Editrice Vaticana. http://www.vatican.va/archive/eng0015/_index.htm.

de la Chapelle, Philippe. 1967. *La Declaration Universelle des Droits de L'Homme et le Catholicisme*. Paris: R. Pichon and R. Durand-Auzias.

Glendon, Mary Ann. 1999. 'Knowing the Universal Declaration of Human Rights'. *Notre Dame Law Review* 73, no. 5: 1153–90.

———. 2001. 'Interview: Professor Mary Ann Glendon Discusses the Role of Charles Malik in Drafting the Universal Declaration of Human Rights'. *All Things Considered*, Public Broadcasting Station, 26 March.

Gould, Carol. 2015. 'A Social Ontology of Human Rights'. In *Philosophical Foundations of Human Rights*, edited by Rowan Cruft, S. Matthew Liao and Massimo Renzo, 177–95. Oxford: Oxford University Press.

Griffin, Miriam. 2017. 'Dignity in Roman and Stoic Thought'. In *Dignity: A History*, edited by Remy Debes, 47–66. Oxford: Oxford University Press.

Harper, Kyle. 2016. 'Christianity and the Roots of Human Dignity in Late Antiquity'. In *Christianity and Freedom*, vol. 1, edited by Timothy Shah and Allen Hertzke, 123–48. New York: Cambridge University Press.

Hatzis, Nicholas. 2011. 'Personal Religious Beliefs in the Workplace: How Not to Define Indirect Discrimination'. *Modern Law Review* 74, no. 2 (March): 287–305.

Hittinger, Russell. 2002. 'Social Pluralism in Catholic Social Doctrine'. *Annales Theologici* 16, no. 2: 385–408.

Insole, Christopher J. 2015. 'A Thomistic Reading of Kant's Groundwork of the Metaphysics of Morals: Searching for the Unconditioned'. *Modern Theology* 31, no. 2: 284–311.

Johnson, M. Glen, and Janusz Symonides. 1998. *The Universal Declaration of Human Rights: A History of Its Creation and Implementation, 1948–1998*. UNESCO.

Joseph, Sarah, and Melissa Castan. 2013. *The International Covenant on Civil and Political Rights: Cases, Materials, and Commentary*, 3rd ed. Oxford: Oxford University Press.

Kant, Immanuel. 1999 [1781, 1782]. *Critique of Pure Reason*. Translated and edited by Paul Guyer and Allen Wood. Cambridge: Cambridge University Press.

———. 2011 [1785]. *Groundwork for the Metaphysics of Morals*. Translated by Mary Gregor and Jens Timmerman. Cambridge: Cambridge University Press.

Kantorowicz, Ernst H. 1957. *The King's Two Bodies: A Study in Mediaeval Political Theology*. Princeton, NJ: Princeton University Press.

Kent, Bonnie. 2017. 'In the Image of God: Human Dignity after the Fall'. In *Dignity: A History*, edited by Remy Debes, 73–98. Oxford: Oxford University Press.

McCrudden, Christopher. 2013. 'Dignity and Religion'. In *Islam and English Law: Rights, Responsibilities and the Place of Shari'a*, edited by Robin Griffith-Jones, 94–106. Cambridge: Cambridge University Press,

Milbank, John. 2013. 'Dignity Rather Than Rights'. In *Understanding Human Dignity*, edited by Christopher McCrudden, 189–206. Oxford: British Academy.

Morsink, Johannes. 2009. *Inherent Rights: Philosophical Roots of the Universal Declaration.* Philadelphia: University of Pennsylvania Press.

———. 2010. *The Universal Declaration of Human Rights: Origins, Drafting, and Intent.* Philadelphia: University of Pennsylvania Press.

Moyn, Samuel. 2010. 'Personalism, Community, and the Origins of Human Rights'. In *Human Rights in the Twentieth Century*, edited by Stefan-Ludwin Hoffman, 85–106. Cambridge: Cambridge University Press.

———. 2011. 'Jacques Maritain, Christian New Order, and the Origins of Human Rights'. In *Intercultural Dialogue and Human Rights*, edited by Luigi Bonanante, Roberto Papini and William Sweet, 55–76. Washington, DC: Council for Research in Values and Philosophy.

Nietzsche, Friedrich. 1911. 'Preface to an Unwritten Book: The Greek State'. In *Early Greek Philosophy and Other Essays*, translated by Maximilian A. Mügge, 1–18. London: Macmillan.

Nowak, Manfred. 1993. *CCPR Commentary*. Kehl am Rhein: Engel.

Paul VI. 1965. *Dignitatis Humanae: On the Right of the Person and of Communities to Social and Civil Freedom in Matters Religious.* http://www.vatican.va/archive/hist_councils/ii_vatican_council/documents/vat-ii_decl_19651207_dignitatis-humanae_en.html.

Pinckaers, Servais. 2005. 'Ethics and the Image of God'. In *The Pinckaers Reader: Renewing Thomistic Moral Theology*, edited by John Berkman and Craig Steven Titus, 130–43. Washington, DC: Catholic University of America Press.

Ramcharan, Robin, and B. G. Ramcharan. 2019. *Asia and the Drafting of the Universal Declaration of Human Rights.* Singapore: Springer.

Rivers, Julian. 2010. *The Law of Organized Religions: Between Establishment and Secularism.* Oxford: Oxford University Press.

———. 2013. 'Justifying Freedom of Religion: Does Dignity Help?' In *Understanding Human Dignity*, edited by Christopher McCrudden, 405–19. Oxford: British Academy.

Rosen, Michael. 2013. 'Dignity: The Case Against'. In *Understanding Human Dignity*, edited by Christopher McCrudden, 143–54. Oxford: British Academy.

Schönecker, Dieter, and Allen W. Wood. 2015. *Immanuel Kant's 'Groundwork for the Metaphysics of Morals': A Commentary*. Cambridge, MA: Harvard University Press.

Trigg, Roger. 2012. *Equality, Freedom, and Religion*. Oxford: Oxford University Press.

Witte, John. 2002. *Law and Protestantism: The Legal Teachings of the Lutheran Reformation.* New York: Cambridge University Press.

———. 2007. *The Reformation of Rights: Law, Religions, and Human Rights in Early Modern Calvinism.* New York: Cambridge University Press.

Chapter Eleven

HOW NOT TO INTERPRET HUMAN DIGNITY: A COMMON FALLACY

Friedrich Toepel

I. The Fallacy of Inferences from One Moral System to Another

The well-known tool for detecting a naturalistic fallacy is G. E. Moore's open question argument from the famous §13 of his *Principia Ethica* (1903, 15).[1] Just as Moore used the argument to show that the word 'good' must denote a non-natural quality, it can be shown that the term 'human dignity' in a legal system purporting to treat major moral systems with the same respect must denote something else than the meaning attributed to human dignity within a particular system. Just as Moore could meaningfully ask whether something conducive to pleasure, for example, is really good, it can be meaningfully asked whether it is really an expression of human dignity that a person is autonomous, that he is created in the image of God, that he is favoured by Allah, that he must be a working individual.

Just as Mackie observed in the second chapter of his *Ethics* that the meaning of good seems to be relative to egocentric commendations (1977, 55, 64), the meaning of human dignity seems to be relative to the perspective of certain moral systems.

It should be noted that the fallacy committed here is closely connected with the naturalistic fallacy of deriving an 'ought' from an 'is'. Moreover, when we contemplate this fallacy more closely, we learn that the temptation consists not so much in inferring a deontic ought from a factual statement. That would be impossible. Persons are rather tempted because they have grown up with a certain moral system, and therefore they tend to generalize the standards of that moral system as being valid also for people of other moral systems or for a legal system. This can easily be done without deriving a deontic ought from a factual statement. The way such persons argue is rather as follows:

(I)

There exists a norm that x ought to be done if situation s obtains [suppressing: according to the moral system A].

---

[1] I hereby wish to thank the audiences at the IVR World Congress in Lucerne, which took place on 8 July 2019 (workshop chaired by Angus J. L. Menuge and Barry W. Bussey), and Ulfrid Neumann's seminar in Frankfurt on 9 January 2020, for inspiring and helpful comments.

Situation s obtains.

There exists a norm that x ought to be done [suppressing: according to the moral system B, or: according to the legal system C].[2]

This seems to be a logically correct syllogism as long as the tacit assumptions in parentheses are not made explicit. Its premises and conclusion consist only of factual statements.

Please note that the first premise and the conclusion are worded in such a way as not to be interpreted as genuine deontic oughts. A deontic ought is characterized by demanding categorically that x ought to be done no matter the circumstances (Von Wright 1983, 153–54, 199–200). The first premise and the conclusion of the syllogism, however, are not worded in such a way[3] and are not meant to be understood as genuine oughts. They are rather formulated as statements which state that a certain norm exists, namely 'x ought to be done', and that is a fact. I use the term 'fact' here as denoting the content of a true statement (Austin 1979b, 118–19, 125, 133; Von Wright 1984, 14). I also intend the facts in the syllogism above to be understood as verifiable facts. The premise 'There exists a norm that x ought to be done if situation s obtains' can at least be regarded as falsified if no person ever acknowledges the existence of such a norm, and it is verified if an empirical survey shows that there are persons who acknowledge the existence of such a norm. In this way the existence of the norm can be regarded as a sociological fact which must be reflected in the codes or actual behaviour of some persons. Thus, a person uttering the syllogism above does not commit the fallacy of deriving an ought from an is, because all premises and the conclusion are purely factual.

But the facts stated are facts of a special sort. They are institutional facts, which means that they require institutions to exist at all (Searle 2010, 10–11). They are in this way contrasted to brute facts which exist independently of any institutions, for example, that the earth is 147.1 million kilometres from the sun. Institutions are systems[4] of constitutive

---

[2] When I presented my paper at the IVR Congress, I formulated 'It is the case that' instead of 'There exists a norm that'. I intended to make the syllogism sound as natural as possible in order to make it easier for my listeners to identify themselves with the syllogism. However, as some complained that syllogism (I) really would fallaciously derive an ought from an is, I decided to make the factual character of the premises more obvious by emphasizing the existence of the norm. Nonetheless, I still believe that 'It is the case that x ought to be done if situation s obtains' is a factual statement, not a genuine deontic ought identical with 'x ought to be done if situation s obtains'.

[3] Although you can, of course, make any words mean anything, as Mr Humpty Dumpty rightly observed (Carroll 2005, 78). However, as also becomes clear in the case of Mr Humpty Dumpty, it is not always practicable to make any word mean anything. You might fall off walls and become a scrambled egg.

[4] Please note that I understand systems in a sociological way here, not as mere theoretical constructs. They exist only if their rules are applied in practice in a way in which Hart characterized the so-called rule of recognition, which exists as 'a complex, but normally concordant, practice of the courts, officials and private persons in identifying the law by reference to certain criteria' (1997, 110).

rules created by a deontic authority.[5] They depend on the recognition of that authority. From a perspective which does not recognize the deontic authority as the competent authority for making the rules, the rules will not exist.

When inferring from the existence of rules within a system A that the same rules do also exist within system B or C, the additional difficulty arises that system A must have been coupled with system B or C in a way that the system B's or C's deontic authority has recognized the rule of system A as also belonging to system B or C. Such a sort of coupling of systems cannot just be presupposed, but must be verified. Therefore, if someone would conclude the following:

(II)

There exists a norm that x ought to be done if situation s obtains according to the moral system A.

Situation s obtains.

There exists a norm that x ought to be done according to the moral system B, or: according to the legal system C.

That is, (I) with the text in parentheses made explicit, then this would be an incorrect inference. If the person would believe that (II) is correct because (III) is correct, he would be deluded:

(III)

There exists a norm that x ought to be done if situation s obtains.

Situation s obtains.

There exists a norm that x ought to be done.

He would have committed a fallacy, just the kind of fallacy which I see people committing when interpreting human dignity in codes of law.[6]

---

5   Searle (2010, 145–73) uses the expression 'deontic power'; Lagerspetz (1995, 153) talks of 'authoritative positions'. Please note that I do not understand the term 'deontic authority' in such a way that only 'authoritarian' systems would fit the description. Under deontic authority I understand any person or body of persons empowered to legislate, execute or judge by the higher-order rules of the system. Without higher-order rules, a group of people is just a community. It cannot be a legal system (cf. Hart 1997, 79–99). Thus, deontic authorities exist with respect to any form of government, even a pure form of direct democracy in which the people as a whole are the deontic authority. Only anarchy is a form of government without any deontic authority. However, according to my view, a completely anarchical state cannot be a state at all.

6   I take the view that this kind of fallacy is also the explanation for many situations in which someone is accused of deriving an ought from an is: people not so much draw illogical inferences – which is a very difficult thing to do indeed – as pick up a statement which they already accept as morally binding because they are familiar with a moral system compatible with that statement, and they unduly generalize it. I know that the term 'naturalistic fallacy' is commonly used to describe the fallacy of deriving an ought from an is. However, as I explained, I believe that this classic naturalistic fallacy occurs much less than is generally assumed. The

Thus, if a rule within the Christian moral system is seen as being created by God, it can only be inferred correctly that this rule also exists within a certain legal system under the condition that the legal system has made the rules of the Christian moral system mandatory. A theocratic state could be an example for such a system. The Islamic states which have internalized the rules of Islam would be another example. If, however, the state is permitting its citizens other perspectives than certain religious ones such as the Christian or the Muslim view, then the inference from the mere existence of rules within these moral systems to the existence in a legal system is fallacious.

II. A Caveat: No Fallacy If Reference to a Certain Moral System Is Made Clear

Now, we have to distinguish very carefully here. Religious moral systems typically claim universalizability. This is plausible. If only the Christian God exists, then accepting the moral rules revealed by Him is an act of sheer self-preservation. The knowledge of God's existence makes the institutional facts existing in this moral system indistinguishable from brute facts. Believing in the existence of the God of the Bible makes it a fact that one who is authorized to pronounce genuine categorical oughts has indeed pronounced them, and everybody should listen. If the adherent of the moral system would intend to say no more than this, he would not commit a fallacy, but only pronounce what is obvious from his perspective. Are adherents to these systems therefore not committing a fallacy when they claim that everyone has the duty to follow the norms of the adherents' particular moral system?

That depends. Such universalized claims may just be interpretations of what the system itself acknowledges. According to the Bible, everyone should worship Jesus Christ as God, therefore also a Muslim or Jehovah's Witness should worship Jesus Christ as God. This is not at all fallacious because these adherents of the Christian moral system do make claims that worshipping Jesus Christ would be a deontic ought for each person, including Muslims and Jehovah's Witnesses. Such a characterization of the situation includes only a claim about Christian morality and that it would be binding for all human beings. It does not include the allegation that worshipping Jesus Christ would also belong to any other moral system like the Muslim or the Jehovah's Witnesses' moral system.

In other words, the Christians need only to be reporting and perhaps endorsing[7] exclusively the norms of the Christian moral system in order to avoid committing a

---

kind of fallacy which I describe in this chapter, like the classic naturalistic fallacy, commits the mistake of declaring something as binding in a certain system because of a fact, namely the sociological fact that the same binding norm exists within another system. Therefore I would be inclined to call this conclusion also a naturalistic fallacy, especially because I am convinced that it is the basis of most fallacies where the one who makes the mistake is accused of deriving an ought from an is. Yet, I do not want to be the source of confusion. For this reason I keep the old terminology and content myself by pointing out the parallel structure of the fallacy described in this chapter and the classic naturalistic fallacy.

[7] Originally, I was tempted to use Hart's (1997, 88–91, 243–44) and MacCormick's (1978, 275–92) distinction between internal, 'detached' and external perspectives for explaining the

fallacy. It is a requirement of honesty to clarify that they are not reporting the norms of any other moral or legal system. Some people just disregard the moral systems of others and make claims about certain universal duties, leaving the other persons who are taking part in the discussion in the dark about the systems to which they are referring. But though such a conduct could be called dishonest or unfair, it is not fallacious because if spelled out, the account can be seen as comprehensible and consistent.

Thus, as long as it is made clear that the speaker regards himself as a worker in the mission field, a fallacy does not arise. The difficulties begin when the speaker feels himself authorized to report that certain norms exist as parts of a moral or legal system merely because they are part of a very different moral system which he, the speaker, endorses without being able to invoke any grounds of justification for such a transfer. An adherent of a moral system having to make a judgement as a member of a legal system is in such a situation. If the legal system does not provide guidance for the interpretation of a certain norm belonging to the legal system and the moral system to which the speaker adheres does take a stance on the problem, then the speaker will be tempted to avail himself of the moral system's stance on the issue.

However, he should restrain himself at this moment. The inference would be fallacious that a certain norm of a legal system C should be interpreted in a certain way because the moral system A takes a certain stance on the problem. This would in particular be a fallacious inference if the deontic authorities of the legal system C have failed to internalize the relevant moral rules of system A.

At least the majority of modern European states view themselves as neutral regarding moral systems so that drawing the inference described from the existence of a moral rule to the existence of a corresponding rule within the legal systems would be fallacious.[8] For international legal systems, neutrality of the system with respect to moral systems is even more urgently needed than with respect to legal systems of nation states.

III. The Variety of Human Dignity Concepts

Now, the question is usually raised whether moral or legal systems, including views on human dignity, are really as diverse as some claim. If the different moral or legal systems only differ minimally, the fallacy which I described in the first section would lose its

---

problem involved. However, the discussion between these authors centres around the question whether a person makes statements about the law as someone for whom the law is a reason to act in a certain way, whether the person is a mere observer and whether he understands what he is describing as an observer (see also Lagerspetz 1995, 148; Patterson 1999, 70). The problem which I describe here is not so much whether an observer only makes his statements as an observer, whether he understands what he is observing or whether he is endorsing the norms, but rather whether his description of the norm content is correct or incorrect. Therefore, I have decided to avoid associations with Hart's or MacCormick's internal, detached and external perspectives.

[8] It cannot be examined in detail here whether this is different in Anglo-American countries in which common law allows for taking into account natural law to some extent.

significance. People may then perhaps not always reason correctly, but at least no serious negative consequences would follow from such inaccuracies because a general sense of what is appropriate and legitimate would compensate for these inaccuracies.

John Mackie's (1977, 36–38) scepticism may not be justified in the field of morality, but at any rate I share his argument from relativity in the field of law and transfer it to the interpretation of human dignity: at some time, there may have existed a definable common meaning for the term 'human dignity'. Whether this has been the case or not, at present human dignity seems to be everybody's favourite concept whichever moral system he has accepted.

What holds true for moral systems in general also holds true for human dignity. Universal acceptance of a certain meaning cannot be taken for granted on account of the variation of moral codes from one society to another.

There are some who, like John Finnis, find this argument 'unimpressive' because proper attention to history and anthropological data would show that the basic forms of human good and the corresponding practical principles would be recognized by human beings in all times and places (1983, 76–78). However, this does not address the core of the issue. There may be some features common to any moral system, but comparing some of the prevailing moral systems in the contemporary world teaches us that at least the edges and concrete formulations of common moral principles differ so vastly that hard cases[9] are bound to occur in which the moral systems contradict each other glaringly (for a very sceptical, theological view, see Montgomery 2005, 13–23). If a legal system has not fully adopted one such moral system, it therefore cannot simply rely on its judges to solve the hard cases by fleshing out the moral principles in the right way. The same is true for the interpretation of the term 'human dignity'.

The most technical meaning which the term ever acquired was developed by Kant. According to his *Groundwork for the Metaphysics of Morals*, for Kant human autonomy is the reason for human dignity (1911, 436) and has as a consequence that each person must treat himself and other human beings as an end in itself and never as a mere means (434). According to this concept, human dignity is inalienable. Yet, of course, there arise considerable difficulties when ascribing dignity to little children, particularly unborn babies, and to psychotic persons who are not able to choose rationally.[10]

For the Judeo-Christian tradition, a human being has dignity on the basis of having been created in the image of God (Gen. 1:27). This kind of dignity is also inalienable. The consequences of ascribing dignity to human beings according to this tradition are controversial, however. It is disputed, for example, whether enemies may be killed or capital punishment may be imposed on human beings in spite of their dignity.

---

[9] 'Hard cases' to be understood in the sense of Dworkin, who used the term for the first time in Dworkin (1975, 1057–109).

[10] When Kant applies his theory, he nevertheless surprisingly often comes to the same conclusion as the Judeo-Christian tradition. However, this is not due to his theory, but to the pietistic milieu in which he grew up and which he took for granted. It is not without reason that Nietzsche calls Kant's way of thinking that of a 'deceitful Christian in the end' ('*eines hinterlistigen Christen zuguterletzt*'; Nietzsche 1919, 81).

Islamic tradition likewise recognizes human dignity because Allah bestowed special favours on the progeny of Adam (Qur'an ('al-Isra'), 17:70). In Islam also, human dignity does not seem to prevent killing of people in war or imposing capital punishment. Islamic scholars have described the wearing of a headscarf as an expression of a woman's (and also a man's) human dignity (e.g. Khan 2003, 110).

Further, the communists used the term. In the Soviet party programs much emphasis was being placed on 'the all-around flourishing of the personality', 'the fullest extension of personal freedom and the rights of Soviet citizens', 'the protection of honor and dignity' and 'the full blossoming of the individual' (Towe 1967, 1270).

This quick overview of the past and present concepts of human dignity already shows clearly enough that they are bound to lead to an impasse sooner or later if they would all be accepted equally as meanings of a legal term 'human dignity'.

IV. 'Wittgensteinian Fideism' Is Not a Possible Solution

At the same time, this diversity of meaning shows that Wittgensteinian Fideism is not an acceptable solution for a legal context. Wittgensteinian fideists do not consider criticism of moral or religious systems as meaningful if they are made from the perspective of someone not endorsing those systems. For them it is only possible to understand these systems by adopting them as a form of life.

However, such a view does not help in international law because such terms as human dignity are not merely intended to be beautiful poetry. They are rather intended to have consequences for solving cases. If a solution is to be acceptable for all the different cultures, the language used to describe the legal standard must be unambiguous. Therefore, interpretations of terms which lead to different or even incompatible conclusions cannot be tolerated.

The view has been christened 'Wittgensteinian Fideism' because the clearest description of it is allegedly by Wittgenstein himself, and, following Wittgenstein, D. Z. Phillips. Whether it is based on a correct interpretation of Wittgenstein or whether it is taken out of context, I do not claim to decide authoritatively. In connection with the issue at hand, this view only serves to demonstrate that insisting on the impossibility of criticism outside a certain belief system is not acceptable in legal contexts.

The view I have in mind quotes Wittgenstein's first 'Lecture on Religious Belief':

> Suppose that someone believed in the Last Judgement, and I don't, does this mean that I believe the opposite to him, just that there won't be such a thing? I would say: 'Not at all, or not always.'
>
> Suppose I say that the body will rot, and another says 'No. Particles will rejoin in a thousand years, and there will be a Resurrection of you.'
>
> If some said: 'Wittgenstein, do you believe in this?' I'd say: 'No.' 'Do you contradict the man?' I'd say: 'No.'
>
> If you say this, the contradiction already lies in this.
>
> Would you say: 'I believe the opposite', or 'There is no reason to suppose such a thing'? I'd say neither.

> Suppose someone were a believer and said: 'I believe in a Last Judgement', and I said: 'Well, I'm not so sure. Possibly.' You would say that there is an enormous gulf between us. If he said, 'There is a German aeroplane overhead', and I said, 'Possibly, I'm not so sure', you'd say we were fairly near. (2007, 53; Phillips 1993, 33 ff.)

I take the view that it is not apparent whether Wittgenstein leaves room for the possibility that one may meaningfully speak of an observer standpoint concerning moral systems at all. In any case, he certainly regards it as decisive for understanding a moral system that you make its norms and presuppositions part of your belief system.[11]

Now, I am not sure whether Wittgenstein accepts the possibility of a dialogue in which one of the speakers endorses a moral system and the other takes an observer standpoint. Nonetheless, in my opinion, Wittgenstein shows that persons can only fully understand each other when they belong to the same moral system. Therefore, there can only be security about the application of norms or principles between persons accepting the same moral system. That means that there is no such security between persons trying to communicate while having internalized different moral systems.

If this would be correct, it could preclude the possibility of legislation in international bodies whose members have accepted different moral systems. Moral systems will contradict each other regarding the interpretation of human dignity, as we have seen. Therefore, if we accept all moral systems, there is no way to choose a solution valid for all. While we obviously cannot agree with such a view, I take it to be a valuable lesson that communication may fail if persons just insist on their respective moral systems without mutual regard for each other. This situation may arise because different moral systems may use overlapping vocabulary so that it may not even be apparent to each of the participants in the conversation which interpretation is used.

There are persons who take advantage of such a situation, and there are persons who are deluded by such a use of language. But whether they consciously exploit ambiguous language or whether they do it in good faith, both commit a fallacy closely related to the famous 'naturalistic fallacy'.

V. Human Dignity and Meaning as Use

If something could be gleaned from the preceding sections of this chapter regarding human dignity, it would be this: that human dignity has a variety of meanings relative to moral systems. Because of the vast spectrum of moral systems, one can never be sure that a meaning attributed to the term will be generally accepted and thus be a suitable interpretation when it is used within a legal system.

---

[11] This could also be expressed by saying that Wittgenstein presupposes that someone understanding a moral system sees the moral system from an internal perspective; see footnote 6.

Therefore, it seems reasonable to look for a solution which is similar to the one already attempted with respect to such words as 'I know' or 'It probably will ...' by Austin (1979a, 76–115) and Toulmin (1964, 47–93), both following the Wittgensteinian proposal to regard the meaning of the words as its use (Wittgenstein 1958, no. 43). The common element of all uses of human dignity seems to be that human dignity has the function of a placeholder for the indispensable elements of personhood ascribed to a human being when personhood is ascribed to it in a moral or legal system.

As moral or legal systems are autonomous or even – speaking with Luhmann (1997, 92–93) – autopoietic ('self-creating'), no overlapping content can be guaranteed. If a new legal system like the German Federal Republic in 1949 uses the term 'human dignity' in its constitution[12] without explaining it and if the previous German legal systems did not make use of that term,[13] the only possibility of interpretation is recourse to existing moral systems making use of the term. There, the difficulties begin because there is no guidance as to which moral notions to discard and which to take over. Accordingly, the judges have wide discretion when interpreting human dignity as used in the constitution. The result is very inconsistent case law.[14]

Incidentally, it should also be noted that because of the dependence of the meaning on an accepting deontic authority, human dignity must indeed be something that the law can confer on human beings. It may not be possible to construct human dignity in a totally arbitrary way. But, certainly, a specific interpretation of the term cannot be part of the moral or legal system if it has not been accepted by the relevant deontic authorities, whether they be part of the deontic authorities' legislative or judicial branches.

It is also not true that religious moral systems may see this differently. They only conceal the deontic authority when they declare that human dignity would be inherent in a person because of human nature. As nature is seen as dictated by God and God is

---

[12] German Constitution, Article 1 (1): 'Die Würde des Menschen ist unantastbar. Sie zu achten und zu schützen ist Verpflichtung aller staatlichen Gewalt' (Human dignity shall be inviolable. To respect and protect it shall be the duty of all state authority).

[13] The Weimar Constitution of 1919 only mentions human dignity en passant in connection with economy in Article 151: 'Die Ordnung des Wirtschaftslebens muss den Grundsätzen der Gerechtigkeit mit dem Ziele der Gewährleistung eines menschenwürdigen Daseins für alle entsprechen' (The regulation of economic life must be in accordance with the principles of justice which have the goal of ensuring an existence in line with human dignity for all). This is a formulation taken over from the first president of the German Workers' Union ('Deutscher Arbeiterverein'), Ferdinand Lassalle.

[14] Examples: According to the German courts, peep shows violate the human dignity of women who participate in them; prostitution and strip-tease dances do not (first decision: German Federal Administrative Court NVwZ 1982, 664). Laser tag games violate the human dignity of the tagged person (German Federal Administrative Court NVwZ 2002, 598). Paintball games do not (necessarily) violate the human dignity of the person hit by the paintball (Higher Administrative Court Mannheim NVwZ-RR 2005, 472; Administrative Court Dresden NVwZ-RR 2003, 848).

understood to be the creator of the relevant moral rules, these rules are also perceived as dependent on the acceptance of a person, namely God.

VI. Recommendation to Avoid the Term 'Human Dignity' in Law

In a pluralistic society, moral rules are a poor guide for the interpretation of human dignity. A Babylonian confusion of the languages used by moral systems prevents clear outcomes. In such a situation people are strongly tempted to commit the kind of fallacy I have described.

Therefore, contemporary legal systems which just use the term 'human dignity' without giving any hint to its interpretation act irresponsibly. Moreover, if my analysis is correct – that human dignity is a placeholder for the indispensable elements of person-hood – then a legal system would also contradict itself when simply leaving the inter-pretation to its (constitutional) judges. Personhood is a core notion of a legal system, for without it a civil law makes no sense. Thus, if a parliament just leaves the interpretation of the elements of personhood to its judges, it declares on the one hand that the matter is of utmost importance and on the other hand that it is not so important because it can be left to the lower authority of the judges to find out what these elements really are.

There can only be one clear solution: to avoid the term and, instead, explicitly define the indispensable elements of personhood in an unambiguous way.

VII. Refuting Some Objections

When this chapter was presented at the IVR Congress in Lucerne, some objections were raised against my statement that the inference from the existence of a norm in one legal or moral system to the conclusion of the norm's existence as part of another legal or moral system is fallacious. I take the view that these objections, for which I thank my learned colleagues, should be addressed here.

1. Metalogic as an Unsuitable Standard

Michał Rupniewski (author of Chapter 9 in this volume) objected against my character-ization of the inference from one moral system to another as a fallacy that I would use a rule of metalogic as a standard in order to disqualify a moral claim, and the rule of metalogic would be unsuitable for that purpose. If I were to assert that certain claims made by a moral system would only be valid for a certain system, then I would, without justification, assume that these claims could not be universally valid, for example.

If I had made such an allegation, it would indeed be unjustified. However, as I tried to clarify in this extended version of my presentation, I did not intend to deny that moral norms can be universally valid as is typically claimed by religious moral systems. My chapter is only concerned with the inference from the norm's existence within one moral system to the norm's existence within another system, particularly within a legal system.

I believe that such an inference is fallacious if no information exists that the norm of system A in the premises of syllogism (I) above has been accepted as authoritative by the system B or C in the conclusion of syllogism (I). That may even be the case if the norm is universally valid. This is so because systems of norms see the world from their own perspective, and the perspectives of different systems may differ. Even if it should therefore be possible that a norm is valid *semper et ubique*, that does not necessarily mean that all moral and legal systems do recognize that to be so. Let us presume that moral system A has got it objectively 'right', and its norms for some reason should be observed always and everywhere. That does not mean that these norms have to be part of moral system B or legal system C as well. It is perfectly comprehensible that the legislature of system C does not recognize the norms of system A and passes a law which contradicts the norms of system A. Then those laws which contradict the norms of system A have become part of system C, although that should not be the case according to the standard of system A or the objective standard. Inferring that nonetheless the norms of system A would be part of system C because of being valid *semper et ubique* would be fallacious.

2. International Norms Presuppose an Inherent Dignity

Iain Benson (author of Chapter 2 of Volume II) pointed out that texts of international law take human dignity to be an inherent concept. Therefore, reference to pre-legal moral systems seems to have been explicitly authorized by such international law and in this way the danger of a fallacy seems to be excluded.

Unfortunately, the problem cannot be solved so easily. It is true that the term 'human dignity' is predominantly seen as a pre-legal term in international legal texts. The International Covenant on Civil and Political Rights provides in Article 10 that 'all persons deprived of their liberty shall be treated [...] with the inherent dignity of the human person'. According to its preamble its rights 'derive from the inherent dignity of the human person'. The European Charter of Human Rights protects human dignity in its Article 1: 'Human dignity is inviolable. It must be respected and protected'. It thereby also seems to presuppose a pre-legal notion by ascribing inviolability to human dignity. The Charter of the United Nations only mentions human dignity in the non-binding part of its preamble, but indicates also that it understands human dignity as something pre-legal, to be found rather than created by legislation when the United Nations see themselves 'determined [...] to reaffirm faith in the [...] dignity and worth of the human person'. The Declaration of Human Rights is a legally non-binding resolution of the General Assembly, but nonetheless it is another indicator that human dignity in international contexts should be understood as an inherent property of persons when it provides in Article 1 that 'all human beings are born free and equal in rights. They are endowed with reason and conscience and should act towards one another in a spirit of brotherhood'.

Yet, dignity being understood as a pre-legal concept does not mean that its content may be arbitrarily chosen by reverting to any moral system whatsoever. Possibly, there are situations in which vagueness of terminology in international law will facilitate passing legislation. But it is irresponsible to keep up such a situation when replacement by more precise terms would be feasible. Otherwise, conflict is inevitable.

Regarding the Declaration of Human Rights, I will only draw attention to the attempt to interpret it as being strictly within a Christian tradition because the two chairpersons of the UN Commission on Human Rights, Eleanor Roosevelt and Charles Malik, were Christians (Moyn 2015). Authors coming from other religious or secular traditions likewise unabashedly attribute human dignity to their favourite tradition. In this way, German philosopher Nida-Rümelin, who was secretary of state for culture in the social-democratic government of Schröder, confidently places human dignity in a Kantian tradition (2005, 136–59). He is quoted by German legal scholars who do not even show a shadow of doubt regarding such an interpretation of human dignity (Petersen 2005, 460–61). This illustrates that treating human dignity as an inherent concept does not guarantee a correct interpretation. For this reason, there is clearly the need of explicitly defining the indispensable elements of personhood in an unambiguous way.

3. Scientific versus Religious Grounding of Human Dignity

Finally, some scholars seem to take the view that secular justifications of human dignity should be ranked higher than religious approaches with respect to their significance for the law. However, looking more closely at the so-called scientific approaches reveals that there is no reliable basis for a concept of human dignity that would make it a priori more important in legal contexts than other concepts.

Which criteria cogently prohibit providing active medical assistance in dying in order to be relieved from severe pain, for example?[15] Which argument cogently prohibits offsetting human interests against each other in a utilitarian way?[16] From what point on should human dignity be attributed to a foetus?

In my opinion, there are no compelling solutions which would exclude alternatives and which would escape the open question argument, and thus there is no other way than directly incorporating fundamental decisions on protected legal interests into the law. If this is not taken seriously, there is no escaping the fallacy described in this chapter, unless the context or the clearly expressed will of the legislator by way of exception allows for an unambiguous interpretation of human dignity in a certain legal document. However, it is very rarely the case that the context or the will of the legislator is sufficiently unambiguous.

The reason why I doubt whether a presumption of correctness should apply regarding a scientific explanation is that we are not in the field of a relevant science such as medicine

---

[15] This is a problem only in conservative countries like Germany where the criminal code contains a provision prohibiting 'killing at the request of the victim; mercy killing' (Section 216, German Criminal Code). Such a provision makes it necessary to distinguish between mere assisting with suicide, which is free of punishment, and causing death according to Section 216 of the German Criminal Code, which is a crime. If the person assisting with suicide would be too active, the court may not any longer assess his behaviour as mere assisting with suicide, but as killing at the request of the victim within the meaning of Section 216. In this context, some German scholars draw the distinction referring to a right to die with dignity (Herdegen 2019). German courts, however, avoid reference to human dignity in this context (for the reasons, see the Jurgeleit (2015, 2714)).

[16] This problem will also become relevant primarily in countries shaped by the Kantian tradition, like Germany, which prohibits the weighing of human life with reference to human dignity.

or psychology when such difficult issues arise. Rather, the questions about the limits and, possibly, the worthiness of protecting human life are problems that at best philosophers could claim for their own terrain.

At the IVR Congress in Lucerne it was argued by the Korean scholar Kim (2019), for example, that an unborn child could not have dignity because dignity would require a human counterpart in the sense of an interpersonal relationship, which a baby in the womb simply could not yet have. How could we come to a conclusion whether such a view would be wrong or right? It would not help adding biological details. I presume that Kim would know that a foetus, at least at an advanced stage, already has all the characteristics of a living human body. The question of whether it should be accorded human dignity cannot be resolved by an increase in biological information. It is, rather, decisive whether or not the concept of human dignity should include an interpersonal relationship as a necessary element.

Of course, arguments for different solutions can be brought forward, and such arguments necessarily will be grounded in certain systems of further assumptions, but no position can a priori have a higher status here that would make it more acceptable from the outset. It is true that a judge cannot simply attach a meaning to the concept of human dignity with which a significant part of the population would not agree, except if the legislator has given him a clear indication that this is its will and if that expression of its will is not unconstitutional. It is true that 'faith divides' (*'Glaube spaltet'*; Neumann 2017, 299); however, that does not only apply to religious positions. It rather applies equally to all belief systems, including philosophical systems. It is not self-evident that human dignity requires at least some elementary form of interpersonal relationship and that a living human being would not per se be entitled to respect of his dignity without such a relationship. It would mean imposing on the people a belief system without any democratic legitimation if a judge adopted such a view, unless the legislator has clearly indicated that this is its intended interpretation.

In this way, I would not juxtapose 'faith' against 'reason'. I would rather see faith as a conviction which can and should be backed by reason. Nor should reason be regarded as a safe tool which ensures against gross errors. For reason is only found in reasoning which is a process of thinking from one proposition to the next by way of syllogisms, often via numerous intermediate propositions. This thought process is thus always relative to certain propositions and necessarily unfinished, because the initial proposition always presupposes further propositions that could in principle be called into question. To a certain extent, this is in contradiction to the fact that the thought process leading to a concrete decision must always be finite and must therefore at some point presuppose premises that are not further examined. But the level which is not taken into account can be precisely the decisive one that makes the whole chain untenable.

Often the thought process is therefore embedded in an apparently well-established belief system to which it is related, and then even careful conclusions can lead to untenable results if they are based on the wrong system.

That means that the judge on the one hand is not entitled to adopt an interpretation, unless the legislature has clearly indicated that this is what it intended. On the other hand, however, it cannot be forbidden for representatives of religious groups or medical scientists to influence the political process by offering reasons in the hope that these will be accepted.

The kind of argument that is needed here consists of a very basic structure and makes use of facts of which nobody can claim to have a superior knowledge. Therefore, I have located such issues as the interpretation of human dignity 'at best' in the field of philosophy because I support the view held by Wittgenstein and Ryle, amongst others, that philosophers are not dealing with a subject which requires a special knowledge.

Wittgenstein insisted in the *Philosophical Investigations* (1958) that philosophical problems were to be solved not by the amassing of new empirical knowledge, but by the rearrangement of what we already know (Kenny 2006, xiii; Wittgenstein 1958, part I, section 109). Ryle seems to have adopted this view from Wittgenstein when he writes in the introduction to his *The Concept of Mind* that the 'philosophical arguments which constitute this book are intended not to increase what we know about minds, but to rectify the logical geography of the knowledge we already possess' (1965, 9).

I find the distinction between individual scientific problems and merely basic philosophical questions also in other thinkers, for example, in Einstein when he writes that 'the man of science is a poor philosopher' (1950, 58) or in Flew when he maintains that

> when you study the interaction of two physical bodies, for instance, two subatomic particles, you are engaged in science. When you ask how it is that those subatomic particles – or anything physical – could exist and why, you are engaged in philosophy. When you draw philosophical conclusions from scientific data, then you are thinking as a philosopher. (2007, 89)

I am convinced that the quest for the correct interpretation of human dignity means being engaged in philosophy in the same way as when you draw conclusions from scientific data. Therefore, there is no special competence for dealing with this problem apart from the fact that philosophers may find the task a bit easier because they have engaged in it more often. For me, it is thus part of the foundation of a democratic state that everyone is allowed to participate in the political discourse without having his voice marginalized a priori because he allegedly fails to meet certain standards of reason. Consequently, concepts resting on religious assumptions cannot be ranked lower than others from the outset.

VIII. Conclusion

I have tried to show that the fallacy of inferring the existence of a norm in a moral or legal system just because it exists in another moral system is a means of unduly influencing a healthy process of democratic decision-making. In the long run, such manoeuvres can be very damaging to a state. Dedicated citizens should consciously avoid them. But they should also not be prevented from participating in the democratic process if they clearly disclose their premises, be they religious or otherwise.

References

Austin, John L. 1979a. 'Other Minds'. In *Philosophical Papers*, edited by James O. Urmson and Geoffrey J. Warnock, 76–116. Oxford: Oxford University Press.

———. 1979b. 'Truth'. In *Philosophical Papers*, edited by James O. Urmson and Geoffrey J. Warnock, 117–33. Oxford: Oxford University Press.

Carroll, Lewis. 2005. 'Through the Looking Glass'. In *Complete Works*, 49–98. London: Collector's Library Editions.

Dworkin, Ronald. 1975. 'Hard Cases'. *Harvard Law Review* 88: 1057–109.

Einstein, Albert. 1950. *Out of My Later Years*. New York: Philosophical Library.

Finnis, John. 1983. *Fundamentals of Ethics*. Washington, DC: Georgetown University Press.

Flew, Antony. 2007. *There Is a God: How the World's Most Notorious Atheist Changed His Mind*. New York: HarperCollins.

Hart, Herbert L. 1997. *The Concept of Law*. Edited by Penelope A. Bulloch and Joseph Raz. Oxford: Clarendon.

Herdegen, Matthias. 2019. 'Art. 1 Abs. 1 para. 89'. In *Grundgesetz: Kommentar begründet von Theodor Maunz und Günter Dürig*, edited by Rupert Scholz, Matthias Herdegen and Hans Klein, 56–57. Munich: C. H. Beck.

Jurgeleit, Andreas. 2015. 'Sterbehilfe in Deutschland: Bestandsaufnahme der gegenwärtigen Rechtslage und Überlegungen zur Reformdiskussion'. *Neue Juristische Wochenschrift* 68, no. 37 (10 September): 2708–14.

Kant, Immanuel. 1911. 'Grundlegung zur Metaphysik der Sitten'. In Kant's *Gesammelte Schriften Bd. IV*, edited by Königlich Preußische Akademie der Wissenschaften, 385–463. Berlin: Georg Reimer.

Kenny, Anthony. 2006. *Wittgenstein*. Oxford: Blackwell.

Khan, L. Ali. 2003. *A Theory of Universal Democracy: Beyond the End of History*. The Hague: Kluwer Law International.

Kim, Young-Whan. 2019. *Rekonstruktion der Diskussion um die Menschenwürde: Menschenwürde als ein normatives Postulat*. Manuscript.

Lagerspetz, Eerik. 1995. *The Opposite Mirrors: An Essay on the Conventionalist Theory of Institutions*. Dordrecht: Kluwer Academic.

Luhmann, Niklas. 1997. *Die Gesellschaft der Gesellschaft*. Frankfurt am Main: Suhrkamp.

MacCormick, Neil. 1978. *Legal Reasoning and Legal Theory*. Oxford: Clarendon.

Mackie, John L. 1977. *Ethics*. Harmondsworth: Penguin Books.

Montgomery, John W. 2005. *Tractatus Logico-Theologicus*. Bonn: Culture and Science.

Moore, Gerald E. 1903. *Principia Ethica*. Cambridge: Cambridge University Press.

Moyn, Samuel. 2015. *Christian Human Rights*. Philadelphia: Pennsylvania University Press.

Neumann, Ulfrid. 2017. 'Das Rechtsprinzip der Menschenwürde als Schutz elementarer menschlicher Bedürfnisse. Versuch einer Eingrenzung'. *Archiv für Rechts- und Sozialphilosophie* 103: 287–303.

New American Standard Bible. 1995. Genesis. Grand Rapids, MI: Zondervan.

Nida-Rümelin, Julian. 2005. *Ueber menschliche Freiheit*. Stuttgart: Reclam.

Nietzsche, Friedrich. 1919. 'Götzen-Dämmerung'. In *Nietzsche's Werke*, Band VIII [vol. 8], 52–174. Leipzig: Alfred Kröner Verlag.

Patterson, Dennis. 1999. 'Explicating the Internal Point of View'. *Southern Methodist University Law Review* 52: 67–74.

Petersen, Niels. 2005. 'The Legal Status of the Human Embryo in vitro: General Human Rights Instruments'. *Zeitschrift für ausländisches öffentliches Recht und Voelkerrecht* 65 no. 2 (1 April): 447–66.

Phillips, Dewi Z. 1993. *Wittgenstein and Religion*. London: Palgrave Macmillan.

Qu'ran, German translation. 1991. *Al-Isra, the 17th Surah*. Stuttgart: Reclam.

Ryle, Gilbert. 1965. *The Concept of Mind*. Harmondsworth: Penguin Books.

Searle, John R. 2010. *Making the Social World: The Structure of Human Civilization*. Oxford: Oxford University Press.

Toulmin, Stephen E. 1964. *The Uses of Argument*. Cambridge: Cambridge University Press.

Towe, Thomas E. 1967. 'Fundamental Rights in the Soviet Union: A Comparative Approach'. *University of Pennsylvania Law Review* 115: 1251–74.

Von Wright, Georg H. 1983. 'Norms, Truth and Logic'. In *Practical Reason: Philosophical Papers Volume I*, 130–209. Ithaca, NY: Cornell University Press.

———. 1984. 'Demystifying Propositions'. In *Truth, Knowledge, and Modality: Philosophical Papers Volume III*, 14–25. Oxford: Basil Blackwell.

Wittgenstein, Ludwig. 1958. *Philosophical Investigations*. Oxford: Basil Blackwell.

———. 2007. 'Lectures on Religious Belief'. In *Lectures and Conversations on Aesthetics, Psychology and Religious Belief*, edited by Cyril Barret, 53–72. Berkeley: University of California Press.

Chapter Twelve

THE NOMINALIST FOUNDATIONS OF CONSTRUCTIVIST DIGNITY

R. Scott Smith

Introduction

Ideas have consequences, which we can see in the history of ethics in the West and how those have played out in law. Largely from the time of Plato through approximately Aquinas, philosophers thought moral principles and virtues were objectively real and universally valid (a view known as *realism*). Moreover, these morals were universals, qualities that in themselves are one thing, yet they can be present in many instances. Thus, philosophers commonly call a universal a *one-in-many*. As such, each instance of a quality, such as dignity, has as its *essence* dignity itself.

However, this view began to change with Ockham, who denied universals and instead embraced nominalism. Since then, the history of Western ethics has been largely a nominalist story. Nominalism has major consequences for ethics in general, and dignity in particular. According to nominalism, everything is particular, such that any two things do not literally share the numerically identical qualities. This means that dignity itself is not something all humans have in common, and, arguably, it does not have an essence. Instead, we could say there are many *dignities*. What then makes all those examples of dignity? It may be just the word we use for them, which fits with the literal meaning of nominalism as being *in name only*.

Nevertheless, if there really are essences to dignity and other morals, then there could be a fact of the matter of *what* kind of thing they are. That is because an essence would be an immaterial entity that defines the kind of thing something is, and it serves as a boundary such that it cannot be something else. However, without essences, there is no 'deeper fact' to what something really is, as Daniel Dennett realizes (1990, 208, 300). In that case, it seems what something is would be 'up to us'.

Now, if nominalism cannot preserve essences, then it seems dignity simply would be our *construct*. Ethical as well as legal theorists have made many attempts to explain how that construction takes place, including, for instance, by our interpretations; what we count as giving our lives meaningfulness and value; or other means. Indeed, I will try to show that this has happened.

To accomplish this, first, I will survey the views of realism and nominalism. Second, I will show how the history of ethics shifted to nominalism after Ockham's influence.

I will show how these views are constructivist, and in this process, I will highlight some contemporary constructivist examples of dignity, including in law.

Third, however, I will argue that nominalism actually will undermine dignity and all other moral qualities. At best, dignity can be nothing but our construct, which I will argue is unsatisfactory. At worst, dignity or any other moral quality cannot even exist on nominalism. In that light, I will explain how nominalism leads us on a desperate quest to secure dignity, yet one that nominalism cannot fulfil. Instead, fourth, I will defend dignity as intrinsic for humans and as an objectively real universal. Any other ontological basis for dignity will fail to preserve the deep need we all have for dignity.

Realism and Nominalism

Plato and Aristotle represent two types of realism. Both believed that *forms*, or universals, exist as immaterial kinds of things, and they can be instanced in various things due to the respective essential natures of the forms themselves and that in which they are exemplified. For example, both affirmed the reality of the cardinal moral virtues, justice, prudence, courage and temperance. These virtues are universals that are appropriate for all human beings due to their essential nature, while they would be inappropriate for dogs due to their nature. For both Plato and Aristotle, each of these virtues is one thing in itself, and yet it can (and should) be present in many humans.

However, the two philosophers disagreed whether a universal could exist apart from its being present in any particulars. For Plato, universals themselves exist apart from their instances in any particular objects (Rodriguez-Pereyra 2015). Therefore, they themselves are *abstract* in the sense of *not* being located in space and time, while their instances can be. On the other hand, Aristotle thought that for a universal to exist, it had to be present in at least one instance (Rodriguez-Pereyra 2015).

Nominalists tend to divide into two general positions. The first is *trope nominalism*, according to which a virtue like justice is real, and it is *simple*. That is, it is just one particular thing (a trope). It is not a combination of two or more things. Nonetheless, we still can indicate many particular dignity tropes; there can be dignity$_1$, dignity$_2$, dignity$_3$ and so on. Here, the numeral is an individuator that reminds us that each trope, whether 1, 2 or 3, is just one particular thing. Unlike universals, it is not the case that each instance shares the numerically identical quality, dignity.

Moreover, tropes, whether virtues like dignity, or colours like red, are inherently qualitative (Maurin 2002, 21). Since tropes are located in space and time, this suggests they would be empirically observable and material (e.g. Campbell 1981, 485–86). Even though they are not abstract in the same way as Plato's universals, nonetheless we still can *consider* tropes abstractly (Williams 1953, 14, qtd in Maurin 2002, 21). This is an epistemic act by means of which we pay attention to various instances of, say, dignity, and generalize from them. Alternatively, we make distinctions by directing our 'attention on some, but not all, of what is presented' (Campbell 1981, 478).

Another major version of nominalism is *austere nominalism*. Like trope theory, all that exists are particular things, and they too are located in space and time. However, unlike tropes, 'there are no characteristics [or qualities per se] but only primitively charactered objects' (Garcia 2015, 107). For example, there is no justice per se, but only just-people.

Yet, to speak that way is imprecise, for it implies that there are people who have that quality. Instead, justice does not add a distinct quality to people. It would be more accurate to speak of just-people, such that there are only particular people *of whom we speak* as being just. This approach lends itself to a linguistic understanding of what unites these various people as all being just. It is not a shared quality they all possess; rather, it is a word we use for them according to our way of speaking.

With these distinctions between realism and nominalism in mind, I will now turn to a survey of the shifts in Western ethics to nominalism and some of its effects in ethics and law.

Western Ethics after Ockham and the Shift to Nominalism

After Ockham, the first major ethical figure I will consider is Thomas Hobbes, who was a proponent of mechanical atomism, on which what is real are mechanisms composed of atoms.[1] Given these metaphysical positions, it is not surprising that Hobbes also was an empiricist, for what is real would be knowable by the five senses. Moreover, there is no room for immaterial entities, so universals do not exist. Instead, Hobbes embraced nominalism.

Hobbes's ethical views fit with his views of reality. *Motions* towards some object cause desires in us for that thing, and those desires are good. On the other hand, motions away from something cause aversions in us, and those are bad (Hobbes 1964 [1651], chapters VI, XV). He is a psychological and ethical egoist, in that we not only in fact act in our own self-interest (prompted by our desires), we also should act in our self-interest. However, as a nominalist, each desire is particular for Hobbes. Since we do and even should act in our self-interest, our interests naturally will conflict. Therefore, it is not surprising that he held that apart from ceding our rights to self-preservation to a sovereign, we would be in a perpetual state of war amongst one another.

While Hobbes also appeals to laws of nature, what he meant by that term had changed. For someone like Aristotle or Aquinas, arguably natural laws exist objectively and universally. Hobbes, however, has no room for such things to exist. Instead, natural laws seem to be our maxims for peaceful coexistence. Accordingly, he seems to be in the same tradition as the sophists, for whom justice is a convention. Likewise, for Hobbes, rights are not inalienable, for they are products of the sovereign. In contrast, inalienable rights, such as the right to life in the Declaration of Independence of the United States, would seem to be intrinsically valid and thus have an essence to them.

Moreover, Hobbes claims that we should regard one another as equals *by nature* (1964 [1651], chapter XIII). Nevertheless, he cannot appeal to an essential nature that all

---

[1]   For further details, please see my *In Search of Moral Knowledge: Overcoming the Fact-Value Dichotomy* (2014). See also chapter 5 of my *Nominalism and Constructivism: Essays in the Ontology of Knowledge* (forthcoming).

humans share, for there are no universals or essences in his views. Given that, it is hard to see how Hobbes can justify this claim, for if we are but mechanisms, it seems some of us function better in various ways than others.

In light of these factors, it is hard to see how Hobbes's views can preserve dignity. First, dignity must be physical; yet, physical stuff can be exhausted descriptively. Yet, that we should treat people with dignity is inherently normative. Second, at best dignity is just a human construct made by the sovereign. In that case, however, dignity is just a power move. It is not an intrinsically valid moral principle, and as such, the sovereign can override or outright reject it if that seems best (Hobbes 1964 [1651], chapter XXX). Third, whose dignity are we talking about, and whose gets to be the standard for treatment of others? For dignity cannot be a universal quality; instead, there are as many dignities as there are people.

Like Hobbes, David Hume embraced mechanical atomism and nominalism. He denied that there are any identities; instead, all our experiences, even of moral qualities such as dignity or justice, are discrete (Hume 1969, 249). He also embraced empiricism, such that all our knowledge comes via the five senses. Accordingly, morals had to fit into his nominalist metaphysic. Further, Hume held that reason does not tell us what is moral or move us to action (Book II, part III, section iii). Instead, Hume believed the prospects of pleasure or pain are what move us to act.

For Hume, what is key for morality is the *moral sense*, that is, sentiment, or feeling, which seems to be what makes an action moral or not. Since all our sentiments are discrete, I may have some particular feeling for wanting such and such, and another person may have a specific feeling for something else. As such, there is no cognitive content to morals. Thus, that we should treat people with dignity seems to be reducible to an emotion, which we could express as 'hurrah, dignity!'

Yet, one's feelings can change. If that happens, it seems the importance of dignity also could change. We might then express that feeling as 'boo, dignity!' Moreover, his view eviscerates dignity and any other moral quality of its normativity. Dignity reduces to nothing more than a descriptive matter of how one happens to feel. Further, even if morals were just a matter of our feelings, they still are particulars on his nominalism. Thus, there is no basis for people to share a common feeling about dignity. In short, Hume's ethics cannot sustain dignity.

Immanuel Kant continued along this nominalist and empiricist path, yet he developed a very different kind of moral theory. Unlike Hobbes or Hume, Kant conceived of morals as *categorical imperatives* (absolute commands), without exceptions. Therefore, whatever one chooses to do, that person should will that to be universal maxim for all to live by. Additionally, we always should treat all humans (including ourselves) as an end, and never merely as a means to an end. Put differently, this shows that Kant believed people are valuable in themselves.

Yet, he did not ground that in a shared essence that all people have, one that defines people as intrinsically valuable, as would the biblical tradition, in which humans are made in God's image (Gen. 9:6). Kant did not follow Plato or Aristotle's belief in real, universal qualities. Instead, we are to *will* our maxims that we devise to apply universally.

Kant thereby introduces an important role for *autonomy*, by which we are to *self-legislate* what would be the case morally for everyone.

To secure the nature of morals as absolute commands, Kant thought they cannot belong to the realm of what is empirically knowable (the *phenomenal* realm), for that realm is contingent and subject to change. However, morals as absolute, unchanging commands would need to be part of a different realm, which he called the *noumena*, the realm of things as they are in themselves. As an empiricist, Kant held that all 'our knowledge begins with experience' (1993a, 25). While he claimed we cannot know things as they are in themselves, he made an exception for morals.

Therefore, for Kant, morals *themselves* are not universals; rather, they are what we *will* to be universally applicable. Moreover, all our experiences are particular, which demonstrates his nominalism. Morals then seem to be particulars that we *generalize* to be applicable to all people. As such, morals are our constructs, for they do not exist independently of us.

Kant's moral theory has had much influence. Autonomy is a major principle in applied ethics in the West today and in the law, such as in laws that permit assisted suicide. Moreover, he offers a philosophical basis for respect for persons as valuable in themselves and not for their functional abilities.

However, Kant also inherited the mindsets of his time about what is real, namely nominalism. This move naturally would influence him to focus on what is empirically observable. Yet, he also was a champion of the Enlightenment; he did not want to forsake the importance of reason on the altar of experience (cf. Kant 1993b, 145). He wed reason and empiricism by maintaining that all our knowledge begins with experience, for our concepts (given by reason) need the contents supplied by experience.

Yet, drawing upon his distinction between the things as we experience them and things as they are in themselves, apart from our experience, Kant's empiricism and nominalism led him to claim that we cannot know things as they are in themselves, apart from experience; we can only know things as they appear to us. While this basic idea lives today in many forms, nonetheless it is a fateful move.

Following Kant, since we cannot know things (people, actions etc.) as they really are; we can only know them as they *appear* to us (appearance$_1$). However, the pattern then repeats: we cannot access appearance$_1$ as it really is, but only as *it appears* to us (i.e. appearance$_2$). Unfortunately, the same move repeats endlessly, such that we cannot get started. This means that even the most egregious violations of dignity cannot even be recognized as such.

This result dooms any abilities to know what the facts are in any case. However, that is not the only problem with Kant's ethics. It seems we cannot know several key things empirically, such as that morals should command us absolutely; humans should be treated as valuable in themselves; and we should universalize our maxims. These seem to be Kant's postulates to make his system work, but if someone (such as Hume) does not agree with his presuppositions, why should that person be obligated to follow them too? This concern seems especially pertinent for oppressive regimes. It seems those in power could will what *they want* to be true for all. However, that would mean morals are just a matter of power. For example, consider how the Nazis involuntarily euthanized the mentally disabled and others under the Aktion T4 program, all in their quest for Aryan racial purity.

Furthermore, on nominalism, it seems we could have a multiplicity of starting points for ethics, rather than Kant's universalized ones. Indeed, unlike Plato's, Aristotle's, or Aquinas's views, there is no human nature to ground ethics. This is because morals are to command us independently of human nature, and there is no human nature that we can know empirically. This result fits with his nominalism, too, for it seems there literally could not be an identical human nature.

Kant's philosophy helped cement the mindset that had been developing through the Scientific Revolution that, given their embrace of mechanical atomism and nominalism, it naturally followed that people would think what is real is empirically knowable. Using empirical methods, and especially Kant's view that we can only know things as they appear to us in experience, people came to see the sciences as the paradigm for know-ledge of facts. On the other hand, they came to view ethics, along with religion, as giving us just personal opinions or preferences (Smith 2014, 97).

The utilitarians, including Jeremy Bentham and John Stuart Mill, followed Kant his-torically, and they continued along the same empiricist and nominalist paths. Accordingly, they had no room for essences and any natural laws. Thus, there are no natural rights, for there is no room for any intrinsically valid morals, or an objective human nature. Instead, right or wrong actions depend on the sum of the good and bad consequences of the *non-moral* good produced directly or indirectly by the consequences of that action or rule. They tried to measure the non-moral good empirically in terms of harms or benefits, and pleasures or pains.

Without any natural rights on their views, we can see a basis for legal positivist theory, which Bentham helped to develop. For him, talk of natural rights was 'nonsense on stilts', for it presupposes that rights exist prior to government (Bentham 2014, 334). Instead, like Hobbes, Bentham maintained that rights are the creation of the law, which in turn the sovereign has commanded. Law, then, is a social construct.

However, there are major problems with utilitarianism. Since there are no intrinsically valid morals, it is conceivable that some morals that we clearly know are valid nonethe-less could turn out otherwise. For example, treating people with dignity could be wrong, and justice could be bad, if the consequences happen to add up that way. But notice that utilitarianism presupposes a prior notion of good even to begin sorting consequences as 'good' or 'bad'. Yet, this prior 'standard' of goodness ends up being just a construct, and without a moral basis for constraining it, it seems there is no intrinsic check upon those in power from defining 'good' in ways that simply perpetuate their positions.

Friedrich Nietzsche was a *naturalist*, such that only the natural exists; there is no super-natural. He further developed this pattern of nominalism, empiricism and materialism. He denied that there are *any* numerical identities and so there are no universals. Instead, we construct things by *taking* them to be identical, when in reality they are only similar, clearly a nominalist move (Nietzsche 1969a, 326). Moreover, there are no enduring selves (Nietzsche 1969a, 324). Our construction of these things reflects the influence of language upon our thought processes: 'even the "one" contains an *interpretation* of the process, and does not belong to the process itself. One infers here according to the usual grammatical formula' (Nietzsche 1969b, 338, emphasis original). The same would apply to moral principles and virtues, for these too are our constructs based on 'our artificial (though convenient) linguistic-conceptual shorthand for functionally unitary products, processes, and sets of relations' (Schacht 1999, 615). In Nietzsche's views, we see a clear move to language in our construction of morality. Since there are no objectively real morals, moral philosophy just is an expression of our will to power (Nietzsche 1969b, 335), a view very much with us today.

Other naturalists have followed Nietzsche, and they have developed a range of views about morals. Yet, understandably, they deny a place for essences or universals. Most also deny any room for morals as immaterial entities; if they do allow for them, it seems they would have to be properties that emerge from, and depend upon, the physical for their existence.

As a sampling of naturalist moral theories, Michael Ruse defends a form of socio-biology in which morals are just a biological adaptation that enable us to survive (2002, 651). Others, such as A. J. Ayer, are *emotivists* – morals are just the expressions of feelings. Simon Blackburn defends *quasi-realism*, a view that focuses on moral ways of speaking while denying the reality of morals (2001, 49). Moreover, Gilbert Harman seems to reduce moral facts to facts of nature (1977, 17), yet he also argues for a form of rela-tivism (2000, 3–19).

Still others include Christine Korsgaard's Kantian, naturalistic ethics. Like other naturalists, Korsgaard believes we live in a disenchanted world without objectively real, intrinsically valid morals (1996, 4). In a world made of matter, we construct ethics by imposing form onto matter, which she sees as Kant's basic project (4–5). That is, we impose our moral concepts onto matter by willing our maxims to be universal for all. In her view, we have universally applicable morals, and yet they are our constructs and are not intrinsically valid.

For James Rachels, his 'bare difference argument' tries to show that right or wrong actions are reducible to the movement of body parts (1986, 111–13), specifically in regards to actively killing a patient versus letting him or her die. He argues that we are just physical beings, and biology does not give us dignity. Rather, our *biographical* life (i.e. the story we have autonomously chosen) gives our lives meaningfulness, value and dignity (chapter 2).

Similarly, Peter Singer thinks persons are sentient, can experience suffering, have a self-concept and form life plans. He explains that 'the life of a fetus (and even more plainly, of an embryo) is of no greater value than the life of a nonhuman animal at a similar level of rationality, self-awareness, capacity to feel and so on, and that because no fetus is a person, no fetus has the same claim to life as a person' (Singer 2011, 151–52). Those, including animals that have these functional abilities, are persons and subjects of moral protection. However, he argues that the unborn and even many infants do not meet these criteria for being counted as persons.

Like Rachels, Singer makes more explicit his position that personhood is linked to the ability to have a self-concept. A criterion for personhood is the *ability to see oneself* as a being 'that might or might not have a future', in order to 'have a desire to continue living' (Singer 2011, 152). Singer also argues that his position does not violate the principle of respect for autonomy, for a being that lacks this quality is not capable of making decisions.

Other bioethicists argue similarly. Alberto Giubilini and Francesca Minerva claim, 'Merely being human is not in itself a reason for ascribing someone a right to life' (2013, 262). Instead, they tie personhood to an individual's ability to form a self-concept that gives one meaning: 'We take "person" to mean an individual who is capable of *attributing* to her own existence some (at least) basic value such that being deprived of this existence represents a loss to her' (262; emphasis added).

Recently, however, Erik Wielenberg has offered an innovative, naturalistic moral theory that incorporates Platonic-like universal morals. For him, moral properties exist as such; they cannot be reduced to matter. Moreover, he distinguishes between a moral *type* (or kind) and its *tokens* (instances). As a type, a moral property seems to be objectively real, and in itself, it would be a universal. Yet, its tokens supervene upon particular physical facts; that is, 'which moral properties are instantiated by a given entity depends entirely on which non-moral properties that entity instantiates' (Wielenberg 2019).

Why do moral properties supervene on non-moral ones? To help answer, he appeals to the 'making' relation. Wielenberg illustrates this supervenience in that 'the *natural* fact that an act is a piece of deliberate cruelty *makes* that act *morally* wrong' (Wielenberg 2014, 16; emphases added). This relation is a kind of causation. We should notice, though, that Wielenberg seems to pack a normative, moral notion – cruelty – into his description of the natural, non-moral properties. Thus, it seems that though he posits the existence of Platonic-like moral universals as moral types, nonetheless it seems he assumes the natural is intrinsically moral. Yet, this move is at odds with naturalism, for he posits essences to natural things. It also begs the question, for a thoroughgoing naturalism of someone like Nietzsche or Ruse, as well as the natural sciences themselves, would deny that cruelty (or kindness) is part of nature.

Moreover, moral properties are epiphenomenal (Wielenberg 2014, 13–14), and thus they have no causal powers. In that case, it is hard to see how we could have knowledge of them. Since according to his view, humans are basically made of physical stuff (except for *qualia* – the felt-qualities of, say, experiences, desires etc.), it seems the way we would need to come to know something is by that thing causing a physical state in us. This could happen, for example, by light waves bouncing off an object, impinging on one's retina and causing a physical state (say, the experience) in the person. Yet, for Wielenberg, since moral properties are epiphenomenal, they cannot cause such states, and so it seems we could not even begin to know them.

Generally, we can notice some patterns in these naturalistic moral views. First, except for Wielenberg, there are no essences to morals (or anything else), and they are not universals. Without essences, however, there are no intrinsically valid morals. This means that while we think we should treat people with dignity and do justice, these core morals could turn out otherwise. Yet, that result runs contrary to the truth we simply know, that these are valid.

Second, it seems there is constructivism running throughout these views. Besides Wielenberg's explicit views, the others all trade upon the naturalistic position that matter can be exhausted by descriptions, but morality is normative. This problem is the naturalistic fallacy: how do we get the moral *ought* from the natural *is*? Korsgaard is perhaps the most direct: we do so by imposing our moral concepts upon the physical, which is a constructive act by which we decide what dignity is, and even that we should respect it. Yet, as we saw earlier, Wielenberg makes much the same move by packing moral notions into natural, non-moral properties. In effect, he thereby makes his view constructivist as well.

The post-moderns continue the same, long-standing nominalist trajectory. Alasdair MacIntyre's revised Aristotelian, and now Thomistic, ethics embraces the virtues, yet cast in his understanding of the later Wittgenstein, including his stress on particulars. For example, MacIntyre argues there is no such thing as rationality as such; instead, there are just the particular rationalities of various 'traditions' (1988, 356). There also is no such thing as language in general; there are only particular languages in their specific, historical contexts (357). Further, his epistemology is historicist; we know only from the standpoints of our historically situated communities (357–58). Therefore, we cannot know anything directly, as it is in itself. Moreover, there is no universal human nature, nor is there a telos (or goal) applicable for all. Instead, we are our bodies, and we are formed by our own narratives, which find their meaningfulness within the context of a local community with its language (MacIntyre 1999, 6; 1982, 217).

One of the many implications of this kind of view is that morals like dignity and justice are the constructs of discrete 'traditions', such as Christianity, according to their formative stories and languages. Yet, there is no essence to language; there are as many languages as there are communities. In addition, since we cannot know dignity as such, it is the construct of each community. In that case, why should we adopt one understanding over another?[2]

As a final set of major ethical views, critical theory (including its progeny such as critical race theory, critical legal studies and queer theory) draws upon nominalism, materialism and historicism. Critical theory developed in the Frankfurt School, and some of its major proponents were Max Horkheimer, Theodor Adorno and Herbert Marcuse. Adorno, for instance, saw our knowledge as historicized (Fagan n.d.; Adorno 1973, 4; Zuidervaart 2015). Marcuse denied the reality of any transhistorical ideals and thus was a nominalist (Farr 2019).

Moreover, we should reject thinking of reality as objectively real with essences and being knowable as such. Such mindsets 'served to establish a single order, a single mode of representing and relating to reality' (Fagan n.d.). Thus, for Horkheimer and Adorno, 'enlightenment is totalitarian' (Adorno and Horkheimer 1997, 24). Furthermore, Marcuse discussed humans in terms of their existence in concrete social conditions as well as their 'essence'. However, as a materialist, one's essence is not some transcendental, immaterial reality. Instead, it is grounded in specific historical settings, and therefore it seems to be nominal.

---

2   While MacIntyre does give an answer, which is by learning the language of an alien 'tradition' as a second first language, I argue that this fails (Smith 2014, chapter 11).

In such settings, Marcuse ties essence to human potential as free, rational beings to achieve the ideals present in a concrete, historically situated culture. In his 'Concept of Essence', Marcuse ties essence with overcoming oppressive existence: 'Materialist theory thus transcends the given state of fact and moves toward a different potentiality, proceeding from immediate appearance to the essence that appears in it. But here appearance and essence become members of a real antithesis arising from the particular historical structure of the social process of life' (1968, 67).

Critical theory focuses on groups of people, and it trades on the belief that disparities between groups are the result of immoral discrimination (Sowell 2018, 100). It adopts the Marxist-like division of people into two groups, the oppressors and oppressed. For Marcuse, a social system (the context of one's existence) that oppresses people distorts and 'erases' one's essence. Morally, our central duty is to liberate the oppressed from their oppressors.

Queer theory illustrates these key positions in its specific areas. It provides 'a way to test the established and stable categories of identity' (University of Illinois 2019), which includes, but is not limited to, sexual identities. For Michel Foucault, there is not an essence that would define sex as what it is (1990; e.g. 69). Judith Butler agrees and explains that 'gender is the repeated stylization of the body, a set of repeated acts within a highly rigid regulatory frame that congeal over time to *produce the appearance* of substance, of a natural sort of being' (1990, 45; emphasis added). This move allows queer theorists to reject 'binary' thinking (e.g. male-female, and heteronormativity) and disrupt such logics as oppressive based on the power of a dominant group.

In general, queer theory resists a static view of life. Instead, it creates indefinite possibilities without limitations. This results in a liberated sexuality, to define oneself according to one's own conceptions (Osinski 2019). Vaughan Roberts agrees: 'You're free – even from nature. Not even our bodies should be allowed to restrict us in our self-definition' (2016, 29). Clearly, with a rejection of essences and universally fixed traits (at least in terms of sexuality), queer theory seems both materialist and nominalist. Moreover, it is historicist in its rejection of any universal vantage points from which we may know what is the case for all humans.

On critical theory, morals, let alone any other property, are material and nominal. Just as we saw with various naturalist ethical theories, it seems morals on critical theory will face the same kinds of problems. It seems, therefore, that dignity, let alone justice and other key morals, is simply a human construct. Yet, that means it is something that can change as the views of people change.

It is no wonder on materialism that critical theorists emphasize equal outcomes. It is not the case that all humans are of equal moral value. If it were so, that would suggest there is a universal quality all humans possess that endows them with that value. Yet, without such immaterial universals, equality has to be redefined along material lines. People vary, however, in their abilities, interests and desires, so it seems unrealistic to expect all people to perform equally in all tasks. Instead, we see attempts to achieve equality in material terms, such as through racial quotas, the redistribution of economic resources and more.

On nominalism (and historicism), critical theory cannot support dignity or justice per se; instead, they are particulars of discrete, historically located people groups. There is not a single, universal definition of dignity, nor is it necessarily a quality that all humans do in fact value. Indeed, this seems to be in line with what we see today, with the claims and desires for people to autonomously define what gives them dignity, so long as it does not harm someone else.

Neil Gorsuch explains that on this mindset, any authority should embrace the *neutrality principle* and 'foreswear any interest in promoting particular moral objectives or ends', since these are not objective and are up to the private choices of individuals (2010, 87). The limit to these private choices is the *harm principle*, which, according to Mill, is that 'the only purpose for which power can be rightfully exercised over any member of a civilized community, against his will, is to prevent harm to others' (2006, 16). By maximizing peoples' liberty to define their identity and what makes them a person of dignity, we achieve the goal of critical theorists to liberate them from oppressive structures.

Yet, if dignity and justice are merely the constructs of particular groups (or individuals), then there will be many dignities and justices. Why then would critical theorists be right, and others wrong? Moreover, the critical theorists' views that dignity and justice are all about power would itself be a power move, one from which we should be liberated. However, if so, that could result in serious indignities being committed. It also seems that there would be no way to adjudicate rationally between rival versions of dignity. If so, then critical theory has no way to recommend itself rationally over other theories of dignity.

Before shifting to examine a deeper issue with nominalism in regards to dignity, I will mention some more examples of how these ideas are playing out in law and public policy. For one, John Rawls's theories have had much influence in political and legal philosophy. He utilizes Kant's basic views in his theory of how we can decide in an 'original position' on principles of justice in order to form a democracy in today's pluralistic setting (Rawls 1993, xvi, xxviii). However, as with Kant, there are no objectively real, universal morals that exist. This means dignity, like justice, is a construct we agree upon and generalize to apply to all people in a given society.

For another, consider Justice Anthony Kennedy's majority opinion in *Obergefell v. Hodges*. Kennedy appealed to personal autonomy in the choice of one's marriage partner and linked that to dignity: 'There is dignity in the bond between two men or two women who seek to marry and in their autonomy to make such profound choices' (*Obergefell v. Hodges* 2015, 13). Denying gays and lesbians this fundamental right to marriage boils down to withholding dignity from them, since they have an 'immutable nature'.[3] Here, I take Kennedy to mean that their being gay or lesbian is hardwired biologically. Therefore, this 'dictates that same-sex marriage is their only real path to this profound commitment' with its 'privileges and responsibilities' and dignity (4).

---

[3]   However, if we have an 'immutable nature' due to our biology, it is hard to see how we can autonomously define ourselves. If so, holding these two concepts together is quite ironic.

Another example comes from *Planned Parenthood v. Casey*, which dealt with a right to privacy in abortion. Justices O'Connor, Kennedy and Souter argued that 'these matters, involving the most intimate and personal choices a person may make in a lifetime, choices central to personal dignity and autonomy, are central to the liberty protected by the Fourteenth Amendment. At the heart of liberty is the right to define one's own concept of existence, of meaning, of the universe, and of the mystery of human life' (*Planned Parenthood v. Casey* 1992, 851).

Additionally, gender identity has many implications for law and public policy. For example, according to the Equal Employment Opportunity Commission in *Macy v. Holder* (Wilson 2012), 'the term "gender" encompasses not only a person's biological sex, but also the cultural and social aspects associated with masculinity and femininity' (7). On the other hand, *gender identity* is 'a person's *internal understanding* of their gender, or someone's *perception* of a person's gender identity. Among other things, gender identity may include a person's *sense* of being male, female, a combination of male and female, neither male nor female, a gender different from the person's sex assigned at birth, or transgender' (Everfi 2019; emphases added).

In October 2019, the US Supreme Court heard oral arguments in the case of *Equal Employment Opportunity Commission v. R. G. & G. R. Harris Funeral Homes Inc.* While that case could have been decided along narrow lines (i.e. may an employer force an employee to dress a certain way for work?), it along with other cases prompted a larger issue, which the Supreme Court took up in *Bostock v. Clayton County GA* (2020). In June 2020, the Court ruled in *Bostock* that 'sex' in Title VII of federal law should include 'gender identity', which is what the sixth circuit federal appeals court had effectively held in *EEOC v. R. G. &. G. R. Harris Funeral Homes* (2018).

Last, let us notice the mindset that has developed for over a century in jurisprudence. For instance, Justice Oliver Wendell Holmes championed the idea that law is divorced from morality, being instead fundamentally about power. Holmes declared, 'Wise or not, the proximate test of a good government is that the dominant power has its way' (2007, 258); and 'a law should be called good if it reflects the will of the dominant forces of the community even if it will take us to hell' (Alschuler 2002, 59). More recently, Roberto Unger explained that in critical legal studies, legal analysis is just 'one more variant of the perennial effort to restate power and preconception as right' (2015, 210).

With this backdrop and analysis in place, I now will turn to examine a further, critical issue with nominalism.

Assessing Nominalism in Relation to Dignity

We have already seen several issues with these various nominalist ethical theories. Yet, another crucial issue remains. Recall that on nominalism, everything is particular; it is just *one* thing. This is the case for both trope theory and austere nominalism. On the former, there simply are many particular 'dignities': dignity$_1$, dignity$_2$, dignity$_3$ and so on. On the latter, there are concrete objects that nonetheless are just one thing: dignified-person$_1$, dignified-person$_2$, dignified-person$_3$ and so on. Yet, on either version, there is just one particular thing – a property or an object.

While it may seem on trope theory that there is a quality (dignity) and an individuator (the numeral), or on austere nominalism there is an object (dignified-person) and an individuator, there is in reality *only one thing*. In that case, we can eliminate either one without real loss. Suppose we eliminate the individuator. Then we are left with just dignity (a quality) or dignified-person (an object), respectively. However, this move leaves us with what seems to be a *universal* – a quality (or object) that is abstract in its being and not particularized.

Suppose, instead, we eliminate the quality or object. In that case, there is just a numeral, yet it does not individuate anything, which is nonsensical. Since there is only one thing, and not two, we can eliminate either the individual or the quality (or object) without any loss in reality. Since we can eliminate the quality (or object) without loss, this means that nominalism cannot sustain their reality. This is important for our discussion, for nominalism cannot preserve any moral qualities, including dignity, justice, equality and more. Nor can it preserve the reality of humans or any other living being. Therefore, at the very best, nominalism leaves us with a view on which we must construct our dignity, meaningfulness and every other quality. In this way, nominalism can be very attractive, for it allows us to think we can define what is good and evil or right and wrong. However, nominalism actually takes away this very ability, for there are no such things, and there is not even any 'we' to do this constructive work. *Nominalism undermines dignity and our very being.*

Yet, we cannot live consistently with such a stark conclusion, for it would require us to reject our everyday experience of our own existence as well as our intuitively obvious recognition that we should treat people with dignity. Thus, nominalism leads us to think we can construct our dignity, yet it is just a matter of power after all. However, in light of the horrors we have experienced in the twentieth century under Soviet and Maoist communism and Nazism, we should resist such a dangerous conclusion. Ironically, this result is something critical theorists recognize but cannot actually prevent on their own logic.

If these nominalist views all fail to preserve dignity and other core morals, to what can we turn?

A Better Way to Ground Dignity

I have claimed that we simply know that we should treat people with dignity. This also seems to be the case with other core morals, including that we should treat people with justice and equality. These morals seem to be intrinsically valid. However, that means they cannot be our constructs; if they were, we could define them as we see fit. Instead, they seem to exist independently of us. Therefore, they seem to be objectively real. Furthermore, each one seems to be a 'one in many', that is, one moral quality, yet it should have many instances/examples. That is, they seem to be *universals*.

While it may seem anachronistic and even unscientific to some to appeal to immaterial qualities and essential natures, nonetheless the consequences of rejecting them, and embracing instead a nominalist view of dignity and other morals, will be disastrous. Rather than freeing people from powerful, paternalistic social structures, it will subject them to domination. Moreover, it will undermine dignity altogether. While we may try to live in ways that deny that conclusion, nonetheless ideas have consequences, which we can see in the very nominalist trends we have been considering in ethics.

Richard Weaver was correct. Similar to Macbeth, he observed 'the witches on the heath' have beguiled us. In our case, these 'witches' guaranteed 'man [*sic*] could realize himself more fully if he would only abandon his belief in the existence of transcendentals' (Weaver 1948, 3). However, while nominalism assures us we can have power to define reality, it cannot deliver. There cannot be any real power, dignity or indignity, justice or injustice, lawfulness or unlawfulness, people or even nominalism itself.

Conclusion

If others do not treat us with dignity, we understandably and quickly feel they have wronged us. Worse, without dignity, we lose our sense of being valuable and that our lives have meaning. Nevertheless, the result of nominalism (as well as materialism, due to a lack of universals and essences) is to deprive us of dignity. Today, we live in light of a long history of shaping influences that lead us to think there is no intrinsic dignity to humans or anything else, and so we must construct it for ourselves, based on our sense, or understanding, of our identity. However, that move reveals our desperation to try to secure some dignity.

While it is true that, in light of various factors, we do construct our own self-concepts, a constructed dignity will not be able to sustain itself. Instead, what we need (and, as I have suggested, *is* the case) is a deeper basis for dignity – one that is objectively real and intrinsically valid.[4]

References

Adorno, Theodor. 1973. *Negative Dialectics*. Translated by E. B. Ashton. New York: Seabury.
Adorno, Theodor, and Max Horkheimer. 1997. *Dialectic of Enlightenment*. Translated by J. Cumming. London: Verso.
Alschuler, Albert W. 2002. *Law without Values: The Life, Work, and Legacy of Justice Holmes*. Chicago: University of Chicago Press.
Bentham, Jeremy. 2014. *Jeremy Bentham's Economic Writings*. Edited by W. Stark. New York: Routledge.
Blackburn, Simon. 2001. *Ruling Passions: A Theory of Practical Reasoning*. Oxford: Clarendon.
Bostock v. Clayton County, Georgia. 2020. 17–1618 US Supreme Court. https://www.supremecourt.gov/opinions/19pdf/17-1618_hfci.pdf.
Butler, Judith. 1990. *Gender Trouble: Feminism and the Subversion of Identity*. New York: Routledge.
Campbell, Keith. 1981. 'The Metaphysic of Abstract Particulars'. In *Midwest Studies in Philosophy VI: The Foundations of Analytic Philosophy*, edited by Peter A. French and Howard K. Wettstein, 477–88. Minneapolis: University of Minnesota Press.
Dennett, Daniel. 1990. *The Intentional Stance*, 3rd printing. Cambridge, MA: MIT Press.
EEOC v. R. G. &. G. R. Harris Funeral Homes. 2018. No. 16–2424. US Sixth Circuit Court of Appeals. http://www.opn.ca6.uscourts.gov/opinions.pdf/18a0045p-06.pdf.
Everfi. 2019. Harassment Prevention Training (US).

[4] While it is beyond the scope of this chapter to argue for such a basis, I have argued elsewhere that the Christian God is the best explanation for such morals (Smith 2014, chapters 12–13).

Fagan, Andrew. N.d. 'Theodor Adorno'. *Internet Encyclopedia of Philosophy*. https://www.iep.utm. edu/adorno/.

Farr, Arnold. 2019. 'Herbert Marcuse'. *Stanford Encyclopedia of Philosophy*. https://plato.stanford. edu/entries/marcuse/.

Foucault, Michel. 1990. *The History of Sexuality*, vol. 1. *An Introduction*. Translated by Robert Hurley. London: Penguin.

Garcia, Robert K. 2015. 'Tropes as Divine Acts: The Nature of Creaturely Properties in a World Sustained by God'. *European Journal for Philosophy of Religion* 7, no. 3: 105–30.

Giubilini, Alberto, and Francesca Minerva. 2013. 'After-Birth Abortion: Why Should the Baby Live?' *Journal of Medical Ethics* 39, no. 5 (May): 261–63. http://dx.doi.org/10.1136/ medethics-2011–100411.

Gorsuch, Neil M. 2010. *The Future of Assisted Suicide and Euthanasia*. Princeton, NJ: Princeton University Press.

Harman, Gilbert. 1977. *The Nature of Morality: An Introduction to Ethics*. Oxford: Oxford University Press.

———. 2000. *Explaining Value: And Other Essays in Moral Philosophy*. Oxford: Clarendon.

Hobbes, Thomas. 1964 [1651]. *Leviathan*. Edited by Francis B. Randall. New York: Washington Square.

Holmes, Oliver Wendell, Jr. 2007. *Collected Legal Papers*. Mineola, NY: Dover.

Hume, David. 1969. *A Treatise of Human Nature*. Edited by Ernest Mossner. Baltimore: Penguin Books.

Kant, Immanuel. 1993a. *The Critique of Pure Reason*. Translated and edited by Carl J. Friedrich. *The Philosophy of Kant: Immanuel Kant's Moral and Political Writings*. New York: Modern Library.

———. 1993b. 'What Is Enlightenment?' Translated and edited by Carl J. Friedrich. *The Philosophy of Kant: Immanuel Kant's Moral and Political Writings*. New York: Modern Library.

Korsgaard, Christine. 1996. *The Sources of Normativity*. Cambridge, UK: Cambridge University Press.

MacIntyre, Alasdair. 1982. *After Virtue*, 2nd ed. Notre Dame: University of Notre Dame Press.

———. 1988. *Whose Justice? Which Rationality?* Notre Dame: University of Notre Dame Press.

———. 1999. *Dependent Rational Animals: Why Human Beings Need the Virtues*. Chicago, IL: Open Court.

Marcuse, Herbert. 1968. *Negations: Essays in Critical Theory*. Boston, MA: Beacon.

Maurin, Anna Sofia. 2002. *If Tropes*. Dordrecht: Kluwer Academic.

Mill, John Stuart. 2006. *On Liberty and the Subjection of Women*. New York: Penguin.

Nietzsche, Friedrich. 1969a. 'Life, Knowledge, and Self-Consciousness'. In *Nineteenth-Century Philosophy*, edited by Patrick Gardiner, 323–31. New York: Free Press.

———. 1969b. 'Prejudices of Philosophers'. In *Nineteenth-Century Philosophy*, edited by Patrick Gardiner, 332–43. New York: Free Press.

Obergefell v. Hodges. 2015. 14–556 US Supreme Court. https://www.supremecourt.gov/opinions/ 14pdf/14-556_3204.pdf.

Osinski, Keegan. 2019. 'Queering Wesley: Holiness in Diversity'. 22 October, Presentation at Crossing the Lines: Interdisciplinary Christian Conversations about Difference Conference. Pt. Loma Nazarene University.

Planned Parenthood v. Casey. 1992. 505 US 833.

Rachels, James. 1986. *The End of Life*. Oxford: Oxford University Press.

Rawls, John. 1993. *Political Liberalism*. New York: Columbia University Press.

Roberts, Vaughn. 2016. *Talking Points: Transgender*. London: Good Book.

Rodriguez-Pereyra, Gonzalo. 2015. 'Nominalism in Metaphysics'. *Stanford Encyclopedia of Philosophy*. http://plato.stanford.edu/entries/nominalism-metaphysics.

Ruse, Michael. 2002. 'Evolution and Ethics: The Sociobiological Approach'. In *Ethical Theory: Classic and Contemporary Readings*, 4th ed., edited by Louis Pojman, 647–62. Belmont: Wadsworth.

Schacht, Richard. 1999. 'Nietzsche, Friedrich Wilhelm'. In *The Cambridge Dictionary of Philosophy*, 2nd ed., edited by Robert Audi, 613–17. New York: Cambridge University Press.

Singer, Peter. 2011. *Practical Ethics*, 3rd ed. New York: Cambridge University Press.

Smith, R. Scott. 2014. *In Search of Moral Knowledge*. Downers Grove, IL: InterVarsity.

Sowell, Thomas. 2018. *Discrimination and Disparities*. New York: Basic.

Unger, Roberto. 2015. *The Critical Legal Studies Movement*. London: Verso.

University of Illinois. 2019. 'Queer Theory: Background'. http://guides.library.illinois.edu/queertheory/background.

Weaver, Richard. 1948. *Ideas Have Consequences*. Chicago, IL: University of Chicago Press.

Wielenberg, Erik. 2014. *Robust Ethics: The Metaphysics and Epistemology of Godless Normative Realism*. Oxford: Oxford University Press.

———. 2019. 12 November, e-mail correspondence with author.

Williams, D. 1953. 'On the Elements of Being: I'. *Rev Metaphys* 7, no. 1: 3–18.

Wilson, Bernadette B. 2012. *Macy v. Holder*. Equal Employment Opportunity Commission Appeal No. 0120120821.

Zuidervaart, Lambert. 2015. 'Theodor Adorno'. *Stanford Encyclopedia of Philosophy*. https://plato.stanford.edu/entries/adorno/.

Chapter Thirteen

ARTIFICIAL DIGNITY: THE HUMANIZING AND DEHUMANIZING IMPLICATIONS OF POLANYI VERSUS TURING'S ONTOLOGY

Andy Steiger

Introduction: Technological Advancement and Human Dignity

Given the rapid technological growth of artificial intelligence (AI) through advancements in machine learning, what was once thought impossible is quickly becoming a reality. It is no longer so far-fetched that humanlike machines will soon be a part of everyday life. People today are divided on whether these continued advancements in AI technologies will lead to the best of times or the worst of times for humankind. History continues to teach that a utopian or dystopian future is largely determined by a society's ability to identify and defend human dignity. Given AI's potential for dehumanization, if we are to avoid the mistakes of our past, our future will depend on people's ability to correctly see the difference between machines and humans.

By developing the work of Michael Polanyi and Alan Turing, the following chapter challenges reductionist perspectives in AI studies that are dehumanizing and explores an alternative foundation that can help navigate the technological future, while upholding the inherent dignity of being human. First (Section 1), a brief history of AI's ontological development is developed within Polanyi and Turing's interactions through tacit knowledge and the imitation game. Second (Section 2), it is demonstrated that Turing's imitation game, as expressed in *strong AI*, undermines the inherent nature of dignity in that it is intrinsically dehumanizing. Third (Section 3), Polanyi's machine ontology is developed as an alternative to the imitation game. Fourth (Section 4), Polanyi's non-reductive approach is contrasted with Turing's reductive approach to explore which best provides a foundation for the nature of human dignity.

1. Artificial Intelligence: Polanyi vs. Turing's Machine Ontology

For a time, Michael Polanyi and Alan Turing both worked at Manchester University in the United Kingdom. Polanyi was a scientist-turned-philosopher and Turing was a mathematician-turned-computer scientist. They both had a keen interest in AI studies and regularly discussed the philosophy of 'intelligent machines' (Hodges 2009, 13). Turing was focused on technological advancement, and Polanyi was concerned with the philosophies behind these advancements. Through their conversations Polanyi encouraged Turing to publish his views and organized formal discussions on the subject. On 27 October 1949, a significant interdisciplinary panel discussion was held on 'The Mind and the Computing Machine', consisting of Michael Polanyi, Alan Turing, M. Newman, M. B. Bartlett, J. Z. Young, D. N. Emmett and others, to examine the question: Can thinking be mechanical? (Scott and Moleski 2005, 215).

Although there is no complete transcript from that dialogue, a rough outline of the proceedings has survived, in which Polanyi is recorded as having argued against mechanical thinking given that the 'semantic function, [is] outside the formalizable system' (*Discussion on the Mind and the Computing Machine* 1949). In reference to cybernetics, Polanyi explains what he means by semantic function:

> I maintain that a formal system of symbols and operations functions as a deductive system only by virtue of unformalised supplements. We must know the meaning of undefined terms, understand what is stated in our axioms and believe it to be true, and acknowledge an implication in the handling of symbols by formal proof. These acts of knowing, understanding and acknowledging are not formalised: they may be jointly designated as the 'semantic operations' of the formalised system. (1952, 313)

This, Polanyi argued, was definitively demonstrated by Gödel through his *incompleteness theorem* in that even mathematics cannot be verified within its own system but requires persons capable of working outside the system (Polanyi 1962, 260–61). Polanyi's point was to emphasize the importance of personal knowledge, referring to the 'unformalized operations' of thinking as tacit knowledge (commonly known today as Polanyi's Paradox), which is encapsulated in his famous axiom: 'We can know more than we can tell' (1966, 4). Specifically, Polanyi argued that the mind operated according to tacit knowledge or unspecified knowledge, which made things like playing chess or diagnosing a disease impossible to code into a machine, given that these activities cannot be completely specified in an explicitly step-by-step fashion to be coded for. Thus, he argued that thinking cannot be programmed into a machine because it cannot be formalized.

Realizing the difficulties raised by Polanyi and others, Turing proposed a creative alternative to the question of a thinking machine. The following year, in 1950, Turing published his famous paper 'Computing Machinery and Intelligence', in which he writes,

> Instead of attempting such a definition I shall replace the question by another, which is closely related to it and is expressed in relatively unambiguous words. The new form of the problem can be described in terms of a game which we call the 'imitation game'. (1950, 433)

Instead of programming a machine to think, Turing proposed designing a machine to imitate thinking. The imitation game is based on deception in which an interrogator, person A (either male or female), is in an isolated room and holds a text-only conversation with person B (male) and person C (female). The goal of the game is for person B to deceive the interrogator into thinking that he is a girl and for person C to convince the interrogator that she is a girl. At the end of the game the interrogator (person A) must correctly identify the gender of both B and C. If B or C are successful in either deceiving or convincing the interrogator, they win.

Turing proposed a version of this game in which either person B or C is swapped with a machine. The question Turing asked was, 'Will the interrogator decide wrongly as often when the game is played like this as he does when the game is played between a man and a woman?' (1950, 433). There are many variations of this game that are commonly known today as the Turing Test. The premise of the Turing Test has remained the same: instead of defining thinking, a machine is programmed to imitate the behaviour of thinking, which Turing believed qualified as thinking and avoided the paradox of an explicit definition.

It is helpful to note that the imitation game was not a new concept; the desire to create an android (derived from the Greek for 'manlike') was coined by Gabriel Naudé in the seventeenth century. By the eighteenth century, people already began to create manlike machines that mimicked their human creators, from Vaucanson's flute-playing android to Kempelen's chess-playing machine called 'The Turk'. In fact, these machines led to new discoveries. For example, Vaucanson's machine shed new insights into music theory and The Turk, which was exhibited across Europe and America competing against and beating both Napoleon and Benjamin Franklin, demonstrated people's interest in these machines and the complexities of creating a thinking machine (Riskin 2016, 115–25). The Turk was exposed as a fake, just a small man cleverly hidden in a box. Over the centuries, the continued interest in these manlike machines has led to technological advancements, such as the universal Turing Machine, in which it is no longer necessary to hide a man in the box, as it uses cleverly devised algorithms. This has raised the philosophical discussion concerning the nature of these machines.

Challenged by Turing and the advancement of computers, Polanyi still affirmed his argument, even given the potential of new technological advancements he called 'automatic operations'. He explained:

The proliferation of axioms discovered by Gödel offers manifest proof that a person operating a logical inference machine can achieve informally a range of knowledge which no operations of such a machine can demonstrate, even though its operations suggest an easy access to it. It proves that the powers of the mind exceed those of a logical inference machine. But we have yet to face the wider problem raised by gunsight predictors, automatic pilots, etc., that is, by machines whose performances range far beyond logical inferences. A. M. Turing has shown that it is possible to devise a machine which will both construct and assert as new axioms an indefinite sequence of Gödelian sentences. Any heuristic process of a routine character – for which in the deductive sciences the Gödelian process is an example – could likewise be carried out automatically. A routine game of chess can be played automatically by a machine, and indeed, all arts can be performed automatically to the extent to which the rules of the art can be specified. While such a specification may include random elements, like choices made by spinning a coin, no unspecifiable skill or connoisseurship can be fed into a machine. (Polanyi 1962, 261, nn 2)

Polanyi was correct – computer science has shown the impracticality of coding a chess programme that considers every possible move – but he failed to see that a machine could be coded with algorithms that *learn* to play chess at a high level. Technologies, such as machine-learning algorithms, have now advanced computers beyond their human creators. For example, in 1996, IBM's computer Deep Blue defeated the world champion chess player Gary Kasparov. In 2011, IBM's machine Watson defeated two of Jeopardy's greatest players. More recently, in 2016, Google's AlphaGo algorithm beat the world Go champion Sedol Lee 4–1, a feat that many thought either impossible or decades from being a reality. The early win was made possible through advances in deep learning and reinforcement learning that allowed the algorithm to compete against itself, which has now advanced to AlphaGo Zero, which is capable of learning the game through playing itself and has gone on to defeat the original AlphaGo programme 100–0 (Silver et al. 2017, 354).

Machine learning has overcome aspects of Polanyi's Paradox through the use of what can be called tacit algorithms such as a confusion matrix, decision trees and neural networks. Inspired by brain neurons, neural networks process large quantities of data through multiple layers called deep learning so as to fine-tune hidden variables that act as a type of weak tacit knowledge. These tacit algorithms have achieved a new level of statistical precision and allow machines to learn more than just games. For example, Polanyi was a physician before going into physical chemistry and from his experience believed it impossible for a machine to accurately diagnose a patient's disease given the high level of skill and tacit variables involved (1969a, 132). However, machine learning algorithms have even demonstrated this level of tacit ability. For example, algorithms have shown an accuracy of determining skin cancer on a par with that of a dermatologist (Esteva et al. 2017, 115–18). Polanyi believed that a machine could not learn these skills because they cannot be communicated in a step-by-step process but require tacit learning through apprenticeship. However, recent advancements in 'deep feature learning' have shown even this is possible; machines can imitate 'component[s] of human expertise learning' (Li et al. 2015).

Turing envisioned the day when computers would learn to play chess or Go in a human versus machine match, but the ultimate challenge would be the imitation game (Turing 1996, 257). Given the advancements in machine learning, there is little doubt that one day a machine will pass at least a simple form of the Turing Test (such as a text-only conversation) and potentially also what is called the total Turing Test (speech and a face-to-face conversation). Given continued technological advancements, the important question that must be considered is not *if* a machine will win the imitation game but *what* the prize will be.

Within computer science two schools of AI have emerged: a weak (cautious or narrow) version and a strong version. Searle coined this distinction, defining weak AI as 'the principal value of the computer in the study of the mind'; whereas, according to strong AI,

> the computer is not merely a tool in the study of the mind; rather, the appropriately programmed computer really *is* a mind in the sense that computers given the right programs can be literally said to *understand* and have other cognitive states. In strong AI, because the programmed computer has cognitive states, the programs are not mere tools that enable us to test psychological explanations; rather, the programs are themselves the explanations. (1980, 417, emphasis original)

Following these distinctions, passing the imitation game, according to Searle, can be interpreted as a weak Turing Test – the machine replicates human behaviour – or a strong Turing Test – the machine is human (2009, 141). Thus, strong AI is commonly associated with the strong Turing Test, becoming more than a game but an ontological test of humanity which Polanyi acknowledged and challenged (1964, 84–85) and Turing embraced, believing machines would one day go beyond humanity (Turing 1996, 259–60).

On 12 July 2017, an indication of how culture views AI and what the prize for winning the imitation game might be was demonstrated when a robot named Sophia was granted citizenship of Saudi Arabia during the tech summit at the Future Investment Initiative. This lifelike machine created by Hanson Robotics is designed to look and act like a human, in everything from skin tone, to facial expressions, to language-processing capabilities. Sophia represents more than another step forward in humanity's drive towards creating innovative technologies; it also represents people's growing propensity to anthropomorphize machines. Consider that although Sophia could not pass either a weak or strong version of the Turing Test, it was still granted citizenship. This not only demonstrates people's ability but also their desire to humanize machines and reveals a human bent towards embracing strong AI. If caution is not taken, this could include more than citizenship of a country but of the human race with all the benefits that come with being a person, as indicated in the Universal Declaration of Human Rights (UDHR, 1948), such as inherent dignity. However, I will argue that following the ethic of the UDHR, granting machines human status does not bring them to the level of humanity; it does the exact opposite – it brings humans down to the level of a machine.

2. Dehumanization: The Danger of Denying and Imitating Dignity

Dehumanization is the very reason that the UDHR was created after World War II. It was a response to such things as eugenics and the atrocities that followed, such as the genocide of the Jews, when persons no longer saw each other as fully human. Historically, people have tended not to question if humans have dignity; rather, they have questioned who qualifies as human, which is at the heart of the dehumanizing nature of strong AI. When people attempt to humanize a robot, by placing it on par with humanity, it has the exact opposite effect: it dehumanizes people by lowering their status to that of a machine. The reason for this is implicit in the UDHR.

The UDHR clearly begins by stating that humans have '*inherent* dignity', meaning that dignity is not bestowed by humans – it is recognized; that is, humans are born with dignity. However, when people attempt to bring a machine to the level of a human, it undermines humanity's dignity because dignity is no longer understood as inherent. The machine earns its humanity, for example, by passing the imitation game. Granting a machine humanity through something like the Turing Test makes dignity no longer inherent but conditional; and herein lies the problem. Depending on how tightly or loosely one draws humanity's lines of demarcation, some people will naturally be included and others excluded. For example, if human dignity is conferred by convincingly imitating a person, what of those humans, such as children or the disabled, who cannot pass the test?

There are many humans unable to communicate sufficiently to pass the Turing Test, in which case this test would grant humanity to some machines and remove it from some humans. Peter Singer uses a similar line of reasoning when he argues against speciesism among animals. He writes:

> We may legitimately hold that there are some features of certain beings which make their lives more valuable than those of other beings; but there will surely be some nonhuman animals, whose lives, by any standards, are more valuable than the lives of some humans. A chimpanzee, dog, or pig, for instance, will have a higher degree of self-awareness and a greater capacity for meaningful relations with others than a severely retarded infant or someone in a state of advanced senility. So if we base the right to life on these characteristics we must grant these animals a right to life as good as, or better than, such retarded or senile human […] This is why when we consider members of our own species who lack the characteristics of *normal* humans we can no longer say that their lives are always to be preferred to those of other animals. (Singer 1975, 19; emphasis added)

What Singer is advocating for here is an imitation game played with animals. Consider that some humans, such as a child or the disabled, are considerably easier for a machine or animal to imitate. But this raises the question: What is 'normal' human behaviour or, in this case, self-awareness that must be mimicked? As well, there are those that will be more demanding interrogators or judges of the Turing Test than others, as demonstrated with Sophia. Who decides what passes as the standard of human behaviour? This can be challenging given a simple flaw within the Turing Test, such as that demonstrated by Warwick and Shah in asking:

> What if the most appropriate response, (as deemed by an entity) to a particular question, is silence? What is the thinking nature of a machine when, rather than responding to an inappropriate or inane question, it does not answer it with an utterance? Why should a truly intelligent machine ingratiate itself with humanlike responses just to be considered human? Is not the truly Turing-intelligent machine the one that knows when and why to be silent? (2017, 287)

It is conceivable that a machine could employ the simple strategy of pleading the fifth, like a person in a court of law, and thereby potentially pass the Turing Test.

As technology advances and increasingly becomes more proficient at mimicking its human creators, caution needs to be taken to avoid the dehumanizing mistakes of the past. It has been recognized that dehumanization, which robs people of their dignity, takes place in one of two ways: by denying people their human nature, equating them with objects or denying their *uniqueness*, equating them with animals (Haslam 2006, 256). As well, there is another form of dehumanization that can be understood as dementalization, the denial of the mind, which does not necessarily constitute a third category, as Haslam explains: 'denial of mind implies a denial of humanness on both of the dimensions' (2014, 37).

All three forms of dehumanization are present in strong AI. First, as strong AI attempts to humanize machines, it simultaneously dehumanizes people because it is predicated on the assumption of what Polanyi called the 'modern scientific outlook' of reductive physicalism. Polanyi, borrowing from Buber, explains that reductive physicalism 'tends towards replacing everywhere the personal I-Thou by an impersonal I-It' (1957, 331). Accordingly, it robs humanity of its *nature* by reducing persons to their biological and physical parts operating according to DNA's code and nature's laws. Second, this also leads to the denial of human *uniqueness*, as people are equated with biological machines – animals made of similar parts but following a different biological code. Thus, the only difference between humans, animals and machines on reductionism is their behaviour. Third, human nature and uniqueness are both denied by reducing the mind or consciousness to brain states, and further by equating events in the brain to either random events of quantum indeterminacy or deterministic events following the laws of Newtonian physics.

Within this three-part framework, the imitation game has introduced developing implications of dehumanization that we are now beginning to study, which may be understood in terms of artificial dignity (AD). For example, it can be argued that a machine that passes a weak Turing Test has a weak level of AD and one passing a strong Turing Test has a high level of AD. This is *not* to say that a machine has real dignity, but the image of humanity that it is imitating has dignity and as such, it has a dehumanizing potential for one's self and society. In robot ethics, this is similar to what Danaher refers to as the 'symbolic-consequences argument' (2017, 107). Danaher demonstrates that symbolic-consequences can be argued at a very basic level with words that reflect an offensive meaning or at a more complex level with machines, such as when an android is used to perform objectionable acts (113–14). Robot sex is a strong example of the consequences of AD and thus will be used to make this point.

Given people's ability to now create humanlike machines for sexual purposes, people can abuse those anthropomorphized relationships. For example, Gutiu writes:

> To the user, the sex robot looks and feels like a real woman who is programmed into submission and which functions as a tool for sexual purposes. The sex robot is an ever-consenting sexual partner and the user has full control of the robot and the sexual interaction. By circumventing any need for consent, sex robots eliminate the need for communication, mutual respect, and compromise in the sexual relationship. The use of sex robots results in the dehumanization of sex and intimacy by allowing users to physically act out rape fantasies and confirm rape myths. (2012, 2)

A gynoid designed to imitate rape fantasies is dehumanizing, but it is not the machine that is being denied its humanity, as it has no humanity to deny; rather, human users are dehumanized by conditioning their view of themselves and other human beings. Gutiu makes a similar point explaining, 'Sex robots cause harm because they provide the user with an illusion of a mutual sexual experience, while also further alienating them from society and normalizing dehumanization of women' (15).

This is the dark side of the imitation game; a sex robot behaves according to the desire of its creator, which raises the concern that this will influence the way that users see and treat the dignity of real people. For example, it has been shown that 'child pornography offending is a valid diagnostic indicator of pedophilia' (Seto and Cantor 2006, 613). That being the case, upholding human dignity requires society to question if people should be allowed to make virtual child pornography. In April 2002, the US Supreme Court found the Child Pornography Prevention Act unconstitutional. Although making and showing sexually explicit pictures of real children is illegal, the manufacture of virtual images is permitted within two categories:

(a) sexually explicit pictures of actual models who appear to be younger than they are, and
(b) computer-generated sexually explicit pictures of children.

Virtual pornography was permitted by the courts because it was determined not to harm a specific child. However, the courts neglected to see the harm caused to users by their actions and the potential harm to those in society that are being dehumanized within the users' worldview.

As technology has moved from virtual pornography to now artificial pornography, it must again be asked if companies should be allowed to make machines in the image and likeness of a child for sexual purposes? The US Congress passed the CREEPER bill in 2017 (Curbing Realistic Exploitative Electronic Pedophilic Robots): 'Specifically, the bill makes it a crime to import, or knowingly use a common carrier or interactive computer service to transport in interstate or foreign commerce, a child sex doll' ('CREEPER Act of 2017' n.d.). Whether or not this bill will be passed into law is yet to be seen, but in the United Kingdom, child sex dolls have led to arrests and imprisonment for 'importing an obscene article' (BBC 2017).

The dangers of dehumanization are clearly documented historically and research continues to show that 'moral action and moral judgment seem to depend on an appreciation of the humanness of others' (Haslam et al. 2012, 203). Considering that these human-like technologies condition a person's worldview, AD raises important ethical considerations that need to be considered. Given the relative ease with which people can rob others of their humanity virtually and physically, and the terrible results that follow in the real world, it is of utmost importance that dehumanization continues to be addressed. This is especially concerning given recent technological advancements in AI and robotics, which make it more important than ever to understand why a machine is not human and what a machine is.

3. Ontology: What Is a Machine?

Polanyi was adamant that a machine was not human. He distinguishes between machines and humans through a commitment to a non-reductive understanding of persons that he called personal knowledge. Highlighting this personal nature of humanity *not* explained via a reductive ontology, Polanyi writes:

> Our existing knowledge of physics and chemistry can certainly not suffice to account for our experience of active, resourceful living beings, for their activities are often accompanied by

conscious efforts and feelings of which our physics and chemistry know nothing. But let us assume for the sake of argument that physics and chemistry could be expanded to account for the sentience of certain physico-chemical systems. It might not be inconceivable that a machine of sufficient complexity would develop conscious thinking, without losing its machine-like character. However, conceived in this sense, conscious thoughts would be the mere accompaniment of automatic operations, on the outcome of which they could exercise no influence. (1962, 336)

Here Polanyi begins to highlight the mind-body problem by differentiating between what can be understood as weak and strong forms of tacit knowledge. A weak form of tacit knowledge is demonstrated in detached machine learning that imitates the operations of the brain, whereas strong tacit knowledge is personal in nature, in that the mind has intentionality: its thoughts are about their objects and have a meaning for a subject. We do not have any good reason to think the states of artificial systems have intentionality. Thus, although machine learning is inspired by humans, it is ontologically distinct and to treat it as the same would be a mistake. Alpaydin notes that an ontology of imitation is not used outside of AI studies; referring to machine learning he writes, 'Our immediate source of inspiration is the human brain, just as birds were the source of inspiration in our early attempts to fly […] nowadays, we see birds and airplanes as two different ways of flying – we call them airplanes now, not artificial birds' (2016, 85–86). No one seriously suggests that an airplane is a bird because it employs aeronautics. In the same way, a machine should not be considered human because it employs neural networks to accomplish tacit feats of intelligence.

   Going even further, Wittgenstein articulated the impossibility of attaining this strong form of tacit knowing by explaining, 'If a lion could talk, we could not understand him' (1953, 223). Gill elucidates Wittgenstein, explaining that for Polanyi, tacit knowledge is where the mind and body collapse into one, meaning we cannot speak 'Lion' because 'we do not share the embodied experiences, emotions, and cultural practices of the Lion's world' (2015, 21). Nagel famously captured the essence of strong tacit knowledge in his essay *What Is It Like to Be a Bat?* writing,

> Reflection on what it is like to be a bat seems to lead us, therefore, to the conclusion that there are facts that do not consist in the truth of propositions expressible in a human language. We can be compelled to recognize the existence of such facts without being able to state or comprehend them. (1974, 441)

Alternatively, it could be asked 'What Is It Like to Be a Human?' A machine cannot be human simply by behaviour, as it does not share the same embodied experience of flesh and blood, which Polanyi argued allows people to relate or empathize with each other, and what he preferred to call 'conviviality' (1961, 245). For example, strong AI can imitate the behaviour of pain (weak tacit knowledge), but humans personally know the experience of pain (strong tacit knowledge), which allows us to understand and relate to one another. Searle made this distinction with his famous Chinese Room Thought Experiment, focusing on the difference between speaking Chinese and knowing Chinese (1980, 417–18).

Although Polanyi did not anticipate that machine learning would rely on weak tacit principles, he did appreciate that one day a machine 'may conceivably simulate these propensities [think, feel, imagine …] to such an extent as to deceive us altogether' (1962, 263). However, he argued against the ontology implicit within the imitation game, explaining: 'A deception, however compelling, does not qualify thereby as truth: no amount of subsequent experience can justify us in accepting as identical two things known from the start to be different in their nature' (263). When it comes to the nature of a machine, Polanyi makes an important distinction between a person and the things persons create, explaining:

> For a machine is a machine only for someone who relies on it (actually or hypothetically) for some purpose, that he believes to be attainable by what he considers to be the proper function of the machine: it is the instrument of a person who relies on it. This is the difference between machine and mind. (262)

Given that machines are created by persons, Polanyi argues that they work within a 'tripartite system' as follows:

I   II   III
Mind→ Machine→ Things to which the machine informally refers. (1952, 314)

Within (III), Polanyi explains that the machine informally refers to 'functions, purpose etc., entertained by the mind', which he called operational principles. Thus, Polanyi concluded that a 'machine can be said to function intelligently only by aid of unspecifiable personal coefficients supplied by the user's mind' (1962, 262).

There exists, according to Polanyi, an ontological dependency between persons and the machines they create that transpires from particulars into composites when setting their operational principles. This is demonstrated in that the particulars, or parts that make up the machine, follow nature's laws, as studied by physics and chemistry, but the composites themselves, which make up the machine, operate according to laws imposed upon them to achieve a desired purpose, as studied within engineering. Polanyi argues that it is the operational principles that ontologically define a composite, such as a machine, via its purpose, explaining:

> The true knowledge of a machine which we have on the upper level is the understating of a *purpose* and of the *rational means* for achieving it; while the knowledge of its physical and chemical topography is *by itself meaningless*, for it lacks any conception of purpose or achievement. It becomes meaningful only when oriented towards establishing the material conditions for the success or failure of a machine. (2014, 52, emphasis original)

Intuitively, people do not define a created composite according to its parts but by its purpose. Polanyi uses the example of a watch to make this point:

> To understand a watch is to understand what it is for and how it works. The laws of inanimate nature are indifferent to this purpose. They cannot determine the working of a watch,

any more than chemistry or physics of printers' ink can determine the concept of a book. (1969b, 152–53)

Although a watch is composed of parts that follow physical chemical laws, it is not and cannot be defined by those parts or laws. The reason for this is that the machine is a composite created by persons, and as such, follows the laws imposed upon those parts to accomplish the purposes it was created for, in the case of a watch to keep time. It is significant to note, in Polanyi's argument, the irreducibility of composites to particulars; the purpose of a machine cannot be arrived at by studying the physical chemical laws of its parts. In the same way, a language cannot be learned by studying the design of the letters alone. This goes back to Gödel's *incompleteness theorem*, in which the meaning of the composites, words or mathematical symbols are defined *outside* the system by persons. According to Polanyi's ontology, an android is a composite and the intentional creation of its human creators, and as such, ought to be defined by its purpose. Therefore, a machine that passes the Turing Test ought to be defined as a successful human imitation machine and not a human. After all, it is called the 'imitation game' and not the 'identity game'. Although a successful imitation machine is not human, it is capable of producing AD, which raises growing concern for a better understanding of what dignity is.

4. Dignity: Whose Approach Best Supports It? Polanyi's or Turing's?

Polanyi and Turing have shown two opposing views. Turing argued for a human ontology of imitation that reduced humans to their behaviour, and Polanyi argued for a machine ontology that is not reducible but the product of the purposeful intention of humans. Thus far the UDHR's use of inherent dignity has managed to coexist with opposing philosophies, such as Polanyi's and Turing's, because it has remained, as explained by Luban, 'strategically silent about what key terms such as "human dignity" are supposed to mean'; Luban subsequently concludes with the concern that 'a concept that can mean anything means nothing' (2007, 68). This is particularly troubling given the UDHR's goal of stopping dehumanization and the mounting challenge to inherent human dignity from recent technological advancements. Kraynak argues that the threat of dehumanization from technology is a serious concern and argues that 'the major challenge of our times is to recover a true and authentic understanding of human dignity and to defend it against threats from modern civilization' (2003, 2).

  In light of Polanyi's development of tacit knowledge, it is not surprising that dignity continues to elude an explicit definition. This may be due to the tacit or non-reductive nature of human characteristics, such as intelligence, intentionality and morality. Alternatively, clarity on what dignity is might be best gained through understanding whose worldview, Polanyi's or Turing's, best supports inherent dignity and what implications follow. It has already been demonstrated that Turing's approach erodes the *inherent* nature of human dignity, whereas Polanyi upholds it by making a clear distinction between man and machine. Now it will be shown that Turing's approach also fails to support the *dignity* of humanity given the intrinsic moral duty owed I-Thou relationships as opposed to I-It relationships. Although Polanyi did not directly address human dignity, he did under-stand his approach as a possible foundation, writing, 'We see before us a way of knowing a human being in the fulness of his dignity through recognizing in him the same powers of understanding by which we are understanding him' (1961, 242).

Polanyi's entire argument shows that reductive physicalism fails to uphold human dig-nity by reducing humanity to either a random or determined collection of I-It parts; in reference to these two implications, he writes,

> It is simply this sort of mechanical reductionism that is the heart of the matter. It is this that is the origin of the whole system of scientific obscurantism under which we are suffering today. This is the cause of our corruption of the conception of man, reducing him either to an insentient automaton or to a bundle of appetites. This is why science denies us the possibility of acknowledging personal responsibility. (Polanyi and Prosch 1975, 25)

Polanyi argued that persons are greater than their parts, since they are relationally responsible to themselves and others. Humanity's responsibility to I-Thou relationships is a key aspect of dignity. Fundamentally, human dignity references moral obligations intrinsic to I-Thou relationships as opposed to I-It relationships. Polanyi's ontology is fundamentally committed to I-Thou relationships in which moral duty necessarily flows. That is, dignity references the moral obligation to value I-thou relationships so as to not reduce them into I-It relationships. The imitation game, however, is funda-mentally based on this dehumanizing reduction of persons to I-It parts and behaviours, which neglects its moral duty to uphold I-Thou relationships of persons. One reason for this is that a reductive ontology denies the existence of morality altogether. There are, however, philosophers that hold to normative realism, such as Wielenberg, who argues for what he calls 'basic ethical facts' that exist necessarily and without an external explanation, such as God, but ultimately he fails to address what obligation one owes those facts (2019, 128).

This is the relational obligation that is inherent to dignity which Wielenberg acknow-ledges, stating, 'Dehumanization is a kind of evil that strikes at the very heart of mor-ality' (137). Thus, he is implicitly arguing that it is morally wrong to treat an I-Thou relationship as an I-It relationship, but fails to explain what duty one owes these moral facts. The point is that duties are owed to persons (I-Thou) and not to moral facts (I-It). If I steal from my neighbour, my obligation to repay is to *him*, not to the moral fact that he has been wronged by theft. It is after all people, not facts, that can be wronged. Taylor, a non-theist, makes this point, writing, 'A duty is something that is owed. [...] But some-thing can be owed only to some person or persons. There can be no such thing as duty in isolation' (1985, 83). He understands the theistic implication of duty being grounded in a person, writing:

> Our moral obligations can [...] be understood as those that are imposed by God. [...] But what if this higher-than-human lawgiver is no longer taken into account? Does the concept of a moral obligation [...] still make sense? [...] the concept of moral obligation [is] unin-telligible apart from the idea of God. The words remain but their meaning is gone. (83–84)

For this reason, Taylor gave up moral obligations, and although Wielenberg appeals to moral facts, there is no obligation to follow them.

Polanyi argued that his approach pointed the way to God, to which he found himself drawn, specifically to Christianity; he writes:

> I have mentioned divinity and the possibility of knowing God. These subjects lie outside my argument. But my conception of knowing opens the way to them. Knowing, as a dynamic force of comprehension, uncovers at each step a new hidden meaning. It reveals a universe of comprehensive entities which represent the meaning of their largely unspecifiable particulars. A universe constructed as an ascending hierarchy of meaning and excellence is very different from the picture of a chance collocation of atoms to which the examination of the universe by explicit modes of inference leads us. The vision of such a hierarchy inevitably sweeps on to envisage the meaning of the universe as a whole. Thus natural knowing expands continuously into knowledge of the supernatural. (1961, 246)

Accounting for one's moral obligation to I-Thou relationships (dignity) would metaphysically require a relational nature that is best understood within the framework of Christian theism. Specifically, it would require that a relational God created humanity with a relational purpose and that humanity has the capacity to understand and obey that moral standard. This places God into an I-Thou relationship with humanity and humanity into an I-Thou relationship with God, one's self and others. Accordingly, dignity would be inherent to humanity due to God's I-Thou relationship with humanity and humanity's intrinsic capacity for I-Thou relationships as persons. Those relationships would be owed dignity given the relational nature of God and morality within an I-Thou relationship. Thus, it is morally wrong to treat an I-Thou relationship as an I-It relationship, which demonstrates that Turing's approach fails to support dignity but Polanyi's framework provides a possible foundation within Christian theism.

Conclusion

This chapter has juxtaposed Polanyi and Turing to elucidate two ontologies, one based on purpose and the other based on imitation. The goal of this enquiry is to highlight the dehumanizing tendencies implicit within the imitation game. Granting humanness to machines undermines the inherent nature of dignity, as specified by the UDHR, and opens the door to dehumanizing certain humans. In order for humanity to retain its understanding of inherent human dignity, anthropomorphized machines must *not* be viewed as human but rather, as proposed by Polanyi's ontology of purpose, as human imitation machines. Although a machine is not human, technological advancements in AI and robotics produce AD, which creates a need for greater clarity regarding what real dignity is. The UDHR leaves human dignity undefined, but this might be necessary, given the tacit nature of humanity. Alternatively, dignity can be elucidated through its metaphysical foundation, which is best supported through Polanyi's non-reductive approach to persons and ultimately founded in a moral lawgiver as demonstrated in Christian theism. If a dystopian future is to be avoided, human dignity must be upheld, and a Polanyian ontology, supported by a Christian framework, provides the necessary clarity to navigate further technological advancements in AI and robotics.

References

Alpaydin, Ethem. 2016. *Machine Learning*. Cambridge, MA: MIT Press.

BBC. 2017. 'Andrew Dobson Jailed for "Child-Like" Sex Doll Import Bid'. https://www.bbc.com/news/uk-england-stoke-staffordshire-40383627.

CREEPER Act of 2017. Pub. L. No. H.R. 4655.

Danaher, John. 2017. 'The Symbolic-Consequences Argument in the Sex Robot Debate'. In *Robot Sex: Social and Ethical Implications*, edited by John Danaher and Neil McArthur, 103–31. Cambridge, MA: MIT Press.

Discussion on the Mind and the Computing Machine. 1949. Interdisciplinary discussion presented at the Manchester University. https://www.turing.org.uk/sources/wmays1.html.

Esteva, Andre, Brett Kuprel, Roberto A. Novoa, Justin Ko, Susan M. Swetter, Helen M. Blau and Sebastian Thrun. 2017. 'Dermatologist-Level Classification of Skin Cancer with Deep Neural Networks'. *Nature* 542: 115–18.

Gill, Satinder P. 2015. *Tacit Engagement: Beyond Interaction*. Cham, Switzerland: Springer International.

Gutiu, Sinziana. 2012. '*Sex Robots and Roboticization of Consent*'. Presented at the We Robot Conference. http://robots.law.miami.edu/wp-content/uploads/2012/01/Gutiu-Roboticization_of_Consent.pdf.

Haslam, Nick. 2006. 'Dehumanization: An Integrative Review'. *Personality and Social Psychology Review* 10, no. 3: 252–64.

———. 2014. 'What Is Dehumanization?' In *Humanness and Dehumanization*, edited by Paul G. Bain, Jeroen Vaes and Jacques-Philippe Leyens, 34–48. New York: Psychology.

Haslam, Nick, Brock Bastian, Simon Laham and Stephen Loughnan. 2012. 'Humanness, Dehumanization, and Moral Psychology'. In *The Social Psychology of Morality: Exploring the Causes of God and Evil*, edited by Mario Mikulincer and Phillip R. Shaver, 203–18. Washington, DC: APA.

Hodges, Andrew. 2009. 'Alan Turing and the Turing Test'. In *Parsing the Turing Test: Philosophical and Methodological Issues in the Quest for the Thinking Computer*, edited by Robert Epstein, Gary Roberts and Grace Beber, 13–22. Dordrecht, the Netherlands: Springer.

Kraynak, Robert P. 2003. 'Defending Human Dignity: The Challenge of Our Times'. In *In Defense of Human Dignity: Essays of Our Times*, edited by Robert P. Kraynak and Glenn Tinder, 1–9. Notre Dame, IN: University of Notre Dame Press.

Luban, David. 2007. *Legal Ethics and Human Dignity*. New York: Cambridge University Press.

Nagel, Thomas. 1974. 'What Is It Like to Be a Bat?' *Philosophical Review* 83, no. 4: 435–50.

Nan Li, Noboru Matsuda, William W. Cohen and Kenneth R. Koedinger. 2015. 'Integrating Representation Learning and Skill Learning in a Human-Like Intelligent Agent'. *Artificial Intelligence* 219: 67–91.

Polanyi, Michael. 1952. 'The Hypothesis of Cybernetics'. *British Journal for the Philosophy of Science* 2, no. 8: 312–15.

———. 1957. 'Scientific Outlook: Its Sickness and Cure'. *Science* 125, no. 3246: 480–84.

———. 1961. 'Faith and Reason'. *Journal of Religion* 41, no. 4: 237–47.

———. 1962. *Personal Knowledge: Towards a Post-Critical Philosophy*. Chicago: University of Chicago Press.

———. 1964. 'The Feelings of Machines'. *Encounter* 22: 85–86.

———. 1966. *The Tacit Dimension*. Chicago: University of Chicago Press.

———. 1969a. 'Knowing and Being'. In *Knowing and Being: Essays by Michael Polanyi*, edited by Marjorie Grene, 123–37. London: Routledge & Kegan Paul.

————. 1969b. 'The Logic of Tacit Inference'. In *Knowing and Being: Essays by Michael Polanyi*, edited by Marjorie Grene, 138–58. London: Routledge & Kegan Paul.

————. 2014. *The Study of Man*. Mansfield Centre, CT: Martino.

Polanyi, Michael, and Harry Prosch. 1975. *Meaning*. Chicago: University of Chicago Press.

Riskin, Jessica. 2016. *The Restless Clock: A History of the Centuries-Long Argument over What Makes Living Things Tick*. Chicago: University of Chicago Press.

Scott, William Taussig, and Martin X. Moleski. 2005. *Michael Polanyi: Scientist and Philosopher*. New York: Oxford University Press.

Searle, John R. 1980. 'Minds, Brains and Programs'. *Behavioral and Brain Sciences* 3, no. 3: 417–57.

————. 2009. 'The Turing Test: 55 Years Later'. In *Parsing the Turing Test: Philosophical and Methodological Issues in the Quest for the Thinking Computer*, edited by Robert Epstein, Gary Roberts and Grace Beber, 139–50. Dordrecht, the Netherlands: Springer.

Seto, Michael C., and James M. Cantor. 2006. 'Child Pornography Offenses Are a Valid Diagnostic Indicator of Pedophilia'. *Journal of Abnormal Psychology* 115, no. 3: 610–15.

Silver, David, Julian Schrittwieser, Karen Simonyan, Ioannis Antonoglou, Aja Huang, Arthur Guez and Demis Hassabis. 2017. 'Mastering the Game of Go without Human Knowledge'. *Nature* 550: 354–59.

Singer, Peter. 1975. *Animal Liberation*. New York: Avon Books.

Taylor, Richard. 1985. *Ethics, Faith and Reason*. Englewood Cliffs, NJ: Prentice-Hall.

Turing, A. M. 1950. 'Computing Machinery and Intelligence'. *Mind* 49: 433–60.

————. 1996. 'Intelligent Machinery: A Heretical Theory'. *Philosophia Mathematica* 4, no. 3: 256–60.

Universal Declaration of Human Rights. 1948. https://www.un.org/en/ga/search/view_doc.asp?symbol=A/RES/217(III).

Warwick, Kevin, and Huma Shah. 2017. 'Taking the Fifth Amendment in Turing's Imitation Game'. *Journal of Experimental & Theoretical Artificial Intelligence* 29, no. 2: 287–97.

Wielenberg, Erik J. 2019. 'Evil and Atheistic Moral Realism'. In *Explaining Evil: Four Views*, edited by W. Paul Franks, 123–39. London: Bloomsbury Academic.

Wittgenstein, Ludwig. 1953. *Philosophical Investigations*. Oxford: Basil Blackwell.

NOTES ON CONTRIBUTORS

Nicholas Aroney is Professor of Constitutional Law at the University of Queensland and a Fellow of the Centre for Law and Religion at Emory University. He has a law degree from the University of Queensland and a PhD from Monash University and has held visiting positions at Oxford, Cambridge, Paris, Edinburgh, Sydney, Emory and Tilburg universities. He is the author of over 130 articles, book chapters and books on constitutional law, comparative federalism, law and religion, and religious freedom, including *The Constitution of a Federal Commonwealth: The Making and Meaning of the Australian Constitution* (2009), *Shari'a in the West* (2010) and *The Constitution of the Commonwealth of Australia: History, Principle and Interpretation* (2015). He is currently co-editing a book titled *Christianity and Constitutionalism*, due for publication in 2021. In 2017–18 he was appointed to the Australian Prime Minister's Expert Panel on Religious Freedom which submitted its report in May 2018.

Paul Copan holds a PhD in philosophy from Marquette University and is currently the Pledger Family Chair of Philosophy and Ethics at Palm Beach Atlantic University (West Palm Beach, Florida). He has done work on topics such as the moral argument for God's existence, human rights, religious liberty, as well as themes related to the intersection of philosophy, theology and science. He has co-edited with Charles Taliaferro *The Naturalness of Belief: New Essays on Theism's Rationality* (2018) and edited the two-volume *Kalam Cosmological Argument* (2017).

David Guretzki, PhD (McGill), is Executive Vice President and Resident Theologian of The Evangelical Fellowship of Canada. He is Adjunct Professor of Christian theology at Briercrest Seminary (Saskatchewan, Canada) and Tyndale University (Ontario, Canada). David's broad research interests include the theology of forgiveness and reconciliation, the intersection of politics and the church in a Canadian context and the theology of the human person. He has published two books on the thought of Swiss theologian Karl Barth. He has testified as an expert witness on court cases in Canada on matters of freedom of conscience and religion. He is executive publisher of *Faith Today*, a bimonthly publication in which he also writes a column.

Hendrik Kaptein is Associate Professor Emeritus of jurisprudence (Leiden University). He is currently researching and writing mainly on (legal) argumentation, issues of legal evidence and proof, legal ethics and criminal law theory, including legal regulation of euthanasia. He is master of the bells of the Old Church, Amsterdam, and member of the boards of non-profit (art) organizations (and a steam locomotive driver). His recent publications include Kaptein et al. (eds), *Legal Evidence and Proof: Statistics, Stories, Logic* (2009), *Logisch? Leren van drogredeneringen* (2017), and Kaptein and van der Velden (eds), *Analogy and Exemplary Reasoning in Legal Discourse* (2018).

Laura Kittel earned her PhD in philosophy from the University of Notre Dame Australia (UNDA), specializing in human rights. She teaches social justice as an adjunct faculty member at UNDA and business ethics at Curtin University. Her previous publications include 'Thomas Jefferson and the Pursuit of Happiness', in *Religious Liberty and the Law: Theistic and Non-Theistic Perspectives*, ed. Angus J. L. Menuge (2018). She has worked at the International Campaign for Tibet in Washington, DC, and presented her research at the United Nations in New York. Originally from Guam and the United States, she lives in Perth, Western Australia. Her current research focuses on human rights, happiness and virtue ethics.

Åsbjørn Melkevik is a Banting Postdoctoral Fellow at the Center of Research in Ethics at the University of Montreal. He was a Fellow-in-Residence at the Edmond J. Safra Center for Ethics at Harvard University. In addition to his book *If You're a Classical Liberal, How Come You're Also an Egalitarian?* (2020), he has published in numerous journals, including *Business Ethics Quarterly*, *Journal of Business Ethics*, *Constitutional Political Economy* and *European Journal of Political Theory*. Åsbjørn specializes in political theory, business ethics and economic ethics.

Bjarne Melkevik, Docteur ès droit (Dr Juris Habil), is a Professor at the Law Faculty of Laval University (Quebec, Canada) where he teaches philosophy of law, legal epistemology, legal methodology, and law and literature. He has published about 25 books in French, which have been translated to Romanian (4 books), Spanish (2), Russian (5), Arabic (6) and Ukrainian (1). He is the author of *Philosophie du droit*, vol. 1 (2010) and vol. 2 (2014), *Habermas, légalité et légitimité* (2012) and *Épistémologie juridique et déjà-droit* (2012).

Angus J. L. Menuge is Chair of the Philosophy Department, and Co-Chair of the Classical Education program at Concordia University Wisconsin. He was raised in England and became an American citizen in 2005. He holds a BA in philosophy from Warwick University and a PhD in philosophy from the University of Wisconsin-Madison. He is author of *Agents Under Fire* (2004) and many articles on the philosophy of mind, philosophy of science and Christian apologetics, and editor of several collections, including *Reading God's World* (2004), *Legitimizing Human Rights* (2013; 2016), *Religious Liberty and the Law* (2017) and, with Jonathan Loose and J. P. Moreland, *The Blackwell Companion to Substance Dualism* (2018). He is past president of the Evangelical Philosophical Society (2012–18).

Michał Rupniewski is Assistant Professor at the University of Łódź, Branch in Tomaszów Mazowiecki, Poland, where he teaches law and philosophy. In his research, he aims to combine jurisprudence, political philosophy and comparative law. He is co-editor of *The Philosophy of Legal Change: Theoretical Perspectives and Practical Processes* (2019) and author of a monograph on John Rawls, published in Polish (2015). His main current interest is human dignity. A monograph tentatively titled *The Status of Personhood: A Theory of Human Dignity in Law* is expected as a result of his research project, pursued at the Faculty of Law and Administration, University of Łódź.

R. Scott Smith, PhD, is Professor of Philosophy and Ethics at Talbot School of Theology. He is the author of *In Search of Moral Knowledge: Overcoming the Fact-Value Dichotomy* (2014) and *Naturalism and Our Knowledge of Reality: Testing Religious Truth-Claims* (2012). He also is the author of 'Social Justice, Economics, and the Implications of Nominalism', *Independent Review* 24:1 (2019), and 'Tropes and Some Ontological Prerequisites for Knowledge', *Metaphysica*, published online 15 August 2019. His research interests focus on the ontology needed to have knowledge, as well as the inabilities of critical theory to preserve justice, dignity and equality.

Andy Steiger is a pastor, Adjunct Professor and President of Apologetics Canada. His PhD work, at the University of Aberdeen, is focused on developing Michael Polanyi's ontology in the area of theological anthropology. Andy's research has focused on current and historical examples of dehumanization and humanization. He is particularly interested in human ontology and dignity in relation to technology. He is the author of *Reclaimed: How Jesus Humanizes in a Dehumanized World* (2020) and *Thinking? Answering Life's Five Biggest Questions* (2015). He created *The Human Project* video series which has won a number of awards, including Best Short Film, Best Documentary Short, Best Foreign Short and People's Choice Award.

Keith Thompson, PhD, is Professor of Law and the Associate Dean at the University of Notre Dame Australia, and he is Adjunct Professor of Law at the University of Fiji. He is the Secretary of SEIROS, an interfaith think tank which researches the economic impact of religion on society. He teaches constitutional law, evidence, legal history and law and religion and has authored many peer-reviewed articles and book chapters. His books include *Religious Confession Privilege and the Common Law* (2011) and *Trinity and Monotheism, a Historical and Theological Review of the Origins and Substance of the Doctrine* (2019).

Friedrich Toepel is Associate Professor of Criminal Law at the Rheinische Friedrich-Wilhelms-University Bonn and Counsel in Dentons' Frankfurt office. His work focuses on the foundations of criminal law, in particular problems of causation, imputation, mens rea and free will. Another main interest of involves problems of expert evidence in criminal procedural law. He is the author of German books on 'Causation and Imputation Regarding Negligent Offences' and 'Expert Evidence in the Law of Criminal Procedure', and he has edited a book titled *Free Will in Criminal Law and Procedure* (2010). He sees himself within the tradition of legal positivism and analytic philosophy. Recent publications also address the issue of a Christian's ability to participate in secular legal systems, which are increasingly hostile to the Judaeo-Christian worldview.

Erik J. Wielenberg is Professor of Philosophy at DePauw University in Greencastle, Indiana. He works primarily in meta-ethics, moral psychology and the philosophy of religion. He is the author of *Value and Virtue in a Godless Universe* (2005), *God and the Reach of Reason: C.S. Lewis, David Hume, and Bertrand Russell* (2008) and *Robust Ethics: The Metaphysics and Epistemology of Godless Normative Realism* (2014).

Claudia Mariéle Wulf, Dr. Phil., Dr. Theol. Habil., worked for years in pastoral care and counselling, and later at the University of Fribourg/CH in fundamental theology. She is now professor of moral theology in Tilburg/NL and leads a praxis of counselling in St. Gallen/CH. Her research, published in monographs, focuses on philosophical anthropology and human dignity (*Freiheit und Grenze*, 2005; *Der Mensch, ein Phänomen*, 2011; *Een antropologie van de christelijke ethiek*, 2012; *Phänomene des Menschseins*, 2014); moral subjects (*Schuld, ins Wort gebracht*, 2011; *Begegnung, die befreit*, 2009); and epistemology in ethics and research (*Was ist gut?* 2010; *Morele denkpatronen*, 2013). She studies the outcomes of traumatic experiences on the person (*Wenn das Ich zerbricht, Psychotrauma*, 2014; translated to English in 2020) and the phenomenon of narcissism (*Narzissten – eine Funktionsanalyse*, 2020) in the context of professional ethics. She is internationally known for her research on Edith Stein.

INDEX

www.ingramcontent.com/pod-product-compliance
Lightning Source LLC
Chambersburg PA
CBHW030836300326
41935CB00036B/171